SECOND EDITION

CATHOLIC BIOETHICS

AND THE GIFT OF

HUMAN LIFE

SECOND EDITION

CATHOLIC BIOETHICS

AND THE GIFT OF

HUMAN LIFE

William E. May

Our Sunday Visitor Publishing Division
Our Sunday Visitor, Inc.
Huntington, Indiana 46750

Nihil Obstat: Rev. Michael Heintz
Censor Librorum

Imprimatur: ✠ John M. D'Arcy
Bishop of Fort Wayne-South Bend
May 8, 2008

The *Nihil Obstat* and *Imprimatur* are official declarations that a book or pamphlet is free of doctrinal or moral error. No implication is contained therein that those who have granted the *Nihil Obstat* or *Imprimatur* agree with the contents, opinions, or statements expressed.

Dedicated to the memory of
Thomas A. Davin (1930-2007),
a great friend who helped me immeasurably
in preparing this revised edition.
Requiescat in pace.

Contents

CHAPTER FOUR
Contraception and Respect for Human Life   127

CHAPTER FIVE
Abortion and Human Life   165

CHAPTER SIX
Experimentation on Human Subjects   213

Introduction to the
Second Edition

Published originally in September 2000, this book needs a thorough revision in order to keep abreast of the rapid developments in the field of bioethics. I delayed revising it because I thought that the Congregation for the Doctrine of the Faith was preparing and would soon issue a major document taking up some of the most debated issues in bioethics on which the Magisterium has not given definitive guidance, issues such as "rescuing frozen embryos," use of methotrexate and salpingostomies to cope with ectopic pregnancies, proper criteria for determining that death has occurred, feeding/hydrating persons in the so-called persistent vegetative state, and others. I thought so because in May 2003 I had the privilege of meeting with Pope Benedict XVI, who at that time, as Joseph Cardinal Ratzinger, was serving as prefect of the Congregation for the Doctrine of the Faith and with whom I had worked from 1986-1997 as a member of the International Theological Commission and afterwards. When we met, I urged him to have the Congregation provide firm guidance for Catholics on these and other issues. Cardinal Ratzinger told me that the Congregation intended to prepare a new document considering issues of this kind and later appointed me to one of the "working groups" assembled under the leadership of Bishop Elio Sgreccia, now the president of the Pontifical Academy for Life, to study these issues and other questions. Four groups of this kind met in Rome during 2004, and later that year work was finished on preliminary reports that were then sent to the Congregation.

In August 2007, some Roman theologians who had, like me, been members of these "working groups" visited me at my office at the Pontifical John Paul II Institute for the Study of Marriage and Family at The Catholic University of America. One of them. Gonzalo Miranda, L.C., of the Pontifical Academy Regina Apostolorum, had participated in the final meeting that Bishop Sgreccia held prior to sending the reports of the different "working groups" to the Congregation. He reported that on the major controverted issues discussed by these groups, e.g., "rescuing frozen embryos," the precise criteria for determining whether a person has died or not, the working groups had themselves been seriously divided and could not reach conclusions acceptable to a majority. He thus thought that the Congregation would not issue a document resolving those debated issues but would rather allow discussion and debate to continue. He and another friend, Joseph Tham, M.D., L.C., also told me that the Congregation might issue shortly a document regarding the feeding/hydrating of "vegetative state" persons and others in order to bring an end to disputes that had arisen as a result of Pope John Paul II's major address on this subject on March 20, 2004. A major document on this matter, dated August 1, 2007, was in fact made public the week of September 10. I now believe that this document from the Congregation, along with John Paul II's March 20, 2004, address, are the most important magisterial statements on issues taken up in the first edition of this work. Naturally, I will consider these in this new edition.

This revised edition includes the following new and/or substantive material: (1) Chapter Three, "Generating Human Life: Marriage and the New Reproductive Technologies," Part 5, " 'Rescuing' Frozen Embryos," has been completely rewritten. Since the publication of this book, literature on this issue has increased dramatically, and it is essential to consider some of the most important studies that have appeared — studies that have not caused me to change my fundamental position but that, however, have forced me to acknowledge some errors in my earlier arguments and to consider very carefully newer arguments advanced against my position. (2) Chapter Four, "Contraception and Respect for Human Life" now takes up contraceptive sterilization. I also judged it necessary to consider the question whether it is morally permissible for married couples to use condoms to prevent the transmission of HIV/AIDS. I think it is not morally permissible, but because some well-known theologians (e.g., Martin Rhonheimer) and cardinals (e.g., Mario Cardinal Martini) approve of this, it is essential to take up this important matter. (3) In Chapter Five, "Abortion and Human Life," I have made minor changes by incorporating or referring to more recent scientific and philosophical studies regarding the beginning of human life and substantively revised the material on coping with ectopic pregnancies and on abortion as "removal" vs. abortion as "killing."

(4) I have thoroughly revised Chapter Six, "Experimentation on Human Subjects," 2.B., "Voluntary Consent in the Non-Therapeutic Situation: Can This Ever Be Morally Required?" I was asked to deliver a major paper on this subject at the 2003 plenary session of the Pontifical Academy for Life. In November 2002, there was a meeting in Rome of persons who

were to give papers at that session. I had written a paper on human experimentation in which I reaffirmed my view, found in Chapter Six, opposing completely proxy consent in the non-therapeutic situation. Because of criticism I received from good authorities faithful to the Magisterium who thought that my position was too restrictive, I was led to change my mind and to conclude that, *in very limited circumstances*, such consent can be morally justifiable. I have thus revised the pages of this chapter devoted to that issue. (5) Also, I have greatly expanded Chapter Six, No. 3, "Research on the Unborn, in Particular, Embryonic Stem-Cell Research." Only two pages were devoted to this issue in the 2000 edition, and since then literature on this topic has exploded, and I have sought to consider the most important developments on this subject. (6) Chapter Seven, "Euthanasia, Assisted Suicide, and Care of the Dying" now incorporates John Paul II's very important March 20, 2004, address, in which he declared that providing persons in the so-called persistent vegetative state with food and hydration is "in principle" morally obligatory as a form of ordinary care. His address, unfortunately, has been attacked and misrepresented by many Catholic theologians. The 2007 document from the Congregation of the Doctrine of the Faith defends Pope John Paul II's address and considers objections brought against it. All of this matter, including John Paul II's address and the recent document of the Congregation for the Doctrine of the Faith, is now included in this chapter. I have also referred to John Paul's address and the CDF document in Chapter One.

Finally, (7) Chapter Eight, "Defining Death and Organ Transplantation," has been completely rewritten, because on August 29, 2000, a few days after the first edition of this book was printed, Pope John Paul II gave an address to the 18th International Congress of the Transplant Society, in which he reaffirmed the criterion I rejected in the first edition. He declared: "[T]he criterion adopted in more recent times for ascertaining the fact of death, namely, the complete and irreversible cessation of all brain activity, if rigorously applied, does not seem to conflict with the essential elements of a sound anthropology" (no. 5). But he also maintained that it was the task of scientists and doctors, not the Magisterium or theologians, to develop criteria to determine whether death has, in fact, occurred. I have thus rewritten this chapter to take his address into account, to consider Alan Shewmon's very detailed commentary on his address, and to provide detailed discussion of post-2000 developments.

I have also made a minor insertion in Chapter One, at the beginning the second full paragraph.

CHAPTER ONE

Church Teaching and
Major Issues in Bioethics

It is important and helpful to begin this book by summarizing the teaching of the Church on major issues in bioethics. I believe that the most important magisterial documents relevant to the topics to be considered in this book are: (1) Pope John Paul II's 1995 encyclical *Evangelium vitae* ("The Gospel of Life"); (2) the Congregation for the Doctrine of the Faith's 1987 *Instruction on Respect for Human Life in Its Origin and on the Dignity of Procreation* (entitled *Donum vitae* in Latin); (3) the same Congregation's 1974 *Declaration on Procured Abortion*; and (4) the same Congregation's 1980 *Declaration on Euthanasia*.

Two important but not major magisterial documents issued since the first edition of this work are Pope John Paul II's March 20, 2004, address, "Life-Sustaining Treatments and Vegetative State: Scientific Advances and Ethical Dilemmas," and the Congregation for the Doctrine of the Faith's "Responses to Certain Questions of the United States Conference of Catholic Bishops Concerning Artificial Nutrition and Hydration," dated August 1, 2007, and released on September 14, 2007. Other magisterial documents, in particular the *Catechism of the Catholic Church* and many addresses of Popes Pius XII and John Paul II, are also quite relevant to matters taken up in this book. In addition, the 1994 *Charter for Health Care Workers* prepared by the Pontifical Council for Pastoral Assistance to Health Care Workers, the 1994 *Ethical and Religious Directives for Catholic Health Care Services* promulgated by the bishops of the United States, and pastoral letters of individual bishops and episcopal conferences bear on topics to be considered. Thus, in chapters to follow, reference will be made to these sources of Church teaching when it is relevant to do so. But the four documents singled out above are of such paramount importance that an exposition of their content and significance will provide a substantive introduction to the major issues in bioethics. In addition, the teaching found in these documents will be referred to time and again in the following chapters; hence, presentation of their principal ideas here will eliminate the need for doing so in later chapters where specific topics taken up in these documents are examined. A simple reference to the matter found in this chapter will suffice.

Rather than consider the four major documents chronologically, I will first take up John Paul II's *Evangelium vitae* because it is by far the most comprehensive and important of the documents. I will then consider the lengthy *Instruction* of the Congregation for the Doctrine of the Faith on issues surrounding the generation of human life, and then that Congregation's declarations on abortion and euthanasia.

1. John Paul II's Encyclical *Evangelium Vitae*

Pope John Paul II's encyclical is a wonderful manifesto eloquently presenting the reasons why human life is of incomparable dignity and, indeed, sanctity. It is also an incisive analysis and critique of the various factors and ideologies underlying the terrible threats menacing human life today, in particular, the life of the weakest members of the human family: the unborn, the severely impaired, the sick, and the dying. It is, above all, an impassioned plea to all people of goodwill to recognize the dignity and sanctity of human life, to defend it from the vicious and at times subtle attacks launched against it today, and to love it as a precious gift from the God whose only-begotten-Son-made-man poured forth his life on the Cross precisely so that everyone might have life in abundance, and in union with him conquer death and rise to everlasting life in fellowship with the Triune God, the Giver of Life and Love.

A. Chapter One: "Present-Day Threats to Human Life"

This chapter begins with a meditation on the story of Cain and Abel in Genesis (nos. 7-9) and goes on to take up in detail the threats menacing human life today. John Paul II goes to the root causes of these threats, zeroing in on the emergence of a perverse idea of human freedom, understood as the autonomous freedom of individuals to be the arbiters of good and evil, right and wrong. This has blinded them to the value of human life, has eclipsed the sense of God and of man as a being of incomparable worth, and has led to the claim that *some* members of the human family, the strong and the able, have the *right* to dispose of the lives of the weak and vulnerable, in particular, the unborn, the "useless," the suffering, and the dying.

John Paul II, mincing no words, correctly claims that today we are confronted "by a culture which denies solidarity and in many cases takes the form of a veritable 'culture of death,'" one "actively fostered by powerful cultural, economic, and political currents which encourage an idea of society excessively concerned with efficiency." It is thus possible, he continues, "to speak in a certain sense of a *war of the powerful against the weak*" which unleashes a "*conspiracy against life,*" a conspiracy involving "not only individuals in their personal, family or group relationships, but go[ing] far beyond, to the point of damaging and distorting, at the international level, relations between peoples and States" (no. 12).

This "culture of death" has its roots in "the mentality which *carries the concept of subjectivity to an extreme* and even distorts it, and recognizes as a subject of rights only the person who enjoys full or at least incipient autonomy and who emerges from a state of total dependence on others" (no. 19). It is likewise rooted in a "*notion of freedom* which exalts the isolated individual in an absolute way, and gives no place to solidarity, to openness to others and service of them" (no. 19), a misunderstanding of freedom which "*leads to a serious distortion of life in society*" (no. 20). This "culture of death" results ultimately in an "*eclipse of the sense of God and of man* typical of a social and cultural climate dominated by secularism" (no. 21). Citing Vatican Council II's Pastoral Constitution on the Church in the Modern World, *Gaudium et spes* (no. 36), which affirmed: "Without the Creator the creature would disappear. . . . But when God is forgotten the creature itself grows unintelligible," John Paul II continues:

> Man is no longer able to see himself as "mysteriously different" from other earthly creatures; he regards himself merely as one more living being, as an organism which, at most, has reached a high stage of perfection. Enclosed in the narrow horizon of his physical nature, he is somehow reduced to being "a thing," and no longer grasps the "transcendent" character of his "existence as man." He no longer considers life as a splendid gift from God, something "sacred," entrusted to his responsibility, and thus also to his loving care and "veneration." (no. 22)

After this incisive critique of the "culture of death," its root causes and effects, John Paul II concludes the first chapter by reviewing "signs of hope," which invite all to commit themselves to welcoming, loving, and serving human life (nos. 26-28). Among these "signs of hope" are many married couples who generously accept children as the supreme gift of marriage; families which serve life and give themselves to the least of their brothers and sisters (abandoned children and elderly persons, handicapped people, teenagers in difficulty); people who generously volunteer to offer hospitality and a supportive environment to the weak; medical scientists, agencies, and organizations mobilizing efforts to bring the benefits of modern medicine to the poor and needy (no. 26); movements and initiatives to raise social awareness to defend human life, particularly the life of the unborn and the sick and dying; the daily struggle of countless people to care for others; a new sensitivity ever more opposed to war as an instrument for resolving conflicts and to the use of capital punishment; concern for the quality of life and the ecology (no. 27). In concluding this chapter, the Holy Father points out that "the unconditional choice for life reaches its full religious and moral meaning when it flows from, is formed by, and nourished by *faith in Christ*" (no. 28).

B. Chapter Two: "The Christian Message Concerning Life"

This chapter first focuses our gaze on Christ, "the word of life" (1 Jn 1:1), in order to show us that the Gospel of Life is "something concrete and personal, for it consists in the proclamation of the *very person of Jesus*" (no. 29), the One who has come to reveal to us the complete truth about man and human life. Jesus, through word and deed, served life — in particular, the life of the poor and the weak. His words and deeds, John Paul II points out, "are not meant only for those who are sick or suffering or in some way neglected by society. On a deeper level they affect the *very meaning of every person's life in its moral and spiritual dimensions*" (no. 32). Jesus himself fully experienced life's contradictions and risks, living poverty throughout his life "until the culminating moment of the Cross: 'he humbled himself and became obedient unto death, even death on a cross. Therefore, God has highly exalted him and bestowed on him the name which is above every name' (Phil 2:8-9)." "It is precisely," the Pope continues, "*by his death* that *Jesus reveals all the splendor and value of life*, inasmuch as his self-oblation on the Cross becomes the source of a new life for all people (cf. Jn 12:32)" (no. 33).

Human life is surpassingly good because "the life which God gives man is quite different from the life of all other living creatures, inasmuch as man, although formed from the dust of the earth (cf. Gn 2:7, 3:19; Job 34:15; Ps 103:14; 104:29), is a *manifestation of God in the world, a sign of his presence, a trace of his glory* (cf. Gn 1:26-27; Ps 8:6)" (no. 34). Jesus brings human life, which is always a precious gift from God, to fulfillment. For Jesus shows us that God, in giving us life, shares something of himself with us precisely so that we can, in union with Jesus, fully participate in the life of the "Eternal

One" by literally becoming his very own children (nos. 37-38). "Eternal life is . . . the life of God himself and at the very same time the *life of the children of God* (cf. 1 Jn 3:1-2). . . . *Here the Christian truth about life becomes most sublime.* The dignity of this life is linked not only to its beginning, to the fact that it comes from God, but also to its final end, to its destiny of fellowship with God in knowledge and in love of him" (no. 38). Human life thus becomes the " 'place' where God manifests himself, where we meet him and enter into communion with him" (no. 39). The life of every human being is sacred and inviolable because God himself personally treasures and cares for it. His commandment that we are not to kill is rooted in the love and reverence due to the life he has given and confided to our trust (nos. 39-41).

Because he loves and trusts us, God allows us to share in his lordship by taking responsibility for human life. Husbands and wives, in particular, are privileged to "become partners in a divine undertaking: through the act of procreation, God's gift [of life] is accepted" lovingly and given the home where it is to take root and grow (no. 43). But "the task of accepting and serving life involves everyone; and this task must be fulfilled above all towards life when it is at its weakest," for Christ himself has told us that what we do to his littlest ones we do to him (cf. Mt 25:31-46) (no. 43).

Human life, God's precious gift, is most vulnerable when it comes into the world and when it leaves the realm of time to embark upon eternity (no. 44). When it comes into the world, it comes from the hand of God himself: "Before I formed you in the womb I knew you" (Jer 1:5; cf. Job 10:8-12; Ps 139: 13-14; 2 Mc 7:22-23). Thus the life of every individual, from its very beginning, is part of God's loving plan for human existence, a truth confirmed and deepened by the incarnation of God's only-begotten Son, who, while still in his mother's womb, was greeted with joy by his cousin John, an unborn child himself, who leapt for joy in Elizabeth's womb when Mary came to visit her cousin, who, despite her advanced age, was "with child" (cf. Lk 2:22-23) (nos. 40-45).

Human life, inescapably bodily in nature, is precious, in itself and to God, at every moment of its existence, even and especially when it is weak, when it suffers, when it draws near to death (nos. 47-48). God's command "You shall not kill" (Ex 20:13; Dt 5:17) is a specific command intended to protect the dignity and sanctity of human life; indeed, the whole of God's law, his wise and loving plan for human existence, fully protects human life. This law finds its fulfillment in Jesus, who shows us the authentic meaning of human life, namely, "that of being a *gift which is fully realized in the giving of self*," in the "*gift of self in love for one's brothers and sisters*" (no. 49).

The Gospel of Life is ultimately fulfilled on the tree of the Cross. From the pierced side of our Redeemer we have given to us "the very life of God." Jesus "proclaims that *life finds its center, its meaning, and its fulfillment when it is given up*" in love (no. 51).

C. Chapter Three: "God's Holy Law"

This chapter is devoted to the intimate bond between the Gospel of Life and the commandment, grounded in self-giving love, that we are not to kill. In this chapter, as he did in the first chapter of his encyclical *Veritatis splendor*, John Paul II begins with a meditation on the Gospel story of the rich young man who asked our Lord what he must do to enter into eternal life and was told that to do so he must keep the commandments (cf. Mt 19:6ff) (no. 52). The Gospel of Life is both a great gift of God and an exacting task for humanity: "In giving life to man God *demands* that he love, respect, and protect life. The *gift* has become a *commandment*, and the *commandment is itself a gift*" (no. 52).

Because it is God's precious gift and is thus sacred and inviolable, human life, particularly when weak and helpless, has God as its "*goel*," its defender (no. 53). The negative commandment "You shall not kill" simply indicates an extreme that can never be exceeded; but it implicitly encourages a positive attitude toward human life. This attitude, deepened and immeasurably enriched by the command that we are to love our neighbor as ourselves, helps to show us the enormity of the crime of murder, the intentional killing of innocent human beings (nos. 53-54).

The Pope, noting that "Christian reflection has sought a fuller and deeper understanding of what God's commandment prohibits and prescribes," reaffirms the Catholic tradition's teaching on the right to self-defense and on the right, and at times the duty, "for someone responsible for another's life, the common good of the family or of the State" to defend life even if one foresees that as a result of legitimately defending one's own or another's life from an unprovoked attack the life of the aggressor may be taken (no. 55). In such instances, one is not violating God's command, nor is one engaging in an act of killing. Rather, one's human act, as specified by the object chosen,[1] is rightly described as an act of legitimate defense and not as an act of killing.

It is in this context that the Pope takes up the question of capital punishment or the death penalty. Here it is important to note that he does not condemn capital punishment as intrinsically evil. Nonetheless, he teaches that, in order to defend the common good from criminal attacks and to punish evildoers for their unjust actions, society "ought not go to the extreme of executing the offender except in cases of absolute necessity; in other words, when it would not be possible otherwise to defend society." He concludes that today, "as a result of steady improvements in the organization of the penal system, such cases are very rare, if not practically nonexistent" (no. 56). In other words, he is saying that under contemporary conditions one ought not to inflict the death penalty. Those wishing to do so have the burden of proving that doing so is absolutely necessary, and John Paul II seriously doubts that this can be so today.

The command "You shall not kill" is absolute, i.e., without exceptions, when it refers to innocent human life, "and all the more so in the case of weak and defenseless human beings, who find their ultimate defense against the arrogance and caprice of others only in the absolute binding force of God's commandment" (no. 57).

In developing this central truth, John Paul II makes it clear that the Church's teaching on the absolute inviolability of innocent human life and on the intrinsic evil of every freely chosen act of deliberately killing innocent human beings has been infallibly proposed by the ordinary Magisterium of the Church. He is *not* solemnly defining this truth by an *ex cathedra* pronouncement, but he definitely claims that this truth pertains to the patrimony of faith as proclaimed by the ordinary and universal Magisterium. He introduces the subject by writing as follows:

> Faced with the progressive weakening in individual consciences and in society of the sense of the absolute and grave moral illicitness of the direct taking of all innocent human life, especially in its beginning and its end, *the Church's Magisterium* has spoken out with increasing frequency in defense of the sacredness and inviolability of human life. The Papal Magisterium, particularly insistent in this regard, has always been seconded by that of the bishops, with numerous and comprehensive doctrinal and pastoral documents issued either by Episcopal Conferences or by individual bishops. The Second Vatican Council also addressed this matter forcefully, in a brief but incisive passage.[2] (no. 57)

Continuing, he then goes on to say:

> Therefore, by the authority which Christ conferred upon Peter and his Successors, and in communion with the Bishops of the Catholic Church, *I confirm that the direct and voluntary killing of an*

innocent human being is always gravely immoral. This doctrine, based upon that unwritten law which man, in the light of reason, finds in his own heart (cf. Rom 2:14-15) is reaffirmed by Sacred Scripture, transmitted by the Tradition of the Church, and taught by the ordinary and universal Magisterium. (no. 57)

Since John Paul II explicitly refers, at the conclusion of the passage just cited, to the teaching of Vatican Council II in *Lumen gentium*, no. 25, it is both useful and necessary, properly to understand the significance of this centrally important passage, to see what the Council Fathers said in the passage referred to. It reads:

> Although the bishops, taken individually, do not enjoy the privilege of infallibility, they do, however, *proclaim the doctrine of the Church infallibly on the following conditions: namely, when, even though dispersed throughout the entire world but preserving for all that amongst themselves and with Peter's successor the bond of communion, in their authoritative teaching concerning matters of faith or morals, they are in agreement that a particular teaching is to be held definitively and absolutely.* (*Lumen gentium*, no. 25; emphasis added)

Note that John Paul II, before invoking the authority conferred upon Peter and his successors, made it a point to call attention to the universal teaching of the bishops and to the teaching of Vatican Council II on the intrinsic and grave malice of every direct and voluntary killing of innocent human beings. Surely this is a teaching on a matter of "morals," and the universal Magisterium agrees in judging that this teaching is to be held definitively and absolutely. Consequently, one can legitimately conclude that here John Paul II is asserting that this truth of Catholic moral teaching has been infallibly proposed by the ordinary and universal Magisterium of the Church, according to the criteria set forth in Vatican Council II's Dogmatic Constitution on the Church, *Lumen gentium*.[3]

Later in this chapter, in condemning the intrinsic evil of direct abortion, John Paul II first reviews the teaching of Scripture (no. 61), the two-thousand-year Tradition of the Church (no. 61), recent papal teaching (no. 62), and the Church's canonical discipline from the earliest times to the present on this question. He then writes:

> Given such unanimity in the doctrinal and disciplinary tradition of the Church, Paul VI was able to declare that this tradition is unchanged and unchangeable (cf. Encyclical Letter *Humanae vitae*, no. 14). There-

fore, by the authority which Christ conferred upon Peter and his Successors, in communion with the Bishops — who on various occasions have condemned abortion and who in the aforesaid consultation [which preceded publication of *Evangelium vitae*], albeit dispersed throughout the world, have shown unanimous agreement concerning this doctrine — *I declare that direct abortion, that is, abortion willed as an end or as a means, always constitutes a grave moral disorder*, since it is the deliberate killing of an innocent human being. This doctrine is based upon the natural law and upon the written Word of God, is transmitted by the Church's Tradition and taught by the ordinary and universal Magisterium [here again John Paul II explicitly refers to *Lumen gentium*, no. 25]. (no. 62; emphasis in original)

Clearly, here John Paul II affirms that the teaching on the grave immorality of direct abortion has been infallibly proposed by the ordinary and universal Magisterium.

Later, in unequivocally condemning euthanasia or mercy killing as always gravely immoral, John Paul II uses similar language:

In harmony with the Magisterium of my Predecessors [here a note refers to the teaching of Popes Pius XII and Paul VI and to *Gaudium et spes*] and in communion with the Bishops of the Catholic Church, *I confirm that euthanasia is a grave violation of the law of God*, since it is the deliberate and morally unacceptable killing of a human person. This doctrine is based upon the natural law and upon the written Word of God, is transmitted by the Church's Tradition and taught by the ordinary and universal Magisterium [again a note refers to *Lumen gentium*, no. 25]. (no. 65; emphasis in original)

The Pope thus affirms here that this truth of Catholic moral teaching has been infallibly proposed by the ordinary and universal Magisterium.[4]

In this chapter, John Paul II also insists that we must have the courage "to look truth in the eye and to call things by their proper names" (no. 58). Truth requires us to say that procured abortion is "the deliberate and direct killing, by whatever means it is carried out, of a human being in the initial phase of his or her existence, extending from conception to birth" (no. 58). The legalization of abortion is "a most serious wound inflicted on society and its culture by the very people who ought to be society's promoters and defenders" (no. 59).

It is also an affront to the dignity of human life to perform experiments on human embryos that are not intended to benefit them. Human life, even in its earliest stages of development, can never be regarded as "biological material" for research or as a source of organs or tissues for transplants: "the killing of innocent human creatures, even if carried out to help others, constitutes an absolutely unacceptable act" (no. 63).

The temptation "to have recourse to euthanasia, that is, to take control of death and bring it about before its time, 'gently' ending one's own life or the life of others" must be totally rejected (no. 64). Although it is morally licit to forgo medical procedures that "no longer correspond to the real situation of the patient, either because they are by now disproportionate to any expected results or because they impose an excessive burden on the patient and his family," "euthanasia is a grave violation of the law of God, since it is the deliberate and morally unacceptable killing of a human person" (no. 65). The same is true of suicide and "assisted suicide." Euthanasia and assisted suicide must be recognized as a "*'false mercy,'* and indeed a disturbing 'perversion' of mercy. True 'compassion' leads to sharing another's pain; it does not kill the person whose suffering we cannot bear" (no. 66). The quite different "*way of love and true mercy*" leads us to recognize, in the pleas of the dying and the suffering, a "request for companionship, sympathy and support in the time of trial . . . a plea for help to keep on hoping when all human hopes fail" (no. 67).

Today, some, at times many, claim that abortion and euthanasia must be regarded as human rights, or at least as legally permissible options if approved by the majority. Unfortunately, the civil law of far too many societies has given legal sanction to such claims (nos. 68-69). When ethical relativism, the root of these tendencies, prevails, it perverts democratic societies. Democracy "cannot be idolized to the point of making it a substitute for morality or a panacea for immorality." The moral value of a democracy depends on conformity to the moral law, whose truths do not depend on changeable "majority" opinions (no. 70).

If sound democracy is to develop, there is an urgent need to "rediscover those essential and innate human and moral values which flow from the very truth of the human being and express and safeguard the dignity of the person: values which no individual, no majority and no State can ever create, modify or destroy, but must only acknowledge, respect and promote" (no. 71). Public authority at times can tolerate moral evils in order to prevent more serious harms to human persons, but "it can never presume to legitimize as a right of individuals . . . an offense against other persons caused by the disregard of so fundamental a right as the right to life." Nor can the legalization of abortion or euthanasia be justified by appeals to respect for the consciences of others, "precisely because society has the right and the duty to protect itself against the abuses which can occur in the name of conscience and under the pretext of freedom" (no. 71). Thus civil laws legalizing the direct killing of innocent human beings through abortion and euthanasia are totally opposed to "the inviolable right to life proper to every individual and thus deny the equality of everyone before the law" (no. 72). Since no human law can authorize such evils, there is a grave obligation in conscience to oppose them; it is never right to obey them or take part in propaganda campaigns in favor of them or to vote for them (no. 73).

John Paul II recognizes that "a particular problem of conscience can arise in cases where a legislative vote would be decisive for the passage of a more restrictive law, aimed at limiting the number of authorized abortions, in place of a more permissive law already passed or ready to be voted on." In such cases,

> when it is not possible to overturn or completely abrogate a pro-abortion law, an elected official, whose absolute personal opposition to procured abortion was well known, could licitly support proposals aimed at *limiting the harm* done by such a law and at lessening its negative consequences at the level of general opinion and public morality. This does not ... represent an illicit cooperation with an unjust law, but rather a legitimate and proper attempt to limit its evil aspects. (no. 73)

A grave obligation of conscience requires persons not to cooperate formally in practices that, even if permitted by civil law, are contrary to "God's law." Such cooperation, which can never be justified, occurs "when an action, either by its very nature or by the form it takes in a concrete situation, can be defined as a direct participation in an act against innocent human life or a sharing in the immoral intention of the person committing it" (no. 74).

The commandment "You shall not kill," by absolutely excluding intrinsically evil acts such as the deliberate killing of innocent human beings, is the point of departure for true freedom because "it leads us to promote life actively, and to develop particular ways of thinking and acting which serve life" (nos. 75-76). The new law of love immeasurably enriches and deepens this commandment: "for the Christian it involves an absolute imperative to respect, love, and promote the life of every brother and sister, in accordance with the requirements of God's bountiful love in Jesus Christ" (no. 77).

D. Chapter Four: "For a New Culture of Human Life"

This chapter is an appeal to proclaim the good news of the "Gospel of Life" and to carry out the work of evangelization, "an all-embracing, progressive activity through which the Church participates in the prophetic, priestly and royal mission of the Lord Jesus" (no. 78). Ransomed by the "author of life" (Acts 3:15) at the price of his blood (cf. 1 Cor 6:30), and made his members by baptism, we are now *the people of life and we are called to act accordingly,*" sent into the world as a people to celebrate and serve life (no. 79). To proclaim Jesus is to proclaim life because he is "the word of life" (1 Jn 1:1). Because of our union with Jesus, we are adopted children of God, members of the divine family (no. 80). We are thus called to proclaim the "living God who is close to us, who calls us to profound communion with himself, who awakens in us the certain hope of eternal life"; we are summoned to affirm "the inseparable connection between the person, his life and his bodiliness" (no. 81).

Teachers, catechists, and theologians must show the anthropological reasons on which respect for every human life is based and help everyone discover how the Christian message "fully reveals what man is and the meaning of his being and existence." The task of proclaiming the Gospel of Life is primarily entrusted to bishops (no. 82).

To carry out our mission, we must foster in ourselves "a contemplative outlook," that "of those who see life in its deeper meaning, who grasp its utter gratuitousness, its beauty and its invitation to freedom and responsibility," accepting reality as a gift and with deep religious awe in order to "rediscover the ability to *revere and honor every person*" (no. 83).

Celebrating the Gospel of Life means celebrating the God of life, the God who gives life (no. 84). It requires us to "appreciate and make good use of the wealth of gestures and symbols present in the traditions and customs of different cultures and peoples" (no. 85). Above all, the Gospel of Life must be celebrated in our daily lives, filled with self-giving love for others. Only in this way can we provide the context within which "heroic actions . . . are born," actions proclaiming the Gospel of Life "by the total gift of self." Such heroism is reflected quietly in the lives of brave mothers "who devote themselves to their own families without reserve, who suffer in giving birth to their children, and who are ready to make any effort, to face any sacrifice, in order to pass on to them the best of themselves" (no. 86).

The Gospel of Life must be proclaimed by works of charity, a pressing need today. In carrying out these works, our attitude must be to "care for the other as a person for whom God has made us responsible." Appropriate and effective programs to support new life in particular must be implemented (no. 87).

A tremendous educational effort is needed to proclaim the Gospel of Life, including the development of centers for natural methods of regulating fertility, for marriage preparation and support, for helping unwed mothers welcome new life and care for it. Needed, too, are communities to help treat people suffering from drug addiction, from AIDS, and for all who are disabled. The elderly and terminally ill must be given the support necessary to sustain them in their final days. This requires a reconsideration of the role of hospitals, clinics, and convalescent homes, which must be "places where suffering, pain and death are acknowledged and understood in their human and specifically Christian meaning" (no. 88).

In proclaiming the Gospel of Life, a unique responsibility belongs to health care personnel: doctors, pharmacists, nurses, chaplains, men and women religious, administrators, and volunteers (no. 89). Effective works of charity need certain forms of social activity and commitment in the political field. Civil leaders have a grave obligation to serve human life through legislative measures. Political leaders must not enact laws "which by disregarding the dignity of the person, undermine the very fabric of society." It is not enough to remove unjust laws; it is necessary to root out the underlying causes of attacks on life, "especially by ensuring proper support for families and motherhood. A *family policy must be the basis and driving force of all social policies*" (no. 90).

The issue of population growth must be addressed by respecting the primary and inalienable responsibility of married couples and families and "cannot employ methods which fail to respect the person and fundamental human rights, beginning with the right to life of every innocent human being" (no. 91).

The family has a decisive responsibility with respect to the Gospel of Life. "This responsibility flows from its very nature as a community of life and love, founded on marriage, and from its mission to 'guard, reveal and communicate love.'" The family is the true "sanctuary of life." It is indeed the "domestic church," summoned to proclaim, celebrate, and serve the Gospel of Life. Married couples are called upon to be givers of life; they must recognize that procreation is "a unique event which clearly reveals that human life is a gift received in order to be given as a gift." They must raise their children in the love and service of God and neighbor (no. 92). To carry out its mission, the family must pray daily, practice solidarity within the home, and extend hospitality and solidarity to others (no. 93).

The neglect or, worse yet, the rejection of the elderly, who have a valuable contribution to make to the Gospel of Life, is an intolerable offense (no. 94).

Because the future of humanity passes through the family, the sanctuary of life, "the *family urgently needs to be helped and supported*." Tragically today, social, economic, and cultural conditions, far from serving the family, make its tasks more difficult. This must change (no. 94).

There is an urgent need for "general mobilization of consciences and a unified ethical effort to activate a great campaign in support of life. All together, we must build a new culture of life" (no. 95). To do this, the first and fundamental step is to form consciences rightly about the incomparable and inviolable worth of every human life and to reestablish the essential link between life and freedom, inseparably related goods of the human person. Of crucial importance in forming consciences is "the rediscovery of the necessary link between freedom and truth." Men must acknowledge that they are God's creatures: "Where God is denied and people live as though he does not exist, or his commandments are not taken into account, the dignity of the human person and the inviolability of human life also end up being rejected or compromised" (no. 96).

Education for life must emphasize its inherent value from its beginning. This demands that young people learn to value their sexuality and come to see the intimate bond between sexuality and authentic human love. Education in sexuality is education in chastity, a virtue enabling persons to respect the "spousal" meaning of the body, the responsibility of married couples to respect the beauty of human procreation and to be open to the gift of life by using natural methods of regulating fertility. Education for life also requires an education in the true meaning of suffering and death (no. 97).

In short, to develop a new culture of life we must have the courage "to *adopt a new life-style*" based on a correct scale of values: "*the primacy of being over having, of the person over things*"; it requires passing from indifference to concern for others, from rejection to acceptance. In developing this culture, everyone has a role. An indispensable one belongs to intellectuals, in particular Catholic intellectuals; likewise universities, especially Catholic universities, and centers, institutes, and committees of bioethics have an indispensable role. So, too, do those involved in the mass media, who should "present the positive values of sexuality and human love, and not insist on what defiles and cheapens human dignity" (no. 98). Women play a particularly important role in developing a new culture of life. They are to bear witness to the meaning of genuine love, especially of love for human life at its inception. Women who have had abortions should remember that the "Father of mercies is ready to give [them] forgiveness and peace," and enable them to re-commit themselves to the service of life (no. 99).

In developing a new culture of life, we must always remember that God, the Giver of Life, is our greatest friend and helper. We need to ask for his help in prayer and fasting "so that the power from on high will break down the walls of lies and deceit: the walls which conceal from the sight of so many of our brothers and sisters the evil of practices and laws which are hostile to life" (no. 100). The Gospel of Life, finally, is not for believers only, but for *everyone*. The value at stake, the value of human life, "is one which every human being can grasp by the light of reason." To be actively pro-life is "to contribute to the renewal of society through the promotion of the common good"; no genuine democracy can exist "without a recognition of every person's dignity and without respect for his or her rights." Nor can true peace exist unless "*life is defended and promoted*" (no. 101).

Conclusion

In the conclusion of his encyclical, Pope John Paul II turns to gaze on Mary, the Virgin Mother so intimately and personally associated with the Gospel of Life (nos. 102-104). She helps the Church to "*realize that life is always at the center of a great struggle* between good and evil, between light and darkness." She helps us realize that "it is precisely in the 'flesh' of every person that Christ continues to reveal himself and to enter into fellowship with us, so that *rejection of human life ... is really a rejection of Christ*" (no. 104). She is the one who helps us face our mission to proclaim life. Like her, we are not "to be afraid," for "with God nothing is impossible" (Lk 1:30, 37) (no. 105).

2. The Vatican *Instruction on Respect for Human Life in Its Origin and on the Dignity of Procreation* (*Donum Vitae*)

On February 22, 1987, the Congregation for the Doctrine of the Faith issued this document, which is divided into an introduction and three principal parts. I will now summarize its contents.

A. Introduction

The Introduction contains five sections. Section 1 deals with biomedical research and Church teaching. The purpose of the document is to put "forward the moral teaching corresponding to the dignity of the person and to his integral vocation" with reference to issues posed by contemporary biomedical research. Section 2 takes up the contributions science and technology can make to the human person. But science and technology are not morally neutral. They require respect for the "fundamental criteria of the moral law," the service of the human person, of his inalienable rights and his integral good according to God's design. Section 3 relates truths about human anthropology to procedures in the biomedical field. Interventions upon the human body affect the human person, especially in the field of sexuality and procreation, where "the fundamental values of life and love are actualized." Biomedical interventions must be morally evaluated in light of the dignity of the human person and his divine vocation. Section 4 proposes two basic criteria for moral judgment in this area, namely, (1) the inviolability of innocent human life "from the moment of conception until death" and (2) the special character of the transmission of human life, which has been "entrusted by nature to a personal act." Section 5 recalls the teaching of the Magisterium, which offers human reason the light of revelation on these two points, holding (1) that human life, from the moment of conception, must be absolutely respected because man is the only creature on earth that God "has wished for himself" and because the spiritual soul of man is "immediately created by God"; and (2) that human procreation requires the responsible collaboration of spouses with God's fruitful love. Human procreation must be realized in marriage through the acts proper and exclusive to spouses.

B. Part I: Respect for Human Embryos

This part has six major sections. Section 1, on respect due to the human embryo, reminds us that "the human being is to be respected as a person from the first moment of his existence." Modern science recognizes that the biological identity of a new human individual is already constituted in the zygote resulting from fertilization. This scientific conclusion gives a valuable indication for discerning by the use of reason a personal presence at the moment of the first appearance of human life: How could a human individual not be a human person?

The moral condemnation of procured abortion is reaffirmed. "Since the human embryo must be treated as a person, it must also be defended in its integrity, tended and cared for, to the extent possible, in the same way as any other human being." This is the principle determining the answers to the moral questions that will follow.

Section 2 deals with prenatal diagnosis. This is licit if the methods used with the informed consent of parents respect the life and integrity of the embryo and the mother without subjecting them to disproportionate risks. It is gravely immoral when the diagnosis is done with the thought of possibly inducing an abortion depending on its results. One must deny to the state or any other authority the right to link in any way prenatal diagnosis and procured abortion.

Section 3, concerned with *therapeutic* procedures on human embryos, affirms that they are licit if they respect the embryo's life and integrity and do not involve disproportionate risks. Procedures menacing the life or integrity of human embryos are illicit.

Section 4 takes up medical *research and experimentation* on human embryos. If the research is intended to benefit the embryo, it can be undertaken provided there is certainty that it will not harm the embryo's life or integrity and provided that proper consent has been given. Research and experimentation not directly therapeutic is absolutely illicit. Moreover, the corpses of human embryos and fetuses must be respected.

Section 5 affirms that it is absolutely immoral to produce human embryos *in vitro* as research material.

Section 6, which deals with procedures for manipulating human embryos engendered by new reproductive technologies, brands as absolutely immoral efforts to obtain a human being asexually through "twin fission," cloning, or parthenogenesis. It likewise brands as immoral efforts to make animal-human hybrids or to gestate human embryos in artificial or animal uteruses, as well as the freezing of embryos, attempts to engineer the "sex" of embryos, etc.

C. Part II: Interventions Upon Human Procreation

Here concern is with "artificial procreation and insemination," i.e., different technical procedures directed toward obtaining a human conception in a manner other than the sexual union of man and woman. This part begins by noting the ideological link between procured abortion and *in vitro* fertilization. This deathly dynamic, however, does not exempt us from a further and thorough ethical study of artificial fertilization, whether heterologous (when the gametic cells used come from persons not married to each other) or homologous (when these cells come from persons married to each other).

(1) *Heterologous Artificial Insemination*

Section 1 deals with the intimate link between marriage and human procreation. From the moral point of view, human procreation must be the fruit of marriage: this is the key principle. Every human being must be accepted as a gift and blessing. The procreation of a new human person must be "the fruit and sign of the mutual self-giving of the spouses." The child has a right to be conceived, carried in the womb, brought into the world and brought up within marriage. The good of society as well demands this. This is the only truly *responsible* way of generating human life.

Thus Section 2 repudiates heterologous artificial fertilization as immoral because it is contrary to the unity of marriage, to the dignity of the spouses, to the right of the child to be conceived and brought into the world in marriage and from marriage. Moreover, the fertilization of a woman who is unmarried or widowed, whoever the donor may be, is not morally justified.

Section 3 rejects "surrogate" motherhood as unacceptable for the reasons given already in repudiating heterologous artificial fertilization.

(2) *Homologous Artificial Insemination*

The key moral principle here is the intimate connection between procreation and the marital act. Three arguments are then given in Section 4, concerned with the connection between procreation and the marital or conjugal act.

(a) There is an inseparable connection, willed by God and unlawful for man to break on his own initiative, between the unitive and procreative meanings of the conjugal act. But artificial fertilization and procreation, even if the gametic cells used come from husband and wife, severs this bond. Fertilization is licitly sought when it is the result of a "conjugal act which is per se suitable for the generation of children to which marriage is ordered by its nature and by which the spouses become one flesh." From the moral point of view, procreation is deprived of its proper perfection when it is not desired as the fruit of a conjugal act, of the one-flesh unity of the spouses.

(b) The "language of the body" likewise shows that it is immoral for spouses to generate human life outside of their marital union, an act inseparably corporeal and spiritual. The origin of a new human person should be "linked to the union, not only biological but spiritual," of husband and wife.

(c) Respect for a human person in his origin requires that he not be treated as a product. When a child is begotten through the conjugal act, he comes to be as a gift from God, a gift crowning the spouses' mutual gift of themselves to each other. When a child is "produced," it comes to be, not as a gift from God, which in truth it is, but as a product of human control.

Section 5 specifically addresses the morality of homologous *in vitro* fertilization and embryo transfer. Even if we prescind from the ideological link between these procedures and procured abortion, the conclusion must be that these ways of generating human life are immoral. They dissociate the begetting of human life from the conjugal act and, in fact, establish the dominion of technology over the origin and destiny of the human person. Conception *in vitro* is not achieved or positively willed as the expression and fruit of a specific conjugal act; in homologous *in vitro* fertilization and embryo transfer, the generation of human persons is objectively deprived of its proper perfection, namely, that of being the result and fruit of a conjugal act expressing the love of husband and wife. The child so obtained has not been respected in his origin.

However a child comes into the world, whether as the fruit of a conjugal act or through these technologies, he must be respected as a person and as a gift from God.

Section 6 deals with homologous artificial insemination. This is rejected because it dissociates the two meanings of the conjugal act. The basic principle is this: if the procedure *replaces* or *substitutes* for the conjugal act, it is immoral; if, however, it *assists* or *helps* the conjugal act to achieve its purpose, it may be morally licit. Masturbation is repudiated as a morally illicit means of obtaining human sperm.

Section 7 treats of the moral criteria for medical intervention in human procreation. The physician is at the service of persons and of human procreation. He does not have the authority to dispose of them or to decide their fate. He is to aid the spouses and not, by his technique, substitute for them.

Section 8 concerns the suffering of spouses who cannot have a child or fear to bring a handicapped child into the world. The desire of spouses for children is natural and legitimate. But they do not have a "right" to a child because the child is not an object but a gift from God. Spouses suffering from sterility must bear their cross.

D. Part III: Moral Law and Civil Law
The inviolable right of every innocent human person and the institution of marriage are moral values and constitutive elements of the civil society and its order.

New technological possibilities require the intervention of political authorities and of legislators. Such intervention should be directed to ensuring the common good of the people through respect for their fundamental rights, the promotion of peace, and public morality. It furthermore ought to preserve the human community from temptations to selfishness and from discrimination and prejudice.

Among fundamental rights are these: (a) every human being's right to life and physical integrity and (b) the rights of the family and of the child.

Political authority may not approve making human beings through procedures exposing them to the grave risks noted in the document. The recognition by positive law of techniques of artificial transmission of human life would widen the breach already opened by the legalization of abortion. The law cannot tolerate, and in fact must forbid, that human beings, even at the embryonic stage of development, be treated as objects of experimentation, mutilated, or destroyed.

Civil law cannot approve techniques of artificial procreation that, for the benefit of third parties, take away what is a right inherent in the spousal relationship; therefore, civil law cannot legalize donation of gametes between persons who are not united in marriage. Legislation ought to also prohibit embryo banks, postmortem insemination, and surrogate motherhood.

Conclusion

In its conclusion, the document issues an invitation to all who can to exercise a positive influence and ensure that, in family and society, due respect is accorded to human life and love. In particular, it invites theologians, above all moralists, to study more deeply and make ever more accessible to the faithful the teaching of the Magisterium in the light of a valid anthropology of human sexuality and marriage.

All are invited to act responsibly in the area proper to each and, like the Good Samaritan, to recognize as a neighbor even the littlest among the children of men.

3. Declaration on Procured Abortion

This document was issued by the Congregation for the Doctrine of the Faith on November 18, 1974, during the pontificate of Pope Paul VI.

Consisting of 27 numbered sections, it is structured as follows: (A) an Introduction (nos. 1-4); (B) In the Light of Faith (nos. 5-7); (C) In the Additional Light of Reason (nos. 8-14); (D) Reply to Some Objections (nos. 15-18); (E) Morality and the Law (nos. 19-23); and (F) a Conclusion (nos. 24-27).

A. Introduction

This stresses that the Church cannot remain silent about the question of abortion because of her obligation to defend man against whatever destroys or degrades him and because the issue is so grave, concerned as it is with human life, the most basic of all man's goods (no. 1). The claim that abortion should be legalized since it does not violate anyone's conscience and reflects legitimate ethical pluralism is specious, because no one can claim freedom of thought as a pretext to attack the rights of others, especially the right to life (no. 2). Thus Christians, both clerical and lay, and notably bishops, have rightly resisted efforts to legalize abortion (no. 3). It is appropriate and necessary for the Congregation for the Doctrine of the Faith, charged with protecting and fostering faith and morals in the Church, to speak out on this matter; all the faithful must realize the need to assent to the truths of faith and morals proposed by the Magisterium. The *Declaration*'s teaching, therefore, lays a serious obligation on the consciences of the faithful (no. 4).

B. In the Light of Faith

Here the document stresses that God is the God of life, not death (no. 5), that the Church's Tradition from earliest times (e.g., the *Didache* of the second century) has always taught that human life must be protected at every stage in its course, including the beginnings (no. 6), despite different opinions regarding the precise time when a spiritual soul is infused. The teaching condemning abortion as gravely sinful, even by those who thought that the soul was not infused at conception, has been consistent throughout Church history and has been forcefully proclaimed by the Magisterium, especially in our day. As Pope Paul VI has said, the teaching of the Church on this matter is "unchanged and immutable" (no. 7).

C. In the Additional Light of Reason

Key points made here are: (1) human beings are persons because they have a rational nature and are radically capable of knowing the truth and making free choices; as a person, a human being is the subject of inviolable rights, among them the right to life (no. 8); (2) as a person, a human being is not subordinate to society but only to God, although a person must subordinate individual interests to the common good of society; his bodily life is a fundamental good (no. 9); (3) conscience must be enlightened to recognize that society is not the source of fundamental human rights but rather is obligated to respect and protect them (no. 10); the first right is the right to life, and society must respect this (no. 11); human life must be respected at all stages of development, from fertilization until natural death (no. 12).

Number 13 of this section is particularly interesting. It declares that modern genetic science confirms belief that all the characteristics of the person are fixed at conception. However, in footnote 19 of this number, the *Declaration* says that it deliberately leaves untouched the question, philosophical in nature, of when the spiritual soul is infused. It does so because "the tradition is not unanimous in its answer and authors hold different views: some think that animation occurs in the first moment of life, others that it occurs only after implantation." But it insists that the moral position it takes on abortion does not depend on the answer to that question, and this for two reasons: (1) Even if one supposes that animation occurs after conception, the life in question is incipiently human, preparing for and calling for a soul in which the nature received from the parents is completed. (2) It is enough that the presence of a soul is at least probable — and the contrary cannot be established with certainty — to show that taking the life of the fetus at least runs the risk of killing a person already in possession of a soul.

It is very important, I believe, to note that in *Evangelium vitae* Pope John Paul II addressed this question when he considered the view of those who "try to justify abortion by claiming that the result of conception, at least up to a certain number of days, cannot yet be considered a personal human life" (no. 60). After explicitly referring to no. 13 of the *Declaration on Procured Abortion*, he then said:

> What is at stake is so important that, from the standpoint of moral obligation, the mere probability that a human person is involved would suffice to justify an absolutely clear prohibition aimed at killing a human embryo. Precisely for this reason, over and above all scientific debates and those philosophical affirmations to which the Magisterium has not expressly committed itself, the Church has always taught and continues to teach that the result of human procreation, from the first moment of existence, must be guaranteed that unconditional respect which is morally due to the human being in his or her totality and unity as body and spirit.

He then concluded by making his own the teaching of *Donum vitae*, namely, that " '*The human being is to be respected and treated as a person from the moment of conception*; and therefore from that same moment his rights as a person must be recognized, among which in the first place is the inviolable right of every innocent human being to life' " (no. 60).

D. Reply to Some Objections

There can be serious reasons or motives for having an abortion (e.g., dangers to the mother's life and health, abnormal condition of the unborn child, extreme poverty, etc.). But life is too fundamental a good to be weighed against even very serious disadvantages. No reason can justify deliberately killing the unborn (no. 14). Women's liberation does not justify abortion (no. 15), nor does sexual freedom (no. 16), nor technological advance (which must be ruled by morality [no. 17]) — nor is birth control the answer (no. 18).

E. Morality and the Law

Cannot a legitimate pluralism legalize abortion, particularly to avoid harm to desperate women who seek abortion clandestinely (no. 19)? While civil law must tolerate some evils, it cannot accept the killing of the unborn (no. 20); civil law is subordinate to natural law, and the state has the obligation to protect the weak from the strong (no. 21). No one can rightly obey a law immoral in itself, nor can anyone take part in campaigns in favor of such laws, nor vote for them, nor collaborate in their application, etc. (no. 22). Law must reform society so that children will be welcomed and received worthily (no. 23).

F. Conclusion

At times heroism is needed to follow conscience and obey God's law, but fidelity to truth is necessary for true progress of human persons (no. 24). A Christian, whose outlook cannot be confined to this world, knows that he cannot measure happiness by the absence of sorrow and misery here below (no. 25). Every Christian must attempt to remedy such sorrows and miseries; while never approving abortion, Christians must work to combat its causes by effective means, including political action and development of suitable institutions to help pregnant women (no. 26). Action will never change unless hearts and minds are changed so that people will consider fertility a blessing, not a curse, and responsible cooperation with God in giving life a privilege and honor. Christians know that in facing these tasks Jesus will help them (no. 27).

4. Declaration on Euthanasia

This *Declaration*, promulgated by the Congregation for the Doctrine of the Faith on May 5, 1980, contains an Introduction, four parts (I. The Value of Human Life; II. Euthanasia; III. The Meaning of Suffering for Christians and the Use of Painkillers; IV. Due Proportion in the Use of Remedies), and a Conclusion.

A. Introduction

Here the document reminds readers of Vatican II's reaffirmation of the dignity of the human person and its unequivocal condemnation of crimes such as abortion, euthanasia, and willful suicide, and also of the Congregation's earlier *Declaration on Procured Abortion*. The Congregation now judges it opportune to set forth Church teaching on euthanasia, particularly in view of progress in medical science and issues this has raised.

B. Part I: The Value of Human Life

This part reaffirms that human life is the basis of all human goods. Most people regard it as sacred; no one may dispose of it at will; and believers regard it even more highly as a precious gift of God's love "which they are called upon to preserve and make fruitful." It then declares:

> 1. No one can make an attempt on the life of an innocent person without opposing God's love for that person, without violating a fundamental right, and therefore without committing a crime of the utmost gravity. 2. Everyone has the duty to lead his or her life in accordance with God's plan. That life ... must bear fruit already here on earth, but ... finds its full perfection only in eternal life. 3. Intentionally causing one's own death, or suicide, is therefore equally as wrong as murder. ... However, one must clearly distinguish suicide from that sacrifice of one's life whereby for a higher cause ... a person offers his or her own life or puts it in danger.

C. Part II: Euthanasia

The document defines euthanasia or mercy killing as "an action or an omission which of itself or by intention causes death, in order that all suffering may in this way be eliminated. Euthanasia's terms of reference, therefore, are to be found in the intention of the will and in the methods used." **NB:** One can kill a person mercifully or commit euthanasia by an act of *omission* as well as by one of commission.

It then articulates the *basic principle*, namely, "nothing and no one can in any way permit the killing of an innocent human being, whether a fetus or an embryo, an infant or an adult, an old person, or one suffering from an incurable disease, or a person who is dying." This is a "question of the violation of the divine law, an offense against the dignity of the human person, a crime against life, and an attack on humanity."

Some people, because of pain, suffering, etc., may ask to be killed mercifully; but many times when they ask for death they are really giving an anguished plea for help and love. What they need, besides medical care, is love.

D. Part III: The Meaning of Suffering for Christians and the Use of Painkillers

Physical suffering is an inevitable part of the human condition; it serves a useful purpose but so affects human psychology that it can become so severe that one wishes to remove it at any cost. Christians recognize that suffering has a special place in God's saving plan as a sharing in Christ's passion and union with his redemptive work. But there is nothing wrong in using painkillers as such so long as their use does not prevent one from carrying out religious and moral duties, even if one foresees that their use may shorten life. Painkillers that cause unconsciousness need special consideration because it is not right to deprive a person of consciousness without a serious reason for permitting this to happen.

E. Part IV: Due Proportion in the Use of Remedies

This is a very important part. The *Declaration* recalls the use in the past Catholic tradition of the distinction between "ordinary" and "extraordinary" means and notes that today — although the principle behind this distinction is good — it is sometimes difficult to understand because of the imprecision of these terms. Thus some today distinguish between "proportionate" and "disproportionate" means. The *Declaration* says that in any event one can make a "correct judgment as to means by studying the type of treatment to be used, its degree of complexity or risk, its cost and the possibilities of using it, and comparing these elements with the result that can be expected, taking into account the state of the sick person and his or her physical and moral resources."

This means that, although it is always gravely immoral to kill a person because of his or her alleged bad quality of life, the condition of a person's life can be used in judging whether a particular medical treatment is "proportionate" or "disproportionate."

In saying this, the *Declaration* in no way supports the proportionalist method of making moral judgments (as some proportionalists have claimed). First of all, the *Declaration* had previously affirmed unambiguously the existence of an absolute moral norm prohibiting an intrinsically evil act, namely, the norm absolutely proscribing the intentional killing of an innocent human being. No proportionalist affirms but rather denies this truth. Second, there are contexts in which judgments of proportionality can be made, *when there is some measure that can be used to compare measurable things.* Here the things to be measured are medical treatments of different types, each with their own risks, hazards, pains, costs, etc., and with their benefits. The judgment to be made in such cases is basically a technical one requiring some help from the medical profession. Moreover, although it is always wrong to kill a person because of the alleged bad quality of his life, a person's physical and moral resources will be such that some can accept treatments that other persons cannot because for some the treatment would be useful and not unduly burdensome whereas for others the treatments would not be useful and would be unduly burdensome. This topic will be considered at length in a later chapter.

The document then notes that it is not always wrong for patients to undergo perhaps hazardous and untried treatments if they so desire, and they can also forgo their use when they are seen not to do what they were supposed to do. Doctors can help greatly in judging whether the investment in instruments, personnel, etc., is just in proportion to the results achieved. No one can force a person to accept a risky or burdensome treatment, etc. If death is imminent, only normal care is required.

Conclusion to Chapter One

This chapter has reviewed in depth the teaching found in four major documents of the Magisterium relevant to the issues to be taken up in this book. The teaching found in Pope John Paul II's encyclical *Evangelium vitae* is pertinent to almost every topic that will be considered, while the teaching set forth in *Donum vitae* is crucially important relative to questions concerning the generation of human life, that presented in the *Declaration on Procured Abortion* is central to the problem of abortion, and that given in the *Declaration on Euthanasia* is, naturally, quite pertinent to issues regarding the care of the dying. In our subsequent study of these specific issues, reference will be made to the documents examined here as well as to other relevant sources of magisterial teaching.

ENDNOTES FOR CHAPTER ONE

1.   On this, see John Paul II, encyclical *Veritatis splendor*, no. 78; see also St. Thomas Aquinas, *Summa theologiae*, 2-2, 64, 7.

2. Here the Pope refers to an incisive passage in *Gaudium et spes*, no. 27, where the Council Fathers had said that "all offenses against human life itself, such as murder, genocide, abortion, euthanasia, willful suicide . . . are criminal; they poison civilization, and they debase their perpetrators more than their victims and militate against the honor of the Creator."

3. The truth of this conclusion is confirmed by what John Paul II subsequently declared in his *motu proprio*, entitled *Ad tuendam fidem* ("To defend the faith"), on May 1998, and by the "explanatory note" on this document prepared by the Congregation for the Doctrine of the Faith. In this note, the Congregation *explicitly* includes the "doctrine on the grave immorality of the direct and voluntary killing of an innocent human being" as an example of a truth proposed as divinely revealed, not through a "defining act," i.e., a truth "solemnly defined by an *ex cathedra* pronouncement of the Roman Pontiff or by the action of an ecumenical council, but through a "non-defining act," i.e., "by the ordinary and universal magisterium of the bishops dispersed throughout the world who are in communion with the Successor of Peter." The Congregation then notes: "Such a doctrine can be confirmed or reaffirmed by the Roman Pontiff, even without recourse to a solemn definition, by declaring that it belongs explicitly to the teaching of the ordinary and universal magisterium." The text of John Paul II's *Ad tuendam fidem* and of the Congregation's explanatory note, entitled "Commentary on the Profession of Faith's Concluding Paragraphs," is found in *Origins: CNS Documentary Service* 28.8 (July 16, 1998). The text of *Ad tuendam fidem* is given on pp. 114-116; that of the commentary on pp. 116-120. See in particular nos. 9 and 11 of the commentary.

4. In its explanatory note on John Paul II's *Ad tuendam fidem*, the Congregation for the Doctrine of the Faith explicitly recalls the teaching of *Evangelium vitae* and cites euthanasia as an example of a truth which, while not revealed, is connected by logical necessity to revealed truth and as one infallibly proposed by the ordinary and universal Magisterium of the Church. See no. 11 of "Commentary on the Profession of Faith's Concluding Paragraphs," in *Origins* (cf. endnote 3).

CHAPTER TWO

Making True Moral Judgments and Good Moral Choices

Before considering, in the following chapters, major bioethical issues, it is fitting and useful to consider first of all the subject of making true moral judgments and good moral choices. It is so precisely because the principles in light of which true moral judgments and good moral choices can be made in our everyday lives as husbands and wives, students, business men and women, or what have you, are the very same principles in light of which true moral judgments and good moral choices can be made in matters pertaining to bioethics.

Upright, virtuous men and women make true moral judgments and good moral choices insofar as doing so has become, as it were, second nature to them. Moreover, faithful Catholics can be confident that they make such judgments and choices by conforming them to the teaching of the Church, which speaks in the name of Christ. But everyone, even the virtuous person, is at times perplexed about what to do, and frequently there is no firm teaching of the Church to which one can appeal in order to make a true moral judgment about some difficult moral problem, and at times it is very difficult to apply such teaching to some complex issues. It is thus worthwhile to reflect more systematically on this matter.

Moreover, it is good for virtuous persons and faithful Catholics to reflect in this way so that they can more intelligently explain both to themselves and to others why they regard some human actions as morally good and others as morally bad, and why the Church's teaching on moral matters is true.

I will proceed as follows: First, I will clarify the meaning of a "human act," its religious and existential significance, and the sources of its moral goodness or badness. I do so because moral judgments bear upon human acts, assessing them for their moral quality. Second, I will consider different kinds of human dignity to show how human freedom of choice is related to truth, to God's wise and loving plan for human existence. Third,

I will consider the relationship between the "good" and human choice and action and the first principle of natural law. Fourth, I will consider the basic normative truths or principles of natural law, i.e., truths enabling us to distinguish between morally good and morally bad alternatives of choice and action. Fifth, I will outline briefly an intelligent way to go about making good moral judgments. Finally, I will consider how the natural law is fulfilled and perfected by the new law of love and what this means for Christians in making moral judgments and choices.[1]

1. The Meaning of a "Human Act"; Its Existential and Religious Significance; the Sources of Its Moral Character

A. The Meaning of a "Human Act"

Human acts are *not* physical events that come and go, like the falling of rain and the turning of leaves, nor do they "happen" to a person. They are, rather, the outward expression of a person's choices, for at the core of a human act is a free, self-determining choice, which as such is something spiritual which abides within the person, determining the very *being* of the person.

The Scriptures, particularly the New Testament, are very clear about this. Jesus taught that it is not what enters a person that defiles him or her; rather, it is what flows from the person, from his or her heart, from the core of his or her being, from his or her choice (cf. Mt 15:10-20; Mk 7:14-23).

Although many human acts have physical, observable components, what is central to them is the fact that they embody and carry out human choices; because they do, they abide within the person as dispositions to further choices and actions of the same kind, until a contradictory kind of choice is made. Thus I become an adulterer and remain an adulterer once I freely adopt by choice the proposal to have sex with someone other than my wife. I commit adultery in the heart even before I engage in the outward, observable act. And I remain an adulterer, disposed to commit adultery again, until I make a contradictory choice, i.e., until I sincerely repent of my adultery, do penance, and commit myself to amending my life and being faithful to my wife. Even then, in a sense, I remain an adulterer because I freely gave myself that identity, but now I am a *repentant* adulterer, resolved to be a faithful, loving husband, and I am a repentant adulterer because I have given myself this identity by my freely chosen act (made, of course, with the help of God's grace) of repentance.

B. The Existential, Religious Significance of Human Acts as Freely Chosen

This great truth, namely, that human acts as freely chosen have an existential, religious significance, has already, to some extent, been brought out in our consideration of the meaning of a human act as a reality shaped by a free, self-determining choice. But this matter is so critically important — it is precisely because human acts as freely chosen have existential and religious significance that eternal life depends on our making *good* moral choices in the light of *true* judgments — that it merits further reflection.

John Paul II eloquently emphasizes this truth at the very beginning of his 1993 encyclical, *Veritatis splendor*, in meditating on the dialogue between Jesus and the rich young man who asked, "Teacher, what good must I do to gain eternal life?" (Mt 19:16). Reflecting on this question, the Holy Father says: "For the young man the question is not so much about rules to be followed, but *about the meaning of life*. . . . This question is ultimately an appeal to the absolute Good which attracts and beckons us: it is the echo of a call from God, who is the origin and goal of man's life" (VS, no. 7). It is, he continues, "*an essential and unavoidable question for every man* for it is about the moral good which must be done, and about eternal life. The young man senses that there is a connection between moral good and the fulfillment of his own destiny" (VS, no. 8).

The rich young man's question has existential and religious significance precisely because it is in and through the actions we freely choose to do that *we determine ourselves* and establish our identity as moral beings. "It is precisely through his acts," the Pope writes, "that man attains perfection as man, as one who is called to seek his Creator on his own accord and freely to arrive at full and blessed perfection by cleaving to him." Our freely chosen deeds, he continues, "do not produce a change merely in the state of affairs outside of man, but, to the extent that they are deliberate choices, they give moral definition to the very person who performs them, *determining his most profound spiritual traits*" (VS, no. 71). Each choice involves a "*decision about oneself* and a setting of one's own life for or against the Good, for or against the Truth, and ultimately for or against God" (VS, no. 65).

To recapitulate: we *determine ourselves, make ourselves to be the kind of persons we are in and through the actions we freely choose to do.* We are free to choose what we are to do and through our choices make ourselves to be the kind of persons we are. But we are *not* free to make what we choose to do to be good or bad, right or wrong. We know this from our own experience, for we know that at times we have freely chosen to do things that we knew, at the very moment we chose to do them, were *morally wrong*. We can, in short, choose badly or well; and if we are to be fully the beings we are meant to be we need to choose well, i.e., in accordance with the truth. We will take this matter up in detail later in this chapter.

C. The Sources of the Morality of a Human Act

The morality of a human act depends on three factors: the *object* of the act, its *end*, and the *circumstances* in which it is done (cf. CCC, nos. 1750-1754; ST, I-II, 18). Of these, the *primary* source of the morality of a human act is the *object*, and no wonder, because the object of the act is precisely what the acting person *chooses to do*. This object is not some physical event in the external world. Since it is precisely what the acting person is choosing to do here and now, he or she ratifies this object in his or her heart and makes himself or herself to be the kind of person willing to do *this*. Thus, if I choose to lie, lying is the object of my act specifying it as an act of lying, and, because I freely choose to lie, I make myself *to be* a *liar*, no matter how I may want to describe myself to others or even to myself.

Pope John Paul II, rejecting some contemporary moral theories utterly incompatible with Catholic faith, has emphasized this great truth. Thus he wrote: "*the morality of the human act depends primarily and fundamentally on the 'object' rationally chosen by the deliberate will*" (VS, no. 78; emphasis in original). In a very important passage that not only well summarizes the Catholic tradition but also bears witness to the truth that a human act is no mere physical happening but rather a reality flowing from the inner core of the person insofar as it is a freely chosen deed, John Paul II goes on to say:

> In order to be able to grasp the object of an act which specifies that act morally, it is therefore necessary to place oneself *in the perspective of the acting person*. The object of an act of willing is in fact a freely chosen kind of behavior. To the extent that it is in conformity with the order of reason, it is the cause of the goodness of the will; it perfects us morally. . . . By the object of a given moral act, then, one cannot mean a process or an event of the merely physical order, to be assessed on the basis of its ability to bring about a given state of affairs in the outside world. Rather that object is the proximate end of a deliberate decision which determines the act of willing on the part of the acting person. (VS, no. 78; cf. ST, I-II, 18)

Note that in this passage John Paul II affirms that the object freely chosen, if it is "in conformity with the order of reason," is the "cause of the goodness of the will" and "perfects us morally." Obviously, if this object is *not* in conformity with the order of reason and is known not to be, then it will be the cause of the badness of the will and will debase us morally. The "order of reason" to which John Paul II refers will occupy us below, in considering the "natural law" or set of truths intended to guide human choices and enable human persons to distinguish between morally good and morally bad alternatives of choice/action.

Note, too, that in this passage John Paul II says that the "object" is also the "proximate end of a deliberate decision which determines the act of willing on the part of the acting person." The "object" is the "proximate" or "immediate" end of an act of willing because it is what one chooses to do here and now. There is also a further or ulterior end of most human actions, the end for whose sake one chooses to do this here and now. This further or ulterior end is a distinct source of the morality of a human act different from the "object" or "proximate end." But both the object or proximate end and the further or ulterior end must be good or in conformity with the order of reason if the human act in its totality is to be morally good. One can choose to do something morally good and in conformity with the order of reason for very bad ulterior ends. Thus one can choose to help carry an elderly widow's groceries into her house in order to gain entry to the house and steal her silverware or computer. The whole action is vitiated by the bad end toward which it is ordered and for whose sake one chose to carry in the groceries.

Frequently, people seek to justify their actions in terms of the further or remote end for whose sake they are done, and at times they even try to re-describe the "object" of their act in terms of its hoped-for benefits. Thus some may seek to justify an abortion by saying that what they are doing — their moral object — is to prevent human suffering (e.g., the suffering that a child afflicted by cystic fibrosis and his family might experience if he is allowed to be born). But this alleged justification is patently false, for the true "object" specifying their act of choice is aborting the unborn child. This is the means chosen, the act done, in order to bring about the remote or further end motivating the act.

The morality of an act also depends on the *circumstances* in which it is done. These, too, can be either good or bad. For instance, it is good to offer charitable correction to a friend, but to do so in front of his children rather than in private is a circumstance affecting the act, turning one otherwise morally good into one morally bad.

Because the morality of a human act, considered in its totality, depends on object (= proximate end), end (further or ulterior end), and circumstances, the act is morally good *only* if *all* these factors are morally good, i.e., in conformity with the order of reason. This is what can be called the principle of plenitude or perfection, expressed in Latin by the dictum *bonum ex integra causa*, which means that the act is morally good if and only if all the factors contributing to its moral quality are good. If *any* of these morally relevant factors is contrary to the order of reason, then the act is morally bad: *malum ex quocumque defectu* — an act is bad if it has any moral defect whatsoever (cf. CCC, nos. 1755-1756; ST, I-II, 18, 1; 18, 4, ad 3; 19, 6, ad 1).

Of these three sources of the morality of a human act, the "object," understood precisely as John Paul II has described it, is primary. An act morally bad by reason of the object freely chosen can never be made good by reason of any end, no matter how noble, or any circumstances, whatever they may be.

2. Kinds of Human Dignity; Human Freedom and God's Wise and Loving Plan for Human Existence

A. Kinds of Human Dignity

According to Catholic tradition, there is a threefold dignity predicable of human persons: (1) the first is intrinsic, natural, inalienable, and an endowment or gift; (2) the second is also intrinsic, but it is an achievement, not an endowment, an achievement made possible, given the reality of original sin and its effects, only by God's unfailing grace; (3) the third, again an intrinsic dignity, is also a gift, not an achievement, but is a gift far surpassing man's nature and literally divinizing him.

The first dignity proper to human beings is the dignity that is theirs simply as living members of the human species, which God called into being when, in the beginning, he "created man in his image . . . male and female he created them" (Gn 1:27). Every human being is a living image of the all-holy God and can therefore rightly be called a "created word" of God, the created word that his Uncreated Word became and is, precisely to show us how much God loves us.

When we come into existence, we *are*, by reason of this intrinsic dignity, *persons*. As God's "created words," as persons, we are endowed with the capacity to know the truth and the capacity to determine our lives by freely choosing to conform our lives and actions to the truth.[2] Yet when we come into existence, we are *not yet* fully the beings we are meant to be. And this leads us to consider the second sort of dignity proper to human persons, a dignity that is intrinsic but an achievement (made possible only by God's never-failing grace), not an endowment.

This second kind of dignity is the dignity to which we are called as intelligent and free persons capable of determining our own lives by our own free choices. This is the dignity we are called upon to *give to ourselves* (with the help of God's unfailing grace) by freely choosing to shape our choices and actions in accord with the truth. In other words, we give ourselves this dignity and inwardly participate in it by making good moral choices, and such choices are possible only in the light of true moral judgments. We give this dignity to ourselves by being true to our natural dignity as persons created in God's image and likeness.

The third kind of dignity is ours as "children of God," brothers and sisters of Jesus, members of the divine family. This kind of dignity is a pure gratuitous gift from God himself. He made us to be the *kind* of beings we are, i.e., persons made in his image and likeness, because he willed that there be beings inwardly capable of receiving, should he choose to grant it, the gift of divine life. And God has chosen to give this utterly supernatural gift to us in and through his Son become man, Jesus Christ. Just as Jesus truly shares our human nature, so, too, do human persons who are re-generated in the waters of baptism share in Jesus' divine nature. As true children of God and brothers and sisters of Jesus, we are called to walk worthily of our vocation *to be* co-workers with Christ, his collaborators in redeeming the world. I will take up the relevance of this dignity for making true moral judgments and good moral choices in section 6 of this chapter. My concern here and in the next two sections is with the second kind of dignity proper to human persons, the dignity that, as intelligent and free persons made in God's image and likeness, they are to give themselves by choosing in accordance with the truth.

B. Human Freedom of Choice and God's Wise and Loving Plan for Human Existence

The nature of this dignity and the relationship between human freedom and God's wise and loving plan for human existence was beautifully developed by Vatican Council II. According to the Council, "the highest norm of human life is the divine law — eternal, objective, and universal — whereby God orders, directs, and governs the entire universe and all the ways of the human community according to a plan conceived in wisdom and in love" (DH, no. 3). Immediately afterwards, the Council went on to say: "Man has been made by God to participate in this law, with the result that, under the gentle disposition of divine providence, he can come to perceive ever increasingly the unchanging truth" (DH, no. 3). Precisely because he can do this, man "has the duty, and therefore the right, to seek the truth" (DH, no. 3). The truth in question here is the truth that is to inwardly shape and guide human choices and actions — moral truth.

The passage concludes by saying that "on his part man perceives and acknowledges the imperatives of the divine law through the mediation of conscience" (DH, no. 3). Another Council document, the Pastoral Constitution on the Church in the Modern World, *Gaudium et spes*, develops this thought in a very significant passage:

> Deep within his conscience man discovers a law which he has not laid upon himself but which he must obey. The voice of this law, ever calling him to love and do what is good and to avoid evil, tells him inwardly at the right moment, do this, shun that. For man has in his heart a law written by God. *His dignity lies in obeying this law*, and by it he will be judged. His conscience is man's most secret core, and his sanctuary. There he is alone with God, whose voice echoes in his depths. By conscience, in a wonderful way, that law is made known which is fulfilled in the love of God and of one's neighbor. (GS, no. 16; emphasis added)

These passages make it clear that human persons give to themselves the dignity to which they are called only by choosing in accord with the truth. They likewise make it clear that God's divine, eternal law, his "wise and loving plan for human existence," is the highest norm of human life. They also affirm that human persons have been so made by God that they can inwardly participate in his divine, eternal law. Although these passages do not explicitly use the expression "natural law" to refer to our intelligent participation in God's eternal law, this is precisely what the expression "natural law" does mean in the Catholic tradition, and the Council Fathers, through official footnotes appended to the text, show that this is precisely how they understand natural law.[3]

3. The Relationship Between the "Good" and Human Choices and Action; the First Principles of Natural Law

Human choices and actions, whether morally good or morally bad, are intelligible and purposeful. Sinful choices, although *unreasonable* and opposed to the "order of reason," are not *irrational, meaningless, or absurd.*

All human choice and action is directed to some end or purpose, and the ends of purposes to which human choices and actions are ordered are considered as "goods" to be pursued. The "good" has the meaning of what is perfective of a being, constitutive of its flourishing or well-being. Consequently, the proposition *good is to be done and pursued and its opposite, evil, is to be avoided* is a proposition to which every human person, as intelligent, will assent (ST, I-II, 94, 2). It is a "principle" or "starting point" for intelligent, purposeful human choice and action. If human persons are to do anything, whether *morally* good or *morally* bad, there must be some "point" in doing it, something promising a benefit to the acting person. The principle that good is to be done and pursued and evil is to be avoided is the first principle or truth of the natural law, and everyone can understand it.

Moreover, this is not an empty principle. It can be specified by identifying the real goods perfective of human persons, aspects of their flourishing or full-being, and these goods are grasped by our practical reason as purposeful ends of human choice and action. St. Thomas identified a triple-tiered set of such human goods, which, when grasped by our reason as ordered to action ("practical reason"), serve as first principles or starting points for intelligent human activity, as starting points for practical deliberation — "What am I to do?" The first set includes being itself, a good that human persons share with other entities; and since the being of living things is life itself, the basic human good at this level is that of life itself, including bodily life, health, and bodily integrity. The second set includes the bodily union of man and woman in order to hand life on to new human persons, who need education and care if they are to flourish, and this is a set of goods that human persons share with other animals, but, of course, in a distinctively human way. The third set includes goods unique to human persons, such goods as knowledge of the truth, especially truth about God, fellowship with other persons in a human community (friendship and justice, peace), and the good of being reasonable in making choices (cf. ST, I-II, 94, 2).

To sum up: the first principles — the "starting points" — or first truths of natural law are the truths (a) that *good is to be done and pursued and evil is to be avoided* and (b) propositions identifying real goods of human existence as the goods that are to be pursued and done and whose opposites are evils to be avoided, propositions such as *life is a good to be pursued and protected, knowledge of the truth is a good to be pursued, friendship is a good to be pursued*, etc. These propositions articulate truths, practical in nature (i.e., relevant to human action), that do not need to be demonstrated as true — their truth is immediately evident for anyone who knows what they mean.

None of these goods is the highest or greatest good, the *Summum Bonum*. God alone is this good. But each of these goods is a real good of human persons, inwardly perfective of them; each is a created participation in the uncreated goodness of God himself. The propositions directing that good is to be done and identifying these as the goods which authentically perfect human persons and which are, consequently, the goods to be pursued in and through human action do not, however, enable us to distinguish, prior to choice, between alternatives of action that are morally good and those that are morally bad. Indeed, even sinners appeal to these goods and the principles directing that they be protected in order to "justify" or, rather, rationalize their immoral choices. Thus a research scientist who unethically experiments on human subjects, failing to secure their free and informed consent because he knows that they will not give it should they be aware of the risks his experiment entails, may try to rationalize his immoral behavior both to himself and others by appealing to the good of knowledge to be gained through his experiments and its benefits for the life and health of other persons.

But, in addition to these *practical* principles of natural law, there are also practical principles that are *moral* in function, i.e., truths that enable human persons to distinguish, prior to making choices, which alternatives are morally good and which are morally bad. I shall now turn to a consideration of these moral or normative truths of the natural law.

4. Normative Truths of Natural Law

St. Thomas Aquinas, in an article devoted to showing that all of the moral precepts of the Old Law can be reduced to the ten precepts of the Decalogue, taught that the twofold law of love of God and neighbor, while not among the precepts of the Decalogue, nonetheless pertained to it as the "first and common precepts of natural law." Consequently, all the precepts of the Decalogue must, he concluded, be referred to these two love commandments as to their "common principles" (ST, I-II, 100, 3 and ad 1). In other words, for St. Thomas the very first *moral* principle or normative truth of natural law can be properly expressed in terms of the twofold command of love of God and neighbor. St. Thomas held this view, obviously, on the authority of Jesus himself, who, when asked, "Teacher, which commandment in the law is the greatest?" replied, citing two Old Testament texts (Dt 6:5 and Lv 19:18), "You shall love the Lord, your God, with all your heart, with all your soul, and with all your mind. This is the greatest and the first commandment. The second is like it: You shall love your neighbor as yourself. The whole law and the prophets depend on these two commandments" (Mt 22:36-40; cf. Mk 12:28-31; Lk 10:25-28; Rom 13:10; Gal 5:14).

In short, for St. Thomas — and the entire Catholic tradition — the very first moral principle of natural law is that we are to love God and our neighbor as ourselves. Moreover, and this is very important, there is an inseparable bond uniting this first *moral* principle of natural law to the first *practical* principle of natural law, which directs us to do and pursue the good and the principles specifying the real goods of human persons that are to be pursued and done. For the goods that are to be done and pursued in human action — the goods perfecting human persons — are in truth *gifts* from a loving God that we are to welcome and cherish, and it is obvious that we can love our neighbors *only* if we are willing to respect fully the goods perfective of them, only by willing that these goods flourish in them, and by being *unwilling* intentionally to damage, destroy, or impede these goods, to ignore them or slight them or put them aside, substituting pseudo-goods for them.

Pope John Paul II has well expressed the indissoluble bond between love for the goods of human existence and love for our neighbor. Commenting on the precepts of the second tablet of the Decalogue, i.e., those concerned with actions regarding our neighbor, he reminds us (as did Aquinas before him) that these precepts are rooted in the commandment that we are to love our neighbor as ourselves, a commandment expressing "*the singular dignity of the human person,* 'the only creature that God has wanted for its own sake'" (VS, no. 13, with an internal citation from GS, no. 22).

After saying this, the Holy Father continues, in a passage of singular importance for grasping the *truth* that is meant to guide our choices and actions, by emphasizing that we can love our neighbor and respect his dignity as a person only by cherishing the real goods perfective of him and by refusing intentionally to damage, destroy, impede, ignore, neglect or in any other way shut ourselves off from what is truly good. Appealing to the words of Jesus, he highlights the truth that "the different commandments of the Decalogue are really only so many reflections on the one commandment about the good of the person, at the level of the many different goods which characterize his identity as a spiritual and bodily being in relationship with God, with his neighbor, and with the material world.... The commandments, of which Jesus reminds the young man, *are meant to safeguard the good of the person, the image of God, by protecting his goods*" (VS, no. 13). The negative precepts of the Decalogue — "You shall not kill; You shall not commit adultery; You shall not steal; You shall not bear false witness" — all these precepts, he concludes, "express with particular force the ever urgent need to protect human life, the communion of persons in marriage," and so on (VS, no. 13).

Here the Holy Father is simply articulating once more the Catholic moral tradition. Centuries ago St. Thomas Aquinas observed that "God is offended by us only because we act contrary to our own good" (SCG 3.122).

In summary: the first *moral principle* of natural law, requiring us to love God and our neighbor as ourselves, directs us, in every one of our freely chosen deeds, to respect fully *every real good* perfective of human persons and to refrain from intentionally choosing to damage, destroy, impede, neglect, ignore, or in any other way fail to honor these goods and the persons in whom they are meant to flourish. This first moral principle of natural law, expressed fittingly in religious language by the twofold commandment of love of God and neighbor, can be expressed in more philosophical language, some contemporary Catholic authors convincingly argue, by saying that "in voluntarily acting for human goods and avoiding what is opposed to them, one ought to choose and otherwise will those and only those possibilities whose willing is compatible with integral human fulfillment" (CMP, p. 184).[4]

In other words, if we are to choose well, in accordance with the truth or order of reason, our basic attitude must be that of persons eager to embrace, revere, and honor the real goods perfective of human persons and the persons in whom these goods are meant to flourish because these goods are *gifts* from God himself, created participations in his own uncreated goodness, and constitutive aspects of the *full being* of the human persons made in his image.

This basic, first principle of morality logically entails various "modes of responsibility," i.e., moral principles specifying ways in which we can fail to love human persons and the goods meant to flourish in them. These are moral principles such as the Golden Rule — we are to do unto others as we would have others do unto us and not do unto others as we would not have them do unto us (cf. Mt 7:12; Lk 6:31; ST, I-II, 94, 4, ad 1) — and the principle that we are not to do evil so that good may come about (cf. Rom 3:8) (on this subject cf. May, p. 103).

In light of the first moral principle of natural law and its modes of responsibility, we can show the truth of more specific moral norms, such as the precepts of the Decalogue, and come to understand that some human acts, as specified by their moral objects, are intrinsically evil and hence absolutely forbidden. If we were willing to make these objects the end of our will act of choice, we would be willing that *evil be* and thus freely make ourselves *evil*-doers.

This truth will be grasped readily if we recall here what was said before about the "object" of a human act, namely, the "freely chosen kind of behavior." Morally good objects are compatible with a love for *all* the goods of human persons and for the God whose gifts these goods are. Human acts specified by such objects are capable of being ordered to God; they specify morally good kinds of human acts, whereas objects opposed to these goods and to the persons in whom they are meant to flourish are not capable of being ordered to God, and such objects specify morally bad kinds of human acts. As Pope John Paul II puts the matter, "reason attests that there are objects of the human act which are by their nature 'incapable of being ordered to God,' *because they radically contradict the good of the person made in his image*" (VS, no. 80). Acts so specified are *intrinsically evil* acts and the specific moral norms proscribing them are *absolute*, i.e., without any possible exceptions.

The Catholic moral tradition — and sound philosophical ethics as well — has recognized that there are human acts of this kind, i.e., human acts specified by "objects" which cannot be chosen by one with a will toward integral human fulfillment, by one who loves all the goods of human persons and the persons in whom these goods are meant to flourish, who regards these goods as precious gifts from God himself. Among such intrinsically evil acts are the intentional (direct) killing of an innocent human being, having sexual relations outside of marriage (fornication, adultery), and the like; norms proscribing such intrinsically evil acts are moral absolutes.

Precisely because the truth of these moral absolutes is so widely denied today, even by some theologians, John Paul II found it necessary to devote his encyclical *Veritatis splendor* to the defense of this truth. He declared that "the central theme of this encyclical . . . is the reaffirmation of the universality and immutability of the moral commandments, particularly those which prohibit always and without exception intrinsically evil acts" (VS, no. 115). He clearly affirms that the truth of these moral commandments is rooted in God's love and in his call to each one of us to be holy as he is holy (cf. Lv 19:2), his commandment that we are to be as perfect as he is perfect (cf. Mt 5:48). "The unwavering demands of that commandment are based upon God's infinitely merciful love (cf. Lk 6:36) and the purpose of that commandment is to lead us, by the grace of Christ, on the path of that fullness of life proper to the children of God" (VS, no. 115).

5. Steps in Making True Moral Judgments

In light of the normative truths of natural law, we can make true judgments regarding the morality of human acts as specified by their "objects,"
i.e., by *what* is proposed as an object of free choice. We have already seen
that there are certain kinds of human acts, as specified by their moral
objects, that we ought never to freely choose to do: intentionally to kill an
innocent human being, to commit adultery or fornication, etc. Obviously,
one cannot intentionally choose to kill an innocent human being without
freely willing that a great evil *be*, namely, the death of that person whose life,
a good of incalculable value, one has chosen to destroy. Similarly, one cannot freely choose to commit adultery without being willing to damage the
incalculable human good of marital fidelity and communion.

What this shows us is that, in considering the moral quality of any proposed alternative of action — any "object" of a human act — one must consider how this proposed action impinges on the *goods* of human persons. If
the proposed action is specified by an object of choice that one *cannot* will
without being willing to damage, destroy, or impede some true good of
human persons, or without being willing to ignore, slight, or repudiate some
real good of human persons, then this proposed action is specified by a
morally bad object and hence not referable to God because it contradicts
the good of persons made in his image.

Moreover, since the morality of human acts, though primarily settled
by the object freely chosen, also depends on the ends for whose sake they
are chosen and done and on the circumstances in which they are done,
these ends and circumstances must also be in accord with the order of reason, i.e., in accord with a love and respect for the goods of human persons.
Actions good by reason of their object can become bad by reason of the end
for which they are chosen or the circumstances surrounding them. Thus,
while it is morally good in itself to sing a beautiful aria — by doing so one
is participating in the good of beauty and perhaps enabling others to do so
as well — it is not morally good to choose to do so in a dormitory at 3 a.m.
and thus disturb the sleep of others. But one can never justify a human act
morally bad by reason of its object (an intrinsically evil act) by *any* end,
however noble (cf. CCC, no. 1756).

To put matters another way: Some proposals of choice (the "objects" of
the act), while relevant to one or perhaps more human goods, are *compatible with a love and respect for all human goods*. Such moral objects are in
accord with the order of reason, and thus acts specified by them can be

rightly chosen. Other proposals of choice, while relevant to one or perhaps more human goods and compatible with a love and respect for *some* human goods, *are not compatible with love and respect for at least one human good*, that good, namely, whose destruction or injury is indeed the "object" of choice. Human acts specified by moral objects of this kind are not in accord with the order of reason and must be judged immoral.

6. The "Fulfillment" or "Perfection" of Natural Law Through the Redemptive Work of Christ

In his introduction to *Veritatis splendor*, John Paul II calls attention to a truth of supreme importance. This is the truth that "it is only in the mystery of the Word Incarnate that light is shed on the mystery of man. . . . It is Christ, the last Adam, who fully discloses man to himself and unfolds his noble calling by revealing the mystery of the Father and the Father's love" (VS, no. 2, citing GS, no. 22). Jesus, in his very person, "fulfills" the law and brings it to perfection and thereby reveals to man his noble calling. As a consequence, to live a moral life means ultimately to follow Christ.

We follow him not by any outward imitation but by "becoming conformed to him who became a servant even to giving himself on the Cross" (VS, no. 21; cf. Phil 2:5-8). Following Christ means "holding fast to the very person of Christ" (VS, no. 19).

But how can we "hold fast" to Christ? We do so by shaping our lives — by making moral judgments and choices — in accord with the sublime truths that Jesus makes known to us. Jesus not only reconfirms the truths of the old law given to Moses (which embodied truths of natural law), he also gives us a new command of love. The old law — as well as the natural law — commands us to love our neighbor as ourselves. The new commandment Jesus gives us still requires this, but it goes beyond it, for Christians, Jesus' brothers and sisters, true children of God, are commanded by him to love one another even as he has loved us, with a healing, redemptive kind of love (cf. Jn 15:12; VS, nos. 18, 20), the kind of self-giving love that finds expression on the Cross.

In his Sermon on the Mount (Mt 5), Jesus specifies for us the nature of this self-giving love. Pope John Paul II, following St. Augustine, St. Thomas, and the Catholic tradition, regards our Lord's Sermon on the Mount as the "*magna charta* of Gospel morality" (VS, no. 15). The Beatitudes of this Sermon "speak of basic attitudes and dispositions in life and therefore they do not," John Paul II says, "coincide with the commandments. . . . [They are], above all, *promises* from which there also flow *normative indications* for the moral life. . . . They are a sort of self-portrait of Christ . . . invitations to discipleship and communion of life with Christ" (VS, no. 16).

The Beatitudes are not optional for the Christian, precisely because they describe the dispositions and attitudes that ought to characterize the followers of Christ. Here we must keep in mind the supreme truth about our existence as Christians and the sublime dignity (cf. the third kind of dignity described above) that is ours as children of God, brothers and sisters of Jesus, members of the divine family.

The Beatitudes of the Sermon on the Mount can be regarded — as Germain Grisez has so well presented matters — as "modes of Christian response." They specify ways of acting (including ways of making good moral judgments) that mark a person whose will, enlivened by the love of God poured into his or her heart, is inwardly disposed to act with the confidence, born of his or her Christian hope, that integral human fulfillment is *indeed* possible and realizable in union with Jesus (cf. CMP, pp. 653-655).

In bearing our cross daily and shaping our judgments, choices, and actions in accord with the truth — and ultimately the truth made known to us by Jesus — we can be confident that the burden he gives us is sweet and his yoke is light because *he is with us!* He is our Emmanuel. And he is, in truth, our Simon of Cyrene, who will help us bear our cross so that we can carry on his work of redemptive love.

ENDNOTES FOR CHAPTER TWO

1.   The following sources are used for this chapter:

Documents of the Church's Magisterium:
(1) *Catechism of the Catholic Church*, abbreviated as CCC.
(2) Vatican Council II, Dogmatic Constitution on the Church, *Lumen gentium*, abbreviated as LG.
(3) Vatican Council II, Pastoral Constitution on the Church in the Modern World, *Gaudium et spes*, abbreviated as GS.
(4) Vatican Council II, Declaration on Religious Liberty, *Dignitatis humanae*, abbreviated as DH.
(5) Pope John Paul II, encyclical *Veritatis splendor* ("The Splendor of Truth"), abbreviated as VS.

Other Sources:

(1) St. Thomas Aquinas, *Summa theologiae*, abbreviated as ST. The *Summa theologiae* is divided into parts, questions, and articles. There are three parts in the *Summa*, and the second part is in turn divided into two parts. The parts will be referred to by roman numerals, the questions and articles by arabic numerals. Thus ST, I-II, 94, 2 means: *Summa theologiae*, First Part of the Second Part, question 94, article 2. Frequently, important material is contained in St. Thomas's responses to the objections he poses at the beginning of each article. These responses are indicated by "ad 1," "ad 2," etc., meaning "response to objection 1," "response to objection 2," etc.

(2) St. Thomas Aquinas, *Summa contra gentiles*, abbreviated as SCG. This work is divided into four books, and the books are divided into chapters. Both will be indicated by arabic numerals, with a period between the arabic numeral designating the book and the arabic numeral indicating the chapter. Thus SCG 3.111 means *Summa contra gentiles*, book 3, chapter 111. This work of St. Thomas has been translated into English as *On the Truth of the Catholic Faith* (New York: Doubleday Image Books, 1955), five volumes.

NB: Perhaps the finest presentation of St. Thomas's moral thought is to be found in John Finnis, *Aquinas: Moral, Political, and Legal Theory* (Oxford and New York: Oxford University Press, 1998), chapters II-V, pp. 20-186.

(3) Germain Grisez, *The Way of the Lord Jesus*, Vol. 1, *Christian Moral Principles* (Chicago: Franciscan Herald Press, 1983). This work will be abbreviated as CMP.

(4) William E. May, *An Introduction to Moral Theology* (second ed.: Huntington, IN: Our Sunday Visitor, 2003). This will be referred to as May.

All the above references are placed in parentheses in the text at appropriate places.

2. A baby, born or preborn, does not, of course, have the *developed* capacity for deliberating and choosing freely, but he has the *natural* or *radical* capacity to do so because he is human and personal in nature. This matter will be taken up in more depth in a later chapter concerned with the moral status of the embryo.

3. Thus, in *Dignitatis humanae,* no. 3, after affirming that God has made man capable of sharing in his law and thus coming to know ever more the unchanging truth, the Council Fathers added an official footnote, in which they refer to three key texts of St. Thomas, namely, ST, I-II, 91, 1; 93, 1; and 93, 2, in which St. Thomas affirms, among other things, that "the

eternal law is unchanging truth, and everyone somehow knows the truth, at least the *common principles of natural law* (even though in other matters some people share more and some less in the knowledge of the truth)" (ST, I-II, 93, 2). Unfortunately, the commonly used English translations of the Documents of Vatican Council II (the "Abbott" edition and the first "Flannery" edition) fail to include this official footnote, which is, however, in the Latin original. Fortunately, subsequent editions of the "Flannery" translation include the footnote.

4.   In suggesting this way of formulating in non-religious and more philo-sophical language the first moral principle of natural law, Grisez and his associates (John Finnis, Joseph Boyle, and myself) are in large measure simply following a suggestion made by the Fathers of Vatican II. As we have seen already, they clearly affirmed that the "highest norm of human life," i.e., the *ultimate norm of morality*, is God's divine, eternal law, in which we participate through the natural law (cf. DH, no. 3). But, in speaking of human action in this world, they also said that the "norm for human activ-ity is this: that, in accord with the divine plan and will, *human activity should harmonize with the genuine good of the human race*, and allow men as individuals and as members of society to pursue their total vocation and fulfill it" (GS, no. 35).

CHAPTER THREE

Generating Human Life: Marriage and the New Reproductive Technologies

Introduction

If the human race is to continue, new human beings must come into existence. It is now possible to "make" human babies in the laboratory through an array of modern reproductive technologies. But, as we all know, the usual way for bringing new human persons into existence is for a man and a woman to engage in genital intercourse, either within marriage and through the marital act or outside of marriage through acts of adultery and fornication or, as the latter is euphemistically called today, "premarital" sex.

No matter how a new human being comes into existence, he or she is something precious and good, a person, a being of incalculable value, worthy of respect, a bearer of inviolable rights, a being *who ought to be loved*.[1] This is true no matter how the child comes to be: whether through the intimate and chaste embrace of husband and wives, through acts of adultery or fornication, or through use of modern reproductive technologies.

This chapter is divided as follows. Part One briefly considers moral issues raised by generating human life through acts of fornication and adultery. Part Two considers at greater length and in depth the bonds intimately uniting marriage, the marital act, and the gift of human life in order to show why, in God's loving plan for human existence, new human life is properly respected when it comes to be in and through the marital embrace and how the generation of human life in and through the marital act is an act of *procreation*, not one of *reproduction*. Part Three takes up in depth the new reproductive technologies; after describing them in some detail, it will set forth ethical and theological arguments to show that it is intrinsically immoral to make use of technologies that generate new human life outside the marital act. Part Four presents criteria for distinguishing between technological interventions that "assist" the marital or conjugal act in being fruitful and those that substitute for it and replace it. Part Five considers the "rescuing" of frozen embryos produced by the new reproductive technologies.

1. Part One: Fornication, Adultery, and the Generation of Human Life

Here we can state straightforwardly that it is *not* good to generate human life through acts of adultery and fornication. It is not good because fornicators and adulterers have not made themselves *fit* to receive the great gift of human life. They do not have the moral capacity to receive this surpassingly great gift because they have not, through their own free and self-determining choices, capacitated themselves to cooperate with God in raising up new life and giving it the home where it can take root and grow.[2] Indeed, practically all civilized societies have, until recently, regarded as irresponsible the generation of new human life through the coupling of unattached males and females. Even today, secular society judges fornicators and adulterers to be acting "responsibly" only if they take care to prevent unwanted pregnancies (and for the most part fornicators and adulterers do not want a pregnancy) by using contraceptives and, should contraceptives fail, abortion as a backup to prevent the birth of an unwanted child (the issues of contraception and abortion will be taken up in depth in later chapters).[3] It is, unfortunately, symbolic of a new barbarism — of the "culture of death" — that many today claim that unmarried individuals have the "right" to generate human life if they so choose, whether through freely chosen genital acts of fornication or adultery or through new laboratory methods of producing new human life.[4]

2. Part Two: Marriage and the Generation of Human Life

Two of the documents examined in Chapter One (*Evangelium vitae, Donum vitae*) testify to the Church's profound love and respect for marriage and the family. Married couples, as Pope John Paul II affirmed, are summoned to be givers of life and to recognize that procreating human life is "a unique event which clearly reveals that human life is a gift received in order to be given as a gift" (*Evangelium vitae*, no. 92). The *Instruction on Respect for Human Life in its Origin and on the Dignity of Procreation* (*Donum vitae*) insisted that the procreation of new human life must be the fruit of marriage and the marital act. As we saw in Chapter One, this document gave three reasons why it is wrong to generate human life outside the marital act: the first was based on the inseparable connection, willed by God and not lawful for man to sunder on his own initiative, between the unitive and procreative meanings of the marital act; the second, on the "language of the body"; the third, on the obligation to regard the child always as a person and never as a product. When children are engendered through the loving embrace of husbands and wives, the "inseparable connection" and the "language of the body" are fully respected, and the children are in no way treated as "products." To show that this is true, I will consider (A) how men and women, by getting married, give themselves rights and capacities that unmarried persons simply do not have. Next (B), I will reflect on the meaning of the marital act as inherently unitive and procreative, and I will then (C) show that the life given in and through the marital act is truly "begotten, not made."

A. Marriage, Marital Rights, and Capacities

Fornicators and adulterers do not have the right either to "give" themselves to one another in genital sex or to "receive" the great gift of human life. They do not have the right to do these things precisely because they have failed to capacitate themselves to do them, to make themselves *fit* to do them.

But husbands and wives, precisely because they have given themselves irrevocably to each other in marriage, have established each other as irreplaceable, nonsubstitutable, nondisposable persons and by doing so have *capacitated* themselves to do things that unmarried individuals simply cannot do: among them, to "give" themselves to each other in the act proper and exclusive to spouses — the marital act — and to receive the gift of life.

In and through his act of marital consent — an act of free self-determination — the man, forswearing all others, has given himself irrevocably the identity of this particular woman's *husband*, while the woman, in and through her self-determining act of marital consent, has given herself irrevocably the identity of this particular man's *wife*, and together they have given themselves the identity of *spouses*. They have established each other as absolutely unique and irreplaceable.[5]

Moreover, in and through the choice that makes them to be husband and wife, a man and a woman give to themselves new capacities and new rights, and they freely take upon themselves new responsibilities. They are now able to do things that unmarried men and women simply cannot do, precisely because the latter have failed to capacitate themselves to do them by getting married. In short, men and women who give themselves irrevocably to each other in marriage have the right and capacity to do what husbands and wives are supposed to do. And among the things that married persons are supposed to do are (1) to give each other a unique kind of love, conjugal or spousal or marital love, (2) to engage in the marital act, and (3) to "welcome life lovingly, nourish it humanely, and to educate it religiously," i.e., in love and service of God and neighbor.

B. The Meaning of the Marital Act

The marital act is not simply a genital act between men and women who happen to be married. Husbands and wives have the capacity to engage in *genital* acts because they have genitals. Unmarried men and women have the same capacity. But husbands and wives have the capacity (and the *right*) to engage in the *marital* act only because they are married, i.e., husbands and wives, spouses. The marital act, therefore, is more than a simple genital act between people who just happen to be married. As marital, it is an act that inwardly participates in their marital union, in their one-flesh unity, a unity open to the gift of children.[6] The marital act, in short, is an act inwardly participating in the "goods" or "blessings" of marriage, i.e., the good of steadfast fidelity and exclusive conjugal love, the good of children, and, for Christian spouses, the good of the "sacrament."

The marital act expresses, symbolizes, and manifests the exclusive nature of marital love, and it does so because it is both a communion in being (the unitive meaning of the act) and the sort or kind of an act in and through which the spouses open themselves to the good of human life in its transmission, to the blessing of fertility (its procreative meaning).[7]

The marital act is unitive, that is, a communion in being or in an intimate, exclusive sharing of personal life because in and through it husband and wife come to "know" each other in a unique and unforgettable way, revealing themselves to each other as unique and irreplaceable persons of different but complementary sex.[8] In and through this act, they become personally "one flesh," renewing the covenant they made with each other when they gave themselves to each other in marriage.[9] In the marital act, husbands and wives "give" themselves to each other in a way that concretely expresses their sexual complementarity, for the husband gives himself to his wife in a receiving sort of way while she in turn receives him in a giving sort of way. His body, which expresses his person as a male, has a "spousal significance," for it enables him to personally give himself to his wife by entering into her body-person and doing so in a receiving sort of way, while her body, which expresses her person as a female, likewise has a "spousal significance," for it is so structured that she is uniquely equipped to receive his body-person into herself and in so receiving him to give herself to him.[10] The marital act thus indeed, as Pope John Paul II has said, speaks "the language of the body."

The marital act is also a procreative kind of an act. In giving themselves to each other in this act, in becoming "one flesh," husband and wife also become one complete organism capable of generating human life. Even if they happen to be sterile, their marital union is the sort or kind of act in and through which human life can be given should conditions be favorable: it is procreative in kind.[11] Moreover, precisely because husbands and wives are married, they have capacitated themselves, as nonmarried persons have not, to cooperate with God in bringing new human persons into existence in a way that responds to the dignity of persons. They have capacitated themselves to "welcome life lovingly, nourish it humanely, and educate it in the love and service of God and neighbor," to give this life the "home" it needs and merits in order to grow and develop.

The marital act, therefore, is not, as Pope Pius XII rightly said, "a mere organic function for the transmission of the germ of life." It is, rather, "a personal action, a simultaneous natural self-giving which, in the words of Holy Writ, effects the union in 'one flesh'. . . [and] implies a personal cooperation [of the spouses with God in giving new human life]."[12] Indeed, as Pope Paul VI put matters, "because of its intimate nature the conjugal act, which unites husband and wife with the closest of bonds, also *make them fit* [the Latin text reads: *eos idoneos facit*] to bring forth new human life according to laws inscribed in their very being as men and women."[13]

The marital act, therefore, precisely as marital, participates inwardly in the goods or blessings of marriage. It is inherently love-giving (unitive) and life-giving (procreative). And this is why the Church teaches that "there is an inseparable connection, willed by God and not lawful for man to break on his own initiative, between the unitive and procreative meaning of the marital act."[14] The bond inseparably uniting these two meanings of the marital act is the marriage itself, and "what God has joined together, let no man put asunder."

The marital act is thus an utterly unique kind of human act. It is a collaborative, personal act executing the choice of the spouses to actualize their marital union and participate in the goods proper to it. It is integrally unitive and procreative, and it speaks the "language of the body."

C. "Begetting" Human Life Through the Marital Act

When human life comes to be in and through the marital act, it comes as a "gift" crowning the act itself. The child is "begotten" through an act of intimate conjugal love; he or she is not "made," treated like a product. Husband and wife do not "make" a baby, just as they do not "make" love, for neither a human baby nor love are "products" one makes. In engaging in the marital act, husbands and wives are not "making" anything. They are, rather, "doing" something, i.e., *giving* themselves to each other as irreplaceable and nonsubstitutable persons complementary in their sexuality, and opening themselves to the gift of human life. They are rightly regarded as "procreating" or "begetting" a child through an act of love; they are *not* "producing" one, "making" one. Their act is properly one of "procreation" and not one of "reproduction."

To grasp this truth properly, it is necessary to understand the difference between "transitive" and "immanent" human activity, between "making" and "doing." In the one mode of human activity, making, the action proceeds from the agent or agents to something produced in the external world by the use of various materials (e.g., cars, cookies, a poem). Such action is *transitive* insofar as it passes from the acting subject(s) to an object or objects fashioned by him or her or them. In this mode of human activity, which is governed by the rules of art, interest centers on the product made, and those that do not measure up to standards are frequently discarded. Thus autoworkers produce cars, cooks bake cakes, novelists write books, and college and university teachers produce lectures and texts. In this mode of human activity, the action perfects (or fails to perfect) the object made, not the agent producing the object — and I would rather have delicious cookies baked by a culinary artist who might, for all I know, be a morally bad person, than inedible ones produced by a saint.

In another mode of activity, doing, the action abides in the acting subject. The action is *immanent* (i.e., within the subject) and is governed by the requirements of the virtue of prudence, not by the rules of art. If the action is morally good, it perfects the agent, who in and through it "makes" himself or herself *to be* the kind of person he or she is, i.e., morally good.[15]

It is important to note that every making involves a doing, for one *chooses* to make something, and the act of choice, whereby we determine ourselves and give ourselves our identity as moral beings, is something we "do." And there are some things that we *can* make that we know we *ought not* to make because a choosing to make them is a morally bad kind of choice, e.g., pornographic films.

The marital act is *not* an act of making or producing. It is not a transitive act issuing from spouses and terminating in some object distinct from them. It is something that they "do." In it they do not "make" love or "make" babies. They *give* love to each other by giving themselves bodily to each other, and they open themselves to the gift of human life. The life begotten through their one-flesh union is not the product of their art, but "a gift supervening on and giving permanent embodiment to" the marital act itself.[16] Thus, when human life comes to be in and through the marital act, we can rightly say that the spouses are procreating or begetting. Their child is "begotten, not made."

3. Part Three: Generating Human Life Through New Reproductive Technologies

Chapter One provided an extended account of the teaching on this matter found in the Vatican *Instruction on Respect for Human Life in its Origin and on the Dignity of Procreation* (*Donum vitae*). Hence there is no need here to repeat this teaching. But I will, prior to describing and offering a moral evaluation of the various methods of generating human life outside the marital act, summarize the teaching of Pope Pius XII on this matter and also the teaching found in the 1997 document issued by the Pontifical Academy for Life on cloning, an issue not treated in *Donum vitae*.

A. The Teaching of Pius XII and the Pontifical Academy for Life
Pius XII died in 1958, twenty years before the birth of Louise Brown, the first baby conceived *in vitro* to be born. Yet he was quite farsighted and in several of his addresses took up the artificial generation of human life.[17] In one address, concerned with artificial insemination either by a third party or by the husband, he articulated the "inseparability principle." His teaching is quite clear, as the following passage shows:

> The Church has . . . rejected the . . . attitude which pretended to separate in procreation the biological activity from the personal relations of husband and wife. The child is the fruit of the marriage union, when it finds full expression by the placing in action of the functional organs, of the sensible emotions thereto related, and of the spiritual and disinterested love which animates such a union; it is in the unity of this human act that there must be considered the biological condition of procreation. Never is it permitted to separate these different

aspects to the point of excluding positively either the intention of pro-creating or the conjugal relation.[18]

Referring specifically to artificial insemination by the husband, he put matters very eloquently:

> To reduce the common life of a husband and wife and the conjugal act to a mere organic function for the transmission of seed would be but to convert the domestic hearth, the family sanctuary, into a biological laboratory. Therefore, in our allocution of September 29, 1949, to the International Congress of Catholic Doctors, We expressly excluded artificial insemination in marriage. The conjugal act in its natural structure is a personal action, a simultaneous and immediate cooperation of husband and wife, which by the very nature of the agents and the propriety of the act, is an expression of the reciprocal gift, which, according to Holy Writ, effects the union "in one flesh." That is much more than the union of two germs, which can be effected even by artificial means, that is, without the natural action of husband and wife. The conjugal act, ordained and designed by nature, is a personal cooperation, to which husband and wife, when contracting marriage, exchange the right.[19]

In another address, he condemned *in vitro* fertilization, at that time only a possibility. In no uncertain terms he declared: "As regards experiments of human artificial fecundation 'in vitro,' let it be sufficient to observe that they must be rejected as immoral and absolutely unlawful."[20]

Although condemning artificial insemination/fecundation by a husband as intrinsically immoral, he declared that "this does not necessarily proscribe the use of certain artificial means destined solely to facilitate the marital act, or to assure the accomplishment of the end of the natural act normally performed."[21] As we have seen, the Vatican *Instruction on Respect for Human Life in Its Origin and the Dignity of Procreation* some thirty years later affirms the legitimacy of technological interventions that "assist" the marital act and do not "replace" it or "substitute" for it.

In June 1997, the Pontifical Academy for Life issued its *Reflections on Cloning*. The document was issued after the success of Scottish scientists in cloning the sheep "Dolly." After noting that cloning "represents a radical manipulation of the constitutive relationality and complementarity which is at the origin of human procreation in both its biological and strictly personal aspects," the Academy pronounces on the morality of cloning: "All the moral reasons which led to the condemnation of *in vitro* fertilization as such and to the radical censure of *in vitro* fertilization for merely experimental purposes must also be applied to human cloning."[22]

B. The New Reproductive Technologies

These include two broad categories: (1) artificial fertilization, which embraces (a) artificial insemination, (b) *in vitro* fertilization and embryo transfer, (c) alternative technologies using male and female gametic cells; and (2) cloning or agametic reproduction.

(1) *Artificial Fertilization*

Fertilization naturally occurs when male sperm (male gametic cells) are introduced into a woman's body through an act of sexual coition and one of the sperm succeeds in penetrating the woman's ovum (female gametic cell) and fertilizing it. Artificial fertilization is brought about when male sperm are not united with the female ovum through an act of sexual coition but by some other means. In artificial *insemination*, male sperm are introduced into the female reproductive tract by the use of a cannula or other instruments, with fertilization occurring when one of the sperm so introduced fuses with the woman's ovum. Fertilization occurs within the woman's body. In *in vitro* fertilization, male sperm and female ova are placed in a petri dish (hence the name *in vitro*, "in a glass") and subsequent fusion of sperm and ovum and fertilization occur outside the woman's body.

Both these forms of artificial fertilization can be either homologous or heterologous. *Homologous* artificial fertilization uses gametic cells of a married couple, whereas *heterologous* artificial fertilization uses the gametic cells of individuals not married to each other (although one or both of the parties may be married to another person).[23]

(a) *Artificial Insemination*

Homologous artificial insemination or artificial insemination by husband (AIH) introduces the husband's sperm into the wife's body by use of a cannula or other instruments. Ordinarily the husband's sperm are obtained through masturbation, although an alternative is intercourse using a perforated condom or, in cases of obstruction of the vas deferens, which serves a conduit for spermatozoa, the surgical removal of sperm from the epididymis, where the sperm are stored.[24]

Some married couples resort to AIH in order to achieve pregnancy when, for whatever reason, the husband is not able to ejaculate within the vagina. It is also used when the husband suffers from oligospermia (when his sperm production is very low and thus makes conception less likely through sexual union) or when some allergy exists that cannot be treated hormonally. Today AIH involves "washing" the sperm in a laboratory procedure to remove antibodies and prostaglandins and to capacitate the sperm for fertilizing the ovum.[25]

With the ability to freeze and store sperm (the cryopreservation of sperm), AIH can also be used to help a widow conceive a child by her own husband's sperm after his death.

Heterologous artificial insemination is usually referred to by the acronym AID, signifying "artificial insemination by a donor." But, as Walter Wadlington correctly observes, "the term 'sperm donor' is a misnomer because compensation of persons supplying semen has been a long-standing practice."[26] It is thus far more accurate to call this form of artificial insemination "artificial insemination by a vendor."[27]

Traditionally, this form of artificial insemination was used by married couples so that the wife could bear a child genetically her own if her husband were infertile or if there was "genetic incompatibility" between the couple; i.e., when the couple were bearers of a recessive genetic defect and there was the likelihood that any child they might conceive might be actually afflicted by this genetic impairment. Today, the procedure is still commonly used for these purposes, but it is now also used by single women who want to bear a child and who, as Wadlington puts it, "do not have a marital or other stable heterosexual partner or by a woman in a life partnership with another woman."[28] It is also used in implementing surrogacy agreements under which a woman will conceive and bear a child who will then be turned over to the sperm provider or another person or other parties after birth.

Because of the danger that the sperm provided by the "vendor" may carry the human immuno-deficiency virus (H.I.V.) and thus threaten the woman and child with AIDS (acquired immune deficiency syndrome), today most doctors engaging in this form of artificial insemination use only frozen sperm from commercial sperm banks which have quarantined the samples long enough to test for H.I.V.[29]

(b) In Vitro *Fertilization and Embryo Transfer*

Until the late 1970s, artificial insemination was the only alternative to sexual union for effecting conception. But in the late 1970s, Patrick Steptoe and Paul Edwards succeeded in bringing to birth a child conceived *in vitro* and transferred a few days after fertilization to her mother's womb. Thus, with the birth of Louise Brown on July 25, 1978, a new mode of human reproduction became a reality: *in vitro* fertilization. It is ironic to note that Louise was born precisely ten years after Pope Paul VI signed his encyclical *Humanae vitae*, which affirmed the "inseparable connection willed by God and unlawful for man to break on his own initiative, between the unitive and procreative meanings of the marital act." *In vitro* fertilization makes it possible for human life to be conceived outside the body of the (genetic) mother, but it is still a form of generating human life that is gametic, i.e., possible only by uniting a male gametic cell, the sperm, with a female gametic cell, the ovum. The new human life is conceived in a petri dish using sperm provided by a man and an ovum provided by a woman. Approximately two days after the fertilization process has been completed, the embryo, which by then has developed to the four-to-eight cell stage, is ready for transfer into a woman's uterus, where it can implant and, if implantation is successful, continue intrauterine development until birth.

Initially, *in vitro* fertilization and embryo transfer (hereafter IVF-ET) was carried out by obtaining a single egg (ovum) from a woman through a laparoscopy, a procedure requiring general anesthesia. When a laparoscopy is performed, the physician aspirates the woman's egg through a hollow needle inserted into the abdomen and guided by a narrow optical instrument called a laparoscope. The first time IVF-ET succeeded, it was carried out in a normally ovulating woman, Louise Brown's mother, whose fallopian tubes had been surgically removed. After a single egg was obtained through laparoscopy, it was fertilized by her husband's sperm *in vitro*, and the resulting embryo was then transferred to her womb two days after the fertilization process was completed.

Today the standard procedure is to overstimulate the ovaries with ovulatory drugs such as Clomid, Pergonal, and Metrodin so that the woman will produce several oocytes for retrieval and subsequent fertilization. Oocytes (ova) produced are retrieved not by laparoscopy, with its requirement of general anesthesia, but by ultrasound-guided transvaginal aspiration, which does not require general anesthesia. This greatly simplifies the procedure. Standard practice today also includes fertilization of many ova, mixing them in the petri dish with sperm (usually collected by masturbation) that have been "washed" to make them more apt to fertilize. Thus several new human zygotes (human beings at the earliest stage of development) are produced and allowed to grow to the early embryo stage. It is now customary to transfer two to four of these early embryos to the womb to increase probability of implantation and subsequent gestation until birth and to freeze and store the others so that they can be used for implantation later if the first attempts are unsuccessful. These "spare" frozen embryos can also be "donated" for research purposes. Eventually, if not claimed by the persons responsible for their manufacture or used in research, the frozen embryos will be destroyed.[30]

IVF-ET can be either homologous or heterologous. Initially, homologous IVF-ET was used almost exclusively for wives whose fallopian tubes had been damaged, to enable them and their husbands to have children of their own. But now this procedure has been extended to include male-factor infertility (oligospermia, for instance) and other cases in which no precise cause for the couple's infertility has been determined.[31] It can also be used, it is now increasingly possible, to help a married couple avoid conceiving a child who could be affected by a genetically inherited pathology. For example, in the summer of 1998 scientists succeeded in identifying and separating male sperm responsible for the conception of female and male children. Male children alone are afflicted by hemophilia. Hence a married couple legitimately worried about conceiving a male child so afflicted can now choose to conceive the child *in vitro*, fertilizing the wife's ovum with sperm provided by her husband but with the assurance that the sperm provided are female-producing and not male-producing sperm. In the future, it is likely that more gametic cells, both male and female, carrying the genes responsible for genetically induced pathologies will be identified and separated, and then only those identified as not carrying the genes causing the maladies can be used for fertilization *in vitro*.

Heterologous IVF-ET can now be used instead of artificial insemination in instances when the husband is completely infertile or when the wife lacks ovaries or when there is genetic incompatibility between the spouses. Sperm "donation" is easier than ova "donation," inasmuch as the latter is complicated by the need to synchronize the menstrual cycles of the woman who "donates" the ova and the wife into whom the embryo is to be implanted. Embryos conceived *in vitro*, as well as sperm and ova, can also be "donated," and embryo donation, like sperm donation, does not require synchronizing the menstrual cycles of different women. Both homologous and heterologous IVF can include implanting the resulting embryo into the womb of a woman other than the one who supplied the ovum, a so-called "surrogate" mother.[32]

As this makes evident, many permutations and combinations of generating human life are now technically feasible as a result of *in vitro* fertilization, among them such procedures as ZIFT (zygote intrafallopian tube transfer), which occurs when the zygote resulting from IVF is inserted into the fallopian tube rather than having the embryo transferred into the womb; and PROST (pro-nuclear tubal transfer), which transfers the very early embryo by use of a laparascope into the fallopian tube.[33]

(c) *Alternative Technologies Using Male and Female Gametic Cells*

Certain contemporary techniques are not, strictly speaking, variants of *in vitro* fertilization inasmuch as fertilization itself occurs, not outside the woman's body in a petri dish, but within a woman's body. Thus these techniques are more closely related to artificial insemination than to *in vitro* fertilization as methods of artificial fertilization. But their development was stimulated by research into *in vitro* fertilization and embryo transfer. In these procedures, sexual union is not required in order to unite male and female gametic cells.

One such technique is called SIFT, or sperm intrafallopian tube transfer. This is sometimes used as an option for infertile couples who have not conceived following AIH. In this procedure, the woman's ovaries are hyperstimulated; this is coupled with a laparoscopy under general anesthesia to inject a "washed" or prepared concentrate of the husband's sperm (or that of a "donor," if necessary) into the fallopian tubes so that conception can occur there.[34]

Another procedure of special interest is GIFT, or gamete intrafallopian tube transfer. This is similar to IVF in that the woman's ovaries are hyperstimulated to produce multiple eggs, which are retrieved either by laparoscopy or ultrasound-guided transvaginal procedures. An egg (or group of eggs) is placed into a catheter with sperm (provided either by masturbation or by the use of a perforated condom during intercourse) that have been treated and "capacitated," with an air bubble separating ova from sperm to prevent fertilization from occurring outside the woman's body. The catheter is then inserted into her fallopian tube, the ovum (ova) and sperm are released from the catheter, and fertilization can then occur within the body of the woman, who can, of course, be the wife of the man whose sperm are used and who could have provided the ovum (ova).[35]

There is currently a debate among theologians over GIFT and some similar procedures, such as LTOT (low tubal ovum transfer) and TOT (tubal ovum transfer). Some hold that GIFT and other procedures can, if used by married persons in a way that avoids procuring sperm through masturbation, be regarded as "assisting" the marital act and not replacing it and hence morally permissible. Others hold that GIFT is definitely a procedure that replaces or substitutes for the marital act and that, therefore, its use is immoral. I will take up this question in Part 4 of this chapter.

(2) *Cloning or Agametic Reproduction*

The February 27, 1997, issue of the journal *Nature* carried the news of the birth of the sheep Dolly through the work of Scottish researchers Ian Wilmut and K. H. S. Campbell and their associates at Edinburgh's Roslin Institute. They succeeded in generating a new sheep by a process called "cloning," or more technically "somatic-cell nuclear transfer."[36] What they did was to produce Dolly by fusing the nucleus of a somatic (body) cell of an adult sheep with a denucleated oocyte, that is, an oocyte deprived of the maternal genome. The genetic identity of the new individual sheep, Dolly, was derived from only one source, namely, the adult sheep whose somatic cell nucleus was inserted into the denucleated oocyte to "trigger" development into a new individual of the species. This procedure can, in principle, be used to generate new human beings whose genetic endowment would be identical to that of the human beings whose somatic cells were inserted into a denucleated human ovum.

A somewhat different procedure, developed by Ryuzo Yanagimachi and his team at the John A. Burns School of Medicine at the University of Hawaii, was used to clone mice and reported in the July 24, 1998, issue of *Nature* magazine. But their work, too, produced a new member of a mammalian species by a procedure that is asexual, or agametic, in nature, inasmuch as it does not require fertilization of the female gametic cell, the ovum, by the male gametic cell, the sperm. Thus, even from a biological perspective, cloning is a far more radical mode of reproduction than artificial insemination or *in vitro* fertilization and their permutations and combinations. As the Pontifical Academy for Life noted in the document previously referred to, cloning "tends to make bisexuality a purely functional leftover, given that an ovum must be used without its nucleus in order to make room for the clone-embryo."[37]

C. An Ethical and Theological Evaluation of the New Reproductive Technologies

(1) *Ethical Reasons Why Non-Marital Ways of Generating New Human Life Are Intrinsically Immoral*

As we saw in Chapter One, the *Vatican Instruction on Respect for Human Life in Its Origin and on the Dignity of Procreation* (*Donum vitae*) briefly sets forth three lines of reasoning to support the conclusion that it is always immoral to generate human life outside the marital act. The first is based on the "inseparability principle," which claims that it is not lawful for man on his own initiative to separate the unitive and procreative meanings of the conjugal act. The second is rooted in the "language of the body," and the third is that non-marital ways of engendering human life change its generation from an act of procreation to one of reproduction, treating the child as if he or she were a product.

I believe that in the first part of this chapter, in reflecting on the meaning of marriage and the marital act, I provided evidence to show that the bond uniting marriage, the marital act, and the generating of new human life is intimate, that the marital act, precisely *as* marital, is inherently both unitive and procreative, and that it speaks the language of the body. Thus I think that in that part of the chapter I offered good reasons to support the first two lines of argument used by *Donum vitae*. There I also emphasized that when a child comes to be in and through the marital act, he or she is "begotten, not made," and that in engaging in the marital act husbands and wives are not "making" anything, either love or babies, but are rather "doing" something, i.e., *giving* themselves to each other in an act that actualizes their marital union and expresses their sexual complementarity, and *opening* themselves to the gift of human life. I thus touched on the third line of reasoning used by *Donum vitae* to show that it is wrong to generate human life outside the marital act, because doing so treats the child as if he or she were a product.

Here I wish to develop this third line of reasoning because I think that it is the one that more clearly shows how seriously wrong it is to generate human life outside the marital act.

In what follows I will focus attention on *homologous* artificial insemination and IVF-ET, i.e., ways of bringing new human life into existence by uniting the gametic cells of husband and wife outside the marital act. I do so because although some people in our society — and perhaps their number is increasing — find the Church's teaching on heterologous fertilization too restrictive of human freedom, most people, Catholic and non-Catholic alike, can understand and appreciate this teaching even if, in some highly unique situations, they might justify heterologous insemination and fertilization. Nonetheless, most people recognize that when a man and a woman marry, they "give" themselves exclusively to each other and that the selves they give are sexual and procreative persons. Just as they violate their marital covenant after marriage by attempting to "give" themselves to another in sexual union, so, too, they dishonor their marital covenant and the uniqueness and exclusiveness of their love and marital union by choosing to exercise their procreative powers with someone other than their spouse, the one to whom they have given themselves, including their power to procreate, irrevocably, "forswearing all others."

But many of these people, including Catholics, find the Church's judgment that *homologous* artificial insemination and IVF-ET are *always* wrong, intrinsically evil, difficult to understand and accept. This is a "hard" teaching, and strikes many as harsh, insensitive, and cruel. They ask, and not without reason, why *must* human life be given *only* in and through the marital act? What evil is being done by a married couple, unable to have children by engaging in the marital act, if they make use of the new reproductive technologies to overcome the obstacles preventing their marriage from being blessed with the gift of children?

It seems obvious that, if homologous artificial fertilization (whether artificial insemination or IVF-ET) is intrinsically immoral, it follows *a fortiori* that this is true of heterologous fertilization and cloning.

To show that even homologous artificial fertilization is intrinsically immoral, I will, as noted earlier, focus on the argument that generating children outside of the marital act, even by procedures making use of gametic cells of husband and wife, changes the generation of human life from an act of "procreation" to one of "reproduction," treating the child as if he or she is a product. I will argue that this is indeed the case, and that it is always gravely immoral to treat a human being, even in his or her initial stages of existence, as a product and not as a person.

The argument to be advanced is intelligible in the light of the distinction, made previously, between "making" and "doing." We have seen already that in engaging in the marital act husbands and wives are not "making" anything, but are rather "doing" something, and that any human life brought into being in and through this act is begotten, not made.

In "making," as we have seen already, the action proceeds from an agent or agents to something in the external world, to a product. In making, interest centers on the product made, and ordinarily products that do not measure up to standards are discarded or, at any rate, are little appreciated and for this reason are frequently called "defective." In making, moreover, the logic of manufacturing is validly applied: one should use the most efficient procedures available, keeping costs as low as possible, etc.

When new human life comes to be as a result of homologous artificial insemination or homologous IVF-ET, it comes to be as the end product of a series of actions, transitive in nature, undertaken by different persons in order to make a particular product, a human baby. The spouses "produce" the gametic materials, which others then manipulate and use in order to make the final product. When these new reproductive technologies are employed, one cannot deny that the child "comes into existence . . . in the manner of a product of making (and, typically, as the end product of a process managed and carried out by persons other than his parents)."[38] With use of these technologies, it is true to say that the child is "made," not "begotten."

Precisely because homologous IVF-ET — like heterologous IVF-ET — is an act of "making," it is standard procedure, as we have seen in surveying the literature describing the technologies, to overstimulate the woman's ovaries so that she can produce several ova for fertilization by sperm, usually obtained most economically through masturbation and then washed and "capacitated" so that they can better do their job; of the resulting new human embryos, some are frozen and kept on reserve for use should initial efforts to achieve implantation and gestation to birth fail; it is also common to implant several embryos (two to four) in the womb to enhance the likelihood that at least one will implant and, should too large a number of embryos successfully implant, to discard the "excess" number through a procedure some euphemistically call "pregnancy reduction." Finally, it is common practice to monitor development of the new human life both prior to being transferred to the womb and during gestation to determine whether it suffers from any defects and, should serious defects be discovered or thought likely, to abort the product that does not measure up to standard. As a form of "making" or "producing," artificial insemination/fertilization, homologous as well as heterologous, leads to the use of these methods, for they simply carry out the logic of manufacturing commodities: one should use the most efficient, time-saving, and cost-effective means available to deliver the desired product under good quality controls.

One readily sees how dehumanizing such "production" of human babies is. It obviously treats them as if they were products inferior to their producers and subject to quality controls, not persons equal in dignity to their parents.

But some people, including some Catholic theologians, note — correctly — that homologous insemination/fertilization does not *require* hyperovulating the woman, creating a number of new human beings in a petri dish, freezing some, implanting others, monitoring development with a view to abortion should "defects" be discovered, etc. They think that if these features commonly associated with homologous insemination/fertilization are rejected, then a limited resort by married couples to artificial insemination/IVF-ET does not really transform the generation of human life from an act of procreation to one of reproduction.

A leading representative of this school of thought, Richard A. McCormick, S.J., argues that spouses who resort to homologous *in vitro* fertilization do not perceive this as the " 'manufacture' of a 'product.' Fertilization *happens* when sperm and egg are brought together in a petri dish," but "the technician's intervention is a condition for its happening, not a cause."[39] Moreover, he continues, "the attitudes of the parents and the technicians can be every bit as reverential and respectful as they would be in the face of human life naturally conceived."[40] In fact, in McCormick's view and in that of some other writers as well, for instance, Thomas A. Shannon, Lisa Sowle Cahill, and Jean Porter,[41] homologous *in vitro* fertilization can be considered an "extension" of marital intercourse, so that the child generated can still be regarded as the "fruit" of the spouses' love. While it is preferable, if possible, to generate the baby through the marital act, it is, in the cases of concern to us, impossible to do this, and hence their marital act — so these writers claim — can be, as it were, "extended" to embrace *in vitro* fertilization.

Given the concrete situation, any disadvantages inherent in the generation of human lives apart from the marital act, so these authors reason, are clearly counterbalanced by the great good of new human lives and the fulfillment of the desire for children of couples who otherwise would not be able to have them. In such conditions, they contend, it is not unrealistic to say that homologous IVF-ET is simply a way of "extending" the marital act.

I believe that it is evident that this justification of homologous insemination/IVF-ET is rooted in the proportionalistic method of making moral judgments. It claims that one can rightly intend so-called pre-moral or nonmoral or ontic evils (the "disadvantages" referred to above) in order to attain a proportionately greater good, in this case, helping a married couple otherwise childless to have a child of their own. But this method of making moral judgments is very flawed and was explicitly repudiated by Pope John Paul II in *Veritatis splendor*.[42] It comes down to the claim that one can never judge an act to be morally bad only by taking into account the "object" freely chosen and that it is necessary, in order to render any moral judgment of an action, to consider it in its totality, taking into account not only its object but the end and circumstances as well. If the end for whose sake something is chosen and done is a "proportionately greater good" than the evil one does by choosing this object (e.g., making a baby in a petri dish), then the act as a whole can be morally good. In Chapter Two, above, this flawed method of making moral judgments was briefly criticized.[43]

Moreover, the reasoning advanced by McCormick and others is rhetorical in character and not based on a realistic understanding of what is involved. Obviously, those who choose to produce a baby make that choice as a means to an ulterior end. They may well "intend" — in the sense of their further intention — that the baby be received into an authentic child-parent relationship, in which he or she will live in a communion of persons which befits those who share personal dignity. If realized, this intended end for whose sake the choice is made to produce the baby will be good for the baby as well as for the parents. But, even so, and despite McCormick's claim to the contrary, their "present intention," i.e., the choice they are making here and now, is precisely "to make a baby" — this is the "object" specifying their freely chosen act. The baby's initial status is the status of a product. In *in vitro* fertilization, the technician does not simply *assist* the marital act (that would be licit) but, as Benedict Ashley, O.P., rightly says, he "*substitutes* for that act of personal relationship and communication one which is like a chemist making a compound or a gardener planting a seed. The technician has thus become the principal cause of generation, acting through the instrumental forms of sperm and ovum."[44]

Moreover, the claim that *in vitro* fertilization is an "extension" of the marital act and not a substitution for it is simply contrary to fact. "What is extended," as Ashley also notes, "is not the act of intercourse, but the intention: from an intention to beget a child naturally to getting it by IVF, by artificial insemination, or by help of a surrogate mother."[45] Since the child's initial status is thus, in these procedures, that of a product, its status is sub-personal. Thus, the choice to produce a baby is, inevitably, the choice to enter into a relationship with the baby, not as its equal, but as a product inferior to its producers. But this initial relationship of those who choose to produce babies with the babies they produce is inconsistent with and so impedes the communion of persons endowed with equal dignity that is appropriate for any interpersonal relationship. It is the choice of a bad means to a good end. Moreover, in producing babies, if the product is defective, a new person comes to be as *unwanted*. Thus, those who choose to produce babies not only choose life for some, but — and can this be realistically doubted? — at times quietly dispose of at least some of those who are not developing normally.[46]

I think that the reasons advanced here to show that it is not morally right to generate human life outside the marital act can be summarized in a syllogism, which I offer for consideration:

- *Major:* Any act of generating human life that is non-marital is irresponsible and violates the respect due to human life in its generation.
- *Minor:* But artificial insemination, *in vitro* fertilization, whether homologous or heterologous, and other forms of generating human life outside the marital act, including cloning, are non-marital.
- *Conclusion:* Therefore, these modes of generating human life are irresponsible and violate the respect due to human life in its generation.

I believe that the minor of this syllogism does not require extensive discussion. However, McCormick, commenting on an earlier essay of mine in which I advanced a syllogism of this kind, claims that my use of the term "non-marital" in the minor premise is "impenetrable," because the meaning of a "non-marital" action is not at all clear.[47] This objection simply fails to take into account all that I had said in my previous essay and in the earlier part of this chapter about the *marital* act.[48]

It is obvious that heterologous insemination/fertilization and cloning are "non-marital." But "non-marital" too are homologous artificial insemination and IVF. Even though married persons have collaborated in these procedures and even though these procedures make use of gametic cells supplied by husband and wife, the procedures are "non-marital" because the marital status of the man and the woman participating in them is accidental and not essential, whereas, as we saw in the first part of this chapter, the marital status of man and woman *is essential* for a *marital* act. Indeed, the marital status of the parties involved in homologous artificial insemination/IVF is utterly irrelevant to the procedures as such. What makes husband and wife capable of participating in these procedures is definitely *not* their marital union, whereas the *marital act* is possible only by reason of their marital union. Their marital status is irrelevant to artificial insemination/IVF because they are able to take part in these procedures simply because, like *unmarried* men and women, they are producers of gametic cells that other individuals can then use to fabricate human life. Just as spouses do not generate human life *maritally* when this life (which is *always* good and precious, no matter how engendered) is initiated as a result of an act of spousal abuse, so they do not generate new human life maritally when what they do is simply provide the materials to be used in making a baby.

The foregoing reflections should suffice to clarify the meaning of the minor premise of the syllogism and to show its truth.

The truth of the major premise is supported by everything said about the intimate bonds uniting marriage, the marital act, and the generation of human life. Those bonds are the indispensable and necessary means for properly respecting human life in its origin. To sunder them is to break the inseparable bond between the unitive and procreative meanings of the conjugal act, to refuse to speak the "language of the body," and above all to treat a child in its initial stage of existence as a product, as something "made," not "begotten." We have seen already that non-marital modes of generating human life change the act generating such life from one of "procreation" or "begetting" to one of "reproducing." Such reproductive modes of generating human life are indeed instances of "making."

(2) *The Basic Theological Reason Why Human Life Ought To Be Generated Only in and Through the Marital Act*

There is a very profound theological reason that offers ultimate support for the truth that new human life ought to be given *only* in and through the marital act — the act proper and unique to spouses, the act made possible only by marriage itself — and not through acts of fornication, adultery, spousal abuse, or new "reproductive" technologies.

The reason is this: human life ought to be "begotten, not made." Human life is the life of a human person, a being inescapably male or female, made in the image and likeness of the all-holy God. A human person, who comes to be when new human life comes into existence, is, as it were, an icon or "created word" of God. Human beings are, as it were, the "created words" that the Father's Uncreated Word became and is,[49] precisely to show us how deeply God loves us and to enable us to be, like him, children of the Father and members of the divine family.

But the Uncreated Word, whose brothers and sisters human persons are called to be, was "begotten, not made." These words were chosen by the Fathers of the Council of Nicaea in A.D. 325 to express unambiguously their belief that the eternal and uncreated Word of God is indeed, like the Father, true God. This Word, who personally became true man in Jesus Christ while remaining true God, is not inferior to his Father; he is not a product of his Father's will, a being made by the Father and subordinate in dignity to him. Rather, the Word is one in being with the Father, equally a divine person. The Word, the Father's Son, was begotten by an immanent act of personal love.

Similarly, human persons, the "created words" of God, ought, like the Uncreated Word, to be "begotten, not made." Like the Uncreated Word, they are one in nature with their parents, persons like their mothers and fathers; they are not products inferior to their producers. Their personal dignity is equal to that of their mothers and fathers, just as the Uncreated Word's personal dignity is equal to the personal dignity of the Father. That dignity is respected when their life is "begotten" in an act of self-giving spousal union, in an act of conjugal love. It is not respected when that life is "made" as the end product of a series of transitive acts of making. Nor is it respected when generated by acts of fornication, adultery, or spousal abuse.

4. Part Four: "Assisted" Insemination/Fertilization

The Church's Magisterium, as we have seen, distinguishes between technological procedures, such as artificial insemination and *in vitro* fertilization, whether homologous or heterologous, which *substitute for or replace the marital act* and procedures which *assist* the marital act in being crowned with the gift of human life. Although married couples ought never to use techniques that replace the marital act, they can legitimately use those that assist it in generating new human life. As Pope John Paul II has said, "infertile couples . . . have a right to whatever legitimate therapies may be available to remedy their infertility."[50]

But there is serious controversy, even among Catholics who defend the truth of the Church's teaching on the generation of human life, regarding the kinds of procedures that assist rather than replace the marital act. After presenting basic criteria to help distinguish procedures that "assist" the conjugal act from those replacing it, I will then examine some specific techniques. We will find that there is a consensus among Catholic theologians regarding some of these procedures, whereas over others there is controversy.

A. Basic Criteria

The basic principle operative here is accurately formulated in the following text from *Donum vitae*:

> The human person must be accepted in his parents' act of union and love; the generation of a child must therefore be the fruit of that mutual giving which is realized in the conjugal act wherein the spouses

cooperate as servants and not as masters in the work of the Creator who is love.[51]

If the child is to be the "fruit" of the marital act, the marital act must be directly related (= have a direct causal relationship) to the origin of new human life. The marital act, in other words, must be the "principal" cause of the conception of the child. It is so because the marital act not only unites husband and wife in an intimate "one-flesh" unity but also directly and personally introduces into the wife's body the sperm of her husband, which then actively seek an ovum in order to fertilize it and cause the conception of the child. Given that the marital or conjugal act is and must be the principal cause of the child's conception if the dignity of human life in its origin is to be respected, then what basic criteria will enable us to determine whether a technological intervention "assists" the marital act rather than "replaces" it or "substitutes" for it?

In an excellent study of this issue,[52] John Doerfler offers a thorough review of relevant literature, offering perceptive critiques of several essays and judging as one of the most helpful an insightful (but neglected) essay by Josef Seifert.[53] Doerfler proposes that the marital act is and remains the principal cause of conception only if the technical procedure either enables it to be performed by removing obstacles preventing the conjugal act from being effective or enables it to be performed by providing active condition(s) for it to exercise its own principal causality (technical procedures of this type will be illustrated below). But the conjugal act is not or does not remain the principal cause of conception if the natural causal process initiated by the marital act and leading to conception is interrupted by the technical means, and it is so interrupted if the technical means terminates or stops the natural causal process, if these means require the husband's sperm to be removed from her body after the marital act has taken place, if conception occurs outside the wife's body, or if the technical means initiates the process anew once it has been stopped. Obviously, too, the conjugal act is not the principal cause of conception if it merely serves as a means for obtaining sperm. These are the major criteria developed by Doerfler[54] (I have in some measure modified and simplified them for presentation here), and in my opinion these are very helpful in enabling us to determine whether a given technical intervention assists or replaces the conjugal act.

From this it follows, I believe, that a procedure assists the marital act if and only if a marital act takes place and the procedure in question either circumvents obstacles preventing the specific marital act from being fruitful or supplies condition(s) needed for it to become effective in causing conception.

With these criteria in mind, I will now examine some specific procedures claimed by Catholic theologians to be licit examples of techniques that "assist" rather than "replace" the conjugal act. As will be seen, there is sharp disagreement among these theologians over some of the procedures to be examined. I will begin with techniques that all commentators, so far as I know, regard as instances of "assisted" insemination or fertilization, and then take up techniques over which controversy exists, offering my own assessment, guided by the criteria developed by Doerfler in his comprehensive study.

B. Acknowledged Instances of Assisted Insemination or Fertilization

(1) *Use of Perforated Condom to Circumvent Hypospadias*
Hypospadias is an anomaly of the male penis in which the urethra does not open at the distal end of the penis but on its underside, close to the man's body. This frequently prevents the husband from ejaculating sperm into his wife's vagina during the marital act. The use of a perforated condom would prevent the husband's sperm from being emitted outside his wife's body and facilitate their entrance into her vagina. This would thus be an instance of a technical means that would *remove an obstacle* to the fruitfulness of the conjugal act; all Catholic theologians who have discussed this procedure agree that it assists and does not replace the marital act and that, consequently, it is morally licit. It surely meets the criteria developed by Doerfler.[55]

(2) *Low Tubal Ovum Transfer (LTOT)*
This procedure, originally designed for women whose infertility was caused by blocked, damaged, or diseased fallopian tubes, relocates her ovum, bypassing and circumventing the area of tubal pathology in order to place the ovum into the fallopian tube below the point of damage, disease, or blockage so that her own husband's sperm, introduced into her body by the marital act, can then effect fertilization. It is called "*low* tubal ovum transfer" because ordinarily the ovum is relocated in the lower part of the fallopian tube (or at times in the uterus itself).

This procedure evidently "removes an obstacle" preventing conception from occurring after the marital act has taken place or provides the conditions necessary if the marital act is to be fruitful. All the procedure does is to relocate the wife's ovum within her body prior to the marital act. The sperm that fertilize the ovum are introduced into her body-person directly as a result of the marital act. This technique clearly meets the criteria set forth by Doerfler.

All Catholic theologians who have addressed this technique agree that LTOT is a morally legitimate way of assisting the marital act.[56]

(3) *Moving Sperm Deposited in the Vagina Into the Uterus and Fallopian Tubes*

Apparently, the fruitfulness of some marital acts is impeded because the husband's sperm do not migrate far enough or rapidly enough into the reproductive tract of his wife, but linger in the vagina or at most migrate only very slowly to those portions of the wife's reproductive tract where conception is most likely to occur, with the result that most of the sperm die before they are able to unite with an ovum and fertilize it.

This obstacle to the fruitfulness of the marital act is removed and the conditions favorable for it to bear fruit can be fulfilled if the physician, after husband and wife have completed the marital act, uses some instrument(s) to propel the sperm deposited in the vagina into the uterus and fallopian tubes. If this is the way the technical intervention occurs, then it seems evident that it merely removes an obstacle preventing the marital act from being fruitful, supplying condition(s) necessary for it to be effective. It thus meets the criteria we have noted before and can rightly be said to assist and not replace the marital act.[57]

C. Controverted Technologies

(1) *Temporary Removal of Sperm or of Ova to "Wash" and "Capacitate" Them*

The procedure just discussed, namely, moving and relocating within the wife's body sperm deposited by her husband during the marital act, may be modified somewhat, requiring the sperm to be removed temporarily from the wife's body or perhaps having her ovum temporarily removed and treated for some pathological condition, and then relocating one or both elements to the fallopian tube where they can unite. Many Catholic theologians who have discussed this procedure believe that it, too, can be regarded as a legitimate assistance of the marital act.[58] This procedure, too, so it seems to them, assists the marital act by removing an obstacle to its fruitfulness or by supplying the conditions under which it can be effective.

Despite my respect for this opinion, I believe that the procedure in question does not truly assist the marital act but rather substitutes for it.

One of the criteria developed by Doerfler in his well-reasoned study and supported by the analysis given by Seifert is that a technical means which stops or terminates the natural causal process initiated by the marital act and then initiates the process anew after its termination can hardly be designated as assisting the conjugal act or the causal process initiated by it.[59] It seems to me quite clear that distinct human acts, specified by their objects, are being chosen and done, and that one of them definitely *stops* or *terminates* a causal process initiated by the other. One of the acts is the marital act; the other is the technical intervention of removing and treating either the sperm introduced into the wife's body by the marital act or the ova present within her body when the marital act occurred, treating them in some fashion. This act is not marital, nor does it assist the causal process initiated by the marital act to be fruitful. It does not assist because it terminates the act in order to do something else, i.e., to treat sperm or ova. A third human act is then required to initiate the causal process that leads to conception, since a new human choice is needed for the reintroduction of sperm and/or ovum into the wife's body. It thus seems clear to me that this procedure substitutes for the marital act and does not assist it.

(2) *Accumulating Sperm From a Series of Marital Acts and Introducing Them Into the Wife's Vagina in Conjunction With a Marital Act*

In order to cope with infertility caused by oligospermia (a condition causing relatively low sperm production by the husband), some theologians propose that the physician collect amounts of sperm from the husband's ejaculate (by morally permissible means, such as use of a perforated condom), conserve and centrifuge such accumulated sperm, and then place this concentrate into the wife's generative tract in association with a marital act (usually prior to one) in order to mix with and fortify the husband's ejaculate during the marital act.

Although some Catholic theologians who accept the teaching of *Donum vitae* think that this procedure assists the marital act,[60] I believe that a proper assessment of what is going on shows that this technique replaces the marital act and does not assist it.

First of all, in this procedure one does not know whether the sperm that fertilize the ovum are sperm introduced into the wife's body by the husband during the marital act or sperm contained in the concentrate obtained by collecting sperm into a perforated condom during previous marital acts. But if the sperm that fertilize the ovum derive from that concentrate, then they simply *cannot* and *must not* be considered as part of the marital act.

They cannot and must not be so considered precisely because they have been *intentionally withheld* from prior marital acts in order to procure sperm in a nonmasturbatory way. The marital act merely serves as an instrument for obtaining sperm. And since one cannot say whether fertilization is caused by sperm introduced into the wife's body by the specific marital act in question or by sperm contained in the concentrate resulting from *deliberately withholding sperm* from prior marital acts, one cannot truly say that the procedure "assists" the specific marital act in question. This procedure clearly violates one of the criteria developed by Doerfler.[61]

(3) *Gamete Intrafallopian Tube Transfer (GIFT) and Tubal Ovum Transfer with Sperm (TOTS)*

GIFT has already been described: the wife's eggs are removed by laparoscopy or ultrasound-guided transvaginal procedures. An egg (or group of eggs) is placed in a catheter with sperm (provided either by masturbation or by using a perforated condom during previous marital acts) that have been treated and "capacitated," with an air bubble separating ovum (ova) from sperm in the catheter while outside the wife's body. Thus fertilization does not take place outside the wife's body. The catheter is then inserted into the wife's body (and this can be done either prior to or immediately following a marital act), the ovum and sperm are released from the catheter, and fertilization and conception can then take place within the wife's body, caused by the concentrate of sperm placed in the catheter and released after its insertion into the wife's body or perhaps by sperm released into her body by the marital act in association with which the catheter is inserted.

Several Catholic theologians — among them, Donald McCarthy, Orville Griese, Peter Cataldo, and John W. Carlson — strongly defend GIFT as a procedure that assists the marital act in being fruitful.[62]

With many others, I disagree completely with this approval of GIFT. First of all, the procedure was originally developed as an offshoot of IVF and the husband's sperm was collected by masturbation. Informed that the Catholic Church condemns masturbation, even as a way of obtaining a husband's sperm, the doctors who used the method suggested that sperm be obtained by using a perforated condom during the marital act. This shows definitely that with GIFT the marital act is merely incidental to the entire procedure, used only as a way of obtaining sperm in a nonmasturbatory way. These sperm, since they have been *deliberately, intentionally withheld from a marital act or series of marital acts*, can then not be said truly to be integral to the marital act when the catheter containing these sperm and

the wife's ovum are inserted into her body. Although subsequent fertilization of her ovum *may* be caused by sperm introduced into her body during
the accompanying marital act, such fertilization would be *per accidens* and
not *per se*. Thus with many others, including Doerfler, Seifert, DeMarco,
Tonti-Filippini, Grisez, and Ashley-O'Rourke, I believe that GIFT definitely substitutes for or replaces the marital act and does not assist it; and
that, therefore, it is immoral to make use of it.[63]

TOTS is similar to GIFT. In this procedure, sperm are procured from
the husband either by masturbation or use of a perforated condom. Sperm
are then placed in a catheter along with the wife's ovum (ova) and separated
by an air bubble, and the catheter is then inserted into the fallopian tube
(hence the name tubal ovum transfer with sperm), where ovum (ova) and
sperm are released and fertilization can then occur. As can be seen, TOTS
is quite similar to GIFT and not similar to LTOT, or low tubal ovum transfer. Like GIFT, it substitutes for the marital act and does not assist it since
the marital act is only incidental to retrieval of sperm and sperm so retrieved
are intentionally withheld from a marital act and hence cannot be regarded
as part of a marital act.

Someone might say that with respect to procedures where reputable
Catholic theologians disagree, and since there is no specific magisterial
teaching on them, Catholics are at liberty to follow whatever view they
prefer as a "probable opinion." This way of looking at the issue is quite
legalistic in my opinion. What one ought to do is examine the arguments
and reasons given by theologians to support their claims to see which is
true and takes into account the realities involved.

D. Conclusion to Part Four; a Word About Fertility Drugs

Some may think that the preceding analysis of procedures to determine
which assist and which replace the marital act may be a bit nit-picking.
Nonetheless, it deals with a real situation. The proper way to "assist" the conjugal act, I think, is to do more research to discover the root causes of
female/male infertility and cure these underlying pathologies. At present, the
usual recommendation to overcome problems posed by blocked fallopian
tubes (not an uncommon cause of inability to conceive) is to have recourse to
IVF-ET. Yet such recourse does not cure the underlying pathology but rather
responds to a human desire. It would be more in line with true medical
research to reconstruct the fallopian tubes surgically or perhaps to attempt a
tubal transplant. Why can't fallopian tubes be transplanted from cadavers just
as kidneys are? This would permanently cure the pathological condition.

Moreover, efforts to overcome infertility through use of hormones are gradually meeting with more and more success. Hormone treatment, to which I will return briefly below, is a type of infertility treatment by drugs, but it does not cause the problems associated with use of hyperovulatory drugs. Although use of hyperovulatory drugs is not intrinsically immoral, their use raises very serious problems. Ordinarily they cause the wife to produce a large number of ova (more than four), which could be fertilized by her husband as a result of the marital act. If all are fertilized and implanted, this can cause serious problems affecting the life and health both of the mother and of the unborn children during pregnancy, leading some doctors who use such drugs to recommend "pregnancy reduction" — a euphemism for injecting potassium chloride into the hearts of some unborn children to kill them — as a means of protecting the health and life of some of the unborn babies. Usually, too, children conceived in this way are born prematurely and must thus spend long periods in the neonatal intensive care unit. This is obviously burdensome to them, and the costs involved are extremely high. The burdens that these children will likely suffer and the extreme expenses involved are likely consequences of using hyperovulatory drugs in an effort to overcome infertility. It seems to me that one ought to avoid these foreseen consequences by not resorting to use of such drugs.

As noted before, hormonal treatments of some causes of infertility have had success. Such treatments and other alternatives have been developed and are being further developed by Thomas W. Hilgers, M.D., at his Pope Paul VI Institute. Dr. Hilgers, a member of the Pontifical Academy for Life, resolutely refuses to use IVF-ET, AIH, GIFT, TOTS and other technologies that substitute for the marital act, but has been able to be of help to many married couples through the programs he has developed.[64] There is hope for couples who have difficulty in conceiving. But all married couples must remember that they do not have a "right" to a child, and that God may give them the cross of childlessness to carry. If he does, they must remember that he will be their Simon of Cyrene, ready to help them bear the cross he gives them.

5. Part Five: "Rescuing" Frozen Embryos[65]

As we have seen, *in vitro* fertilization requires that an ovum be removed from the body of a woman and then fertilized by male sperm in a petri dish. Because the procedure may fail or the newly conceived embryo not implant in the womb, standard procedure is to retrieve several ova and fertilize them all. One or several may be immediately implanted, but others may be held in a state of virtual suspended animation through the process of *cryopreservation*. In this procedure, an embryo — a living human person at the earliest stages of his/her life, we must not forget — is "frozen" by being put into a reservoir of liquid nitrogen. Because of various circumstances, some, in fact many, embryos frozen in this way will be left stranded in this absurd state, prisoners in what the late and great French geneticist Jerome Lejeune appropriately called "concentration cans."[66] As a result, today thousands of embryonic human beings are now so imprisoned, left orphans even before their birth. The question thus arises, what can be done on behalf of these human persons?[67]

Is it morally permissible for a woman to have a biologically unrelated, abandoned and frozen human embryo transferred from the freezer to her womb (= Heterologous Embryo Transfer — HET), to nurture it until birth as a means of protecting its life? The Magisterium has no clear teaching on this question, although some claim that passages in *Donum vitae* require a negative answer. Catholic theologians and philosophers are sharply divided: some maintain that it is absolutely immoral; others, that a *married woman* can justly do so, prenatally adopting the child and committing herself to be its adoptive mother, but that an *unmarried woman* cannot and would be guilty of abandoning the child at birth by giving it up for adoption and could only be regarded as a *surrogate*; still others, and I am among them, claim that while it may be preferable that a married woman do this, an unmarried woman can justly choose to have the embryo transferred from freezer into her womb to nurture it until birth and then give it up for adoption.

A. Does *Donum Vitae* Itself Provide an Answer?

As noted, some authors maintain that certain texts in *Donum vitae* require a negative answer, e.g., Msgr. William B. Smith, professor of moral theology at St. Joseph's Seminary, Dunwoodie, NY, and Nicholas Tonti-Filippini, professor of bioethics at the John Paul II Institute for Studies on Marriage and the Family in Melbourne, Australia. Both also develop arguments to support their claim that this is absolutely immoral, and I will examine these arguments later. But what of the texts of *Donum vitae* to which they appeal?

Smith appeals both to a specific passage in *Donum vitae* and to the "principled conclusion" of the document.[68] The specific passage states: "In consequence of the fact that they have been produced *in vitro*, those embryos which are not transferred into the body of the mother and are called 'spare' are exposed to an absurd fate, with no possibility of their being offered safe means of survival which *can be licitly pursued*."[69] Commenting, Smith says: "No safe means that *can licitly be pursued!* Perhaps the CDF did not intend to address this precise case, but I read here a first principled insight indicating that this volunteer 'rescue' is *not* a licit option."[70]

Geoffrey Surtees and Germain Grisez[71] have pointed out that Smith has taken this important passage out of context. It occurs in a section where *Donum vitae* is concerned with using embryos produced *in vitro* as subjects of experimental research. Thus, as Grisez says, the "sentence Smith quotes should not be understood as referring to the action of a rescuer who has in no way participated in the wrongs that have brought the embryonic persons to be and left them to their absurd fate, but to the options available to those wrongly involved in IVF."[72]

The "principled conclusion" of *Donum vitae* to which Smith appeals is its teaching on the moral relevance of the bond uniting the procreative and unitive meanings of the conjugal act and between the goods of marriage, along with the unity and dignity of the human person which require that "the procreation of a human person be brought about as the fruit of the conjugal act specific to the love between spouses."[73] Since the projected "rescue" of the frozen embryo is not procreation of this kind, Smith concludes that it cannot be morally licit.[74]

This is true. The passage, however, is concerned explicitly with the *generation of new human life*. In the case at hand, that life has *already been generated*, and all parties to the debate agree that the way in which it was generated, namely, through IVF, was intrinsically immoral. But the woman who seeks to protect this child's life by having it moved from the freezer to her nurturing womb in no way shares in that grave evil. Her freely chosen act *does not bear on the generation of human life*. Thus the "principled conclusion" to which Smith appeals to support his claim is not relevant.

Tonti-Filippini cites the following passage from *Donum vitae*, II A 1: "Coniugum autem fidelitas, in unitate matrimonii, secumfert mutuam observantiam erga ius utriuslibet, ad hoc ut alter pater et mater fiat solummodo per alterum. (The fidelity of the spouses in the unity of marriage involves reciprocal respect of their right to become a father or mother only through each other)."[75] He acknowledges that this passage refers to the *generation of new human life* and thus does not bear *directly* on the question. Nonetheless, fundamental to his negative answer is his claim that the capacity to become impregnated and to carry pregnancy and give birth is a capacity that belongs only in marriage and that this passage supports this claim. This argument will be considered below.

B. Truths Accepted by All Parties to the Debate

Before giving reasons supporting an affirmative answer and replying to objections, I think it important to emphasize the truth of propositions held by all parties to the debate. An affirmative answer in no way denies any of these propositions, despite the claims of some who reject that answer. The propositions are the following:

1. *It is intrinsically evil to generate human life by means other than the conjugal act.*
2. *The "fidelity of the spouses in the unity of marriage involves reciprocal respect for the right to become a father and a mother only through each other."* This is the passage, as noted already, to which Tonti-Filippini appeals.
3. *It is intrinsically evil for a woman to serve as a surrogate mother.*[76]
4. *"The use of the natural, generative instinct and function is lawful in the married state only, and in the service of the purposes for which marriage exists."*[77]

However — and this is crucial — although it is intrinsically evil to *generate* human life by means other than the conjugal act, it is *not* intrinsically evil for a woman to allow herself to become pregnant by means other than the conjugal act. Fornication and adultery, of course, are intrinsically evil, and one reason why they are is that fornication and adultery are opposed to the *good* of any child who could be conceived as a result. But a woman who fornicates or commits adultery cannot seek to prevent the conception of a child as a result of her fornication or adultery because it is intrinsically evil to contracept. If a child is conceived, she is obliged to nurture it in her womb until birth, i.e., to become pregnant.[78] Moreover, nurturing a child immorally generated by acts of fornication and adultery is to do something good, not evil, since doing so protects the life of the child. As will be seen, some opponents of an affirmative answer do so because they claim that it is intrinsically evil for a woman to allow herself to become pregnant by means other than the conjugal act. I agree that women who *cause* a pregnancy by engaging in fornication, adultery, artificial insemination, and *in vitro* fertilization commit intrinsically evil acts in *causing* the pregnancy, but allowing themselves to *become* pregnant as a result is not to do something intrinsically evil.

C. Central Moral Considerations

The following moral considerations are central to any answer, affirmative or negative, to our question.

1. *"The morality of a human act depends primarily and fundamentally on the 'object' rationally chosen by the deliberate will. . . .* In order to be able to grasp the object of an act which specifies that act morally, it is therefore necessary to place oneself *in the perspective of the acting person.* The object of the act of willing is in fact a freely chosen kind of behavior. . . . By the object of a given moral act, then, one cannot mean a process or an event of the merely physical order, to be assessed on the basis of its ability to bring about a given state of affairs in the outside world. Rather that object is the proximate end of a deliberate decision [choice] which determines the act of willing on the part of the acting person" (Pope John Paul II, *Veritatis splendor,* 78).[79]

2. "Reason attests that there are objects of the human act which are by their nature 'incapable of being ordered to God' because they radically contradict the *good* of the person made in his image. These are the acts which in the Church's moral tradition have been called 'intrinsically evil' (*intrinsece malum*): they are such *always and per se,* in other words, on account of their very object, and quite apart from the ulterior intentions of the one acting and the circumstances" (John Paul II, *Veritatis splendor,* 80).

3. Those acts whose morally specifying object "radically contradict the good of the person made in his image" do so precisely because they violate the "good of the person" by violating *his goods,* e.g., goods such as life itself and the marital communion (cf. *Veritatis splendor,* 13).

4. "We offend God only by acting contrary to our own *good*" (Thomas Aquinas, *Summa contra gentiles,* 3.122).

In light of these propositions, it follows, first, that one *cannot* equate the *natural species of an act* and its *moral species* and that the *object* morally specifying an act *cannot* be identified with a physical event capable of causing a state of affairs in the world. It follows, second, that it is morally wrong for a woman, married or single, to have a biologically unrelated abandoned and frozen unborn child transferred from the freezer to her womb to nurture it there until birth as the chosen means of protecting its life *if* the object of her choice violates one or more of the goods intrinsic to human persons, goods such as life itself or the marital communion. Opponents of the position I defend claim that the object freely chosen violates some good or goods of human persons, whereas I and others claim that the object freely chosen in no way does so, but is rather completely compatible with love and respect for every good perfective of human persons.

D. Reasons Supporting an Affirmative Answer

It is first necessary to identify the "object" morally specifying the human act chosen as the *means* to protect the life of the frozen and abandoned unborn child generated immorally by *in vitro* fertilization. As I have emphasized already, following Pope John Paul II, this object "*cannot mean a process or an event of the merely physical order, to be assessed on the basis of its ability to bring about a given state of affairs in the outside world.*" It cannot, in short, be identified with the *natural species* of the act. The object, on the contrary, "*is the proximate end of a deliberate decision [choice] which determines the act of willing on the part of the acting person,*" and to grasp this object one must place oneself "in the perspective of the acting person." To put matters another way, the "object" is precisely what the person is *choosing to do* here and now (see *Veritatis splendor*, 78, and the Thomistic texts cited above). In this case, the acting person is the woman; what she is choosing to do here and now, i.e., the "moral object" which is also the *proximate end* of her deliberate choice, is precisely "to transfer this unborn human baby from the freezer to her womb and to nurture it there until birth." This is the *means* she chooses to save the child's life, and the saving of its life is the *further* or *remote end* of her act. This freely chosen object includes her being pregnant, insofar as pregnancy is required in order to nurture the child in her womb.

Is this freely chosen object opposed to any good of human persons? The goods of human persons that come into focus in making a choice of this kind certainly include the following: the good of *human life itself*, the good of human sexuality as inherently *unitive and procreative*, and the good of *marriage* and of the *marital act*. The object freely chosen is obviously not opposed to the good of human life itself; rather it protects the good of the life of the unborn child. Nor is it opposed, as are fornication, adultery, artificial insemination, *in vitro* fertilization, and other means of generating life in the laboratory, to the good of human life in its transmission. The baby to be transferred to the womb already exists and it is his life that is relevant. Although this human person ought not to have been generated in the way it was, this new person now exists; and like babies conceived through the conjugal act, or through IVF and other new "reproductive technologies," or through fornication, adultery, or rape, it has the same immeasurable worth and deserves the same loving care as any other human person.

This object is also not opposed to the unitive/procreative good of human genital sexuality insofar as in choosing this object the woman is *not* choosing to exercise her genital powers, i.e., the *moral object* specifying her act is *not* to engage in genital, generative sex. She is not violating the norm proposed by Pius XII and cited above, namely, "*The use of the natural, generative instinct and function is lawful in the married state only, and in the service of the purposes for which marriage exists.*" Since this is so, this object is also not opposed to the good of marriage and the good of the marital act. The woman is *not* choosing to give herself in an act of genital union to someone other than her spouse, nor is she choosing to engage in the conjugal act or in *any* sexual act. Thus her choice does not violate any relevant human good but rather serves to protect and nurture the good of human life.

The *end* for whose sake this choice is made is also good, namely, the saving of the life of an already living unborn child who otherwise will die.

In addition, the woman is in no way cooperating in the evil of *in vitro* fertilization nor is she choosing to bear the child for the benefit of other persons, as a surrogate mother does, but rather for the benefit of the child. The nurture she proposes to give does not involve her in the wrongs already done to the baby, and it will be given for the baby's good and not the good of other persons. The woman is not cooperating in any evil project undertaken by the technicians whose aid is needed in transferring the baby from the freezer to her womb. On the contrary, while they usually cooperate in immoral activities, on this occasion these technicians are cooperating with the woman in treating the baby as a person whose life is intrinsically good and worthy of protection.

To avoid scandal, the woman should take care to let it be known that she regards *in vitro* fertilization and surrogate mothering as intrinsically evil, that babies produced artificially are human persons of incalculable value and in need of protection, and that her only interest is to protect an abandoned unborn baby's life.[80]

E. Objections

Two major kinds of objections are leveled against this position. The first kind maintains that it is *intrinsically evil* for *any* woman, married or single, to make the choice defended here. There are two variants of this kind of objection. The first variant affirms, rightly, that it is intrinsically evil to serve as a surrogate mother, and then alleges that any woman who chooses to have a biologically unrelated, abandoned, unborn child transferred to her womb to nurture it there is doing precisely this, namely, serving as a surrogate mother.[81, 82] The claim that the woman rescuing the frozen embryo is serving as a surrogate mother is simply not true. It ignores the precise meaning given to a "surrogate" mother in *Donum vitae* and the reason why that document condemns surrogacy. *Donum vitae* says that a "surrogate" mother is one who carries the pregnancy with a "pledge to surrender the child once it is born to the party who commissioned or made the agreement for the pregnancy."[83] However, the woman in our affirmative answer, whether married or single, is definitely not carrying the child on behalf of other parties who have commissioned the pregnancy. She is serving only the unborn child. Despite the fact that the understanding of "surrogacy" entertained by these authors (Smith and Pacholczyk) differs from the understanding of surrogacy given by *Donum vitae*, I will consider Pacholczyk's view more fully below when criticizing his claim that HET is a fundamental violation of the good of marital sexuality, a claim central to the second variant of the claim that she is engaging in an intrinsically evil act. The second variant holds that it is intrinsically wrong for any woman to allow herself to become pregnant by means other than the conjugal act.[84] This variant is a very serious objection, and the different kinds of arguments used to support it require detailed criticism.

The second kind of objection, while defending the moral liceity of a *married* woman's "adopting" a frozen and unborn embryo and having it transferred from the freezer to her womb, maintains that it is not morally licit for an *unmarried* woman to do so, because she is not capable of giving the child the home to which it has a right and is willing to abandon it after birth.[85] This objection also requires a more detailed response.

(1) *It Is Intrinsically Evil for a Woman to Allow Herself to Become Pregnant by Means Other Than the Conjugal Act*

Before examining the major arguments making this claim, I simply want to point out that the claim is demonstrably false. Earlier in this section, I emphasized that although it is intrinsically evil to fornicate or commit adultery, it is *not* intrinsically evil for a woman who fornicates or commits adultery to allow herself to become pregnant. Indeed, she is obliged *not to contracept* in order to prevent the conception of a child and also *not to abort* a child already conceived to prevent its implantation into her uterus. She is obliged to conceive a child if conception is possible and also to nurture in her womb any child who might be conceived as a result of her act of fornication of adultery. In addition, a woman's choice to nurture a child in her womb is to choose to do something *good*, not *bad*.

Moreover, *Donum vitae* itself *seems* to propose that the woman who has had a child conceived *in vitro* is *under a moral obligation* to have her unborn child implanted in her womb, where she can nurture it and carry it to term. I think that the following passage *can be* interpreted in this way, although I recognize that it need not be. The passage is the following: "In consequence of the fact that they have been produced *in vitro*, those embryos **which are not transferred into the body of the mother** and are called 'spare' are exposed to an absurd fate, with no possibility of their being offered safe means of survival which can be licitly pursued" (*Donum vitae,* I 6; boldface added).

The document clearly indicates that embryos "produced *in vitro*" would *not* be exposed to this "absurd fate" if they were transferred into the body of their mothers, indicating, so it seems to me, that the mothers of these embryos are obliged to have their children transferred to their wombs and nurtured. However, one cannot be obliged to do what is intrinsically wrong. Therefore, the claim that it is intrinsically evil for a woman to allow herself to become pregnant by means other than the conjugal act, so it seems to be, is falsified. It is also instructive to point out that *Donum vitae* explicitly calls the woman whose ovum was fertilized *in vitro* to "make" the baby its "mother."[86]

Interestingly, Mary Geach attempts to answer this argument. She notes that Helen Watt had claimed that a woman who had conceived a child by IVF and has embryos in store is obliged to bear them and that one cannot be obliged to do what is evil in itself.[87] Geach attempts to answer this objection by claiming that certain passages from St. Thomas seem to lead to the conclusion that at times we can be obliged or at least permitted to do what is intrinsically evil.[88] The problem with this reply is that even if that were Aquinas's view, it would be one of those rare instances in which he made a bad mistake, but in fact the texts cited simply do not support Geach's claim. For instance, in *Summa theologiae* I-II, 19, 6, reply, St. Thomas is discussing whether an *erroneous conscience* can excuse the person of the evil done — it can, if the ignorance is not culpable. But my point is that the claim that it is intrinsically evil to allow oneself to become pregnant by means other than the conjugal act is surely false, and its falsity militates against accepting their position.

Nonetheless, it is important to examine the principal arguments advanced to support this. I will consider the positions developed by Geach, Tonti-Filippini, and Pacholczyk.

(a) *Geach on the "Moral Object" Necessarily Entailed in HET*

In a series of essays, Geach has argued that any woman who seeks to rescue a frozen embryo by having it transferred from freezer to her womb to nurture it is engaging in a highly defective form of the marital act, and is thus damaging what Geach calls her "reproductive" integrity. Thus Geach holds that the "good" violated by this act is the good of the woman's reproductive integrity.

Geach maintains that what is essential for the woman's part in the marriage act is that she performs "an act of admission whereby she allows an intromission of an impregnating kind to be made into her." But this is precisely the kind of act performed by a woman who voluntarily has an unrelated human embryo placed in her womb. In other words, the *object* morally specifying the woman's act and making it to be the kind of act it is is this kind of act. But, and this is central to Geach's argument, this kind of act, from the woman's point of view, is the marital act. As a result, the woman who willingly has this embryo placed in her womb is engaging "in a highly defective version of the marital act." Her act is thus an unchaste act, an intrinsically evil act, and an act that destroys her reproductive integrity. It is intrinsically evil.[89]

Toward the end of her essay in *What Is Man, O Lord?*, Geach thus summarizes her position: "by allowing the impregnating insertion one is performing an act which is *like a marital act* in its spiritual essence, an essence which requires that the father of the child be playing his part. If one does without him, one is exploiting oneself: for to exploit someone is to use that person as a means in a way which ignores and cuts across that person's ends and goods. The end and the good of one's womb is in relation to the father of the child as well as to the child."[90]

A fundamental error in Geach's analysis is the fact that she confuses the *natural species* of an act with its *moral species*. I think that an act of *heterosexual intercourse*, whether the conjugal act, an act of adultery, an act of fornication, or act of incest is, in its *natural species*, a *generative kind of act*, and, that since pregnancy follows generation of a child, an act of *heterosexual intercourse* (including a marital act) may be viewed, in its *natural species*, in the way Geach describes it, i.e., as an intromission of an impregnating kind. But this is *not*, as I stressed earlier in this section, the proper way to describe the act in its *moral species*, nor is it the proper way to identify the *object morally specifying* the act freely chosen. In fact, if the woman is married, and if she engages in an act of heterosexual intercourse with her own husband but in doing so *chooses* the act as a means of gratifying libidinous desire and views her husband as simply a male body to use in this way, the *object morally specifying* her choice is *adultery* as both St. Thomas and Pope John Paul II have affirmed. In the case at hand, the *object morally specifying* the woman's choice is precisely to have an abandoned and frozen unborn child moved from the freezer to her womb to nurture it there. Although this object includes becoming pregnant, since she must be pregnant if she is to nurture the child, it is just as fallacious to claim that her act in its moral species is a "highly defective version of the marital act" (as Geach does) as it would be to claim that a legitimate act of capital punishment is an act of homicide.[91] In short, Geach simply fails to identify properly the *object morally specifying the act in question.*[92]

(b) *Tonti-Filippini on HET as Marital Infidelity*
Tonti-Filippini recognizes that the passage from *Donum vitae* insisting that the fidelity of marriage requires spouses to recognize that they have the right to become parents only through each other[93] was meant to apply to *heterologous fertilization* and not to *heterologous embryo transfer*; nonetheless, he claims that "impregnation has a particular significance and that the Congregation's statement . . . would rightfully apply to achieving motherhood by impregnation outside of the conjugal relationship."[94] He therefore devotes a major section of his essay (pp. 83-102) to argue that pregnancy outside of marriage constitutes infidelity to marriage. According to him, the intimate union of mother and child in pregnancy is utterly unique; in marriage this union is an "extension and embodiment of the union between the woman and her husband." He insists "that having given herself, her psychosomatic unity, faithfully, exclusively, totally, and in a fully human way in marriage, a woman is not free to give herself to being impregnated with a child from outside of marriage in this way. . . . This is so because her generative capacity, which . . . includes or is at least so linked to her capacity to become pregnant and to bear a child in her womb, and is not merely her capacity to produce ova and to express her love in the conjugal act, belongs to the marital union, and hence may not be given outside marriage."[95]

This, in essence, is Tonti-Filippini's exegesis of the passage from *Donum vitae*, II A 1. His argument is that becoming pregnant is for a woman the continuation of generating human life and that, since the woman has given over to her husband exclusively her generative power, becoming pregnant by means other than the marital exercise of her generative power is intrinsically evil. I think that Tonti-Filippini has, like Geach, sought to equate the natural species of an act with its moral species, and the object morally specifying the act with its "ability to bring about a given state of affairs in the external world" (cf. *Veritatis splendor*, 78). He has not properly identified the object morally specifying the act by putting himself within the perspective of the acting person, by viewing this object as the proximate end determining her act of choice.

Although Tonti-Filippini does not, in my opinion, clearly identify the *object* morally specifying her act, it seems to be that for him this object is to exercise her generative power, which includes pregnancy, with someone who is not her spouse and that therefore she is being unfaithful to her marriage because of the intimate bonds uniting marriage, the marital act, and the generation of human life. But in the case at hand, the woman is definitely *not* choosing to engage in a genital or marital act, nor is she choosing to generate human life apart from her husband; her object is precisely to have the embryo transferred to her womb to nurture it there as a means of protecting its life, and, as we have seen, this object in no way violates any human good.

Moreover, as E. Christian Brugger has remarked,

> Tonti-Filippini fails to show how his positive conception of the place and purpose of pregnancy in marriage and procreation *gives rise to an irrevocable negative norm* excluding a woman's becoming pregnant outside of the context of the conjugal act. His error, as I see it, is he invests a sui generis *moral* significance in gestational motherhood without providing convincing reasons explaining why such a status is required by the nature of marriage, the marital act of the mother-child gestational relationship. That is, he invests an a priori sui generis moral significance in gestational motherhood per se, i.e. apart from procreation, apart from the bringing about of new human life, and then argues that becoming a gestational mother by other means is always immoral. Tonti-Filippini's conception of biological pregnancy leads him to apply moral norms to it in a way not taught or even implied, as far as I know, anywhere in Catholic moral teaching.[96]

(c) *Pacholczyk on Pregnancy as Integral to Procreation and HET as Violating the Integrity of Marriage*

Central to Pacholczyk's argument that HET is intrinsically evil is his claim that pregnancy is integral to procreation. According to him, *Casti connubii* 17 shows that "*birth seems to be the significant threshold where procreation ends and education begins*," and that consequently "pregnancy is an essential and integral dimension of procreation." He offers an exegesis of *Donum vitae* II A 1 (see footnote 9) according to which this text teaches us that it is *only* through marriage that "a woman is capacitated to conceive and give birth to a child, i.e., to enter into the pregnant state."[97] According to Pacholczyk, it thus follows that in HET

> one is trying to assume the role of gestational mother without having conceived that same embryo through a conjugal act with one's husband. This is in actuality the essence of surrogacy, understood broadly, which violates ... the goods of motherhood and procreation by implanting an extra-corporeally-generated embryo into one's uterus. ... [But] we have to respect *the integrity of marriage* and the way in which we are intended to invoke the procreative powers of our bodies. This is meant to occur only in and through exclusive acts of conjugal self-giving between husband and wife, which have pregnancy and birth as their natural sequelae and finality.[98]

There are several serious problems with Pacholczyk's analysis. First of all, as was pointed out earlier in this section, the passage from *Donum vitae* to which he, with Tonti-Filippini, appeals has to do explicitly with *generating* human life. But in HET, human life has *already been generated*, albeit immorally.[99] But the text in no way requires one to regard pregnancy as an "essential and integral dimension of procreation," as our author claims. Moreover, to interpret *Casti connubii* 17 as affirming what Pacholczyk affirms is an instance of *eisegesis*, not *exegesis*, insofar as the text does not declare pregnancy to be an essential dimension of procreation but simply declares that the "procreation and education of children is the primary end of marriage" and cites Augustine to the effect that children are to be "begotten lovingly and educated religiously."[100] Pacholczyk goes well beyond what Pius XI asserts as true.

Nurturing in the womb, or being pregnant, is an essential and integral dimension of an unborn baby's development, but this child is generated at the time of conception/fertilization and pregnancy is not an integral and essential dimension of this.

Moreover, Pacholczyk, with Geach and Tonti-Filippini, seems to me to identify the *moral species* of a human act with its *natural species*, and to consider the *object morally specifying* the act the same as the physical event having the capacity to bring about a state of affairs in the external world.

(d) *Austriaco's Argument Based on the Father's Role in Conception/Pregnancy*

Austriaco, a Dominican priest with a doctorate in biology, first sets forth the Church's teaching on marriage and the bonds linking marriage, the marital act, and the generation of human life, and concludes that this teaching, in principle, rejects *heterologous embryo transfer*. He then cites scientific studies showing that husband and wife engaging in the conjugal act during their fertile period give each other more than what is needed for the child's conception. They suggest that the husband's semen deposited during the marital act appears to condition his wife's immune system so that it will not reject his immunologically unique molecular signature, one inherited by the child generated. Austriaco then declares:

> In light of these discoveries, we can now say that a husband, as part of his total self-donation during the conjugal act, gives his wife the capacity to implant and to gestate the child they both conceive together. Consequently, in its fundamental structure... the conjugal act... is biologically ordered towards *both* the conception and the gestation of a child. Thus, both the procreation and the gestation of a child contribute to the unitive good of marriage because both are ends that are attained by both spouses working together. Putting it another way, the conjugal act is unitive because it is procreative and gestative in kind.... *Both* parents are involved not only in begetting their child but also in caring for him from the earliest days of his life.[101]

He then concludes that *heterologous* embryo transfer violates the *unitive good* of marriage just as *homologous* fertilization *in vitro* does. But unlike Tonti-Filippini and Pacholczyk, who think it *intrinsically evil* for the woman whose ovum was fertilized *in vitro* to have the child so generated into her womb, Austriaco believes that *homologous* embryo transfer is justifiable.[102]

I maintain that Austriaco's argument to show that heterologous embryo transfer is intrinsically evil because it violates the unitive good of marriage suffers the same fatal flaw as the arguments advanced by Geach, Tonti-Filippini, and Pacholczyk, namely, a confusion of an act's *natural species* with its *moral species* and a failure to take into account that the primary source giving an act its *moral species* is the *object* freely chosen as the proximate (not remote) end of the acting person, in this case the woman, and that one *cannot* identify this object with processes in the external world capable of bringing about various states of affairs but only by viewing it from the acting person's perspective.[103]

(e) *Summarizing Conclusion to the Objection That HET Is Intrinsically Evil Because It Violates Marriage or the Conjugal Act or a Woman's Reproductive Integrity*

Geach, Tonti-Filippini, Pacholczyk, and Austriaco have many beautiful and true things to say about the intimate bonds linking marriage, the marital act, and the generation of human life with which I agree wholeheartedly. In fact, long before they wrote on these issues I had written extensively on them, repudiating *in vitro* fertilization ten years *before* the Congregation for the Doctrine of the Faith issued *Donum vitae*. I had argued, and still argue, that any act of generating human life that is not marital (e.g., fornication, adultery, artificial insemination, *in vitro* fertilization) is intrinsically immoral and violates the good of marriage.[104] Moreover, I think that I was one of the first theologians to note that the English text of *Humanae vitae*, 12, is not well translated. The English text states that "the conjugal act . . . capacitates them [the spouses] for the generation of new life, according to laws inscribed in the very being of man and woman." I noted that the Latin text does *not* say that the conjugal act "capacitates them" but rather that "it makes them *fit* or *worthy*" (*eos idoneos facit*).[105]

I thus fully appreciate the truth and beauty of what these authors say about the bonds linking marriage, the marital act, and the generation of life in the development of their arguments against HET. The problem is that all this simply does not address the issue at hand and is based on a confusion between the natural species of an act and its moral species.

(2) *It Is Intrinsically Evil for an Unmarried Woman to Become Pregnant With an Abandoned and Orphaned Embryo and Give It Up for Adoption After Birth*

Some authors, preeminently Helen Watt and John Berkman, reject the position defended by Geach et al. and hold that a married woman can rightly choose to pre-adopt the orphaned and abandoned, frozen, unborn child, first giving it a home in her womb and then, with her husband, giving it the home it needs to grow as a human person. But they claim that it is morally wrong for an unmarried woman to have the unborn child transferred to her womb from the freezer to nurture it and then to give it up for adoption after birth.[106] Both Watt and Berkman regard doing so as a form of surrogacy. Berkman explicitly recognizes that he and Watt are not limiting surrogacy to the "contractual view," which, "on a literal reading, is arguably the viewpoint expressed by *Donum vitae*."[107] I contend that this is not "arguably the viewpoint expressed by *Donum vitae*" but is precisely what this document teaches, as the following passage from *Donum vitae* makes clear:

> By "surrogate mother" the Instruction means: a) the woman who carries in pregnancy an embryo implanted in her uterus and who is genetically a stranger to the embryo because it has been obtained through the union of the gametes of "donors." She carries the pregnancy with a pledge to surrender the baby once it is born to the party who commissioned or made the agreement for the pregnancy. [Or] b) the woman who carries in pregnancy an embryo to whose procreation she has contributed the donation of her own ovum, fertilized through insemination with the sperm of a man other than her husband. She carries the pregnancy with a pledge to surrender the child once it is born to the party who commissioned or made the agreement for the pregnancy. (*Donum vitae*, II A 3, asterisk footnote)

Be that as it may, let us consider more fully the objection raised by Watt and more forcibly by Berkman.

The argument can be summarized as follows: a woman who freely chooses to have an unborn baby implanted in her uterus as a means of saving its life becomes that baby's gestational mother and by doing so accepts responsibility for the child. This responsibility is essentially adoptive; she has, in other words, chosen to adopt the child. But the choice to adopt the child is incompatible with the intention to give the child up later for adoption or otherwise. Thus this argument concludes that a woman should never choose to gestate an embryo that she does not also intend to raise.

Berkman says that analogies used by Germain Grisez and me in earlier writings[108] (e.g., that the woman is acting in the way that foster parents do; that her action is similar to that of a wet nurse) are false analogies and that the rescuing woman is the one who is "ultimately responsible" for the child and because of this responsibility is guilty of "abandoning" the child if she intends to give the child up for adoption after birth.[109]

Berkman argues that choosing to gestate another's embryo ipso facto entails becoming that embryo's social mother because the true nature of motherhood requires this. According to him, motherhood by definition entails an irrevocable covenant between mother and child; the woman who gestates an embryo becomes its mother and enters into an irrevocable covenant with the embryo. Just as it would be immoral for a couple to adopt a born child with the intention to give it up later for adoption, so, too, it would be immoral to choose to gestate an embryo with the intent to give the child up for adoption after birth.[110]

I think that Brugger has provided a strong counterargument to Berkman. I will here set forth his counterargument in detail:

> What is the ground for saying that gestational motherhood always entails a permanent covenant with the child? Why couldn't a person become someone's emergency adoptive mother...? Why isn't such a woman rightly called the child's mother? She has *exclusive* and *full* responsibility for the child's welfare; she does not care for the child *for* someone else; she cares for him for his sake; she accepts and carries out every responsibility of social parenthood, but temporarily. Berkman argues that any person could become another's guardian for a time because there is nothing essentially parental in that; but a gestational mother takes on a unique, irreplaceable role that unequivocally establishes her as the child's mother. But this still begs the question, why is the designation "parenthood" denied to the emergency adoptive parent? What about her moral responsibility for the child is not truly parental? Saying simply that it is not permanently covenantal is circular ("she does not become the child's gestational mother and therefore she does not become its true mother"). Why is gestational mother "true motherhood" and emergency adoptive motherhood not? Perhaps because what the emergency adoptive mother does could be done by any guardian? But this is not fully accurate. It can be done only by those who judge correctly that they have the resources to care well for the child for this important period, and by those who are *willing* to make the sacrifice of time and effort, willing to set aside other pursuits in which they might otherwise rightly engage but which are incompatible with this choice, willing to undergo the suffering of being up at night with the child, the economic cost of providing for the child, the psychological suffering of worrying about the child (after all, there is *no one* else responsible). What morally relevant parental responsibility does the emergency adoptive parent lack? Berkman argues that gestational motherhood is motherhood in its fullest sense, but fails to show how the gestational mother's motherhood is essentially a different kind of motherhood — except to the extent that it entails a different kind of biological relationship — from emergency adoptive motherhood. He fails to show why the biology gives rise to an irrevocable mothering duty, while the very real and grave duties accepted in the choice to become one's emergency adoptive parent do not. To

sustain his argument Berkman needs to overcome the objection that he has illicitly invested biological gestation with moral normativity (i.e., the charge of biologism).[111]

The crucial issue is whether the woman whose action I defend is doing something immoral in (a) nurturing the frozen and abandoned unborn baby in her womb and (b) in giving her up for adoption after birth. Both Watt and Berkman agree that (a) can be morally justifiable. They repudiate (b). But it is surely not intrinsically evil for an unmarried gestational or even an unmarried generative and gestational mother to give the child up for adoption after birth — and if she does so precisely *for the good of the child*, she is doing *good*, not *evil*.

Here I wish to say that my earlier efforts[112] to answer Berkman's objection were inadequate. I emphasized that his objection was based on the woman's prior intention to give up (and for him this means "abandon") the child after birth. In the "Colloquy" section of my first response, I claimed that this was not the woman's *present intention*, i.e., the object freely chosen, but was a *further intention*. In his reply, Berkman insisted that the intention to give up the child after birth was indeed part of the chosen object. In my second response, I erroneously granted that this intention was part of the *object* freely chosen. It is not. It is an intention *with which* the single woman does choose to have the frozen embryo transferred to her womb and nurtured there until birth. But it is a *further or remote intention*, not the *present intention or object of choice*, precisely because the woman *could choose to keep the baby after birth* (e.g., if she married while pregnant). Similarly, I may choose to give a lecture with the further intention of giving a stipend received for it to Catholic Charities and change my mind because on the day before the talk my wife had a serious operation that will not be covered fully by insurance.

Conclusion

I have provided reasons to show that it is morally permissible for a woman, whether married or single, to adopt by choice the proposal to have an abandoned and frozen unborn child, a human embryo immorally generated by *in vitro* fertilization, transferred from what Jerome Lejeune termed "concentration cans" into her womb to nurture it there by becoming pregnant with it as the *means* to protect its life. This woman is not acting as a surrogate mother, nor is the object of her choice one incompatible with a love for any good perfective of human persons made in God's image. I have also responded to the principal objections leveled against this position.

ENDNOTES FOR CHAPTER THREE

1. This truth, a matter of Catholic faith, will be discussed in more detail below in the chapter on abortion. In his book *Love and Responsibility*, trans. H. T. Willetts (New York: Farrar, Straus, Giroux, 1981; reprinted, San Francisco: Ignatius Press, 1993), Karol Wojtyla (Pope John Paul II) expressed matters this way: "A person is the kind of good which does not admit of use and cannot be treated as an object of use and as such the means to an end. . . . A person is a good towards which the only proper and adequate attitude is love."

2. Centuries ago St. Augustine rightly and wisely noted that one of the principal *goods* of marriage is the good of children, who are "to be received lovingly, nourished humanely, and educated religiously," i.e., in the love and service of God and neighbor. See his *De genesi ad literam*, 9.7 (*PL* 34.397).

3. It is worth noting here that the principal reason St. Thomas gave to show that fornication is intrinsically evil is that acts of fornication may cause (and are known to cause) the conception of new human life, that the life thus generated would be deprived of the home to which it has a right, and that, therefore, by fornicating one was unjustly exposing children who could be generated by fornication to this deprivation. He observed that one might try to prevent their conception by contraceptive acts, but he judged contraception to be even more gravely immoral insofar as it constitutes an attack on the survival of the human species. See his *Summa contra gentiles*, 3.122.

4. I realize that many women valiantly struggle to care for children whom they have conceived out of wedlock. Their caring for these children is *good,* and I praise them for it. Despite this, it is *not* good for them to conceive children in this way nor for their children to be deprived of the home that only loving spouses can provide — as these valiant women themselves realize. Nor is it good for the males who impregnate women outside of marriage to place themselves in a position where they cannot properly carry out their obligations to the women they have made pregnant nor to the children they have fathered.

5. As the German theologian Helmut Thielicke put the matter: "Not uniqueness establishes the marriage, but marriage establishes the uniqueness." *The Ethics of Sex* (New York: Harper, 1964), p. 95.

6. Here see John Paul II's perceptive observations in his commentary on Genesis 2: "The unity of which Genesis 2:24 speaks ('and the two will be one flesh') is without doubt the unity that is expressed and realized in the conjugal act. The biblical formulation, so extremely concise and simple, indicates sex, that is, masculinity and femininity, as that characteristic of man — male

and female — that allows them, when they become one flesh, *to place their whole humanity at the same time under the blessing of fruitfulness*" (emphasis added). See Pope John Paul II, *Male and Female He Created Them: A Theology of the Body*, Translation, Introduction, and Index by Michael Waldstein (Boston: Pauline Books & Media, 2006), 10.2, p. 167. This book is the new and definitive translation of Pope John Paul II's famous Wednesday Audiences on the "Theology of the Body," given from September 5, 1979, through November 28, 1984. "10.2" means that this text is found in Audience number 10, paragraph no. 2. Henceforth this work will be referred to as TOB, with Audience and paragraph numbers given, followed by page number.

7. On this, see Pope Paul VI, encyclical *Humanae vitae*, no. 12; Pope John Paul II, Apostolic Exhortation on the Role of the Christian Family in the Modern World (*Familiaris consortio*), no. 32; *Catechism of the Catholic Church*, no. 2369.

8. On this, see Pope John Paul II, TOB, 20.1-5, pp. 204-208, " 'Knowledge' and Procreation" (Gn 4:1). Here the Pope notes that in the conjugal act, whereby they come to "know" each other, husband and wife "reveal themselves to one another with *that specific depth of their own human 'I,' which precisely reveals itself also through their sex*, their masculinity and femininity" (20.4, p. 207). "Thus, the reality of conjugal union in which man and woman become 'one flesh' contains in itself a new and definitive discovery of the meaning of the human body in its masculinity and femininity" (20.5, p. 208).

9. On this, see John F. Kippley, *Sex and the Marriage Covenant: A Basis for Morality* (Cincinnati: Couple to Couple League, 1991), pp. 7-12, 76-86.

10. The ideas briefly set forth here are developed by me at more length in *Marriage: The Rock on Which the Family Is Built* (San Francisco: Ignatius, 1995), chap. 2, "Marriage and the Complementarity of Male and Female." See also Robert Joyce, *Human Sexual Ecology: A Philosophy of Man and Woman* (Washington, DC: University Press of America, 1980), pp. 35-50.

11. On this, see Robert P. George and Gerard V. Bradley, "Marriage and the Liberal Imagination," *The Georgetown Law Review* 84 (1995), 301-320; Germain Grisez, "The Christian Family as Fulfillment of Sacramental Marriage," a paper delivered to the Society of Christian Ethics Annual Conference, September 9, 1995 (unpublished manuscript, on file with *The Georgetown Law Review*).

12. Pope Pius XII, Address to the Italian Union of Midwives, October 21, 1951, text in *The Catholic Mind* 50 (1951), 61.

13. Pope Paul VI, encyclical *Humanae vitae*, no. 12. My translation.

14. Ibid., no. 12.

15. Classic sources for the distinction between *transitive* and *immanent* action, between making and doing, and the significance of this distinction are: Aristotle, *Metaphysics,* Bk. 9, chap. 8, 1050a23-1051b1; St. Thomas Aquinas, *In IX Metaphysicorum,* Lect. 8, no. 1865.

16. Catholic Bishops' [of England] Committee on Bioethical Issues, *In Vitro Fertilization: Morality and Public Policy* (London: Catholic Information Services, 1983), no. 23.

17. Four of his addresses take up this issue: (1) Allocution to the Fourth International Conference of Catholic Doctors, September 29, 1949; text in *Papal Teachings on Matrimony,* ed. The Benedictine Monks of Solemnes, trans. Michael J. Byrnes (Boston: St. Paul Editions, 1963), pp. 381-385; (2) Allocution to Italian Catholic Midwives, October 29, 1951, in ibid., pp. 405-434; (3) Allocution to the Second World Congress on Fertility and Human Sterility, May 19, 1956, in ibid., pp. 482-492; and (4) Allocution to the Seventh Hematological Congress, September 12, 1958, in ibid., pp. 513-525. He discussed artificial insemination in all four of these addresses, and in no. 3 he explicitly took up *in vitro* fertilization.

18. Allocution to the Second World Congress on Fertility and Human Sterility, ibid., p. 485.

19. Allocution to Italian Catholic Midwives, ibid., pp. 427-428.

20. Allocution to the Second World Congress on Fertility and Human Sterility, ibid., p. 470.

21. Allocution to the Fourth International Congress of Catholic Doctors, ibid., p. 559.

22. Pontifical Academy for Life, *Reflections on Cloning* (Vatican City: Libreria Editrice Vaticana, 1997), pp. 10, 14.

23. It is instructive to note that in his article on artificial insemination in the widely used and influential *Encyclopedia of Bioethics,* Luigi Mastroianni included under "homologous" fertilization procedures "utilizing the semen of the husband *or designated partner*" (emphasis added) ("Reproductive Technologies, Introduction," in *Encyclopedia of Bioethics,* ed. Warren T. Reich [2nd rev. ed.: New York: McGraw Hill, 1995], 2207). Inasmuch as this edition of the *Encyclopedia* now includes an essay entitled "Marriage and *Other Domestic Partnerships*" (emphasis added) by Barbara Hilkert Anderson (pp. 1397-1402), Mastroianni's apparent equation of husbands with "designated partners" is not too surprising.

24. See Mastroianni, "Reproductive Technologies, Introduction," 2207.

25. On this, see David S. McLaughlin, M.D., "A Scientific Introduction to Reproductive Technologies," in *Reproductive Technologies, Marriage, and*

the Church, ed. Donald G. McCarthy (Braintree, MA: The Pope John Center, 1988), pp. 55-56.

26. Walter Wadlington, "Reproductive Technologies, Artificial Insemination," *Encyclopedia of Bioethics*, 2220.

27. George J. Annas, "Artificial Insemination: Beyond the Best Interests of the Donor," *Hastings Center Report* 9.4 (August 1979), 14-15, 43.

28. Wadlington, "Reproductive Technologies, Artificial Insemination," 2217.

29. See McLaughlin, "A Scientific Introduction to Reproductive Technologies," p. 57.

30. On this, see Mastroianni, "Reproductive Technologies, Introduction," 2209-2210; Andrea L. Bonnicksen, "Reproductive Technologies, In Vitro Fertilization and Embryo Transfer," *Encyclopedia of Bioethics*, 2221-2224; and McLaughlin, "A Scientific Introduction to Reproductive Technologies," pp. 58-59.

31. Mastroianni, "Reproductive Technologies, Introduction," 2211.

32. See Bonnicksen, "Reproductive Technologies, In Vitro Fertilization and Embryo Transfer," 2222.

33. On these and other technologies, see McLaughlin, "A Scientific Introduction to Reproductive Technologies," pp. 60-62.

34. Ibid.

35. Ibid. See also Mastroianni, "Reproductive Technologies, Introduction," 2211-2212.

36. "Somatic-cell nuclear transfer" is the expression used to describe mammalian cloning by the National Bioethics Advisory Commission in its document, released in June 1997: "Cloning Human Beings: The Report and Recommendations of the National Bioethics Advisory Commission." A summary of this report is printed in *Hastings Center Report* (September-October, 1997), 7-9.

37. Pontifical Academy for Life, *Reflections on Cloning*, pp. 10-11.

38. Catholic Bishops' (of England) Committee on Bioethical Issues, *In Vitro Fertilization: Morality and Public Policy*, no. 24.

39. Richard McCormick, *The Critical Calling: Reflections on Moral Dilemmas Since Vatican II* (Washington, DC: Georgetown University Press, 1989), p. 337. The internal citation is from William Daniel, S.J., "In Vitro Fertilization: Two Problem Areas," *Australasian Catholic Record* 63 (1986), 27.

40. Ibid.

41. See Thomas A. Shannon and Lisa Sowle Cahill, *Religion and Artificial Reproduction: An Inquiry Into the Vatican "Instruction on Respect for Human*

Life" (New York: Crossroads, 1988), p. 138; Jean Porter, "Human Need and Natural Law," in *Infertility: A Crossroad of Faith, Medicine, and Technology*, ed. Kevin Wm. Wildes, S.J. (Dordrecht/Boston/London: Kluwer Academic Publishers, 1997), pp. 103-105. It should be noted that Shannon and Cahill, using an argument proportionalistic in nature — that is, that it can be morally permissible to intend a so-called nonmoral evil (e.g., heterologous generation of human life) should a sufficiently greater nonmoral good be possible (e.g., providing an otherwise childless couple with a child of their own) — insinuate that, if the spouses consent, recourse to third parties for gametes and even to surrogate mothers might not truly violate spousal dignity or unity. See *Artificial Reproduction. . .*, p. 115.

42. See Pope John Paul II, encyclical *Veritatis splendor*, nos. 71-83. An excellent collection of essays on this encyclical is *Veritatis Splendor and the Renewal of Moral Theology*, eds. J. A. DiNoia, O.P. and Romanus Cessario, O.P. (Chicago: Midwest Theological Forum, 1999).

43. For critiques of proportionalism see my *An Introduction to Moral Theology* (second ed.: Huntington, IN: Our Sunday Visitor, 2003); Germain Grisez, *The Way of the Lord Jesus*, Vol. 1, *Christian Moral Principles* (Chicago: Franciscan Herald Press, 1983), chap. six; Martin Rhonheimer, "Intrinsically Evil Acts and the Moral Viewpoint: Clarifying a Central Teaching of *Veritatis splendor*," in *Veritatis Splendor and the Renewal of Moral Theology*, pp. 161-194.

44. Benedict Ashley, "The Chill Factor in Moral Theology," *Linacre Quarterly* 57.4 (1990), 71.

45. Ibid., 72.

46. The argument just advanced was set forth originally in an earlier essay I wrote on this issue: "*Donum Vitae*: Catholic Teaching on Homologous *In Vitro* Fertilization," in *Infertility: A Crossroad of Faith, Medicine, and Technology*, pp. 73-92, especially pp. 81-87, making use of material developed by Germain Grisez, Joseph Boyle, John Finnis, and me in our essay " 'Every Marital Act Ought To Be Open to New Life': Toward a Clearer Understanding," *The Thomist* 52 (1988), 365-426.

47. McCormick, "Notes on Moral Theology," *Theological Studies* 45 (1984), 102.

48. Here I must note that in her essay, "Human Needs and Natural Law" (see endnote 41), Jean Porter claims that my argument supporting *Donum vitae* is based on a "Kantian" sexual ethics that "gives pride of place to autonomy" (pp. 100-101). She even claims that I "dissent" from Catholic teaching in my analysis of the marital act because of my emphasis on the role of intention in determining the moral significance of human actions. Porter's criticisms are ludicrous and can only be attributed to a woeful ignorance of

Thomistic moral theory and the teaching of John Paul II in *Veritatis splendor*. I may dissent from a "Suarezian" understanding of natural law, which Porter perhaps employs along with her own proportionalism, but I am by no means Kantian. As far as the role of intention in determining morality is concerned, has Porter read St. Thomas, *Summa theologiae*, II-II, 64, 7 (for instance), where he clearly says that "moral actions are specified according to what is intended and not by what lies outside the scope of one's intentionality" (the Latin text reads: *"morales autem actus recipiunt speciem secundum id quod intenditur, non autem ab eo quod est praeter intentionem"*)?

49. It is important to stress here that Christian faith proclaims that the Word Incarnate, although not a human *person*, is still a *human being, a man*. Christian faith rejects docetism, the doctrine that the Uncreated Word only seemed to become human and ceased so appearing after the resurrection.

50. Pope John Paul II, "To my brother bishops from North and Central America and the Caribbean assembled in Dallas, Texas," in *Reproductive Technologies, Marriage and the Church*, p. xv.

51. *Donum vitae*, II B 4, 7.

52. Rev. John Doerfler, *Assisting or Replacing the Conjugal Act: Criteria for a Moral Evaluation of Reproductive Techniques*, unpublished 1999 S.T.L. dissertation on file at the John Paul II Institute for Studies on Marriage and Family, Washington, DC. A substantive summary of his study has appeared in *Anthropotes: Rivista di Studi sulla Persona e Famiglia*. He has briefly summarized his work in "Technology and Human Reproduction," *Ethics & Medics* 24.8 (August 1999), 3-4.

53. Josef Seifert, "Substitution of the Conjugal Act or Assistance to It? IVF, GIFT and Some Other Medical Interventions. Philosophical Reflections on the Vatican Declaration 'Donum Vitae,'" *Anthropotes: Rivista di Studi sulla Persona e Famiglia* 4 (1988), 273-286.

54. See Doerfler, *Assisting or Replacing the Conjugal Act*, pp. 89-90.

55. See, for example, Thomas J. O'Donnell, S.J., *Medicine and Christian Morality* (2nd rev. ed.: New York: Alba House, 1991), p. 238.

56. See, for instance, the following: Donald T. DeMarco, "Catholic Moral Teaching and TOT/GIFT," in *Reproductive Technologies, Marriage and the Church*, pp. 122-139; Nicholas Tonti-Filippini, " 'Donum Vitae' and Gamete Intra-Fallopian Tube Transfer," *Linacre Quarterly* 57.2 (May 1989), 68-79; Benedict Ashley, O.P., and Kevin O'Rourke, O.P., *Health Care Ethics: A Theological Analysis* (4th ed.: Washington, DC: Georgetown University Press, 1997), pp. 242-247; Germain Grisez, *Difficult Moral Questions*, Vol. 3 of *The Way of the Lord Jesus* (Quincy, IL: Franciscan Press, 1997), pp. 244-249.

57. See Grisez, *Difficult Moral Questions*, p. 248; Orville N. Griese, *Catholic Identity in Health Care: Principles and Practice* (Braintree, MA: Pope John XXIII Medical-Moral Research and Education Center, 1987), pp. 443-44; John W. Carlson, "Interventions Upon Gametes in Assisting the Conjugal Act Toward Fertilization," in *Infertility: A Crossroad of Faith, Medicine, and Technology*, pp. 110-111; Tonti-Filippini, " 'Donum Vitae' and Gamete Intra-Fallopian Tube Transfer," 70.

58. This seems to me to be the position of Grisez, Griese, and Carlson (see preceding endnote for bibliographical details).

59. On this, see Doerfler, *Assisting or Replacing the Conjugal Act*, pp. 89ff.

60. Two Catholic theologians explicitly accepting this procedure are: O'Donnell, *Medicine and Christian Morality*, p. 238; Griese, *Catholic Moral Identity in Health Care*, p. 46.

61. Good critiques of this procedure are provided by Grisez, *Difficult Moral Questions*, pp. 247-249; Tonti-Filippini, " 'Donum Vitae' and Gamete Intrafallopian Tube Transfer."

62. The most extensive and initially plausible defense of GIFT is given by Peter J. Cataldo. His most detailed effort to justify it is found in his essay, "The Newest Reproductive Technologies: Applying Catholic Teaching," in *The Gospel of Life and the Vision of Health Care*, ed. Russell Smith (Braintree, MA: Pope John XXIII Medical-Moral Research and Education Center, 1996), pp. 61-94. A briefer presentation of his argument is given in "Reproductive Technologies," *Ethics & Medics* 21.1 (January 1996), 1-3. See also Donald . McCarthy, "Infertility Bypass," *Ethics & Medics* 8.10 (October 1983), 1-2; McCarthy, "Catholic Moral Teaching and TOT/GIFT: A Response to Donald T. DeMarco, in *Reproductive Technologies, Marriage, and the Church*, pp. 140-145; Griese, *Catholic Identity in Health Care*, pp. 47-49.

63. For Doerfler, in addition to the study referred to in endnote 52, see his "Is GIFT Compatible with the Teaching of *Donum Vitae*?" *Linacre Quarterly* 64.1 (February 1997), 41-47. See also Grisez, *Difficult Moral Questions*, pp. 246-248; Tonti-Filippini, " 'Donum Vitae' and Gamete Intrafallopian Tube Transfer," 68-89; DeMarco, "Catholic Moral Teaching and TOT/GIFT," in *Reproductive Technologies, Marriage, and the Church*, pp. 122-140; Ashley/O'Rourke, *Health Care Ethics*, pp. 246-247; Seifert, "Substitution of the Conjugal Act or Assistance to It . . . ?"

64. Personal letter from Thomas W. Hilgers, M.D., June 9, 1999. He has developed the *Creighton Model Fertility/Care System* for helping married couples experiencing difficulties in conceiving.

65. An earlier draft of this section was presented at the Westchester Institute's First Annual Scholars Forum, "On the Morality of Heterologous Embryo

Transfer," October 28-29, 2004, at the Hyatt Regency Hotel in Washington, DC. That draft was published in somewhat modified form in *The National Catholic Bioethics Quarterly* (*NCBQ*) 5.1 (Spring 2005) and in final form as "The Object of the Acting Woman in Embryo Rescue" in *Human Embryo Adoption: Biotechnology, Marriage, and the Right to Life*, eds. Rev. Thomas V. Berg, L.C., and Edward J. Furton (Philadelphia/Thornwood: The National Catholic Bioethics Center/The Westchester Institute for Ethics & the Human Person, 2006), pp. 135-163. This section is a slightly modified version of "The Object of the Acting Woman in Embryo Rescue." I am grateful to the National Catholic Bioethics Center and the Westchester Institute for permission to use material from *Human Embryo Adoption*. In it, I correct errors that I made in the section devoted to this matter in the first edition of this book (pp. 94-107) and in articles published between 2002-2005. My most serious error was the claim that "becoming pregnant" was *not* included in the object morally chosen by the woman who seeks to protect the life of an abandoned, unborn, frozen embryo. I am most grateful for the constructive criticism given earlier drafts of this section by Kevin Flannery, S.J., Nicanor Austriaco, O.P., Germain Grisez, and E. Christian Brugger.

66. Jerome Lejeune, *The Concentration Can* (San Francisco: Ignatius Press, 1992).

67. One highly immoral way of handling frozen embryos has already occurred to entrepreneurs in the United States, namely, the formation of business enterprises eager to locate and distribute abandoned frozen embryos to couples anxious to have a child. One such entity, called "Creating Families, Inc.," is located in Denver, CO. Although this company is careful to claim that it does not accept "fees" for its work in "creating families," it nonetheless solicits "donations" for its services, and it is somewhat naïve to think that the profit motive is not operative (see the Web site of Creating Families, Inc.: http:/www.creatfam.com/embryodononor.html). Similarly, the Columbia Presbyterian Medical Center in New York can provide an already frozen embryo for $2,750, as opposed to the $16,000 needed to cover the entire IVF-ET procedure (on this, see Brian Caulfield, "Souls on Ice: With Frozen Embryo Technology, Life's Sanctity is Lost," *National Catholic Register*, 74.1 [January 4-10, 1998], 15).

68. Msgr. William B. Smith, "Rescue the Frozen?" *Homiletic and Pastoral Review* 96.1 (October 1995), 72-74.

69. *Donum vitae*, I 5 (emphasis added), cited by Smith, ibid., 72.

70. Ibid.

71. Germain Grisez, *The Way of the Lord Jesus*, Vol. 3, *Difficult Moral Questions* (Quincy, IL: Franciscan Press, 1997), p. 242, footnote 188. Geoffrey Surtees, "Adoption of a Frozen Embryo," *Homiletic and Pastoral Review* 96 (August-September 1996), 8-9.

72. Grisez, p. 242, footnote 188.

73. *Donum vitae,* II 4, cited by Smith, ibid., 74.

74. Ibid. I believe that I have accurately summarized Smith's point here; nonetheless, this particular section of his essay does not seem to be clearly articulated.

75. Nicholas Tonti-Filippini, "The Embryo-Rescue Debate: Impregnating Women, Ectogenesis, and Restoration from Suspended Animation," *Rescuing Frozen Embryos*, pp. 73-74.

76. See *Donum vitae,* II A 3.

77. Pope Pius XII, "Address to Italian Union of Midwives" (Allocutio "Vegliare con sollecitudine" October 29, 1951), *Acta Apostolicae Sedis* 43 (1951). The Italian text reads: "La retta norma è dunque questa: l'uso della naturale disposizione generativa è moralmente lecito soltanto nel matrimonio, nel servizio e secondo l'ordine dei fini del matrimonio medesimo" (no. 60, at 852).

78. On this, see, for example, St. Thomas Aquinas, *Summa contra gentiles*, 3.122, where the Common Doctor, after showing that simple fornication is evil because it is opposed to the good of the life of the child who could be conceived as a result, goes on to say that preventing its conception by contraception is an even greater evil.

79. Here the Pope is making the same point that St. Thomas Aquinas made when he distinguished clearly between the *natural species* of an act and its *moral species.* Thus the *natural species* of an act might be *killing* or *sexual intercourse*, but its *moral species* could be *homicide* or legitimate *self-defense* or *the conjugal act* or *adultery,* depending on the *intention* — primarily the intention at the heart of the *voluntas eligens*, i.e., choice. As a matter of fact, both Thomas and John Paul II recognize that a husband can commit adultery with his own wife *if* he is choosing intercourse with her merely as a means of satisfying his lustful desires and looks on her not as his wife but as a female body meant to gratify his desires.

    On the Thomistic distinction between the *natural species* of an act and its *moral species*, see *Summa theologiae*, 1-2, 1, 3; 2-2, 64, 7; and, for the crucial role of intention as *choice, voluntas eligens*, see in particular *In Sent. II*, 40, 1 2c: ". . .voluntas dupliciter potest considerari: vel secundum quod est intendens, prout in ultimum finem fertur; vel secundum quod est eligens, prout fertur in obiectum proximum, quod in finem ultimum ordinatur.

Si consideretur primo modo, sic malitia voluntatis sufficit ad hoc quod actus malus esse dicatur; quia quod malo fine agitur malum est. Non autem bonitas voluntatis intendentis sufficit ad bonitatem actus: quia actus potest esse de se malus, qui nullo modo bene fieri potest. *Si autem consideretur voluntas secundum quod est eligens, sic universaliter verum est quod a bonitate voluntatis dicitur actus bonus, et a malitia mala"* (emphasis added). See also *De Malo*, 2, 2, ad 1.

Regarding a husband/wife committing adultery with his own wife/her own husband, see St. Thomas, *Supplement to the Summa theologiae*, 49, 6 (= *In IV Sent.*, 31, 2, 3), and John Paul II, *"Man and Woman He Created Them": A Theology of the Body*, Waldstein trans. (Boston: Pauline Books & Media, 2006), 43.2-3, pp. 298-299.

80. This argument is clearly presented by Germain Grisez, *Difficult Moral Questions*, Vol. 3 of his *The Way of the Lord Jesus* (Quincy, IL: Franciscan Press, 1997), Question 51, pp. 239-244.

81. Msgr. William B. Smith, "Rescue the Frozen," 72-74. See also Smith, "Response," *Homiletic and Pastoral Review*, 96:11-12 (Aug.-Sept. 1996), 16-17.

82. See also Tadeusz Pacholczyk, "Frozen Embryo Adoptions Are Morally Objectionable," in *The Catholic as Citizen: Debating the Issues of Justice. Proceedings from the 26th Annual Conference of Catholic Scholars*, ed. Kenneth Whitehead (South Bend, IN: St. Augustine's Press, 2004), pp.84-101.

83. *Donum vitae*, 2 A 3, asterisk footnote.

84. This objection is developed in different ways primarily by the following: (1) Mary Geach, "Rescuing Frozen Embryos," *What Is Man, O Lord?*, pp. 217-230, and her presentation at the Westchester Institute's Scholars Forum, published as "The Female Act of Allowing an Intromission of Impregnating Kind," *Human Embryo Adoption*, eds. Thomas V. Berg, L.C., and Edward Furton, pp. 251-271; (2) Nicholas Tonti-Filippini, "Embryo Rescue Debate: Impregnating Women, Ectogenesis, and Restoration from Suspended Animation," presented at the Westchester Institute's Scholars Forum and published in *Human Embryo Adoption*, pp. 69-113; "Nicholas Tonti-Filippini Replies," in the "Colloquy" section of *The National Catholic Bioethics Quarterly* 4.1 (Spring 2004), 11-12; (3) Tadeusz Pacholczyk, essay cited in footnote 82, presented in shorter form as "Some Moral Contraindications to Embryo Adoption," in *Human Embryo Adoption*, pp. 37-53; and (4) Nicanor Austriaco, O.P., "On the Catholic Vision of Conjugal Love and the Morality of Embryo Transfer," presented at the Westchester Institute's Scholars Forum and published in *Human Embryo Adoption*, pp.115-133; (5) Christopher Oleson, "The Immorality of Heterologous Embryo Transfer," given at the Westchester

Institute's First Annual Scholars Forum and published as "The Nuptial Womb: On the Moral Significance of Being 'With Child,' " in *Human Embryo Adoption*, pp. 165-195. Here I will consider Geach, Tonti-Filippini, Pacholczyk, and Austriaco. I will refer to texts in *Human Embryo Adoption*, except for Pacholczyk, for whom I use the text cited in endnote 82, and also some claims made by Geach in her essay in *What Is Man, O Lord?* I will not consider Oleson's argument insofar as it is quite similar to Tonti-Filippini's.

85. On this, see Helen Watt, "Are there any circumstances . . . ," in *Issues for a Catholic Bioethics*, pp. 347-352. The view is most strongly championed by John Berkman, "Gestating the Embryos of Others: Surrogacy? Adoption? Rescue?" *The National Catholic Bioethics Quarterly* 3.2 (Summer 2003), 309-330, and "John Berkman Replies," in the "Colloquy" section of *The National Catholic Bioethics Quarterly* 4.1 (Spring 2004), 12-13. In what follows, I will center attention on Berkman's presentation of this view.

86. In "The Embryo Rescue Debate ..." published in *The National Catholic Bioethics Quarterly*, Tonti-Filippini refused to call the woman the baby's mother and held that the woman whose ovum was fertilized *in vitro* is obliged *not to have the child transferred to her womb*. In the revised version in *Human Embryo Adoption*, p. 101, he calls her "mother."

87. See Watt, "Are there any circumstances . . . ," 348.

88. See Geach, "Rescuing Frozen Embryos," 226, footnote 12, where she indicates that Aquinas teaches this in the following passages: *Summa theologiae*, I-II, 19, 6, reply 3; II-II, 62, 2, obj. 2; III, 64, 6, reply 3; *De Veritate*, 17, 4, reply 8.

89. Here I have summarized the argument given in the sources identified in endnote 84.

90. "Rescuing Frozen Embryos," 228 (emphasis added).

91. Although John Paul II in *Evangelium vitae*, 56, urges that capital punishment be used *only* if there are no other means of protecting society, he does not condemn capital punishment as intrinsically immoral. On this, see St. Thomas Aquinas, *Summa theologiae*, 1-2, 1, 3.

92. An excellent critique of Geach's position, and in particular her claim that pregnancy is a continuation of the marital act, is given by Christopher Tollefsen, "Could Human Embryo Transfer Be Intrinsically Immoral?" in *Embryo Adoption and the Catholic Moral Tradition*, eds. S. Brakman and D. Weaver (Dordrecht, The Netherlands: Springer, 2008).

93. Tonti-Filippini, "The Embryo Rescue Debate . . . " in *Human Embryo Adoption*, pp. 81-82.

94. Ibid., p. 84. Tonti-Filippini's position has in essence been adopted by Christopher Oleson, "The Nuptial Womb: On the Moral Significance of Being 'With Child,'" in *Human Embryo Adoption*, pp. 165-195.

95. Ibid., p. 84.

96. E. Christian Brugger, "A Defense by Analogy of Heterologous Embryo Transfer," *Human Embryo Adoption*, pp. 207-208, revised version of "The Morality of Heterologous Embryo Transfer," given at the Scholars Forum and published in *The National Catholic Bioethics Quarterly* 4.1 (Spring 2004).

97. Pacholczyk, "Frozen Embryo Adoptions...," 89 (for *Casti connubii* 17) and 92 (for *Donum vitae* II 1 A).

98. Ibid., 94.

99. I think that when human life is generated in the laboratory by *in vitro* fertilization and other "new reproductive methods," it is truly *generated*, and human life is *conceived*, but it is *not "procreated"* in the true sense. These laboratory methods have, as I have argued many times, transformed "procreation" to "reproduction."

100. This is the way Augustine is cited in *Casti connubii*. The full text of Augustine (*De genesi ad litteram*, 7, 9), however, to which a footnote in the encyclical refers, says that "children are to be welcomed lovingly, nourished humanely, and educated religiously."

101. Austriaco, "On the Meaning of the Conjugal Act and the Morality of Embryo Transfer," manuscript pages 9-10.

102. Ibid., manuscript page 132.

103. In some e-mail exchanges, Father Austriaco informed me that he was not identifying the moral species of the act with its natural species but simply noting the moral relevance of the husband's contribution to implantation and gestation. He offered an analogy: Just as it would be morally wrong for a woman intentionally to become pregnant if she *knew* that she could not carry the baby to term but that it would definitely miscarry because of the harm this would cause the baby, so too a woman who *knows* that her husband's sperm contributes to a successful implantation and gestation would not *intentionally* become pregnant with the child of another person because of the harm this would cause the marriage and her husband. To which I reply that in the former case, although the harm caused the child might be an unintended side effect, the woman would violate the norm of fairness or the Golden Rule, whereas in the latter case any harm done, if harm is done, is surely not intended, and if the husband consents, a necessary condition if the rescuing woman is married, no unfairness is done either. But

I think that no harm is done to the marriage or the marital act since the marital act is by no means chosen.

104. See the following publications: *Sex, Marriage and Chastity: Reflections of a Layman, Spouse, and Parent* (Chicago: Franciscan Herald Press, 1981), esp. pp. 9-19, 80-90; *Human Existence, Medicine, and Ethics: Reflections on Human Life* (Chicago: Franciscan Herald Press, 1977), pp. 39-67; " 'Begotten, not Made': Reflections on the Laboratory Generation of Human Life," in Pope John Paul II Lecture Series in Bioethics, ed. Francis J. Lescoe and David Q. Liptak, Vol. I, *Perspectives in Bioethics.* (Cromwell, CT: Pope John Paul II Bioethics Center, 1983), pp. 31-60; " 'Begotten, Not Made': Further Reflections on the Laboratory Generation of Human Life," *International Review of Natural Family Planning* 10.1 (Spring 1986), 1-22; "The 'Simple Case' of In Vitro Fertilization," *Linacre Quarterly* 55.1 (February 1988), 29-36; "Catholic Moral Teaching on In Vitro Fertilization," in *Reproductive Technologies, Marriage, and the Church*, ed. Donald McCarthy (Braintree, MA: Pope John XXIII Medical-Moral Research and Education Center, 1988), pp. 107-121; *Catholic Bioethics and the Gift of Human Life* (Huntington, IN: Our Sunday Visitor, 2000), pp. 73-86.

105. See *Marriage: The Rock on Which the Family Is Built* (San Francisco: Ignatius, 1995), p. 69.

106. See the essays identified in endnote 84.

107. Berkman, "Gestating the Embryos of Others," 317.

108. On this, see Grisez, work cited in endnote 71.

109. Berkman, "Gestating the Embryos of Others," 325.

110. Ibid., 329.

111. Brugger, "The Morality of Heterologous Embryo Transfer," 22-23 of typescript. See the published version of this essay elsewhere in *NCBQ* 4.1 (2004).

112. See May, "The Embryo Rescue Debate," in the "Colloquy" section of *The National Catholic Bioethics Quarterly* 4.1 (Spring 2004), 9-10. Berkman, in a later essay, "Virtuous Parenting and Orphaned Embryos," *Human Embryo Adoption*, pp. 13-35, seeks to rebut Brugger's criticism, but does so by offering his own understanding of "surrogate motherhood," one quite different from that given in *Donum vitae* itself.

CHAPTER FOUR

Contraception and Respect for Human Life

Introduction

Contraception is usually considered an issue in sexual ethics rather than one proper to bioethics. But, as I hope to show here, contraception is very much relevant to respect for human life inasmuch as it is not, of itself, a *sexual* act but rather an *anti-life* kind of act. It is indeed the "gateway to abortion"; widespread social acceptance of contraception has led to the "culture of death" described by John Paul II in his encyclical *Evangelium vitae.*

The suggestion that contraception is "anti-life" and has led to the "culture of death" will offend many people, both Catholic and non-Catholic, who do not regard contraception as an anti-life kind of act and who can see no connection whatsoever between contraception and the "culture of death." For most people in our society, Catholic and non-Catholic as well, contraception by married persons is regarded as "natural." It is the obvious thing to do if there are good reasons for avoiding a pregnancy; and the suggestion that there is a link between contraception and the "culture of death" is considered outrageous, in particular, by married couples who are "pro-life" but nonetheless believe that there is nothing wrong with contraception.

This is illustrated by some of the contributors to the December 1998 symposium on contraception in the journal *First Things.* Gilbert Meilaender, a Lutheran theologian known widely for his opposition to abortion, and Philip Turner, an Anglican theologian also "on the side of life," in their joint contribution expressed the view that "contraceptive intercourse may sometimes be a fitting means by which husband and wife aim to nourish simultaneously the procreative and unitive purposes of their marriage."[1] Similarly, the editor of *First Things,* James Nuechterlein, reflecting on the symposium in a subsequent number of the journal, began by observing that he and his wife did not want children immediately because of their circumstances, although, had she become pregnant, "we would not for a moment have considered abortion. But," he continued, neither for a moment did we morally hesitate to practice contraception. We no more debated whether we would use contraception than we debated whether we would, in the fullness of time, have children. Of course we would someday, God willing, have children; in the meantime we would practice (non-abortifacient) contraception. This was not, for us, a matter of presuming on God's providence. It seemed rather a right use of reason in fulfilling the various goods of our marriage. We intended both the unitive and the procreative goods of marriage, but not necessarily both in every act of love.[2]

Concluding, Nuechterlein said: "The point of this self-revelation is to suggest how utterly typical that view was and is. There is nothing singular in our experience. I believe it is, mutatis mutandis, the experience of most Protestant couples of our generation and after."[3]

Note that Nuechterlein refers to the common experience of contemporary *Protestants* (and this, seemingly, was also in the mind of Meilaender and Turner). However, it is no doubt true that a great majority of Catholic couples agree with these writers. On reading their essays, in fact, I was reminded of the views set forth in the celebrated "Majority Papers" of the Papal Commission on Population, the Family, and Natality.[4] Two passages from these papers — to which I will return later for closer examination — seem in particular to express the view articulated by these contributors to *First Things*.

In one passage, the Majority justify contraception by married couples as an intelligent use of reason to control biological nature:

> The true opposition is not to be sought between some material conformity to the physiological processes of nature and some artificial intervention. For it is natural for man to use his skill in order to put under human control what is given by physical nature. The opposition is to be sought really between one way of acting which is contraceptive [in the sense of selfishly excluding children from marriage] and opposed to a prudent and generous fruitfulness, and another way which is in an ordered relationship to responsible fruitfulness and which has a concern for education and all the essential human and Christian values.[5]

In another passage, they justify the use of contraception by married couples by distinguishing between individual acts of sexual union within marriage and the totality of the marriage. According to them,

When man interferes with the procreative purpose of individual acts by contracepting, he does this with the intention of regulating and not excluding fertility. Then he unites the material finality toward fecundity which exists in intercourse with the formal finality of the person and renders the entire process human. Conjugal acts which by intention are infertile or which are rendered infertile are ordered to the expression of the union of love; that love, however, reaches its culmination in fertility responsibly accepted. For that reason other acts of union are in a certain sense incomplete, and they receive their full moral quality with ordination toward the fertile act. Infertile conjugal acts constitute a totality with fertile acts and have a single moral specification.[6]

The "single moral specification" of such acts, as the Majority makes clear, is "the fostering of love responsibly toward a generous fecundity."

In this view, what married couples who use contraception as a way of spacing children *in* their marriage and not of excluding them *from* their marriage are doing is simply using appropriate means for nourishing both the procreative and unitive purposes of marriage. This is their "intention" — as Meilaender/Turner and Nuechterlein indicate in the passages previously cited — and surely this intention is not immoral.

This way of viewing the use of contraception by married couples who have serious reasons to avoid having children, at least for a time, is quite common in our society. Many, Catholic and non-Catholic alike, who hold it regard abortion with horror, and they also unambiguously judge sex outside of marriage to be immoral. But they can see nothing wrong with the "responsible" use of contraception within marriage, nor do they believe that there is some inexorable link between contraception and the "culture of death."

This widely held view, however, is mistaken. For centuries, Christian writers regarded contraception an "anti-life" kind of act. In fact, one of the contributors to the *First Things* symposium, Alicia Mosier, an editorial assistant of the journal, forcefully expressed this view. She began by emphasizing that the issue does not center on the "artificiality" of the means used to prevent conception but with the nature of contraception itself. As she said, "what is wrong is contraception itself: the deliberate will, the choice, to subvert the life-giving order and meaning of the conjugal act."[7] Commenting on Pope Paul's description of contraception as "every action... which proposes... to render procreation impossible,"[8] she wrote:

Proposing to render procreation impossible means, simply put, willing directly against the order of intercourse and consequently against life.... Couples who contracept introduce a countermeasure... whose sole purpose is to make it impossible for a new life to come to be. Contraception is an act that can only express the will that *any* baby that might result from *this* sexual encounter not be conceived.... [I]t manifests a will aimed directly against new life.[9]

Mosier's way of expressing this view echoes the argument against contraception mounted by Germain Grisez, Joseph Boyle, John Finnis, and me in 1988.[10] But, as noted already, she articulates a position that was traditional in the Church, both East and West, both Catholic and Protestant, from the early days of Christianity to the mid-twentieth century. It is found in such Church Fathers as John Chrysostom, Ambrose, and Jerome; in medieval theologians such as Thomas Aquinas; in the canon law operative in the Roman Catholic Church from the mid-thirteenth century until 1917; in the thought of reformers such as John Calvin; and in the teaching of the *Roman Catechism*, popularly known as the *Catechism of the Council of Trent*. There is no need here to recapitulate this tradition. In the accompanying note, I cite representative witnesses.[11] There is thus a long and respected Christian tradition that judges contraception to be anti-life, expressing a will that is indeed at the heart of the "culture of death."

Here I will show why contraception is intimately related to the culture of death and, indeed, is the gateway to this culture. I will begin by considering Pope John Paul II's thought regarding the roots of the culture of death and his way of relating contraception to that culture. I will then take up his claim that the difference, anthropological and moral, between contraception and recourse to the rhythm of the cycle is enormous and involves ultimately "irreconcilable concepts of the human person and of human sexuality." This section will show that the acceptance of contraception is based on a dualistic anthropology of the human person and a consequentialist/proportionalist understanding of the morality of human acts: an anthropology and moral perspective central to the "culture of death." This section will likewise show how confusing and misleading talk about "intentions" can be. I will follow this with an analysis of the human act of contraception to show that it is and cannot not be anti-life, and that this is *the* reason why contraception is indeed the gateway to the "culture of death." In conclusion, I will consider contraception as an act both anti-love and anti-life, utterly incompatible with the "culture of life" and the "civilization of love." In an appendix, I will briefly consider the morality of seeking to prevent conception if a woman is in danger of being raped or has already suffered this violence to herself.

1. Pope John Paul II on the Roots of the Culture of Death and Contraception's Relationship to It

In the first chapter of his encyclical *Evangelium vitae*, Pope John Paul II identifies two roots of the "culture of death." This culture, he says, is rooted, first of all, in the "mentality which *carries the concept of subjectivity to an extreme* and even distorts it, and recognizes as a subject of rights only the person who enjoys full or at least incipient autonomy and who emerges from a state of total dependence on others" (no. 19). It is rooted, secondly, in a "*notion of freedom* which exalts the isolated individual in an absolute way" (no. 19).

Of these two roots, the first is most relevant for showing the relationship of contraception to the culture of death. At its heart is the idea that only those members of the human species who enjoy at least "incipient autonomy," i.e., individuals with exercisable capacities of reasoning and will, are *truly* persons with rights that ought to be recognized by society. This mentality, John Paul II points out, "tends to *equate personal dignity with the capacity for verbal and explicit,* or at least perceptible, *communication*" (no. 19). On this view a "person" is preeminently a subject aware of itself as a self and capable of relating to other selves; and not all members of the human species are persons in this understanding of "person." This idea, as will be seen later, fits in well with the anthropology underlying the acceptance of contraception.

In the first chapter of *Evangelium vitae*, John Paul II also discusses the relationship between contraception and abortion, whose justification and legalization is, of course, a hallmark of the "culture of death." To the common claim that contraception, "if made safe and available to all, is the most effective remedy against abortion," John Paul II replied:

> When looked at carefully, this objection is clearly unfounded. It may be that many people use contraception with a view to excluding the subsequent temptation of abortion. But the negative values inherent in the "contraceptive mentality" — which is very different from responsible parenthood, lived in respect for the full truth of the conjugal act — are such that they in fact strengthen this temptation when an unwanted life is conceived. . . . Certainly, from the moral point of

view contraception and abortion are *specifically different* evils: the former contradicts the full truth of the sexual act as the proper expression
of conjugal love, whereas the latter destroys the life of a human being;
the former is opposed to the virtue of chastity in marriage, the latter
is opposed to the virtue of justice and directly violates the divine commandment "You shall not kill." (no. 13)

It is important to emphasize that here John Paul II does *not*, as did the
long Christian tradition noted above, identify contraception as an "anti-
life" kind of act, akin to murder. He rather characterizes it as an "anti-love"
kind of act, one that, as he says elsewhere, "falsifies" the meaning of the
conjugal act as one in which the spouses give themselves unreservedly to
one another.[12] But he nonetheless insists that despite their differences "contraception and abortion are often closely connected, as fruits of the same
tree," and he points out that the close link between the two "is being
demonstrated in an alarming way by the development of chemical products,
intrauterine devices and vaccines which, distributed with the same ease as
contraceptives, really act as abortifacients in the very early stages of the
development of the life of a new human being" (no. 13).

John Paul II obviously sees a real and substantive link between contraception and abortion and — through it — the "culture of death." But he does
not here *directly* relate contraception to the culture of death. For him, contraception directly violates marital chastity and not the good of human life.

2. Contraception vs. "Recourse to the Rhythm of the Cycle": Their Anthropological and Moral Differences, One Ultimately Entailing "Irreconcilable Concepts of the Human Person and of Human Sexuality"

In his apostolic exhortation on the *Role of the Christian Family in the
Modern World* (*Familiaris consortio*), Pope John Paul II made the following
bold claim:

> In the light of the experience of many couples and the data pro-
> vided by the different human sciences, theological reflection is able to
> perceive and is called to study further *the difference, both anthropologi-
> cal and moral,* between contraception and recourse to the rhythm of the
> cycle: it is a difference which is much wider and deeper than is usu-
> ally thought, one which involves in the final analysis *two irreconcilable
> concepts of the human person and of human sexuality.* (no. 32)[13]

Perhaps many people who *practice* contraception — and many who *practice* periodic abstinence — are not consciously aware of the difference between these two ways of exercising responsible parenthood, but the difference is profound. I will show this by examining the rationale used to defend the legitimacy of contraception in order to disclose its underlying anthropology and moral methodology. I will then contrast this by presenting the anthropology and moral methodology on which the practice of natural family planning or periodic abstinence or what John Paul II calls here "recourse to the rhythm of the cycle" is based.

A. Contraception: Its Underlying Anthropology and Moral Methodology

A dualistic understanding of the human person and of human sexuality is at the heart of the defense of contraception. This anthropology regards the body as an instrument of the person, a good for the person insofar as it is a necessary condition for goods and values intrinsic to the person; the latter, so-called personalistic goods and values, are those whose existence depends on their being consciously experienced. This anthropology underlies several key arguments given to support contraception, in particular, that defending contraception as the exercise of intelligent human dominion over nature and that justifying it on the basis that it is in harmony with the nature of *human* sexuality.

Several passages from the Majority documents of the Papal Commission illustrate the first line of reasoning, based on humankind's dominion over the world of nature. I cited one of these at the beginning of this chapter, in which the authors stressed that "it is natural for man to use his skill in order to put under human control what is given by physical nature."[14] In another passage they declare that, "in the matter at hand," namely, contraception,

> [T]here is a certain change in the mind of contemporary man. He feels that he is more conformed to his rational nature, created by God with liberty and responsibility, when he uses his skill to intervene in the biological processes of nature so that he can achieve the institution of matrimony in the conditions of actual life, than if he would abandon himself to chance.[15]

In yet another passage, the majority emphasized that "it is proper to man, created in the image of God, to use what is given in physical nature in a way that he may develop it to its full significance with a view to the good of the whole person."[16]

These passages make it clear that those defending contraception con-sider the biological fertility of human persons and the biological processes involved in the generation of new human life as physical or biological "givens." Human fertility, in other words, is part of the world of subhuman or subpersonal nature over which persons have been given dominion. The majority theologians of the Papal Commission, in fact, assert that "biolog-ical fertility ... ought to be assumed into the human sphere and be regulated within it."[17] Obviously, if the biological fecundity of human persons is intrinsically human, it does not need to be "assumed into the human sphere." Nothing assumes what it already is or has of itself. This passage is a clear assertion of dualism.

In other words, in this view human fertility is in and of itself a biolog-ical given belonging to the physical, not human, world over which the per-son has been given dominion. Biological givens, such as fertility, confront the person who is to control and regulate them by "assuming" them into the human and personal sphere, i.e., by making use of them when they serve "personalist" goods and by suppressing or impeding them when their con-tinued flourishing inhibits participation in these goods, whose existence, as noted already, depends on their being consciously experienced.

The notion that human biological fertility is, of itself, subhuman and subpersonal is closely related to the understanding of human sexuality cen-tral to the defense of contraception. One of the major reasons for chang-ing Church teaching on the matter, the majority theologians argued, is the "changed estimation of the value and meaning of human sexuality," one leading to a "better, deeper, and more correct understanding of conjugal life and the conjugal act."[18] According to this understanding, *human* sexu-ality, as distinct from *animal* sexuality, is above all relational or unitive in character. As one theologian put it, "the most profound meaning of human sexuality is that it is a relational reality, having a special significance for the person in his relationships."[19] Human sexuality, as some other theological defenders of contraception contend, "is preeminently ... the mode whereby an isolated subjectivity [= person] reaches out to communion with another subject. Embodied subjectivity reaches out to another body-subject in order to banish loneliness and to experience the fullness of being-with-another in the human project."[20]

Proponents of this understanding of human sexuality acknowledge that human sexual union can be procreative — or, to use the term that the more secularistic of them prefer, "reproductive." Yet in addition to these "biolog-ical" needs, sexual union serves other, more personal values, those, namely, whose existence depends on their being consciously experienced. The fact that such union, at times, results in the conception of a new human being has, in the past and even today, frequently inhibited the realization of these more personal purposes. But today — and this is *the* important consideration — it is possible through efficient methods of contraception to sever the connection between the procreative and unitive or relational dimensions of human sexuality.

The more radical, secularistic proponents of contraception sever this connection totally. As George Gilder so perceptively observed over a quarter of a century ago,

> The members of the sex coalition go well beyond a mere search for better contraceptives. They are not satisfied merely to control the biological tie between intercourse and childbirth. They also want to eliminate the psychological and symbolic connections. . . . By far the most frequent and durably important long-term use of sex, they would say, is the fulfillment of the physical and psychological need for orgasmic pleasure and the communication of affection. For these purposes, sex is most adaptable if it is not connected with procreation, if it is regarded as a completely separate mode of activity.[21]

It cannot be denied that many people in the Western (and increasingly the non-Western) world regard the emergence of contraceptive technologies as a truly liberating event. They believe that the effective use of contraceptives enables human persons to liberate the *personal* and *human* purposes of sexuality and of genital intercourse from the tyranny of biology. Many today would agree with the claim of the well-known British writer, Ashley Montagu, that

> The pill provides a dependable means of controlling conception. . . . [T]he pill makes it possible to render every individual of reproductive age completely responsible for both his sexual and his reproductive behavior. *It is necessary to be unequivocally clear concerning the distinction between sexual behavior and reproductive behavior.* Sexual behavior may have no purpose other than pleasure . . . without the slightest intent of reproducing, or it may be indulged in for both pleasure and reproduction.[22]

The majority theologians of the Papal Commission, and Protestant authors such as Meilaender, Turner, and Nuechterlein, would not go so far as Montagu and other secular supporters of contraception and sever completely the bond between the unitive and procreative meanings of human sexuality. Nonetheless, they deem the relational or unitive meaning its *personal*, as distinct from its procreative or *biological*, significance, the latter needing to be assumed into consciousness in order to become human and personal. Coupling this understanding of human sexuality with the dominion that human persons have over their biological fertility, they contend that if the continued flourishing of biological fecundity inhibits the expression of the relational or unitive meaning of sexuality, it is then licit to suppress this "biological given" so that the *personal*, relational good of sexuality can be realized. They do not want to sever the bond between the unitive (personal) and procreative (biological) meaning of our sexuality for the *whole* of the marriage, but they think it proper intentionally to separate them in *individual acts* if doing so is thought necessary for serving the procreative-unitive meaning of marriage as a whole. Biological fertility is, for them, a lesser good — a good *for* the person (something like a coat), not a good *of* the person. For them, goods *of* the person are goods whose existence depends on being consciously experienced. Since fertility does not so depend, it is not this kind of a good. On the other hand, they consider the union made possible by sexual coition — the unitive or relational aspect of our sexuality — to be a good *of* the person because its existence and flourishing depends on being consciously experienced.

The foregoing has clearly shown the dualistic anthropology and understanding of the human person and of human sexuality crucial to major arguments used to justify contraception. This anthropology distinguishes the person, i.e., the conscious subject of experiences (or, as John Paul II noted in *Evangelium vitae*, no. 19, the subject having "the capacity for verbal and explicit, or at least perceptible, communication"), from the *body* that this person uses, now for this purpose, now for that. If the person is really not his or her own body, then the person's sexuality can be "liberated" from regulation by biological laws and used for "interpersonal communication" or the "fostering of conjugal love."

This anthropology or understanding of the human person is central to the "culture of death." For, if the person is not his or her own body, then, as Germain Grisez has noted, "the destruction of the life of the body is not directly and in itself an attack on a value intrinsic to the human person." Continuing, he said:

> The lives of the unborn, the lives of those not fully in possession of themselves — the hopelessly insane and the "vegetating" senile —

and the lives of those who no longer can engage in praxis or problem solving, become lives no longer meaningful, no longer valuable, no longer inviolable.[23]

The dualistic anthropology that has led to the justification of abortion on the grounds that the life thus taken, while "biologically" human, is not "meaningfully" human or the life of a "person," and to the justification of euthanasia on the grounds that it serves the needs of the "person" when biological life becomes a burden, is thus definitely operative in the ideology behind contraception, even if this is not acknowledged by many.

I turn now to consider the *moral methodology* employed in the justification of contraception, in particular, contraception by married couples. This methodology is clearly evident in the argument based on the distinction between individual or "isolated" marital acts and marriage as a whole or totality. This argument acknowledges (as Montagu and the most secular advocates of contraception do not) that procreation is indeed a good of marriage, and that marriage and children go together. But, this argument claims, the procreative good of marriage is properly respected and honored even when individual acts of marriage are deliberately made infertile, as long as those acts are ordered to the expression of love and to a generous fecundity within the marriage as a whole.

It will be useful here to review this very illuminating passage. It reads:

> When man interferes with the procreative purpose of individual acts by contracepting, he does this with the intention of regulating and not excluding fertility. Then he unites the material finality toward fecundity which exists in intercourse with the formal finality of the person and renders the entire process human.... Conjugal acts which by intention are infertile or which are rendered infertile are ordered to the expression of the union of love; that love, however, reaches its culmination in fertility responsibly accepted. For that reason other acts of union are in a certain sense incomplete, and they receive their full moral quality with ordination toward the fertile act.... Infertile conjugal acts constitute a totality with fertile acts and have a single moral specification.[24]

The "single moral specification" or moral object of this totality is the fostering of love responsibly toward a generous fecundity.

Note that this passage considers "recourse to the rhythm of the cycle" or periodic abstinence as simply another way of contracepting; it equates "acts which by intention are infertile," that is, marital acts chosen while the wife is not fertile, and acts "which are rendered infertile." The authors, in other words, see absolutely no *moral* difference between contraception and "recourse to the cycle." The latter is simply another way of contracepting.[25] They do so because they consider the moral "intentions" to be the same in both cases. Their "intention" is to avoid a pregnancy, perhaps for very serious and good reasons. I will return to this issue below.

The central claim of this passage is that the moral object specifying what couples who "responsibly" contracept individual acts of marital congress are doing is "fostering love responsibly toward a generous fecundity." Their aim, their "intention," as Meilaender and Turner later put it in their *First Things* essay, is to "nourish simultaneously the procreative and unitive purposes of their marriage."

This claim is rooted in the idea that we can identify the moral object specifying a human act *only* by considering the act in its "totality." According to this method of making moral decisions, it is not possible to determine the moral species of an action — its "moral object" — without taking into account the "intention" or end for whose sake the choice is made along with the foreseeable consequences for the persons concerned. If one does this, so the argument goes, one can conclude that, if the choice to contracept individual acts is directed to the end of nourishing conjugal love so that the good of procreation can also be served, then one can rightly say that *what* the spouses are doing — the *moral object* of their choice — is to foster conjugal love toward a generous fecundity, obviously something good, not bad.

But this reasoning is specious. It is so because it *re-describes* the contraceptive act, in fact, a whole series of contraceptive acts, in terms of hoped-for benefits. The *remote* or *further* end for whose sake the couple contracepts individual acts of sexual union may indeed be to nourish simultaneously the unitive and procreative goods of marriage. This end is indeed "intended." And this end, this "intention," is good. But "intended" also is the *choice* to contracept — and the couple cannot *not choose*, cannot *not intend*, to contracept. But this specious moral reasoning conceals this "moral object." This reasoning, moreover, relies on a faulty understanding of the marital *act*. According to this reasoning, which re-describes the spouses' behavior in terms of hoped-for benefits, the marital act is intended to foster love between spouses, to unite them. But it is not, as such, intended to be open to the gift of life; rather the marriage *as a whole* in which particular acts occur is so intended. Its proponents would surely hold that spouses ought not, in choosing to unite genitally, freely intend to set aside its unitive dimension. Why, then, do they hold that they can freely intend, in uniting genitally, to set aside its procreative dimension? They can do so only because, as we have seen, they regard this dimension as merely "biological," a "lesser" good than the "personal" good of being sexually united.

The moral methodology used, in other words, is consequentialistic. It fails to recognize that the morality of human acts, as we saw in Chapter Two and as John Paul II has so correctly said, "depends primarily and fundamentally on the 'object' rationally chosen by the deliberate will."[26] With respect to contraception, that object is *not* "to foster love responsibly toward a generous fecundity" or to nourish simultaneously the unitive and procreative goods of marriage. Precisely what this object is will be taken up below. My point here, however, is that the consequentialist moral reasoning used in this central argument to justify contraception is plausible only because it re-describes the object of choice — contraception — in terms of the hoped-for benefits of contracepting individual acts of sexual union.

We have now seen the anthropology and moral methodology underlying the defense of contraception. The anthropology, a dualistic one, regards the person primarily as a subject of enduring experiences who uses his or her body now for this purpose, now for that. It likewise locates the *human* and *personal* meaning of human sexuality in its *relational* significance, i.e., its ability to allow two subjects of enduring experiences to enter into deep interpersonal union, while regarding the *procreative* meaning of human sexuality as of itself subpersonal, part of the subhuman world of nature over which the person has been given dominion. This anthropology, as has been shown, is central to the "culture of death."

The moral methodology employed is a form of consequentialism or proportionalism, one that re-describes chosen deeds in terms of their hoped-for benefits and by doing so conceals their true nature. This moral methodology is also central to the specious rationalizations used to justify the killings characteristic of the "culture of death." Thus abortion is not recognized as the intentional killing of an unborn child but is rather re-described as an act protecting the mother's health or the family's stability or something of this kind; rather than being called killing, euthanasia is re-described as helping persons to die with dignity, etc.

B. Recourse to the Rhythm of the Cycle: Its Underlying Anthropology and Moral Methodology

The anthropology supporting the practice of periodic continence as the way to harmonize the requirements of conjugal love with respect for the good of procreation is holistic; i.e., it regards the human person as a unity of body and soul. The person is, in the unity of body and soul, the subject of moral actions.[27] On this anthropology, the body and bodily life are integral to the person, goods *of* the person, not merely *for* the person.

Human persons are, in other words, body persons. When God created Man, he did not, as some dualistic-minded defenders of contraception claim, create "an isolated subjectivity . . . who experiences existence in [either] a female body-structure . . . [or] a male body-structure."[28] Quite to the contrary, God, in creating *human* persons, created bodily, sexual persons: "male and female he created them" (Gn 1:27). The human body expresses the human person; and since the human body is inescapably either male or female, it expresses a man-person or a woman-person. Precisely because of their sexual differences, manifest in their bodies, the man-person and the woman-person can give themselves to each other bodily. Moreover, since the body, male or female, is the expression of a human person, a man and a woman, in giving their bodies to each other, give their *persons* to each other. The bodily gift of a man and a woman to each other is the outward sign, the sacrament, of the *communion of persons* existing between them. The body is, therefore, the means and the sign of the gift of the male-person to the female-person. Pope John Paul II calls this capacity of the body to express the communion of persons the *spousal meaning* of the body.[29]

In addition, human fertility or fecundity is *not* some subhuman, subpersonal aspect of human sexuality. As Vatican Council II clearly affirms, "Man's sexuality and the faculty of generating life wondrously surpass the lower forms of life" (Pastoral Constitution on the Church in the Modern World, *Gaudium et spes*, no. 51). Pope John Paul II pointedly observes that human fertility "is directed to the generation of a human being, and so by its nature it surpasses the purely biological order and involves a whole series of personal values" (apostolic exhortation *Familiaris consortio*, no. 11). The procreative meaning of human sexuality, in this non-dualistic anthropology, is *not* subhuman or subpersonal, in need of "being assumed" into the human. It is human and personal to begin with.

The rationale supporting recourse to the rhythm of the cycle does not judge the morality of human acts in terms of hoped-for results or of the anticipated overall proportion of good and evil that will come about. It holds, rather, that the morality of human actions depends on both the *end intended* and the *object chosen* and, because chosen, also *intended*. It distinguishes between the ulterior or remote end for whose sake one chooses to do *this*, and the proximate or immediate end, which is precisely the freely chosen object. Both end intended and object chosen must be morally good, i.e., in conformity with right reason; if either is not in accord with the truth, then the entire action is vitiated. But the primary source of the morality of the act is, as noted above, the "object" freely and rationally chosen by the acting subject. This is precisely *what one chooses to do*. The moral methodology underlying the practice of contraception ignores this object, the immediate end of one's choice to do *this* here and now, and focuses on the remote end or further intention of the act, i.e., the reason why one chooses to do this here and now. As we have seen, this consequentialist methodology conceals and keeps hidden from view the precise object of one's freely chosen act and *re-describes* it in terms of its hoped-for benefits, the remote end intended by the acting person, the object of one's "further" intention.

The non-consequentialist way of making moral judgments on which recourse to the rhythm of the cycle is based recognizes, as Pope John Paul II emphasizes, "that there are objects of the human act which are by their nature 'incapable of being ordered' to God, because they radically contradict the good of the person made in his image." Continuing, the Pope says:

> These are the acts which, in the Church's moral tradition, have been termed "intrinsically evil" (*intrinsece malum*); they are such *always and per se,* in other words, on account of their very object, and apart from the ulterior intentions of the one acting and the circumstances. (*Veritatis splendor,* no. 80)

We need now to examine the moral object specifying the act of contraception in order to show that it is indeed an anti-life kind of act.

3. Contraception: An Anti-Life Act

In order to pass moral judgment on contraception, it is first necessary to know precisely what we are speaking of. It is essential to provide an accurate description of the kind of human act an act of contraception is and then to judge whether it is a human act in accordance with right reason, with the truth, or not, and, if not, why not.

We have seen already that human acts are specified primarily by the "object" freely and rationally chosen by the deliberate will. But what is the "object" freely chosen in contraception? Pope Paul VI offers a good description when he says that the Church's teaching on the immorality of contraception excludes "every action, whether in anticipation of the conjugal act, or in its accomplishment, or in the development of its natural consequences, proposes [the Latin text reads *intendat*], either as end or as means, to impede procreation [here the Latin text reads: *ut procreatio impediatur*]" (*Humanae vitae*, no. 14). Paul here refers to the conjugal act, since his encyclical was concerned with contraception by married couples. But, if "conjugal act" is changed to "genital act," Paul's description accurately identifies the "object" morally specifying an act as contraceptive, whether within marriage or not.

As this description shows, the object freely chosen and willed by someone who engages in an act of contraception is precisely to impede the beginning of a new human life or to impede procreation. It is reasonable to think that a certain kind of behavior — genital behavior — is the kind of behavior in and through which new human life can come to be. If one does not want that life to come to be, perhaps for very good reasons (e.g., the woman's health, inability properly to care for a new baby, etc.), one therefore chooses to do something to impede the beginning of the new human life that one believes that genital behavior might initiate. If one did not reasonably think that this kind of behavior — genital behavior — could result in the beginning of a new human life, one would have no reason to contracept. If one wanted that life to come to be, obviously one would not contracept in order to impede its beginning. Contraception makes sense, i.e., is an *intelligible* human act, only because one does not want new human life to come into existence as a result of another kind of human activity, namely, genital activity. As Mosier so well put it in the essay cited early in this work, "contraception is an act that can only express the will that *any* baby that might result from *this* sexual encounter not be conceived. . . . [I]t [thus] manifests a will aimed directly against new life."[30]

This analysis of the object specifying an act as one of contraception makes it clear that contraception, although related to genital/sexual acts, is not itself a sexual or genital act. Fornication, adultery, masturbation, and marital coition are sexual/genital acts. But if a fornicating couple, an adulterous couple, or a married couple contracept, they choose to do something distinct from the genital act they likewise choose to engage in. In other words, they choose (a) to engage in genital coition and (b) to do something prior to, during, or subsequent to their freely chosen genital coition precisely to impede procreation, i.e., to impede the beginning of the new human life that they reasonably believe could begin in and through the freely chosen genital coition. The act specified by the second choice, (b), is the act of contraception. It is not even necessary for the person who contracepts to engage in genital coition. For instance, suppose a father provides a home for his newly married daughter and her husband. His daughter and her husband abhor contraception, deeming it a grave moral evil. They would never contracept, although perhaps they plan to practice periodic continence until they can move into their own quarters. But the girl's father, in order to make sure that she does not conceive while living in his house, regularly puts contraceptive pills into his daughter's cereal in the morning. He is the one who is choosing to contracept, not his daughter.[31]

Since the contraceptive act is distinct from any sexual act to which it is related, it cannot be considered a part or element of a sexual act and justified on the alleged grounds that it is merely a part of a larger whole, for instance, the marital or conjugal act. This, in essence, is what the specious argument considered above seeks to do, namely, to justify contraception as simply an aspect of a totality of marital acts that nourish both the unitive and procreative goods of marriage. But, as has now been made clear, contraception is not a part or aspect of any marital act or series thereof; it is a distinct kind of human act, specified by the choice to impede the beginning of new human life, either as an end or as a means to some further end, one perhaps good in itself.

Since contraception is specified precisely by the choice to impede the beginning of new human life, it is an anti-life kind of act, one expressing a contra-life will. It is precisely because contraception is specified by a contra-life will that it was, as we saw earlier, regarded for centuries as analogous to homicide by Christian writers. This analogy, a contemporary author rightly says, "no longer surprises us if we look not exclusively at the material nature of the behaviour in the two cases [contraception and homicide], but rather at the intention or movement of the will that has recourse to contraception. Ultimately, in fact, the decision is rationalized and motivated by the judgment: 'It is not good that a new human person should exist.' "[32] Contraception is always seriously wrong because it is always gravely immoral to adopt by choice the proposal to damage, destroy, or impede the good of human life.

If the contraception fails and a child is conceived despite the steps taken deliberately to prevent its life from beginning, the child comes to be as an "unwanted" child. This does not mean that those who sought to prevent his or her conception will now resort to abortion — for they may resolutely have set their hearts and minds against abortion, as did Nuechterlein and his wife, as we have seen. But one can hardly say that a child conceived despite efforts to prevent its conception is a "wanted child." Its initial status is that of an unwanted child and is so because its parents have intentionally done something to "unwant" it, namely, to contracept, to impede the beginning of its life.

This is not true of couples who have "recourse to the rhythm of the cycle" or to periodic abstinence and who avoid irresponsibly causing a pregnancy by abstaining from the marital act at times when they believe that the wife is fertile and hence could conceive.[33] It is true that, like a contracepting couple, they do not "want" to have a child in the sense that they do not, for good reasons, want to cause a pregnancy. But not wanting to have a child in this sense is quite different from not wanting to have the child one could have as a result of *this freely chosen act of sexual union* and then freely choosing to do something to *impede that prospective child's coming into being*. Couples who contracept do not "want" a child in this second sense, and hence if it does come to be despite their contraceptive efforts to prevent it from coming to be, it comes to be as an "unwanted" child. But a child conceived by a couple having recourse to the rhythm of the cycle does not come to be as an "unwanted" child because they have done nothing to "unwant" this particular child. He or she may be a "surprise" baby, but not an "unwanted" baby.[34]

4. Contraception: Both Anti-Love and Anti-Life

As we have seen, the principal argument proposed by John Paul II as pope against contraception is that it violates marital love and falsifies the language of the body: the natural dynamism of the conjugal act, which is ordered to the procreation and education of children and the mutual love of the spouses, is overlaid with an objectively contradictory language: a refusal to give oneself fully to the other (see Pope John Paul II, apostolic exhortation *Familiaris consortio*, no. 32).[35] For John Paul II, contraception directly violates marital love and marital chastity and only indirectly is opposed to the good of human life.

This argument, which has featured prominently in John Paul II's teaching on marriage and on the malice of contraception, was well expressed by Paul Quay, S.J., in the early 1960s and has been developed by Dietrich von Hildebrand, Mary Joyce, and others.[36] I believe it true that, by contracepting, a married couple fail to give themselves to each other fully and unreservedly. Yet the "not-giving" entailed is *not* the object specifying the choice to contracept, and most married couples who do contracept would vehemently deny that they are refusing to give themselves to each other. Nuechterlein, in his *First Things* article, illustrates this. He says that "if someone had told us [his wife and himself] that we were 'withholding our fertility' from one another' [or 'not giving themselves to one another'] he would have met with blank incomprehension."[37] The "not-giving" is *praeter intentionem* or outside the scope of the intentions of the married couples who are contracepting. It is, I believe, an *effect* or *consequence* of their contracepting their sexual union, but for the most part they do not consciously recognize this. It is surely *not* "the proximate end of a deliberate decision which determines the act of willing on the part of the acting person," as John Paul II himself describes the object morally specifying a human act in *Veritatis splendor*, no. 78. Indeed, contracepting married couples commonly attempt to justify their choice to contracept by claiming that contraception *is necessary* in order for them to express their love for each other. I will return to this issue later.

Although the argument summarized here is the principal one used by John Paul II to show that it is wrong for married couples to contracept, in some of his writings he has focused attention on the anti-life character of contraception. Thus, in a homily during a Mass for youth in Nairobi, Kenya, he pointed out that the fullest sign of spousal self-giving occurs when couples willingly accept children. Citing *Gaudium et spes*, no. 50, he said: "That is why *anti-life* actions such as contraception and abortion are wrong and are unworthy of good husbands and wives."[38] Moreover, writing as the philosopher Karol Wojtyla, Pope John Paul II had earlier written that the ultimate end served by the sexual urge in human persons, men and women, "is the very existence of the [human] species. It follows therefore that that urge, on account of its very own nature, aims at the transmission of life, because on that depends the good of the human species."[39]

In addition, the human sexual urge aims at transmitting *personal* life, and the love of husband and wife, the philosopher Wojtyla argued, is shaped by this good. Indeed, as he says:

> Looked at more closely and concretely, these two persons, the man and the woman, facilitate the existence of another concrete person, their own child, blood of their blood, and flesh of their flesh. This person is at once an affirmation and a continuation of their own lives. The natural order of human existence is not in conflict with love between persons but in strict harmony with it.[40]

Thus John Paul II clearly recognizes the anti-life nature of contraception. It is both *anti-love* and *anti-life*. In his papal writings on marriage and the family, John Paul has obviously concluded that he can best persuade married couples to reject contraception by stressing its character as an act incompatible with conjugal love. And, if we think clearly about things, this is true, even if the precise "object" of contraception is to impede the beginning of new human life and *not* the "not-giving of spouses to one another."

Spouses cannot contracept merely by taking thought. They do so by choosing to do something to their body-persons, and different contraceptives work in different ways to "impede procreation." I here omit discussion of devices allegedly "contraceptive" that are either definitively abortifacient (e.g., morning-after pills, Norplant) or may "work" by preventing implantation in the event that conception occurs (e.g., the pills in use today and, for the most part, IUDs). I hence limit consideration to the so-called barrier (condoms, diaphragms, etc.) and "chemical" (spermicidal jellies and the like) methods.

Now consider this. A person does not put on gloves to touch a beloved one tenderly, unless one thinks that some disease may be communicated. But is pregnancy a disease? And is not the use of condoms, diaphragms, spermicidal jellies, and the like similar to putting on gloves? Do husband and wife really become "one flesh" if they must arm themselves with protective gear before "giving" themselves to each other genitally? The answers to these questions are obvious, and they help us see why the argument that contraception is anti-love and a falsification of the "language of the body" is true. Spouses who must "protect" themselves from each other in such ways are "not giving" themselves unreservedly to each other as bodily, sexual beings, even if this "not giving" is "outside the scope of their intention."

Contraception is thus anti-love as well as anti-life. It is utterly incompatible with the "culture of life" and the "civilization of love." It is rather the gateway to the "culture of death." This is implicit in the slogan frequently on the lips of those who defend our contraceptive culture by saying that "No unwanted child ought ever to be born." This banal slogan typifies the "culture of death," which seeks to avert the tragedy of an "unwanted child" by preventing its coming into being through contraception, and, should this fail, by abortion. It is utterly opposed to the truth that "no person, i.e., no human being, whether born or unborn, male or female, young or old, genius or demented, ought ever to be unwanted, i.e., unloved." And the only way to build a civilization in which every human person is indeed wanted is to respect both the love-giving (unitive) and life-giving meanings of human sexuality and marriage.

5. Sterilization

Partly because of the dangers of the pill and IUDs, more and more people are resorting to sterilization as a means of preventing conception. Naturally, those who justify contraception use the same reasoning to justify sterilization, although dissenting Catholic theologians usually require a "greater proportionate reason" to justify sterilization since it is very difficult to reverse.[41] Many advocate sterilization as the most appropriate way to cope with the problems faced by a couple who have serious reasons to avoid a pregnancy, for instance, if a pregnancy would endanger the mother's life or if there were a serious risk of generating a child crippled by a severe recessive genetic defect such as Tay-Sachs disease.

A. Why Contraceptive Sterilization Is Morally Wrong

The Church's Magisterium has constantly taught that contraceptive or direct sterilization is always gravely immoral.[42] The Church, along with theologians faithful to her teachings, distinguishes between direct or contraceptive sterilization and "indirect" sterilization. The former is an act specified by the choice to impede procreation from freely chosen genital acts; it is thus contraceptive in nature no matter what further good ends are appealed to in order to "rationalize" this contraceptive choice. Contraceptive sterilization is just as much anti-life and anti-love as are other methods of contraception. So-called indirect sterilization is an unintended side effect of medical procedures morally specified by the choice to remove pathological reproductive organs (ovaries, wombs, testes, etc.) or to inhibit their natural functioning when such functioning (e.g., abnormal hormonal production) aggravates a pathological condition within the person.

Contraceptive sterilization is not only, as is contraception by other means, an anti-life kind of act, it is also an act of mutilation and is therefore more seriously wrong than other methods of contraception.

From the time of *Humanae vitae* through the 1990s, revisionist theologians time and again sought to justify contraceptive sterilization by interpreting the principle of totality as a form of proportionalistic moral reasoning. They argued that contraceptive sterilization is morally good if necessary to prevent a future pregnancy that may be hazardous to the life of the mother or may result in the conception of a severely handicapped child, and in this way contribute to the "total" well-being of individuals and families.[43] In essence, this is an argument that some hoped-for good-to-come can justify the willingness to do evil here and now.

B. Medical Dangers of Tubal Ligation

Several Catholic moralists, among them Bernard Häring, C.Ss.R., and Richard A. McCormick, S.J., recommended tubal ligation, one form of contraceptive sterilization, as the best way, morally and medically, of helping families cope with serious problems that arise when a wife is told that her life might be endangered should she get pregnant.[44] They redescribed the act of sterilization in terms of its hoped-for benefits by calling it a "marriage-saving" act. Ironically, tubal ligation is *not always effective*. As Hanna Klaus, M.D., has noted, women who choose tubal ligation run the risk of subsequently conceiving and of having a tubal pregnancy that can seriously threaten their lives and that are frequently not considered by medical personnel precisely because of their history of sterilization. As Klaus has written:

> Female sterilization by tubal ligation has been shown to be less effective than previously thought. Most publications say 2% failure now. . . . Depending on the type of sterilization performed and the age of the woman, the risk of ectopic pregnancy, if there is post-surgical conception, is quite high and persists into menopause. For women who have been sterilized before the age of 30 the likelihood of ectopic pregnancy ranges from 1.2 per 1000 for postpartum open surgery to 31.9 per 1000 for bipolar coagulation. . . . If a woman has symptoms of an ectopic pregnancy she should be investigated immediately and aggressively irrespective of the history of sterilization.[45]

Because we live in a technological age, the temptation to resort to sterilization either of husband or wife to cope with difficult problems is understandable because it is touted by many in our culture as the most "effective" way of handling serious problems. One can, in light of Dr. Klaus's studies, call this assumption into doubt, and one can also ask serious questions about the "love" a husband has for his wife if he allows her or requires her to undergo a tubal ligation in order to avoid a pregnancy and run the risk of having an ectopic pregnancy later, particularly when effective use of modern methods of natural family planning have been shown to be 99 percent effective in helping a couple avoid a pregnancy by periodic abstinence.[46]

C. Moral Dangers of Contraception and Sterilization

The most serious danger of contraception and of sterilization is to the good of the person who chooses any form of contraception. A grave sin, like contraception/sterilization, is something freely chosen. And, as we saw in Chapter Two, our choices *last* insofar as they are self-determining. Contraceptive sterilization is not only *physically* mutilating but *spiritually* so. This self-mutilation lasts until the person repents and freely chooses to do penance and to reform his/her life.

Moreover, studies now show that contraception — and today in the United States contraceptive sterilization is the most popular method — contributes greatly to divorce and the breakup of families precisely because women in particular feel "used" by their husbands.[47]

D. What to Do if One Has Been Sterilized?

Ought couples of whom one or both have been sterilized abstain entirely from the conjugal act or try to have the sterilization reversed? There is no Church teaching explicitly devoted to this issue. Grisez believes that general principles indicate a negative answer to both questions at least for most cases.[48] However, he maintains that those who repent of being sterilized must consider their responsibilities consciously and that some couples will judge correctly that they still should seek to have children if they can and that they can and should accept the burdens attempts to reverse the sterilization might involve. He likewise notes that repentant couples could sin by deliberately rejoicing over their self-inflicted sterility and then "in order to maintain and confirm their repentance and verify its sincerity to themselves and each other, they should abstain during periods which would be fertile except for the sterilization."[49]

I agree with Grisez, although I think that *if* surgery to correct the sterilization does *not* impose the kind of serious burdens Grisez speaks of, then the sterilized party should seek to have it reversed. I also think that a single person should do so prior to getting married *if*, again, doing so imposes no grave burdens. Such a sterilized person is free to marry because sterilization, whether caused by some pathology or deliberately done as a contraceptive measure, is not a diriment impediment to marriage.

John Kippley, the founder and first president of the Couple to Couple League differs from Grisez and me. He believes that sterilized couples are morally obliged to abstain from intercourse during times that would otherwise be fertile.[50]

An interesting discussion of this matter is provided by Janet Smith and Christopher Kaczor in their 2007 book *Life Issues, Medical Choices: Questions and Answers for Catholics*.[51]

6. Condoms and Prevention of HIV

In June 1988, writing as the president of the Fellowship of Catholic Scholars, I addressed the question whether or not a married couple could licitly use condoms to prevent the transmission of HIV and AIDS. I noted that I was sure that it "would loom large in the future." I noted that some theologians (e.g., James Alison, O.P., of England and Norman Ford, S.D.B., of Australia) justified such use. They argued that such use of condoms is not contraceptive, because their present intention is not to prevent conception but rather to avoid the transmission of a deadly disease, and they pointed out that the indirectly intended contraceptive effect of using the condoms is not the means to the good. I said that I could agree with these theologians in judging that the use of condoms for such a purpose may not be contraceptive, and that this can be seen if we consider the case of a couple when the wife is past menopause. Contraception for such a couple is not even an alternative of choice. Thus I granted that use of condoms by spouses to prevent the transmission of AIDS is not necessarily immoral by reason of being contraceptive (although I realize now and should have noted then that such use surely can be and in all likelihood is contraceptive for many married couples who wish to prevent the conception of a child who might be afflicted with AIDS).

However, I held that such use, even if not wrong because contraceptive would nonetheless be seriously morally wrong. I argued that condomistic intercourse is of itself an "unnatural" or perverted sexual act, and cannot be regarded as a true act of marriage. The Catholic tradition repudiated condomistic intercourse not only because it was usually chosen as a way of contracepting but also because it was against nature. I noted that older theologians judged that in such intercourse the male's semen was deposited in a *vas indebitum* or "undue vessel." Although this language is not in favor today, the judgment it embodied is true. When spouses choose to use condoms, they change the act they perform from one of true marital union (the marriage act) into a different kind of act. What John Paul II called the "language of their bodies" is totally changed. In the marital act, their bodies speak the language of a mutual giving and receiving, the language of an unreserved and oblative gift. Condomistic intercourse does not speak this language; it mutilates the language of the body, and the act chosen is more similar to masturbation than it is to the true marital act.

I concluded the 1988 essay by saying that I had discussed the matter with *lay, married theologians* who accepted Church teaching and that all of them, with one exception, who later, it seemed to me, changed his mind, immediately rejected spousal condomistic sex as utterly depraved and in no way marital intercourse.[52]

Almost sixteen years later, Martin Rhonheimer, a priest of the prelature of Opus Dei and a highly regarded moral philosopher who teaches at the Università della Santa Croce in Rome, presented in some detail an argument similar to that advanced by Alison and Ford to justify this practice. This article, "The Truth About Condoms," appeared in the July 10, 2004, issue of the influential British journal *The Tablet*.[53]

In April 2007, Carlo Cardinal Martini, retired cardinal-archbishop of Milan and considered among the *papabili* in the conclave after the death of John Paul II in April 2005, endorsed condom use by married couples to prevent transmission of HIV, and other high-placed clerics, among them Godfried Cardinal Danneels of Belgium and George Cardinal Cottier, O.P., former theologian to John Paul II, also did so.

I thus present here arguments to show that such condom use is intrinsically evil and that it is wrong to counsel such use as the "lesser evil." I wish to express my thanks especially to my colleagues Luke Gormally and John Finnis in articulating the arguments. One of the finest published essays on the topic is Gormally's "Marriage and the Prophylactic Use of Condoms";[54] he presented an abbreviated version of this argument in his essay "Note on the Use of a Condom by a Spouse within Marriage to Prevent the Transmission of HIV,"[55] on which I based material on this subject in my book *Standing with Peter: Reflections of a Lay Theologian on God's Loving Providence*.[56]

A. It Is Intrinsically Evil for Spouses to Use Condoms as a Means of Preventing Their Intercourse From Transmitting HIV Because Such Intercourse Is Not *Per Se* Apt for Generation and Is Hence "Non-Marital"

The Magisterium has constantly and firmly taught that sexual intercourse is morally good only if it is a "marital" (or "conjugal") act; any other use of the sexual faculty is gravely wrong. The use of condoms by spouses to prevent their intercourse from transmitting HIV is intrinsically wrong because it renders their sexual acts non-marital by making them *per se* inapt for generation. This is true whether or not such use is also contraceptive. Paragraph 1 of Canon 1061 defines the act by which marriage is consummated, to which "marriage is by its nature ordered and by [which] the spouses become one flesh" as one in which the "spouses have in a human manner engaged together in a conjugal act in itself apt (*per se aptus*) for the generation of offspring." Documents of the contemporary Magisterium (e.g., Congregation for the Doctrine of the Faith, *Decretum circa impotentiam quæ matrimonium dirimit* [May 13, 1977], *AAS* 69 [1977], 426) confirm the age-old *sensus fidelium* and teaching of theologians that the intercourse of spouses, even those who are temporarily or permanently infertile, is marital *if* it culminates in an act that, if conditions beyond their control allowed, could result in conception, gestation, and birth.

Couples who use a condom to prevent HIV transmission do *not* engage in an act *per se* apt for generation because by their use of a condom they intend — and cannot not intend — to change what they do together so that it will not include what couples who want to conceive include, i.e., the deposit of semen in the vagina. The use of a condom intentionally makes the act one that is *not per se* apt for generation. This judgment is not "physicalistic," for it is rooted in the fact that the behavior freely chosen would definitely *not* be chosen by a couple wanting to conceive. Such a couple would not do what the condom-using couple, even if they have no contraceptive intent, choose and do: prevent ejaculation into the vagina.

B. Such Use of Condoms by Spouses Is Intrinsically Wrong Because It Renders Such Acts "Non-Marital" by Making Them Unfit for "One Flesh" Union

Condomistic or condomized sexual intercourse is not only inapt for generation, but it is also inapt for truly uniting the couple "as one flesh." Paul VI taught that "marital" acts are spousal sexual acts of a unitive-generative kind and that the unitive and procreative meanings of sexual intercourse are indissolubly linked (see *Humanae vitae*, no. 12). By deliberately rendering their sexual acts inapt or unfit for making them "one flesh," entering into a bodily union made possible by their sexual complementarity, the couple make those acts inapt for conjoining their hearts and bodies in marital union.[57]

In his Wednesday catecheses from 1979 to 1984, and in other writings on "the nuptial mystery," Pope John Paul II explored at length the nature of the marital act as revealing and reverencing the dignity of the human being, integrated bodily and spiritually, and differentiated sexually as man and woman.[58] Building upon Paul VI's teaching, John Paul taught that the "gift of the self" in the marital act is a kind of "sacrament of the person," signifying and effecting in bodily activity the gift of self between spouses in a love that is total, reciprocal, and complementary. To withhold an essential component of that act — the communication of that, which, in normal circumstances, makes it both unitive and potentially procreative — is intrinsically wrong. Intentionally introducing a physical barrier to the unitive-procreative aptitude of one-flesh union is utterly incompatible with the "language of the body," for now the spouses no longer "give" their bodies — their person — to each other; they speak a "lie." Condomistic or condomized intercourse cannot therefore express marriage in "the language of the body."

C. Such Use Is Also Intrinsically Wrong Because It Is Frequently Done With Contraceptive Intent

Many couples who use condoms to prevent the transmission of HIV between the spouses also aim to prevent transmission of HIV to a child *by preventing such a child from being conceived*. In such a case, the use of a condom is undoubtedly contraceptive in intent, even if avoiding transmission to the uninfected spouse is also a goal. The act is one of contraception and intrinsically wrong.

D. Such Use Cannot Be Approved as "The Lesser of Two Evils"

Some have argued that approving such use of condoms would be a case of permitting a lesser evil (rendering the marital act non-marital and often also contraceptive) in order to prevent a greater evil. But sexual intercourse of a kind not *per se* apt for generation is, like all other non-marital sexual intercourse, *intrinsically evil*, prohibited by an exceptionless moral norm. For the reasons authoritatively elaborated in *Veritatis splendor*, such an action cannot be rightly advised or chosen.[59]

This argument is based on a grave misunderstanding of what traditional Catholic teaching had in mind when it spoke of "permitting the lesser evil." Traditional use of the phrase related to the *toleration* or "non-impeding" of the sins of *other* persons, but *not* to what one may licitly choose to do himself or herself. But those advocating the use of condoms by married couples as a way of avoiding the transmission of a disease and preventing death by HIV urge the *spouses* to choose the evil of condomistic, i.e., non-marital, intercourse. But as seen already, such intercourse is *not* marital, and it is only to the marital act that spouses have a right. The Church has always taught that it is incompatible with an authentic sense of moral responsibility deliberately to choose what is known to be morally wrong, however good and desirable one's further purpose might be.

Moreover, it is an error to assume, as many do, that the only choices available to a couple, one of whom is infected with HIV, are to engage in marital intercourse at the risk of lethal infection or to engage in an inherently non-marital kind of sexual activity. On the contrary, spouses with similar and even lesser reasons at times in charity and prudent integrity choose abstinence. By that choice they affirm rather than undermine the foundation of their marriage in a communion of persons which precedes (and has priority over) their one-flesh union.[60] The more serious the risks associated with sexual intercourse, the greater will be the reason to abstain.[61]

Appendix: Preventing Conception When in Danger of Rape or After Rape

As we have seen, contraception is an intrinsically evil act and can never be morally justified. Contraception, as a human, moral act is specified by the object freely chosen, and this object is precisely *to impede the beginning of new human life that one reasonably foresees may come into existence through freely chosen genital acts.* Moreover, the *object specifying* a human act, as we have seen and as St. Thomas and Pope John Paul II make clear, is *not* merely some physical performance or outward behavior but is rather shaped by the present *intention* of the acting person: it is precisely what the acting person is freely choosing to do;[62] in contracepting, one is choosing to impede the beginning of a new human life that one believes might begin through a freely chosen genital act.

If a woman is in serious danger of being raped (for instance, if she is in an area where invading soldiers have already raped the women they have encountered), she has a right to protect herself from the rapist's sperm and the further violation to her bodily and personal integrity that his sperm could cause. Were she to use some device that would prevent the rapist's sperm from penetrating her ovum (e.g., a diaphragm or spermicidal jellies), the *object* specifying her act would *not* be *to impede the beginning of a new life that could begin through her freely chosen genital act,* but rather *to protect herself from further bodily and personal violation by a rapist,* and a human act, specified by this object, is *not* an act of contraception nor does it violate any moral norm. The woman has absolutely no obligation to permit the rapist's sperm to penetrate and fertilize her ovum, because she has not consented to a genital act but has rather refused such consent and has been sexually violated by the rapist. In a fine passage, Germain Grisez has put the matter this way:

> Rape is the imposition of intimate, bodily union upon someone without her or his consent, and anyone who is raped rightly resists so far as possible. Moreover, the victim (or potential victim) is right to resist not only insofar as he or she is subjected to unjust force, but

insofar as that force imposes the special wrong of uniquely intimate bodily contact. It can scarcely be doubted that someone who cannot prevent the initiation of this intimacy is morally justified in resisting its continuation; for example, if a woman who awakes and finds herself being penetrated by a rapist need not permit her attacker to ejaculate in her vagina if she can make him withdraw. On the same basis, if they cannot prevent the wrongful intimacy itself, women who are victims (or potential victims) of rape and those trying to help them are morally justified in trying to prevent conception insofar as it is the fullness of sexual union.

The measures taken in this case are a defense of the woman's ovum (insofar as it is a part of her person) against the rapist's sperms (insofar as they are parts of his person). By contrast, if the intimate, bodily union of intercourse is not imposed on the woman but sought willingly or willingly permitted, neither she nor anyone who permits the union can intend at the same time that it not occur. Hence, rape apart, contraceptive measures are chosen to prevent conception not insofar as it is the ultimate completion of intimate bodily union but insofar as it is the beginning of a new and unwanted person.[63]

In other words, the moral object specifying the rape victim's (or potential rape victim's) human act is *not* to prevent the conception of a new human person but rather to prevent ultimate completion of an unjust act of sexual violence.

Similarly, a woman who has suffered the horrible violence of being raped, but who has not, prior to being raped, sought to protect herself from further violence from the rapist's sperm, can legitimately protect herself from the further violation that would be done to herself were the rapist's sperm to penetrate her ovum. Thus Directive 36 of the *Ethical and Religious Directives for Catholic Health Care Services*, promulgated by the National Conference of Catholic Bishops of the United States in 1994, reads as follows:

A female who has been raped should be able to defend herself against a potential conception from the sexual assault. If, after appropriate testing, there is no evidence that conception has occurred already, she may be treated with medications that would prevent ovulation, sperm capacitation, or fertilization. It is not permissible, however, to initiate or to recommend treatments that have as their purpose or direct effect the removal, destruction, or interference with the implantation of a fertilized ovum.[64]

In other words, human acts can legitimately be taken to protect the woman who has been raped from being made pregnant by the rapist's sperm. Such acts are *not acts of contraception,* which is intrinsically evil and can *never* be morally justified. Such acts are not acts of contraception because the *object* freely chosen and morally specifying them is *not* the impeding of a new human life that could begin through a freely chosen genital act (= definition of contraception) but is rather the *protecting of the raped woman from further violence by the rapist.*

ENDNOTES FOR CHAPTER FOUR

1. Gilbert Meilaender and Philip Turner, "Contraception: A Symposium," *First Things* 88 (December 1998), 24.

2. James Nuechterlein, "Catholics, Protestants, and Contraception," *First Things* 92 (April 1999), 10.

3. Ibid.

4. Pope John XXIII established this Commission, whose function was exclusively to offer advice to the Pope, in 1963. After Pope John's death, Pope Paul VI ordered that it continue its work. The Commission's original charge was to determine whether the newly discovered "anovulant" pill was indeed a contraceptive (as Pope Pius XII had judged in an address given to a Congress of Hematologists on September 12, 1958, less than a month before he died), but it soon began to open up the entire issue of contraception. The Commission soon divided into a "minority," which held that the Church's teaching on the immorality of contraception is true and cannot change, and a "majority," which held that contraception by married couples can be justified. The Commission completed its work in 1966. Although its findings were supposed to have been given *only* to the Holy Father, the Commission's papers were leaked to the press in July 1967 and published in the United States in the *National Catholic Reporter.* The Commission issued four documents; all can be found in *The Birth-Control Debate: Interim History from the Pages of the National Catholic Reporter,* ed. Robert Hoyt (Kansas City: National Catholic Reporter, 1969). One, expressing the minority view, was entitled in Latin "*Status Quaestionis: Doctrina Ecclesiae Eiusque Auctoritatis,*" and is given the title "The State of the Question: A Conservative View" in the Hoyt volume. Three documents set forth the majority position: (1) a rebuttal of the minority view ("*Documentum Syntheticum de Moralitate Nativitatum*" in Latin; entitled "The Question Is Not Closed: The Liberals Reply" in Hoyt); (2) the final theological report of the majority ("*Schema Documenti de Responsabili Paternitate*" in Latin and called "On

Responsible Parenthood: The Final Report" in Hoyt); and (3) a pastoral paper, written in French under the title *"Indications Pastorales"* ("Pastoral Approaches" in Hoyt).

An interesting account of the Commission and its work, written by one fully in agreement with the "majority" position, is given by Robert McClory, *Turning Point: The Inside Story of the Papal Birth Control Commission, and How Humanae Vitae Changed the Life of Patty Crowley and the Future of the Church* (New York: Crossroad, 1995).

5. "On Responsible Parenthood," in Hoyt, p. 88.

6. "The Question Is Not Closed," in ibid., p. 72.

7. Alicia Mosier, "Contraception: A Symposium," *First Things* 88 (December 1998), 26.

8. A better translation of the Latin text of *Humanae vitae* to which Mosier refers is "to impede procreation" insofar as the Latin reads *"ut procreatio impediatur."*

9. Alicia Mosier, "Contraception: A Symposium," *First Things* 88 (December 1998), 26-27.

10. See Germain Grisez, Joseph Boyle, John Finnis, and William E. May, " 'Every Marital Act Ought To Be Open to New Life': Toward a Clearer Understanding," *The Thomist* 52 (1988), 365-426; reprinted in *The Teaching of Humanae Vitae: A Defense* (San Francisco: Ignatius Press, 1988), pp. 33-116.

11. See, for instance, the following:

(1) St. John Chrysostom, *Homily 24 on the Epistle to the Romans*, PG 60.626-627: "Why do you sow where the field is eager to destroy the fruit? Where there are medicines of sterility? Where there is murder before birth? You do not even let a harlot remain only a harlot, but you make her a murderess as well. Do you see that from drunkenness comes fornication, from fornication adultery, from adultery murder? Indeed, it is something worse than murder and I do not know what to call it; for she does not kill what is formed but prevents its formation. What then? Do you contemn the gift of God, and fight with his law? What is a curse, do you seek as though it were a blessing? Do you make the anteroom of birth the anteroom of slaughter? Do you teach the woman who is given to you for the procreation of offspring to perpetuate killing?" Cited by John T. Noonan, Jr., in his *Contraception: A History of Its Treatment by Catholic Theologians and Canonists* (Cambridge, MA: The Belknap Press of Harvard University, 1965), p. 98. On pp. 91-94 of this work, Noonan shows that contraception, along with abortion, was considered equivalent to murder in such early Christian writings as the *Didache* and the *Epistle to Barnabas*. As Noonan shows in later sections of his work, e.g., pp. 146,

232-237, this tradition perdured in the Church for centuries.

(2) St. Thomas Aquinas, *Summa contra gentiles*, Bk. 3, chap. 122: "Nor, in fact, should it be deemed a slight sin for a man to arrange for the emission of semen apart from the proper purpose of generating and bringing up children . . . the inordinate emission of semen is incompatible with the natural good of preserving the species. Hence, after the sin of homicide whereby a human nature already in existence is destroyed, this type of sin appears to take next place, for by it the generation of human nature is impeded."

(3) The *"Si aliquis"* canon, which was integrated into the canon law of the Church in the *Decretum Greg. IX*, lib. V, tit., 12, cap. V, and was part of the Church's canon law from the mid-thirteenth century until 1917, clearly likened contraception to murder. It declared: "If anyone for the sake of fulfilling sexual desire or with premeditated hatred does something to a man or a woman, or gives something to drink, so that he cannot generate or she cannot conceive or offspring be born, let him be held as a murderer." Text in *Corpus iuris canonici*, ed. A. L. Richter and A. Friedberg (Leipzig: Tauchnitz, 1881), 2.794.

(4) In its treatment of marriage, the *Roman Catechism* declared: "Whoever in marriage artificially prevents conception, or procures an abortion, commits a most serious sin: the sin of premeditated murder" (Part II, chap. 7, no. 13). It should be noted that Pope Paul VI explicitly refers to this text in a footnote to no. 14 of *Humanae vitae* (footnote no. 16), precisely where Paul defines contraception as every act prior to intercourse, during it, or in the course of its natural effect that proposes (the Latin text reads *intendat*), either as end or as means, to impede procreation (*ut procreatio impediatur*).

(5) John Calvin, in his commentary on the sin of Onan in Genesis 38, had this to say: "Onan not only defrauded his brother of the right due him, but also preferred his semen to putrefy on the ground. . . . The voluntary spilling of semen outside of intercourse between man and woman is a monstrous thing. Deliberately to withdraw from coitus in order that semen may fall on the ground is doubly monstrous. For this is to extinguish the hope of the race and to kill before is born the hoped-for offspring. . . . If any woman ejects a foetus from her womb by drugs, it is reckoned a crime incapable of expiation, and deservedly Onan incurred upon himself the same kind of punishment, infecting the earth by his semen in order that Tamar might not conceive a future human being as an inhabitant of the earth." *Commentaries on the First Book of Moses Called Genesis*, ch. 38:9,10; quoted in Charles D. Provan, *The Bible and Birth Control* (Monongahela, PA: Zimmer Printing, 1989), p. 15. Provan points out that the editor of the *unabridged* series of Calvin's Commentaries, published by Baker Book House, has omitted the commentary on these two verses of Genesis.

12. See, for instance, his apostolic exhortation *Familiaris consortio* (*The Role of the Christian Family in the Modern World*), no. 32.

13. On this, see Paul F. deLadurantaye, " 'Irreconcilable Concepts of the Human Person' and the Moral Issue of Contraception: An Examination of the Personalism of Louis Janssens and of Pope John Paul II," *Anthropotes: Rivista di Studi sulla Persona e la Famiglia* 13.2 (1997), 433-456. This essay is a summary of deLadurantaye's 1997 S.T.D. dissertation under the same title at the John Paul II Institute for Studies on Marriage and Family, Washington, DC.

14. See endnote 5, above.

15. "The Question Is Not Closed," in Hoyt, p. 69.

16. "On Responsible Parenthood," in Hoyt, p. 87.

17. "The Question Is Not Closed," in Hoyt, p. 71.

18. "On Responsible Parenthood," in Hoyt, p. 89.

19. Louis Janssens, "Considerations on *Humanae Vitae*," *Louvain Studies* 2 (1969) 249.

20. Anthony Kosnik et al., *Human Sexuality: New Directions in American Catholic Thought* (New York: Paulist, 1977), p. 83.

21. George Gilder, *Sexual Suicide* (New York: Quadrangle Books, 1973), p. 34.

22. Ashley Montagu, *Sex, Man, and Society* (New York: G. P. Putnam's, 1969), pp. 13-14; emphasis in original.

23. Germain Grisez, "Dualism and the New Morality," *Atti del congresso internazionale Tommaso d'Aquino nel suo settimo centenario*, vol. 5, *L'agire morale* (Naples: Edizioni Domenicane Italiane, 1977), p. 325.

24. "The Question Is Not Closed," in Hoyt, p. 72.

25. In fact, some Catholic advocates of contraception, for instance, Rosemary Ruether and Louis Janssens, claim that with barrier methods of contraception one puts a "spatial" barrier between ovum and sperm, whereas with the use of periodic abstinence one puts a "temporal" barrier between ovum and sperm. Thus Ruether writes: ". . . sexual acts which are calculated to function only during the times of sterility are sterilizing the act just as much as any other means of rendering the act infertile. *It is difficult to see why there should be such an absolute moral difference between creating a spatial barrier to procreation and creating a temporal barrier to procreation*" ("Birth Control and Sexuality," in *Contraception and Holiness: The Catholic Predicament*, Introduced by Thomas D. Roberts, S.J. [New York: Herder and Herder, 1964], p. 74; emphasis added).

26. Pope John Paul II, encyclical *Veritatis splendor* (*"The Splendor of Truth"*), no. 78.

27. See ibid., no. 48. In this section of his encyclical, Pope John Paul II explicitly refers to defined Catholic teaching on the unity of the human person as a unity of body and soul, namely, the Council of Vienne, Constitution *Fides Catholica, DS* 902; Fifth Lateran Council, Bull *Apostolici Regiminis, DS* 1440; and Vatican Council II, Pastoral Constitution on the Church in the Modern World (*Gaudium et spes*), no. 14. See footnotes 66 and 67 to no. 48 of *Gaudium et spes*.

28. Anthony Kosnik et al., *Human Sexuality: New Directions in American Catholic Thought*, pp. 83-84.

29. The "spousal meaning" of the body is developed in many of the addresses of Pope John Paul II on the "theology of the body." See, in particular, Pope John Paul II, *Man and Woman He Created Them: A Theology of the Body*; Translation, Introduction, and Index by Michael Waldstein (Boston: Pauline Books & Media, 2006), General Audiences 14 (pp. 181-185), 15 (pp. 185-190), and 15 (pp. 190-194). This is the definitive translation of John Paul II's "theology of the body." On this issue, see my essay, "Marriage and the Complementarity of Male and Female," chap. 2 of my *Marriage: The Rock on Which the Family Is Built* (San Francisco: Ignatius, 1995), pp. 39-66.

30. Mosier, "Contraception: A Symposium," p. 27.

31. In criticizing an earlier version of the argument given here (see endnote 10 above for bibliographical details of the Grisez et al. argument), Janet Smith accused the authors of "subjectivism" and of failing to recognize that "what one intends to do is defined as good or bad *independently of any act of the will*" (Janet Smith, *Humanae Vitae: A Generation Later* [Washington, DC: The Catholic University of America Press, 1991], p. 355). This criticism overlooks the fact that Paul VI, in order to reject every sort of contraception, had to define it in terms of the intention to impede procreation. Smith's critique, in fact, completely misunderstands the Grisez et al. argument; nowhere in her critique does she even report on the *arguments* given by Grisez et al. to show why it is always wrong to have an anti-life will. For a response to her criticisms, see William E. May, "A Review of Janet Smith's *Humanae Vitae: A Generation Later*," *The Thomist* 57 (1993), 155-161.

32. Carlo Caffarra, "*Humanae Vitae* Venti Anni Dopo," in "*Humanae Vitae: 20 Anni Dopo: Atti del II Congresso Internazionale di Teologia Morale* (Milan: Edizioni Ares, 1989), p. 192; English translation in *Why Humanae Vitae Was Right: A Reader*, ed. Janet Smith (San Francisco: Ignatius, 1993), p. 267.

33. I acknowledge that some individuals *can* abuse "recourse to the rhythm of the cycle," regarding it merely as another way of impeding new human life. Such individuals have, in fact, a "contraceptive mentality," and may

decide to impede new life by this means rather than by barrier or chemical means for aesthetic or hygienic reasons. St. Augustine, who used a primitive form of "fertility awareness" (refraining from having sex with his mistress during certain periods), testifies to this, for in his *Confessions* he acknowledges that his son Adeotatus "was conceived against our wills," but that, once born, he forced Augustine and his mistress to love him (see Book 4, chap. 2). Such individuals are, in effect, putting a "temporal barrier between sperm and ovum" (as Rosemary Ruether claims) precisely in order to impede procreation. But those who have "recourse to the rhythm of the cycle," choosing to abstain, not as a means of impeding procreation but of not causing a pregnancy when it would not be prudent to do so, do not have this anti-life will. If told that they "are putting a temporal barrier between sperm and ovum," they would rightly find the charge incomprehensible. Augustine would not find it so because he apparently thought that this was precisely what he was doing, for he was contracepting.

34. The argument briefly set forth in this section is developed at much greater length by Grisez et al. in the essay referred to in endnote 10 above. It is masterfully presented by Grisez in Vol. 2, *Living a Christian Life*, of his *The Way of the Lord Jesus* (Quincy, IL: Franciscan Press, 1993), pp. 506-519.

35. Pope John Paul II develops this argument in many of his papal writings. Janet Smith provides an excellent synthesis of his thought on this matter in her *Humanae Vitae: A Generation Later*, pp. 98-129. See also Paul deLadurantaye, work cited in note 13 above.

36. See Paul Quay, S.J., "Contraception and Conjugal Love," *Theological Studies* 22 (1961), 18-40. See also Mary Joyce, *The Meaning of Contraception* (Collegeville, MN: The Liturgical Press, 1969), Dietrich von Hildebrand, *The Encyclical Humanae Vitae: A Sign of Contradiction* (Chicago: Franciscan Herald Press, 1969), and John Kippley, *Sex and the Marriage Covenant: A Basis for Morality* (Cincinnati: Couple to Couple League, 1991), pp. 50-76. In *Contraception and the Natural Law* (Milwaukee: Bruce, 1964), pp. 33-35, Germain Grisez offers an appreciative critique of this argument as expressed by Paul Quay.

37. Nuechterlein, "Catholics, Protestants, and Contraception," 10.

38. Pope John Paul II, "Homily at Mass for Youth, Nairobi, Kenya," *L'Osservatore Romano*, English ed., August 26, 1985, no. 8, p. 5; emphasis added. In saying this, John Paul II was in some ways also reaffirming the thought of Pope Paul VI, who referred to *Humanae vitae* as a defense of life "at the very source of human existence," and, citing the teaching of *Gaudium et spes*, no. 51, on abortion and infanticide, added: "We did no more than accept this charge when, ten years ago, we published the Encyclical *Humanae vitae*. This document drew its inspiration from the inviolable

teachings of the Bible and the Gospel, which confirms the norms of the natural law and the unsuppressible dictates of conscience on respect for human life, the transmission of which is entrusted to responsible fatherhood and motherhood" (Paul VI, "Homily on the Feast of Sts. Peter and Paul," *L'Osservatore Romano*, English ed., July 6, 1978, no. 2, p. 3).

39. Karol Wojtyla, "Instynkt, milosc, malzenstwo," *Tygodnik Powszechny* 8 (1952), 39. Quoted in John M. Grondelski, *Fruitfulness as an Essential Dimension in Acts of Conjugal Love: An Interpretative Study of the Pre-Pontifical Thought of John Paul II* (New York: Fordham University Press, 1986), p. 49. I am indebted to Paul deLadurantaye for calling this text to my attention. This entire section of this chapter owes much to the final portion of deLadurantaye's unpublished S.T.D. dissertation, *"Irreconcilable Concepts of the Human Person" and the Moral Issue of Contraception: An Examination of the Personalism of Louis Janssens and Pope John Paul II*, especially pp. 259-280. As noted in endnote 13 above, a summary of this excellent study is provided in the journal *Anthropotes*.

40. Karol Wojtyla, *Love and Responsibility*, trans. H. Willetts (New York: Farrar, Strauss, Giroux, 1981), pp. 53-54. See *Evangelium vitae*, no. 81: "The meaning of life is found in giving and receiving love, and in this light human sexuality and procreation reach their true and full significance."

41. See, for example, Charles E. Curran, "Sterilization: Exposition, Critique, and Refutation of Past Teaching," in *New Perspectives in Moral Theology* (Notre Dame, IN: Notre Dame University Press, 1976), pp. 207-211.

42. See, for example, Pope Paul VI, *Humanae vitae*, no. 14; National Conference of Catholic Bishops, *Ethical and Religious Directives for Catholic Health Care Services* (Washington, DC: United States Catholic Conference, 1995), no. 53.

43. A remarkable presentation of this view is given by Martin Nolan, "The Principle of Totality," in *Absolutes in Moral Theology*, ed. Charles E. Curran (Washington, DC: Corpus Books, 1968). Paul Ramsey provided a brilliant critique of Nolan in his *The Patient as Person* (New Haven: Yale University Press, 1970), pp. 178-181.

44. On this, see Bernard Häring, *Medical Ethics* (Notre Dame, IN: Fides, 1973), p. 90. Richard McCormick, *How Brave a New World: Dilemmas in Bioethics* (New York: Doubleday, 1981), p. 272.

45. Hanna Klaus, M.D., "The Reality of Contraception," available at www.catholic.net/RCC/Periodicals/Dossier/sept97/reality.html.

46. On this, see Richard Fehring, D.N.Sc., R.N., Stella Kitchen, and Mary Shivanandan, *An Introduction to Natural Family Planning*, ed. Therese Notare (Washington, DC: USCCB, 1999), "A Word About Effectiveness."

47. See W. Bradford Wilcox, "Social Science and the Vindication of Catholic Moral Teaching," in *The Church, Marriage, & the Family: Proceedings from the 27th Annual Convention of the Fellowship of Catholic Scholars, September 24-26, 2004, Pittsburgh, PA,* ed. Kenneth Whitehead (South Bend: St. Augustine's Press, 2007), pp. 330-340.

48. Grisez, *Living a Christian Life* (Quincy, IL: Franciscan Press, 1993), p. 545: "On the one hand, having repented sterilization, married couples have the same right to intercourse and reasons for it which other couples have after the wife's menopause. On the other hand, there usually are good reasons not to try to have the operation reversed: doing so involves costs and other burdens, the attempt often fails to restore fertility, and even if it were to succeed many such couples would have no moral obligation to try to have a child."

49. Ibid.

50. On this, see his *Sex and the Marital Covenant: A Basis for Morality* (Cincinnati, OH: The Couple to Couple League, 1991), pp. 209-212.

51. See their book *Life Issues, Medical Choices: Questions and Answers for Catholics* (Cincinnati: Servant Books, published by St. Anthony Messenger, 2007), Question 34, pp. 95-97.

52. William E. May, in *Fellowship of Catholic Scholars Newsletter*, Vol. 11, No. 23 (June 1988), pp. 1-2.

53. *The Tablet* did not see fit to publish my letter responding to Rhonheimer's piece.

54. In *The National Catholic Bioethics Quarterly* 5.4 (Winter 2005).

55. In *Faith Magazine*, July-August 2006.

56. *Standing with Peter: Reflections of a Lay Theologian on God's Loving Providence* (Bethune, SC: Requiem Press, 2006), pp. 87-88.

57. One argument that has been proposed for this is as follows: Biologically, every animal, whether male or female, is a complete individual with respect to most functions: growth, nutrition, sensation, emotion, local movement, and so on. But with respect to reproduction, each sexual animal is incomplete, for a male or a female individual is only a potential part of the complete organism that reproduces sexually. This is true also of men and women: as mates who engage in sexual intercourse suited to initiate new life, they complete each other and become an organic unit. In doing so, it is literally true that "the two of them become one body" (Gn 2:24).

58. There are several editions of John Paul II's Wednesday catecheses of these topics, most recently *Man and Woman He Created Them: A Theology of the Body*, trans. Michael Waldstein (Boston: Pauline Books & Media, 2006).

59. *Veritatis splendor*, §§56-64, 79-82, esp. 80. Cardinal Joseph Ratzinger, "On *The Many Faces of AIDS*: Letter to Archbishop Pio Laghi," May 29, 1988: "In the case here under discussion, it hardly seems pertinent to appeal to the classical principle of tolerance of the lesser evil on the part of those who exercise responsibility for the temporal good of society. In fact, even when the issue has to do with educational programs promoted by the civil government, one would not be dealing simply with a form of passive toleration but rather with a kind of behaviour which would result in at least the facilitation of evil."

60. John Paul II, *Man and Woman He Created Them*, 19, no. 5.

61. Abstinence is not necessarily the only reasonable alternative to condom use. While it is not reasonable for an HIV infected spouse to demand marital intercourse when his/her spouse is unwilling to be exposed to the attendant risks, it may be reasonable for an uninfected spouse willingly to accept the risks associated with marital intercourse in these circumstances. These risks will vary according to which of the spouses is infected, the phase of the menstrual cycle during which intercourse occurs, the stage of infection and the efficacy of medication in reducing infectivity. Likewise a couple, one of whom is infected, cannot be condemned as necessarily unreasonable for having intercourse with a view to having a child. Clearly a decision to accept any risk of HIV transmission, whether to oneself or one's child, demands honest and careful consideration of one's responsibilities, wise counsel, prayerful discernment, moral fortitude and great prudence.

62. For St. Thomas, see, for example, *Summa theologiae*, 2-2, 64, 7: "moral acts are specified by what is intended, not by what falls outside the scope of one's intentionality" (*actus autem morales recipiunt speciem secundum id quod intenditur, non autem ab eo quod est praeter intentionem*). For Pope John Paul II, see encyclical *Veritatis splendor*, no. 78.

63. Germain Grisez, *The Way of the Lord Jesus*, Vol. 2, *Living a Christian Life* (Quincy, IL: Franciscan Press, 1993), p. 512.

64. National Conference of Catholic Bishops, *Ethical and Religious Directives for Catholic Health Care Services* (Washington, DC: United States Catholic Conference, 1995), Directive 36.

CHAPTER FIVE

Abortion and Human Life

Introduction: Structure of This Chapter

Although Chapter One set forth in some detail the Church's teaching on abortion, I begin this chapter with a résumé of that teaching, particularly in order to clarify that teaching on the "definition" of abortion, the question of "ensoulment," and the distinction between "direct" and "indirect" abortion. After a presentation of relevant scientific data, I then defend the proposition that it is reasonable to believe that most people begin at fertilization* and unreasonable to deny this (in defending this proposition, I criticize opposing views).

I do so because the great majority of the arguments advanced to justify abortion, either throughout the entire pregnancy or at least during its early stages, contend that the being killed by abortion is not a human person. Next I consider the special gravity of abortion and the fallacies characterizing the major arguments used to justify it as a woman's right even if one grants that it kills a human person. I then focus on the distinction made by some thinkers today between abortion as "killing" and abortion as "removal" and the argument that the latter can, under certain conditions, be morally justified. Debates among Catholic theologians on the proper moral management of ectopic pregnancies are then considered.

The chapter, therefore, is divided as follows: (1) Résumé and Clarification of Church Teaching; (2) Some Relevant Scientific Data; (3) It Is Reasonable to Believe That Most People Begin at Fertilization and Unreasonable to Deny This; (4) The Special Moral Gravity of Abortion, a Woman's "Right" to Abortion, the Difference Between a "Right" and a "Liberty"; (5) Abortion as "Removal" vs. Abortion as "Killing"; (6) The

---

* As we will see in this chapter, the only persons who do not begin at fertilization are some monozygotic twins or triplets, etc., of whom *one* may come into existence after fertilization whereas another, so it will be argued, was in being from fertilization onward.

Management of Ectopic Pregnancies. The issue of experimenting on unborn human life is taken up in Chapter Six.

1. Résumé and Clarification of Church Teaching

The *Catechism of the Catholic Church* succinctly summarizes the teaching of the Church — reviewed extensively in Chapter One — on the inviolability of human life from its beginning and on the grave moral evil of abortion. Here it will be useful to cite two passages from the *Catechism*, along with their internal citations from Scripture, from the second-century document called the *Didache* (also known as *The Teaching of the Twelve Apostles*), and from Vatican Council II:

> Human life must be respected and protected absolutely from the moment of conception. From the first moment of his existence, a human being must be recognized as having the rights of a person — among which is the inviolable right of every innocent being to life (cf. CDF, *Donum vitae* I, 1). "Before I formed you in the womb I knew you, and before you were born I consecrated you" (Jer 1:5; cf. Job 10:8-12; Ps 22:10-11). "My frame was not hidden from you, when I was being made in secret, intricately wrought in the depths of the earth" (Ps 139:15). (CCC, no. 2270)
>
> Since the first century the Church has affirmed the moral evil of every procured abortion. This teaching has not changed and remains unchangeable. Direct abortion, that is to say, abortion willed either as an end or a means, is gravely contrary to the moral law. "You shall not kill the embryo by abortion and shall not cause the newborn to perish" (*Didache* 2, 2: SCh 248, 148; cf. *Ep. Barnabae* 19, 5: PG 2, 777; *Ad Diognetum* 5, 6: PG 2, 1173; Tertullian, *Apol.* 9: PL 1, 319-320). "God, the Lord of life, has entrusted to men the noble mission of safeguarding life, and men must carry it out in a manner worthy of themselves. Life must be protected with the utmost care from the moment of conception: abortion and infanticide are abominable crimes" (*Gaudium et spes*, no. 51 § 3). (CCC no. 2271)

Moreover, as we saw in Chapter One, Pope John Paul II clearly affirmed that the teaching of the Church on the grave immorality of procured or direct abortion has been infallibly proposed by the ordinary and universal Magisterium of the Church. Mincing no words, he spoke as follows:

[B]y the authority which Christ conferred upon Peter and his Successors, in communion with the Bishops — who on various occasions have condemned abortion and who . . . , albeit dispersed throughout the world, have shown unanimous agreement concerning this doctrine — *I declare that direct abortion, that is, abortion willed as an end or as a means, always constitutes a grave moral disorder*, since it is the deliberate killing of an innocent human being. This doctrine is based upon the natural law and upon the written Word of God, is transmitted by the Church's Tradition and taught by the ordinary and universal Magisterium. (*Evangelium vitae*, no. 62; emphasis in original)

A. The Definition of Abortion

Shortly before making this powerful declaration, John Paul II had defined direct or procured abortion as "the deliberate and direct killing, by whatever means it is carried out, of a human being in the initial phase of his or her existence, extending from conception to birth" (*Evangelium vitae*, no. 58; emphasis in original). Note that here the Pope defines abortion as an act of "killing" and not as the "expelling" from the mother's womb of a living but not yet viable fetus. Some older manuals of Catholic moral theology had defined abortion in this way and used other terms, e.g., "craniotomy," "embryotomy," "feticide," to describe interventions that deliberately caused the death of the unborn child but did not do so by "expelling" it from the womb.[1] I bring this matter up here because of its relevance to the distinction made today by some scholars between abortion as "killing" and abortion as "removal," a matter to be consider later.

B. "Ensoulment" or Infusion of the Immortal Soul

We saw also in Chapter One that the Magisterium of the Church has not expressly committed itself to the position that individual human personal life begins at conception. As John Paul II declared in *Evangelium vitae*, when commenting on the views of those who seek to justify abortion by claiming that the result of conception, at least for a time, cannot be considered personal human life, "what is at stake is so important that, from the standpoint of moral obligation, the mere probability that a human person is involved would suffice to justify an absolutely clear prohibition of any intervention aimed at killing a human embryo." He concluded by saying: "Precisely for this reason, over and above all scientific debates and those philosophical affirmations [concerning the precise moment when a spiritual soul is infused] to which the Magisterium has not yet expressly committed itself, the Church has always taught and continues to teach that the result of human procreation, from the first moment of its existence, must be guaranteed that unconditional respect which is morally due to the human being in his or her totality and unity as body and spirit" (no. 60).[2]

In speaking in this way, Pope John Paul II voices the age-old tradition of the Church. No matter what their own personal views regarding the moment when the spiritual soul was infused into the body, the Apostolic Fathers, the early Christian apologists, the Fathers and Doctors of the Church, both East and West — indeed, the entire tradition — unanimously condemned procured or direct abortion of any kind as utterly immoral.[3] Thus, for example, the Greek Church Father St. Basil the Great declared that whoever purposely destroys a fetus is a murderer, and it makes no difference whatsoever whether it is formed (animated by a spiritual soul) or unformed (not yet so animated).[4]

I believe that the individual personal human life of most people begins at conception/fertilization and that empirical evidence supports this belief. Later in this chapter, this issue will be explored in depth. But it is very important to emphasize here that the Church's teaching on the grave immorality of procured or direct abortion deliberately leaves the question open for discussion. As we saw in Chapter Four, a long tradition in the Church regarded contraception as a gravely immoral *anti-life* kind of act, analogous to murder. It is thus obvious that during the centuries when all Christians judged contraception and abortion as gravely immoral, theoretical differences regarding the precise moment of "ensoulment" or infusion of an immortal soul to "form" the fetus made little or no difference in the practical judgment that every attempt to terminate pregnancy was absolutely immoral, no matter when this attempt was made.[5]

C. "Direct" vs. "Indirect" Abortion

In *Evangelium vitae*, Pope John Paul II, like his predecessors in the chair of St. Peter and along with the *Catechism of the Catholic Church*, condemned as intrinsically evil and gravely immoral every act of "procured" or "direct" abortion. Moreover, he clearly defined the meaning of "direct" or "procured" abortion. Explicitly referring to and citing from the teaching of Pope Pius XII,[6] John Paul II said that "direct" abortion includes every act tending to destroy human life in the womb "whether such destruction is intended as an *end* or only as a *means* to an end" (no. 62). By direct or procured abortion, then, one means a human act specified morally as an act of *killing the unborn*. It is so specified because its "object" as a human act is precisely the destruction of unborn human life. This "object" is either the *end* for the sake of which the act is done, or, more frequently, the *means chosen* in order to bring about some *further* end. In any event, this "object" is the *proximate end* willed by the agent; it is the *proximate end* specifying a freely chosen human act, which may also be willed as a *means* to some "further" or "ulterior" end that may have motivated the act (e.g., to avoid the embarrassment of out-of-wedlock pregnancy, to prevent the birth of a child probably suffering from some genetically induced malady, etc.). And this "object" is precisely the aborting or killing of unborn human life. That life's abortion (killing) cannot *not* be willed by the acting person.[7]

In so-called indirect abortion, the killing of the unborn child or its abortion is *not* the object of the act, neither as end nor as means. It is, rather, as the passage already cited from Pope Pius XII (see endnote 6) makes clear, the foreseen but "unintended" consequence or result of a medical procedure that itself is specified as an act of healing a sick woman or protecting her life. Neither the end intended nor the means chosen to attain the end in question is the abortion or killing of the unborn. This is foreseen as an inevitable and unavoidable result of the deed chosen to protect or heal or safeguard the mother's life, but it is *not willed by the acting person*. It is "outside the scope of his or her intentions," and can be justified if there is urgent need to protect a great good, such as the life of the mother, and no other alternatives can be used to do so. Thus, for instance, it is morally permissible for a woman suffering from cancer of the uterus to have a hysterectomy or undergo radiation therapy to cure the cancer or protect her from dying of it even if she is pregnant and realizes that the unborn child will die as a result of the hysterectomy or radiation therapy, provided that no alternative therapies exist and those that do exist cannot be postponed until after the baby's safe delivery. The "abortion" in such conditions is no more "directly" willed than is one's baldness, which one foresees will occur as a result of undergoing chemotherapy for a life-threatening cancerous condition. The "baldness" is surely "outside the scope of the agent's intention" and is definitely *not* willed in any way. Similarly, in cases of so-called indirect abortion, the abortion or death of the unborn child is also "outside the scope of the agent's intention" and is definitely *not* willed in any way, even "indirectly." The abortion, understood as the death of the unborn child, is in no way willed by the acting person, neither as end nor as means. It is precisely an *unintended* side effect of an action good in itself because the "object" specifying it is precisely the saving or protecting of the mother's life. The unborn child's death is thus not "intended" in any way.

2. Some Relevant Scientific Data

I will first consider an important essay by Nicanor Pier Austriaco, O.P., and I will then show the relevance of an article by Patrick Lee and Robert George.

In a most important essay, Austriaco summarizes "a systems biology view of the beginning of human life." Addressing the issue of fertilization and embryogenesis, Austriaco reviews the biology by describing the molecular and cellular events at the beginning of life. Fertilization, traditionally the point that marks the origin of the human organism, "is initiated by fusion of the sperm and egg. . . . Between eleven and eighteen hours after insemination, the two pro-nuclei, one from each of the gametes, become visible and eventually unite, forming the embryonic nucleus with its complete set of forty-six chromosomes. About thirty hours after sperm-egg fusion, the first cell division occurs, and two-to four-cell stage embryos can usually be observed by day two. By day three, the embryo reaches the eight cell stage. Sometimes between days two and three, the embryonic genome is activated representing the transition of control from maternally-derived to embryonically-derived molecules. By day five, the embryo appears as a ball of cells, called the blastocyst, which is ready for implantation in his mother's womb. This sequence of orchestrated changes makes up the early stages of human development called embryogenesis."[8]

He then gives an analysis of the human egg or oocyte before it is in a state called meiotic arrest. "In a sense, the egg is a structured collection of *inert molecules awaiting activation* (emphasis added). . . . In this state the egg only has a lifespan of about twenty-fours after it has been expelled by the ovary. It cannot maintain itself and soon depletes its energy resources. If it is not fertilized, the system will deteriorate, collapse, and the egg will die."[9]

The fusion of egg and sperm (fertilization) has two effects. First of all, by introducing paternally derived molecules into the network of maternally derived molecules it initiates a new structure, an entirely new system or organism. Second, fertilization

> triggers a change in the dynamics of the egg by reorganizing and reactivating the interconnected network of inert maternal molecules in its contents . . . trigger[ing] the chain of reactions and molecular interactions that drive cell division and differentiation. If left alone, this self-driven, self-perpetuating process of molecular interactions will continue for nine months and beyond, transforming the living system

called an embryo into the living system called a gurgling eight pound baby. Whereas the living system before fertilization only had a lifespan of twenty-four hours, the new living system after fertilization now has a span of seventy or eighty for those who are strong. Furthermore, since this new system is capable of independent and self-sustaining existence, it is an organism. Fertilization is the paradigmatic example of cell-to-organism transition.[10]

Summarizing, Austriaco says that from the systems perspective "the beginning of life should be understood, first and foremost, as the transformation of one dynamic system, the egg, into another, the embryo. The *egg is a cell*, an embodied process in stasis that has only a life expectancy on the order of hours because it *is not self-sustaining*. . . . In contrast, the *embryo is an organism*, an embodied process that has a life expectancy on the order of decades precisely because *it has the ability to sustain itself as an independent entity*. It is a dynamic system which arises from the necessary interactions among the mix of molecules that is created by the fusion of the egg and the sperm, and it manifests itself as the visible and morphological changes which we call human development."[11]

It is easy to see, after this summary of Austriaco's essay, why standard embryology texts locate the beginning of the human individual at fertilization, not at implantation (cf., for example, William J. Larsen, *Human Embryology*, 3rd ed. (2001); Keith Moore and T. V. N. Persaud, *The Developing Human, Clinically Oriented Embryology*, 7th ed., 2003; and Ronan O'Rahilly and Fabiola Mueller, *Human Embryology and Teratology*, 3rd ed., 2000. But some people claim that at implantation maternal signaling factors transform a bundle of cells into a human organism. However, as Patrick Lee and Robert George point out, "there is much dispute about whether any such maternal signaling actually occurs. As Hans-Werner Denker observes, it was once assumed that in mammals, in contrast to amphibians and birds, polarity in the early embryo depends upon some external signal, since no clear indications of bilateral symmetry had been found in oocytes, zygotes, or early blastocysts. But this view has been revised in light of emerging evidence: '[I]ndications have been found that in mammals the axis of bilateral symmetry is indeed determined (although at first in a labile way) by sperm penetration, as in amphibians. Bilateral symmetry can already be detected in the early blastocyst and is not dependent on implantation.' "

Continuing, Lee and George write:

Denker refers specifically to the work of Magdalena Zernicka-Goetz and her colleagues at Cambridge and that of R. L. Gardner at Oxford, which shows that polarity exists even at the two-cell stage.

The test of whether a group of cells constitutes a single organism is whether they form a stable body and function as parts of a whole, self-developing, adaptive unit. Compaction, cavitation, the changes occurring earlier to facilitate these activities, and implantation — all of these activities are clear cases of the cells acting in a coordinated manner for the sake of a self-developing and adaptive whole. In other words, such activities are ordered to the survival and maturation of the whole, existing embryo. This fact shows that the unity of the blastomeres (the cells of the early embryo) is *substantial* rather than incidental; the blastomeres are integrated parts of a functional whole, not separate parts that lead to the creation of a whole. This is compelling evidence that what exists from day 1 to day 6 is not a mere aggregate of cells but a multi-cellular organism.... The actions of the embryo from day 1 to day 6 are clearly part of a unitary development toward human maturation. None of the events occurring in the embryo could reasonably be interpreted as creating a new and distinct direction. Implantation does not change the *nature* (kind of being) of the embryo; it is an event in the unfolding life of a whole human organism, not the initiation of an entirely new organism.[12]

3. It Is Reasonable to Believe That Most People Begin at Fertilization and Unreasonable to Deny This

Here I will defend the position that the individual personal human life of most people begins at conception/fertilization. This position, of course, is denied by many. It is denied first of all by those who claim that the being killed by abortion is not even a *human being*, let alone a person. It is denied also by many who grant that the being killed by abortion is a *human being* or *member of the human species*, but who contend that it simply cannot be regarded as a *person* with rights. Still others adopt one or another variant of the "gradualist" view, which holds that at some point during gestation the entity that was conceived *becomes* human and personal in nature. There are many variants to this view, with some holding that a human person is in existence early on in the process — for instance, at implantation — while others claim it does not become a person until some later stage — say, the formation of the neocortex of the brain, the presence of all organ systems, viability, etc. This view, which has wide rhetorical appeal, regards early abortions (those done prior to the event that marks the beginning of personal as opposed to merely biological life, whatever that event might be) as morally permissible, while abortions done later are questionable, and the later an abortion the closer it is to being wrong or more seriously wrong. Among the finest presentations and critiques of these different views are the studies by Patrick Lee in *Abortion and Unborn Human Life* and by Robert George and Christopher Tollefsen in *Embryo: A Defense of Human Life*, and I urge readers to consult these rigorously argued works.[13] Many others have also examined this matter in depth, and my obvious debt to them will be noted throughout.

I will first briefly consider some opinions, unfortunately common in our society, that are utterly incompatible with what we *know* about human procreation. I will then take up positions that at least seem more plausible. The falsification of the even more plausible views will help corroborate the claim that it is reasonable to hold that the human personal life of most people begins at conception/fertilization and that it is unreasonable to deny this.

There is no need to waste time with the utterly rhetorical and/or euphemistic assertions identifying the being brought into existence at fertilization as "protoplasmic rubbish" or a "gobbet of meat"[14] or a "blueprint"[15] or "gametic materials" or the "product of conception,"[16] or only a "part of the mother's body."[17] Such views, which rely on rhetoric and the abuse of language, are patently either false or totally inadequate in light of what we actually *know* about the process of human generation. They simply cannot be and ought not to be taken seriously.

Another common set of claims, slightly more credible, that deny the humanity and *a fortiori* the personhood of the human zygote and early embryo, appeal to the fact that these organisms do not "appear" to be human or persons. Pictures and drawings of human beings at these stages of development *seem* to support claims of this kind. "How," they ask, "can you say that an organism with no face or hands or feet or organs can possibly be a human being, much less a person?" Or, "How can an organism no larger than the period at the end of a sentence possibly be regarded as a human being, a person?" Germain Grisez points out that arguments of this kind are plausible "because they use imagery and directly affect feelings. Usually, in judging whether or not to apply a predicate [such as *human being* or *person*] to an experienced entity, one does not examine it to see whether it meets a set of intelligible criteria; instead, one judges by appearances, using as guide past experience of individuals of that kind." However, he continues, such claims can be falsified by pointing out "that, while the particular difference [between a human zygote or early embryo and embryos and fetuses at a later stage of development] is striking because of the normal limits of human experience, nevertheless entities that are different in that way certainly are living human beings."[18] Stephen Schwarz, whom Grisez commends, has identified the element common to these denials of humanity and/or personhood to the zygote and early embryo and has responded to it decisively. He points out that all these objections are "based on the expectation that what is a person must be like us. It must be the right size (a size like ours); it must have a level of development comparable to ours; it must look like us; it must, like us, be conscious."[19]

But, he continues, "these are not true criteria for being a person [or for being a human being]." They are rather "simply expressions of our expectations, of what we are used to, of what appears familiar to us. It is not that the zygote fails to be a person [or human being] because it fails these tests; rather, it is we who fail by using these criteria to measure what a person [or human being] is."[20]

It is unreasonable to expect that a human being in the first stages of his or her development will look like a familiar human being, or like a newborn baby or a four-year-old or a teenager, or like a mature adult or a wheelchair-bound elderly man or woman. The way these persons "appear" during the early stages of their development says nothing of the status of their *nature* or *being*. Each of us develops and unfolds his or her personality every day of our lives, and we were developing and unfolding them before we were born, just as we do so afterwards because we were alive then. This ought not to cause anyone surprise. "Horton," one of Dr. Seuss's lovable characters, hits the nail on the head in *Horton Hears a Who* when he says, "A person's a person, no matter how small."

Another claim denying personhood to the unborn, or at least to many unborn human beings, is widely held today, but it too is readily falsifiable. It is the claim that personhood is a status conferred on entities by others, and it is, surprisingly, held by many in our society. Proponents of this view contend that personhood is a *social status* conferred on an entity by others, and that an entity is a *person* only when recognized by others as a person. They believe that this view is supported by the truth that persons exist only with other persons — personhood is *relational* in character.

One advocate of this view, Marjorie Reiley Maguire, proposes that the personhood of the unborn "begins when the bearer of life, the mother, makes a covenant of love with the developing life within her to birth. . . . The moment which begins personhood . . . is the moment when the mother accepts the pregnancy." And, if she does not accept it and decides to abort the "developing life within her," that life must be regarded as not a person, for personhood has not been bestowed on it.[21]

This position, of course, leads to the absurdity that the same being can be simultaneously both a person and not a person; it is a "person," for instance, if at least one person, say its father, recognizes and esteems it as a person; but it is not a "person" if another person, say its mother, refuses to consider it a person. This claim presupposes that human meaning-giving *constitutes* persons; the truth is that human meaning-giving and human societies *presuppose* human persons.[22]

I will now consider and rebut more plausible views that deny personhood to the unborn. These have been well identified by Grisez, who offers excellent critiques of them.[23] In what follows, I will use somewhat different categories than the ones he uses, but mine are essentially the same. The principal positions of this kind are the following: (A) personhood requires exercisable cognitive abilities; (B) personhood is dependent on sense organs and a brain (= the "delayed hominization" position); (C) individual persons, as phenomena such as twinning and the "wastage" of embryos prior to implantation indicate, are formed only two weeks after fertilization.

A. Personhood Requires Exercisable Cognitive Abilities

This view, widely held today, contends that for a human being to be regarded as a person, he or she must have developed at least incipiently exercisable capacities or abilities for understanding, choice, and rational communication. Many who hold it — and among its more influential proponents are Michael Tooley, Daniel Callahan, and Peter Singer[24] — are willing to grant that a human being, in the sense of a living biological member of the human species, is in existence from conception/fertilization or at any rate very early afterwards. But they contend that membership in the human species is not a sufficient criterion for personhood because only some members of the human species acquire the property or set of properties necessary if an entity is to be regarded as a "person." In fact, some who hold this position assert that those who believe that membership in the human species is of great moral significance are guilty of a form of discrimination, *speciesism*, a prejudice similar to such immoral prejudices as *racism*. Prominent among those who make this claim is Peter Singer, the champion of "animal rights," who contends that it is far more immoral to torture a kitten than it is to kill an unborn child or a young infant with a debilitating condition such as Down syndrome.[25] In this view, not only are unborn children nonpersons but so, too, are newborns and, apparently, adult humans who no longer possess exercisable faculties of knowledge, recognition, consciousness, etc.

The reasoning behind this claim is fallacious. It fails to distinguish between a *radical* capacity or ability and a *developed* capacity or ability. A radical capacity can also be called an *active*, as distinct from a merely *passive*, potentiality. An unborn baby or a newborn child, precisely by reason of its membership in the human species, has the *radical capacity or active potentiality* to discriminate between true and false propositions, to make choices, and to communicate rationally. But in order for the child — unborn or newborn — to *exercise* this capacity or set of capacities, his radical capacity or active potentiality for engaging in these activities — predictable kinds of behavior for members of the human species — must be allowed to develop. But it could never be developed if it were not there to begin with. Similarly, adult members of the human species may, because of accidents, no longer be capable of actually exercising their capacity or ability to engage in these activities. But this does not mean that they do not have the natural or radical capacity, rooted in their being the kind of beings they are, for such activities. They are simply inhibited by disease or accidents from exercising this capacity. Similarly, members of the species "bald eagle" have the *radical* capacity or *active* potentiality, rooted in their being the kind of beings they are, to soar loftily in the air; eaglets who have not as yet *developed* this capacity and adult eagles whose wings have been broken are not able to *exercise* this capacity, but the fact that this capacity is not presently exercisable does not mean that it is not a radical capacity or active potentiality rooted in the nature of all members of the species "bald eagle" and not merely potential in a passive sense.

A human embryo has the *active* potentiality or *radical* capacity to develop *from within its own resources* all it needs to exercise the property or set of properties characteristic of adult members of the species. One can say that the human embryo is a human person *with potential*; he or she is *not* merely a *potential person*. Those, like Tooley and Singer, who require that an entity have *exercisable* cognitive abilities, recognize that the unborn have the *potentiality* to engage in cognitive activities. But they regard this as a merely *passive* potentiality and fail to recognize the crucially significant difference between an *active* potentiality and a merely *passive* one. In his excellent development of the significance of this difference, Patrick Lee makes two very important points. The first concerns the *moral* significance of the difference between an *active* and a merely *passive* potentiality. An active potentiality means "that the same entity which possesses it is the same entity as will later exercise that active potentiality. With a passive potentiality, that is not so; that is, the actualization of a passive potentiality often produces a completely different thing or substance [e.g., oxygen has the passive potentiality to become water when appropriately combined with hydrogen]." Lee's second key point answers the question "Why should higher mental functions or the capacity or active potentiality for such functions be a trait conferring value on those who have it?" The proper answer is that such functions and the capacity for them are "of ethical significance not because [these functions] are the only intrinsically valuable entities but because entities which have such potentialities are intrinsically valuable. And, *if the entity itself is intrinsically valuable, then it must be intrinsically valuable from the moment that it exists.*"[26]

The claim that not all human beings are persons but that only those who possess exercisable cognitive abilities are to be so regarded, moreover, is marked by debates among its advocates over precisely *which* ability or abilities must be exercisable if an entity is to be classified as a "person." This claim thus inevitably leads to arbitrary and unjust criteria for "personhood." A group of Catholic thinkers in England gives a devastating critique of this arbitrariness, and it is worthwhile to cite it at some length because it so ably pinpoints the arbitrariness involved:

> The rational abilities necessary to these [cognitive] abilities are various, and come in varying degrees in human beings. If actual possession of such abilities is a necessary condition of the claim to be treated justly, questions will have to be faced precisely *which* abilities must be possessed, and how developed they must be before one enjoys this claim to be treated justly. And these questions can be answered only by *choosing* which to count as the relevant abilities and precisely how developed they must be to count. But any such line-drawing exercise is necessarily arbitrary. . . . Arbitrary choices may be reasonable and unavoidable in determining some entitlements. . . . But if one's understanding of human worth and dignity commits one to being arbitrary about who are to be treated justly (i.e., about who are the very *subjects* of justice), it is clear that one lacks what is recognisable as a framework of justice. For it is incompatible with our fundamental intuitions about justice that we should determine who are the subjects of

justice by arbitrary choice. The need for a non-arbitrary understand-ing of who are the subjects of justice requires us to assume that *just treatment is owing to all human beings in virtue of their humanity*. This indispensable assumption is also intrinsically reasonable. It is true that the distinctive dignity and value of human life are *manifested* in those specific exercises of developed rational abilities in which we achieve some share in such human goods as truth, beauty, justice, friendship, and integrity. But the necessary rational abilities are acquired in virtue of an underlying or radical capacity, *given with our nature as human beings*, for developing precisely those abilities.[27]

The "only-those-with-exercisable-cognitive-abilities-are-persons" claim is also dualistic because it sharply distinguishes between the "person," the subject with exercisable cognitive abilities, and the living human body, which the person, as it were, possesses. It is, of course, true that human persons can do things — think, make free choices, etc. — which show that they are *more* than their bodies and that they are also (or can be) consciously experiencing subjects with cognitive abilities. But, as Grisez notes, "persons can be more than their bodies without being realities other than their bodies, since a whole can be more than one of its parts without being a reality other than that part."[28] There is not one being who breathes, eats, sleeps, feels bodily pain, etc., and another being who thinks, chooses, and is aware of his rights, etc. The same subject, the same *human being, is* the living human body and the subject of cognitive activities. The dualistic view of man underlying the claim denying personhood to human beings who lack *exercisable cognitive abilities* is, therefore, a false understanding of man, male and female.[29]

A final comment on this position is that, as Grisez has said, it simply misses "what *person* means in ordinary language," where the word refers to a living, human individual.[30] The legitimate application of this term to non-adult human beings is rooted in its use in referring to adult human beings, who regularly think of their personhood not as a trait that they have acquired at some time in their lives but as an aspect of their very being. If one asks a person when he or she was born, he or she will spontaneously say that he or she was born on his or her day of birth, clearly implying that the person so responding considers himself or herself to be identical in being with the one born on that day. And were one to ask a person, "When were *you* conceived?" the person addressed would spontaneously reply "Approx-imately nine months before I was born," thereby implying that he or she regards himself or herself as the very same being, i.e., person, conceived and born.[31]

B. Personhood Depends on Sense Organs and a Brain: The "Delayed Hominization" Theory

Unlike the claim just considered, this position repudiates a dualistic understanding of the human person; nonetheless, its advocates contend that the early human embryo cannot be considered a person because it lacks sense organs and a brain, material organs necessary for exercising human cognitive and volitional powers.

Among its proponents are several Roman Catholic philosophers and theologians, the more influential of whom are Joseph Donceel, S.J., Thomas A. Shannon, and Allan Wolter, O.F.M.[32] These writers seek to rehabilitate the "delayed hominization" theory of St. Thomas Aquinas. According to this view, the human embryo undergoes a substantial change from a sub-human entity to a human, personal entity, and does so when its body becomes sufficiently organized to be fit matter for the infusion of a spiritual soul. Donceel proposes that the body formed at conception is capable only of biological, not rational actions. It is capable of the latter only when the neural integration of the entire organism has been established, and this occurs only around the twentieth week of gestation when the cerebral cortex is present, and Shannon and Wolter hold a similar view. Their central claim is that what specifically distinguishes human and personal nature as superior to that of other animals is reason, and that the necessary condition for reasoning is the operation of the cerebral cortex. Thus it is only after formation of the cerebral cortex that a *personal* as distinct from a merely *animal* body, fit for reception of a spiritual soul, is in being. It is at this point that the entity in question undergoes a substantial change; i.e., it changes from being a nonpersonal entity into a person. They realize that it is absurd to suggest that babies undergo a substantial change after birth, even though they cannot actually engage in thought until some time later in their development. They thus hold that the developed brain itself is not the bodily basis for intellectual activities but only its precursor, but they hold that this is all that the hylomorphic theory of St. Thomas requires.

The attempt by Donceel, Shannon/Wolters, and others to rehabilitate the "delayed hominization" theory in order to justify early abortions fails on several counts. First of all, these modern authors, in contrast to St. Thomas, assume that abortion of a pre-personal entity might be justified. But, as we saw earlier, various opinions during patristic and medieval times on the infusion of the spiritual soul in no way changed their judgment that procured abortion was always gravely immoral. All Christian writers, including St. Thomas, absolutely condemned all deliberate abortion, no matter whether the embryo/fetus was "formed" or not.

Secondly, the attempted rehabilitation of the "delayed hominization" theory is philosophically untenable, and untenable on *Thomistic* grounds in light of what we *know* about the process of human generation. Many writers, among them Grisez, Lee, Benedict Ashley, Albert Moraczewski, Jean Siebenthal, Mark Johnson, and others have shown this very clearly.[33] Here I will summarize the critiques given by Grisez and Siebenthal.

Grisez first points out that even after birth, babies cannot think and make choices, the rational actions characteristic of human persons and capacity for which distinguishes human, personal nature from subhuman, subpersonal nature. Thus, as the advocates of the delayed hominization theory themselves admit, the beginning of the brain's development during the gestation period cannot be the bodily basis required for specifically personal acts but only its precursor. Since this precursor satisfies the requirements of St. Thomas's theory, why cannot precursors at earlier stages of development satisfy them? Moreover, modern biology demonstrates that every human embryo has from the very beginning a specific developmental tendency, including the epigenetic primordia or sources for the development of *all* its organs, including the brain. The fact that a spiritual soul can exist only in matter able to receive it does not entail the conclusion that a human zygote cannot receive it, since it has within itself the active potency to develop all its organs. Grisez then concludes that the assumption on which this theory rests, namely, that the human embryo is at first a pre-personal entity and only later becomes personal, "posits two entities where only one is necessary to account for the observed facts. But entities," he continues, "are not to be multiplied without necessity. Consequently, the view that the embryo becomes a person when the brain begins to develop should be rejected, and the personal soul should be considered to be present from conception."[34]

Siebenthal's refutation of this view is most interesting because he roots it in a careful analysis of the thought of St. Thomas himself — to whom Donceel, Shannon, and others appeal for support. Siebenthal first stresses that for St. Thomas the origin of the *human body* coincides with the infusion of a spiritual or intellectual soul. For St. Thomas, *human* flesh gets its being — its *esse* — from the human intellectual soul.[35] Since St. Thomas himself mistakenly thought, because he relied on the inadequate biological knowledge of his day, that in human generation the male seed was alone the active element, he concluded that the body first formed from the maternal blood by this seed was only vegetative in nature; later, a substantial change occurred and a new body, this time animated by an animal soul, was formed; finally, another substantial change occurred and a new body, human in nature and animated by an intellectual soul, came into being. But note that for St. Thomas the *bodies* first generated were *not human* in nature. He thus concluded that there was a radical discontinuity between the bodies formed during gestation. Siebenthal's point is that St. Thomas, were he alive today and cognizant of the biological evidence known today, would not hesitate in concluding that the *body* that comes to be when fertilization is completed is indubitably a *human* body and hence that its organizing and vivifying principle can only be a *human soul*, an intellectual or spiritual soul.[36]

Today, in addition to those advocating the "delayed hominization" theory, several thinkers believe that authentically human and personal life begins only once the brain has developed in the unborn. They do so because they think that a functioning brain is an essential property of a human being. Scholars taking this position draw an analogy between the end and the beginning of human life. They note that today a widely accepted criterion to show that death has occurred and that a living human person no longer exists is the irreversible cessation of the functioning of *the entire brain, including the brain stem*. Since we can say that a person is dead, i.e., no longer alive and among us, when his or her brain in its entirety has irreversibly ceased to function, then why can we not say that human, personal life begins when the fetus acquires a functioning brain?[37]

Even if it is granted that irreversible cessation of all the functions of the entire brain, including the brain stem, is an acceptable criterion that death has occurred, the analogy invoked is not accurate, as Lee, in particular, clearly shows. While it is true that what we say about the end of human life should be consistent with what we say about its beginning, advocates of this view locate the analogy in the wrong place, i.e., in a *functioning brain*, and not in the *unity of the organism*. Irreversible cessation of all functions of the entire brain may indeed show that death has occurred, because in a mature human being the brain is the organ that integrates the functioning of all the systems of that mature human being. Hence, when the brain ceases to function (totally and irreparably) in a mature human being, all other tissues and organs cease to form a unified organism. A human being is essentially an organism, albeit a specific type, and so if the tissues and organs cease to constitute an organism, then the human being has ceased to be. But, since being an organism expresses in a very general way what a human being is, it is impossible for an organism to come to be at one time and, remaining the *same* organism, become human at a later time. Hence, "if an organism at one time is the same organism as a human organism at a later time, then the organism at the earlier time is a human organism also, the same human organism as the one which exists at a later time."[38] Proponents of this view must acknowledge that, before the formation of the brain in the developing biological organism, there is something in that organism during its zygotic and early embryonic stages that definitely integrates all its living activities — the essential function carried out by the brain in that same organism at later states of its existence. It is impossible to declare the organism dead or deny that it is identifiably biologically as a member of the human species as distinct from other animal species. The organism is alive, human in nature, and has within itself the active potential to develop its own brain. One cannot say this of the nonliving corpse of a person declared dead because there is certainty that there is irreversible cessation of all the functions of the entire brain, which serves, in the mature human, as the integrating, organizing factor.[39]

C. Individual Personhood Cannot Be Established Before Implantation

Another challenge to the thesis defended here, namely, that most persons begin at fertilization, is raised by those who contend, on the basis of certain facts (or alleged facts), that the thesis in question is unreasonable and that it is simply not possible for *individual human persons to come to be prior to implantation.*

The two major facts appealed to in support of this claim are the following: (1) the enormous "wastage" of life prior to implantation and (2) the phenomenon of monozygotic twins (triplets, etc.) and the possibility of "fusion" or recombination of two or more zygotic individuals into a different individual prior to implantation. As I will now show, the first of these alleged "facts" is highly questionable. The second raises some difficulties but definitely does *not*, as those who appeal to it claim, "rebut" the idea that human personal life begins at conception.

(1) The question of "wastage": Some people, mainly Catholic theologians, contend that the loss or wastage of "fertilized eggs," "zygotes," "blastocysts" and other clusters of human genetic cells prior to implantation is so vast that it is highly unreasonable to call these entities "persons."[40] In fact, Shannon and Wolter say that "to ascribe such bungling of the [reproductive]

process [as this "wastage" implies] to an all-wise creator would seem almost sacrilegious."[41]

The argument, in brief, is this: *Major:* An all-wise and providential God would not create new human persons made in his own image and likeness and then let them die even before they can be implanted in the wombs of their mothers. *Minor:* But enormous numbers of the beings resulting from human fertilization die before they can be implanted in the womb. *Conclusion:* Therefore, it is unreasonable and even sacrilegious to call these entities persons made in the image and likeness of God.

What can be said in response? First of all, the minor can be seriously challenged. Those who pose this problem cite studies claiming that from 40 to 60 percent of all "fertilized eggs" and their progeny are "wasted" prior to implantation. But if one carefully examines the studies in question — as several scholars have done, in particular, W. Jerome Bracken, C.P.[42] — one soon discovers that most such losses are the result of such severe chromosomal defects that the individual in all likelihood lacks the proper complement of genetic material for formation of a *human* body animated by a *spiritual* soul. In other words, the "fertilized eggs" that are "wasted" were not, in a great number of cases, individual human beings to begin with because of severe abnormalities in the process of fertilization.

How about the major? We are not God, and do not know his mind. We need to remember that, for most of human history, infant mortality was very high. Would those who invoke the "fact" of "fetal wastage" to support their claim that it is unreasonable and even sacrilegious to say that individual personal life begins at conception want to deny that the millions of babies who have died in infancy were not persons and that an all-wise God would allow such "bungling" of the infancy period?

(2) The question of monozygotic "twinning" and possible "fusion" or "recombination" of zygotes: It is a fact that two or more twins (triplets, etc.) known as "monozygotic" twins, etc., can be derived from the zygote (the human baby in its unicellular stage) formed after conception/fertilization but before implantation in the womb of the mother. It is also a possibility that a human individual might form from the "fusion" or "recombination" of two original zygotes (whether this possibility has ever in fact occurred in humans is not known). This fact and this possibility have led some to conclude that it is not possible for an *individual human person* to be in existence from fertilization, and that it is impossible for individual human persons to exist prior to implantation (a process that takes place approximately two weeks *after* fertilization and after which twinning is not possible).

Many today champion this position. It has been perhaps most extensively presented by an Australian Catholic priest, Norman Ford, S.D.B., in his highly influential book *When Did I Begin? Conception of the Human Individual in History, Philosophy, and Science,*[43] and by many others, for instance, Michael Coughlan.[44]

According to Ford, Coughlan, and others who hold this position, the zygote and the very early or "pre-implantation" embryo (or, as they prefer to call it, the "pre-embryo," a term that ought not be employed, as Angelo Serra and Roberto Columbo emphasize in an important study[45]) is *genetically and biologically human* and distinct from its parents; but it is not as yet an *ontologically distinct human individual* until after "gastration," the formation of the "primitive streak," and implantation, events after which twinning and recombination cannot take place. What exists during this time of gestation, they insist, is not an ontologically distinct human individual but rather a colony of cells held together in an artificial way, each with the active potentiality and "totipotential" to become more than one human individual.

This is the basic claim made by proponents of this view. Shannon and Wolter, who adopt this view, attempt to strengthen it by appealing to the work of the biologists C. A. Bedate and R. C. Cefalo,[46] who contend that the early embryo or "pre-embryo" must receive information from the mother before a distinct human individual can begin to exist.

Before offering a definitive rebuttal to the claims made by Ford and others on the basis of the phenomenon of twinning and the possibility of recombination, I will first comment on Shannon and Wolter's assertion that the pre-implantation embryo lacks the genetic information necessary for being a distinct human individual and must receive it from its mother. This contention has been devastatingly rebutted by the embryologist Antoine Suarez, who shows that contemporary research into early embryonic development definitively proves that "during pregnancy the embryo does *not* receive any messages or information from the mother able to control the mechanisms of development or to produce the type of cellular differentiation necessary for building the tissues of the new human adult." To the contrary, recent empirical research supports the conclusion that "*the pre-implantation embryo is the same individual of the human species (the same animal) as the adult into whom the pre-implantation embryo can in principle develop.*"[47]

The claims made by Ford and others based on the phenomenon of twinning have been subjected to devastating criticism by many, including philosophers, theologians, and embryologists. Among the more incisive critiques are those given by Grisez, Lee, Ashley/Moraczewski, Nicholas Tonti-Filippini, Anthony Fisher, and Angelo Serra/Roberto Columbo.[48] Here I will summarize the principal reasons given by these authors to show that the Ford-et-al. hypothesis is untenable.

The Ford-et-al. view claims that in the early embryo (or "pre-embryo") prior to implantation, formation of the "primitive streak," etc., the various cells within the *zona pellucida* (the membrane surrounding the zygote and early embryo) are all "totipotential," i.e., each *can* become distinct individual human persons (monozygotic twins, triplets, etc.), all with the same genetic endowment. Their thesis, as we have seen, is that while this entity is *biologically and genetically human* and distinct from its parents, it is not yet an *ontologically distinct* human individual person. It is rather a *colony* of individual cells, each capable of developing into a distinct human person.

However, as embryologists such as R. Yanagimachi and Antoine Suarez note in summarizing what is scientifically known about mammalian fertilization, "fertilization in mammals normally represents the beginning of life for an individual."[49] In light of all the evidence, the claim that cell division in the early embryo actually gives rise to a colony of really distinct individuals "until a small army of them form the true human individual" is not at all plausible.[50] Ford and those who agree with him think that the individual cells within the early embryo have the *active* potentiality to become individual human beings — and if so, then they would so develop unless some accident prevented such development. But they do not have such "active" potentiality; their "totipotentiality" is not "active" but hypothetical. It is hypothetical because for it to be actualized some extrinsic cause must separate the individual cells within the pre-implantation embryo. We can grant that during the early stages of its development (i.e., prior to implantation) the individual cells of the embryo are as yet relatively unspecialized and therefore *can* become whole human organisms *IF* they are divided and have an appropriate environment after division. But, as Patrick Lee points out, "this does not in the least indicate that prior to such an extrinsic division the embryo is an aggregate rather than a single, multicellular organism," and one identifiably of the human species, distinct from other members of the species.[51]

The crucial question raised by such phenomena as monozygotic twinning and possible recombination is this: Do they, *of themselves*, demonstrate that the "ontological" human individual comes into being only after implantation? The attempts to demonstrate this by Ford and others are very implausible and rest on the presupposition, not credible, that the individual cells within the *zona pellucida* surrounding the early embryo have the *active* potentiality to become individual human persons. But if they did have an *active* potency of this kind, then they would *all* become individual persons, and this is absurd. Thus, as Grisez says, "contrary to what Ford asserts (without argument), in those zygotes which develop continuously as individuals the facts do not evidence an *active* potentiality to develop otherwise. Rather, at most the facts show that all early embryos could *passively* undergo division or recombination."[52]

In short, the argument that individual human persons *cannot* begin at fertilization because of such phenomena as identical twinning is based on appearances and alleged common sense, but it fails to prove what it claims to prove. It is far more likely, as Ashley/Moraczewski and others argue, that identical twinning is a developmental accident and that the coming into being of identical twins can be explained reasonably as a mode of asexual reproduction (cloning).[53]

Twinning and similar facts in no way compel us to conclude that individual human persons do not begin to be at conception/fertilization. It is possible that *some* human individuals begin to be between fertilization and implantation, but *most* human individuals do come to be at fertilization/conception; it is reasonable to hold that they do and unreasonable to claim that they do not. I believe that this section of this chapter has provided evidence and arguments to support the truth of this proposition.

4. The Special Moral Gravity of Abortion, a Woman's "Right" to Abortion, the Difference Between a "Right" and a "Liberty"

Here I will first reflect on the unique moral gravity of abortion. I will then comment on some of the principal arguments, passionately advanced, by those who claim that a woman has a "right" to abortion, and conclude by considering the crucial difference between a "right" and a "liberty" and the relevance of this distinction to the issue of abortion.

A. The Unique Moral Gravity of Abortion

Abortion, as we have seen, is the intentional killing of an innocent human person. As we saw in Chapter Two, the intentional killing of *any* innocent human person is an intrinsically evil act insofar as it is utterly opposed to *love* of the person made in the image and likeness of God. But the intentional killing of unborn human children and of infants has a unique kind of gravity. Human life, the life of human persons, is a magnificent gift from God, a truth that John Paul II develops eloquently in Chapter Two of his encyclical *Evangelium vitae*. Although we saw this in detail in Chapter Two, it is useful here to summarize what he had to say there and elsewhere.

Human life, the Pope reminds us, is surpassingly good because "the life which God gives man is quite different from the life of all other living creatures, inasmuch as man, although formed from the dust of the earth (cf. Gn 2:7; 3:19; Jb 34:15; Ps 103:14; Ps 104:29), *is a manifestation of God in the world, a sign of his presence, a trace of his glory* (cf. Gn 1:26-27; Ps 8:6)" (*Evangelium vitae*, no. 34). Human life indeed is the " 'place' where God manifests himself, where we meet him and enter into communion with him" (no. 38). This great truth is immeasurably deepened and enriched by the incarnation of God's only-begotten Son, his uncreated Word, who for love of us became, like us, God's "created word." And his Son, Jesus, has made known to us not only who we are — God's created "words," his living images — but also who we are meant to be! As John Paul II reminds us, "Eternal life . . . is the life of God himself," and at the same time "is *the life of the children of God* (cf. 1 Jn 3:1-2). . . . *Here the Christian truth about [human] life becomes most sublime.* The dignity of this life is linked not only to its beginning, to the fact that it comes from God, but also to its final end, to its destiny of fellowship with God in knowledge and love of him" (no. 38).

God so loves us and wills that we share in his creative work that he entrusts to us in a special way the gift of new human life. This life, as the Pope reminds us, is entrusted "to each and every other human being." "But," he continues, it "is entrusted in a special way . . . to woman, precisely because the woman, in virtue of her special experience of motherhood, is seen to have a *specific sensitivity* towards the human person and all that constitutes the individual's true welfare, beginning with the fundamental value of life."[54] New human life comes to be in and through the intimate union of man and woman (a union honored, as we saw in Chapter Three, only when *marital*). In its beginnings, this life is particularly vulnerable and dependent on others for its well-being. It is a gift to be welcomed and received with love, as each one of us knows. How grateful we must be if the man and the woman who gave us life welcomed our coming! And how sad it must be should one come to know that they did not, even if they did not kill one in the womb. Yes, the intentional killing of children, and in particular unborn children — and each one of us was, when we came into existence, an unborn child — has a particular gravity, a betrayal, as it were, of a sacred trust committed to our care. We must remember that God's eternal Word, his only-begotten Son, became man — became truly one of us — as a helpless and utterly dependent unborn child in the womb of his mother. He is one with unborn children in the wombs of their mothers.[55]

Unfortunately, many today, because of the contraceptive/abortifacient culture in which we live, fail to realize this truth or to take it into account. But it *is* a truth, one we must have the courage to face, even as we seek to care compassionately for women who experience pregnancies "unwanted" for one reason or another.

B. A Woman's "Right" to an Abortion

In our society, many claim today that a woman has a "right" to an abortion. It will be, I think, worthwhile to consider some of the major arguments given to support this claim, and then to show why they are not good arguments. In the final section of this part, I will show that the alleged "right" to an abortion is not a right at all but rather a supposed "liberty," one that cannot be genuine insofar as it is nonexistent in view of the unborn child's authentic "right" to life.

As Sidney Callahan remarks in an interesting essay,[56] the most highly developed feminist arguments for the morality and legality of abortion can be found in Beverly Wildung Harrison's *Our Right to Choose* (Boston: Beacon Press, 1983) and Rosalind Pollack Petchesky's *Abortion and Woman's Choice* (New York: Longmans, 1984). Callahan identifies four major strands of argumentation. Of these, the one dependent on the claim that the unborn child cannot be regarded a person has already been sufficiently rebutted. Another, claiming that abortion is necessary if women are to be considered socially equal to men, simply avoids facing the basic questions. The other two lines of argument, however, are very popular, somewhat more plausible, and appeal to many people today. They should therefore be confronted, the truth they inadequately express acknowledged, and their specious character identified.

The two arguments in question are: (1) the woman's moral right to control her own body, and (2) the moral necessity of autonomy and choice in personal integrity. The first claims that in choosing an abortion a woman is simply exercising a basic right of bodily integrity. If she does not choose to be pregnant, she should not be compelled to be so against her will. It is *her* body that is involved, and intimately so. If no one can be compelled to donate an organ to another or to submit to other invasive procedures on his or her own body for however noble a cause, why should women be so compelled just because they happen to become pregnant? This would seem especially the case, as another feminist author, Judith Jarvis Thomson, claimed in a celebrated essay originally published in 1970,[57] if the woman has taken precautions not to become pregnant by using an effective contraceptive. The alternatives, on this argument, are these: either *compulsory pregnancy* or the right to terminate a pregnancy, i.e., have an abortion. Of these two alternatives, this argument contends, the second is obviously the right moral one, for it alone recognizes the woman's right to bodily integrity.

The second argument holds that in order for a woman to be a full adult in the moral sense, not only does she have a right to *bodily* integrity but also to make and keep commitments and determine her own lifestyle. In order to do this, she must have control over reproduction, because if she does not she is not capable of keeping prior and present commitments, and/or of making future ones, particularly in the areas of family, work, and education. A right to abortion is integral to a woman's adult, mature responsibility and autonomy.[58]

With respect to the first argument, it simply refuses to take into consideration the truth that abortion affects the body and bodily integrity of the unborn child, whose life is destroyed by it, far more than it does the body and bodily integrity of his or her mother. As Callahan so well says in her critique of this argument, during pregnancy "one's own body no longer exists as a single unit but is engendering another organism's life. This dynamic passage from conception to birth is genetically ordered and universally found in the human species. Pregnancy is not like the growth of a cancer or infestation by a biological parasite; it is the way every human being comes into the world. Strained philosophical analogies fail to apply: having a baby is not like rescuing a drowning person, being hooked up to a famous violinist's artificial life-support system,[59] donating organs for transplant — or anything else."[60]

Proponents of this argument are correct in saying that civil law protects, and rightly so, one's own bodily integrity and considers as a crime against the person any invasions of that person's body without free and personal consent. This is the kernel of truth in the argument that gives it some plausibility. But the same civil law clearly and rightly holds that it is wrong and criminal to intentionally harm the bodies, bodily integrity, and lives of *other persons*, of other *bodies*. Although the protection that civil law thus affords has been unjustly removed from the unborn, it clearly recognizes the difference between invasive procedures affecting one's own body and attacks on the body of another. Thus the argument is specious.

The second major argument advanced by feminists is rooted in the individualistic understanding of human autonomy so prevalent in our culture, an understanding that refuses to recognize that human persons can exist only within a community of persons, and that our freedom to choose is not independent of the truth and is not the same as the autonomy to determine what is right and what is wrong (cf. Chapters One and Two). The truth it contains, making it somewhat plausible, is that we must make commitments in our lives and be faithful to them. But these commitments, which are particular choices affecting broad areas of our lives, must themselves be morally good and in accord with the truth, and we may have to set some aside, once made, in the light of moral responsibilities which we have either freely taken upon ourselves or which have been placed on us (e.g., caring for an injured person when we are the only ones able to do so, even if this means sacrificing something worthwhile in itself).

C. The Difference Between a "Right" and a "Liberty"

There is a great deal of talk in our society today about "rights." As we have seen, many claim that a woman has a "right" to an abortion; pro-lifers, on the other hand, claim that the unborn child has a "right" to life. How is it possible to distinguish between authentic rights and alleged rights? I believe that the distinction between a right in the strict sense or a "claim right" and a "liberty" or a "liberty right" is most helpful here. In what follows, I will paraphrase and to some extent simplify the brilliant discussion of this matter presented by John Finnis in chapter 8 of his *Natural Law and Natural Rights*.[61]

Very frequently, particular in popular discussions (as on TV talk shows, etc.), people talk about rights as two-term relations between persons and one subject-matter or *thing* (e.g., a woman's right to an abortion, an innocent person's right to life, a worker's right to a just wage, a smoker's right to smoke, etc.). In order to distinguish a right in the strict sense, or what can be called a "claim right," from a liberty or a "liberty right," it is necessary to speak of a three-term relationship between two persons (or groups of persons) and an act of a specific type. If we do so, we can speak of a claim-right as follows:

> *A* (= a person or group of persons, or all persons if we are speaking of basic human and inalienable rights of human persons) has a

right (a "claim right") that *B* (= another person or group of persons or all persons) should *x* (= some specifiable act), if and only if *B* has a *duty* to *A* to *x*.

To illustrate: Innocent human persons (= A) have a *right* in the sense of a claim right to life if and only if innocent human persons (= A) have a right that all other persons (= B) have a duty to innocent human persons (= A) to forbear from intentionally killing them (= x). In other words, the right of innocent human persons to life, if genuine, means that all other persons have an obligation or duty *not to kill them* intentionally. Applying this to unborn children, we can say: Unborn children have a strict right or claim right to life if, and only if, unborn children (= A) have a right that their mothers and other persons (= B) have a duty to unborn children *to forbear from aborting them, i.e., intentionally killing them* (= x). And, as we have seen already, this right is genuine because all persons, including mothers, have a strict obligation or duty to forbear from intentionally killing innocent human persons, and abortion is the intentional killing of an innocent human person.

Note that with respect to a right in the strict sense, a claim right, the action in question is required, not of the right-holder, but of other persons. With reference to the right to life, the action required is first and foremost an act of forbearance (of refusal to kill intentionally) required of all who must respect this right. With respect to abortion, the action in question is not an action of the unborn, but an action of others (mothers, etc.) and is again an act of forbearance, of refusing intentionally to kill the unborn by aborting them.

What about the alleged "right" of a woman to an abortion? If we express this, not as a two-term relationship between a person (a woman) and a thing (an abortion), but in a three-term relationship between two persons and a specifiable action, we see that the alleged right is really a "liberty" claimed by women. It can be put generally as follows:

B (= a person, group of persons, etc.) has a *liberty* relative to *A* (= a person, a group of persons, etc.) to *x* (= some specifiable act), if and only if *A* has no claim right that *B* should not *x*.

Translating this talk about the woman's alleged "right" to an abortion into this language, we have the following: A woman (= *B*) has a liberty relative to the unborn baby (= *A*) intentionally to abort it (= *x*) if and only if the unborn baby (= *A*) has no claim right that the woman (= *B*) should not abort it (= *x*). But, as we have seen, the unborn has the claim right that his or her mother (and others) forbear from aborting it. Consequently, the liberty (and not right) claimed by women to abort is spurious.

There are, of course, many genuine liberties or "liberty rights," e.g., the right to worship God, the right of persons of the opposite sex to marry and have children, etc.

5. Abortion as "Removal" vs. Abortion as "Killing"

Patrick Lee puts the title of the fourth chapter of his excellent book on abortion in the form of a question: "Is abortion justified as nonintentional killing?" In it he examines the view that abortions, or at least many of them, can be justified because they are not intentional killings of innocent human persons but are rather to be regarded as "indirect" abortions, or abortions that are not intended. As we have seen, the Magisterium condemns procured or "direct" abortion, i.e., acts in which the abortion is intended either as end or as means, but recognizes that under certain conditions one can rightly engage in an act which has abortion as a foreseen, even inevitable, yet unintended effect. In such instances, the abortion is unintended or nonintended.

If abortion is *defined* as the "removal" or "expulsion" of a living but not yet viable unborn child from the womb of his or her mother, then the question posed by Lee as the title of his chapter is intelligible, for it is at least conceivable that some "removals" or "expulsions" of a living but not yet viable unborn child from his or her mother's womb might not have as its moral object, either as end or as means, the killing or death of the unborn child. Assume, for the sake of argument, that the unborn child in the womb of a woman diagnosed with cancer of the uterus could be removed from her womb and placed in an artificial womb for the three months necessary for it to become viable. The woman is in danger of dying from the cancer, and traditionally Roman Catholic moralists (and the Magisterium) would justify the woman's having a hysterectomy or undergoing chemotherapy to protect her from dying of cancer even though it was foreseen that the unborn child would die as a result of the hysterectomy or chemotherapy. The reasoning was that the "removal" of the child from the mother's womb — the abortion itself — and consequent death were not "directly intended" but only foreseen as unavoidable but not intended effects of the hysterectomy or chemotherapy. It seems obvious that it would be far better, if it were possible, to save the life of the unborn child in such instances by "removing" him or her from the mother's womb to an artificial womb than to "allow" him or her to die as a foreseen but nonintended result of the chemotherapy or hysterectomy. But one would, in this instance, definitely *intend* the "removal" of the unborn child from the mother's womb; one could not *not* intend this. Thus, if abortion is defined as "removal," then it seems that in at least some instances (like the hypothetical one I just gave) a "direct abortion" would be morally justifiable. This is the kind of issue with which Lee is concerned, and I will reflect on his treatment of this issue below.

But before doing so, it seems only obvious to note that if we *define* abortion as the *intentional killing of an innocent unborn child*, then it is not possible to distinguish between abortion as "removal" and abortion as "killing." If abortion is *defined* as the *intentional **killing** of an unborn child*, then directly intended *removals* of the unborn from their mothers' wombs cannot be considered *abortions*, **if** the *killing or death of the unborn* is intended neither as end nor as means, i.e., is not intended at all. But, as we have seen and as I emphasized in the first section of this chapter, Pope John Paul II in *Evangelium vitae* defines abortion as the *intentional killing of the unborn*. I will return to the relevance of this. I will begin, however, by summarizing and reflecting on Patrick Lee's analysis.

A. Lee's Analysis and Position

The question Lee poses is whether direct abortions, or at least many abortions (understood as removing or expelling nonviable unborn children from their mother's wombs), can be justified because they are nonintentional killings of innocent human persons.

He notes that this line of justifying abortions (or most abortions) was developed by Judith Jarvis Thomson in her celebrated "In Defense of Abortion" article,[62] and Lee's first concern is to reject her claim that the great majority of abortions can be justified as nonintentional killings. She argued that even if we grant that the unborn baby is a human person with a right to life, this does not mean that it has a right to everything it needs to support its life, particularly the use of a woman's body. According to Thomson, no woman has the right to *kill* the fetus, but no woman has the obligation to let it use her body for life support *unless* she has voluntarily assumed this duty; and, particularly if she has tried to avoid conception by using contraceptives, very frequently she has not assumed that duty. Therefore, Thomson concludes, she can expel the unborn child from her body even if she knows that it will die as a result.

In short, she argues that there is a real difference between intentional killing or securing someone's death and causing death as a side effect. Many abortions are not intentional killings because the objective of the women having them is not the securing the death of the child they are carrying; they are rather cases of causing death as a side effect of "removing" the unborn child from the womb, justifiable when one has no obligation to allow the unborn child use of one's womb and one simply wants its removal. Consequently, many abortions are morally right even if we grant that the unborn child or fetus is a person.[63]

Lee grants that the distinction between intentional killing and causing death as a side effect is valid (and I agree, as can be seen from what was said above). But he argues, and rightly so, that the great majority of abortions are intentional killings because those who procure them want to get rid of the unborn. However, he continues, even if some abortions (= "direct" abortions understood as intentional "removals" of living but not yet viable unborn children from their mothers' wombs) are not intentional killings, they are not, for the most part, morally justified. He then distinguishes two types of abortion cases that are not (or at least need not be) intentional killings and in which the mother's life is not significantly in danger. In one type of case, the man and the woman freely choose to have sex, realizing that by doing so the woman can conceive (even if they use contraceptives). In such a case, even if one grants that the "object" of the abortion is not the securing of the child's death but its "removal" so that the woman could, for instance, maintain her figure, "removing" it and thereby "causing its death" as a foreseen side effect is gravely immoral because, Lee writes, "(a) they have a specific duty to the child because they placed him or her in that dependent relationship, and (b) the harm caused to the child is immensely worse than the harm that the woman (and others involved) is avoiding by having the abortion." In a second type of case, abortion is performed because of rape or incest. Here (a) does not apply, but because of (b) and other factors, such as the unborn child's innocence and the moral significance of the mother's biological relationship to it, abortion is not morally justified here either, even if it is not an instance of intentional killing but rather of intentional removal. It is not morally justified because it is grossly unjust and unfair and thus violates the moral principle of fairness or the Golden Rule in a serious way.[64]

Lee thus concludes that in the great majority of cases, one cannot justify direct abortion as "removal" rather than as "killing' because the death of the unborn child can and ought to be prevented; there are grave moral reasons why "allowing" its death would be seriously immoral.[65] But Lee then goes on to argue that in cases in which the mother's life is significantly in danger, then permitting the death of the unborn child as a foreseen but not intended side effect of its removal could be morally justifiable. It is so, he says, "if the choice to save the mother rather than the child is fair" — for example, if both cannot be saved — because in such cases "it seems that it would be causing the child's death as a side effect and with a grave reason to do so." Lee says that he has no *philosophical* objections against (direct) abortion, understood as "removal" and not as "killing," in such cases, but in a footnote he advises his readers to follow the teaching of the Church if the act is against Catholic teaching.[66]

B. Critique

It is thus evident that Lee thinks that some abortions, clearly *intended* and hence "direct," can be justified in very special cases when necessary to save the mother's life as "removals" causing the death of the unborn child as a foreseen but *not intended* effect of its removal and an effect that one can rightly "permit." His position was set forth originally by Grisez (whom Lee follows on this matter) in his 1970 massive study, *Abortion: The Myths, the Realities, and the Arguments*. Grisez applied St. Thomas Aquinas's analysis of killing in self-defense,[67] the classic source for the principle of double effect, to some sorts of procedures, for instance craniotomies and salpingostomies, that Catholic moral theologians — who, as we have seen at the beginning of this chapter, *defined* abortion as the "expulsion" of a living but not yet viable unborn child from the womb — considered "direct" abortions and therefore intrinsically immoral. Grisez argued (as does Lee in his book) that under certain conditions when such procedures are used, the death of the unborn child need be neither the end intended nor the means chosen and that, therefore, it is possible to regard the evil done by these procedures, namely, the death of the unborn child, as not intended and therefore justifiable.[68] As did Lee later, Grisez maintained that this was a position he had reached as a philosopher, but that, should Catholic teaching judge otherwise, Catholics like himself were not at liberty to set that teaching aside and act on the basis of his analysis.[69]

As indicated at the very beginning of this section, when I considered the possibility of "removing" an unborn child from the womb of a mother about to undergo a hysterectomy or chemotherapy (to save her life from cancer) to an artificial womb, I think that the distinction between abortion as "killing" and abortion as "removal" is a valid distinction, and is relevant to the issue of abortion when it is *defined* as the removal or expulsion of a nonviable fetus from the mother's body, and that if abortion is defined is this way, then some "direct" abortions are, at least in principle, justifiable. It is obvious, however, that if "direct" abortion, i.e., abortion intended either as end or as chosen means, is *defined* — as it is by Pope John Paul II — as the "killing" of an innocent unborn person, then all "direct" abortions are gravely immoral and in no way justifiable.

In the first edition, I rejected the defense offered by Grisez, Boyle, and Lee of craniotomy as an example of abortion as "removal" but not of "killing." I thought their analysis faulty; in particular, I thought their claim that the "object" morally specifying the act was to alter or change the dimensions of the baby's skull was simply a specious way of "redescribing" the act. I thus accepted the critique of their argument by Kevin Flannery, S.J.

I have since changed my mind. Before describing why I did, it is important, I think, to describe what a craniotomy is. The following description of it was sent to me by e-mail on October 20, 2007, by a great pro-life Catholic obstetrician-gynecologist, John Bruchalski, M.D.:

> The technical definition of a craniotomy is the surgical procedure where the physician creates a hole in the cranium (crani-otomy). The most common practical situation would be when a pre-born child has water on the brain, hydrocephalus. In that case the craniotomy is accomplished by an 18g needle[,] where the skull is punctured and fluid drained to decompress the child's skull enough to affect vaginal delivery. *The intent in that case is to affect delivery[,] not to kill the child* [my emphasis]. In a D&X abortion [= partial-birth abortion], the craniotomy is to kill the child and enable the delivery of the head. Today, a cesarean section would be done in most cases to safely deliver the child and "save" the mother's life in most medical situations. The intention of doing a craniotomy with anything other than a needle is the death of a child to save the mother's life. Craniotomy is the direct, intended destruction of the child in most medical cases where it is recommended as a therapy for delivery to protect the life of the mother. Cesarean sections are able to be done safely and quickly.[70]

It now seems to me that Boyle, in essence, put the matter correctly in a passage cited and criticized in the first edition. Boyle pointed out that in the case under consideration "the death of the fetus in no way contributes to the continuation of labor and thus to saving the mother's life, and thus the bringing about of this effect just as such is not a means to these ends. . . .

[I]t is not the *killing* which removes the threat; the means here appears to be the craniotomy itself insofar as it alters the dimensions of the skull *in order to* allow labor to proceed. It is the dimensions of the baby's skull being altered and not its being dead which saves the mother's life." I have also been led to change my mind by studying the article jointly published in *The Thomist*, in January 2001, by John Finnis, Germain Grisez, and Joseph Boyle, entitled " 'Direct' and 'Indirect': A Reply to Critics of Our Action Theory."

There they show that both Thomas Aquinas (cf. *In II Sent.* d. 40, a. 2, c and ad 2-3, *De Malo*, q. 2, a. 2, ad 8, *S. T.* 2-2, q. 64, a. 7, *In V Metaphysics*, lect. 2, no. 9) and John Paul II (*Veritatis splendor*, no. 78) make it clear that the object morally specifying a human act *cannot be identified with a process or an event in the physical order* (what Thomas called the *natural species* of an act as distinct from its *moral* species) but is rather precisely what the acting person is *choosing to do* here and now, and that this object can be grasped only from the perspective of that acting person. It is thus possible that the very same physical performance, e.g., a craniotomy in its *natural species*, can be, if viewed *from the perspective of the acting person*, either the choice to engage in a partial-birth abortion (a morally bad object of choice) or the choice to reduce the size of the baby's head so that it or its corpse can be removed from the birth canal (an object of choice not in itself immoral), foreseeing as a nonintended side effect the death of the child, a death that could be accepted under the principle of double effect.

Finnis, Grisez, and Boyle respond to the charge that the Magisterium has condemned their view by acknowledging that toward the end of the nineteenth century the Holy Office (now the Congregation for the Doctrine of the Faith) issued three documents concerning craniotomies. But, they emphasize, "*none of these documents taught that craniotomies are intentional killings or morally wrong.*" But those documents did declare that one might not *teach* that craniotomies could be done and that craniotomies cannot safely be done. Our authors then write: "However, since the Holy Office did not assert that craniotomy is immoral, its responses cannot ground an argument against a position such as ours," inserting a footnote in which they write: "Our position is shared by some theologians completely faithful to the Church's magisterium, e.g., Marcellino Zalba, S.J." — Zalba, I want to note, was a member of the minority commission of the "papal birth control commission" that defended the Church's teaching against contraception prior to *Humanae vitae*, and subsequently heroically defended *Humanae vitae* and as a result suffered terribly.

Finnis, Grisez, and Boyle affirm that they regard as a truth of faith the Church's teaching that the intentional killing of the unborn is *always gravely immoral*. Their position, however, is that "a doctor could do a craniotomy, even one emptying a baby's skull, without intending to kill the baby — that is, without the craniotomy being a direct killing." Here they insert another footnote in which they acknowledge that *even if such killing is not directly intended or direct killing it could often be gravely wrong and that there might be reasons for condemning the practice of craniotomy other than that it is direct killing and that Catholics who reject their opinion certainly ought to form their consciences in the light of Church teaching in the light of faith.*[71]

I have come to accept their argument that a craniotomy could indeed *not* be a direct, intentional killing of the unborn and that its death could be accepted as a nonintended but foreseen consequence of an act not morally bad in itself. However, so far as I know, the Magisterium, although not declaring craniotomy in the case envisioned to be morally wrong, nonetheless still teaches that it is *not safe to teach* that craniotomies can be performed and also that *craniotomies are not safe*. Since neither our authors nor I have the right to instruct the faithful, whereas the Magisterium has both the right and the duty, I conclude this part of this chapter by citing an important passage from Grisez's 1970 massive and superb defense of the unborn, *Abortion: The Myths, the Realities, and the Arguments* (Cleveland/New York: Corpus Instrumentorum), pp. 345-346:

> Roman Catholic readers may notice that my conclusions about abortion diverge from common theological teachings, and also diverge from the official teaching of the Church as it was laid down by the Holy Office in the nineteenth century. I am aware of the divergence, but would point out that my theory is consonant with the more important and more formally definite teaching that direct killing of the unborn is wrong. I reach conclusions that are not traditional by broadening the meaning of "unintended" in a revision of the principle of double effect, not by accepting the rightness of direct killing or the violability of unborn life because of any ulterior purpose or indication.

He then continues:

> Most important, I cannot as a philosopher limit my conclusions by theological principles. However, I can as a Catholic propose my philosophic conclusions as suggestions for consideration in the light of faith, while not proposing anything contrary to the Church's teaching as a

practical norm of conduct for my fellow believers. *Those who really believe that there exists on this earth a community whose leaders are appointed and continuously assisted by God to guide those who accept their authority safely through time to eternity, would be foolish to direct their lives by some frail fabrication of mere reason instead of by conforming to a guidance system designed and maintained by divine wisdom.* (emphasis added)

I want to note here that Martin Rhonheimer, in a book scheduled for publication by The Catholic University of America Press in 2008, *Killing in Vital Conflicts*, also claims that craniotomies to save the mother's life do not violate the virtue of justice and hence are not morally wrong.

6. The Management of Ectopic Pregnancies

Currently, there is a debate among non-dissenting Catholic theologians regarding the legitimacy of different methods of managing ectopic pregnancies, specifically tubal pregnancies. Before taking up this debate, I will briefly describe ectopic pregnancies, their frequency, and current medical procedures available for their management. I will also summarize relevant material from the *Ethical and Religious Directives for Catholic Health Care Services* promulgated by the bishops of the United States in November 1994.

A. Ectopic Pregnancies and Their Frequency

An ectopic ("out of place," from the Greek *ek*, out of, and *topos*, place) pregnancy occurs when a developing new human person does not implant in the uterus, where it belongs, but elsewhere in the mother's body, usually in the fallopian tube or, more rarely, in the ovary, the cornua, the abdomen, or the cervix. Such pregnancies pose serious risks to the mother's life because of the danger of hemorrhage. During the last thirty years, there has been an alarming increase in the number of ectopic, and particularly tubal, pregnancies. The principal factors responsible for this increase include the alarmingly growing number of sexually transmitted diseases, especially pelvic inflammatory disease, tubal sterilization, the use of intrauterine devices or progesterone contraceptive pills, and *in vitro* fertilization.[72]

B. Medically Available Procedures for Coping With Ectopic Pregnancies

Medical authorities recognize four major treatment procedures for managing ectopic pregnancies: (1) "expectant" therapy; (2) drug therapy;

(3) conservative surgical treatment; and (4) radical surgical treatment.[73] (1) "Expectant" therapy simply means that nothing is done and one simply waits for the tubal pregnancy to resolve itself by spontaneous abortion or miscarriage. This may occur in as many as 64 percent of the cases. (2) Drug therapy involves the uses of methotrexate (MTX). MTX interferes with the synthesis of DNA and resolves tubal pregnancies by attacking the trophoblast, i.e., the outer layer of cells produced by the developing baby, connecting it to its mother. According to the scientific literature, actively proliferating trophoblastic tissue "is exquisitely sensitive to this effect [interference with the synthesis of DNA], which forms the rationale for its use in the treatment of ectopic pregnancies."[74] Under (3), "conservative surgical treatment," are included (a) partial salpingectomy or removal of the portion of the fallopian tube *affected* by the tubal pregnancy, i.e., that portion of the tube containing the tubal pregnancy, with subsequent resectioning of the fallopian tube and (b) salpingostomy, procedures in which an incision is made in the affected part of the fallopian tube and the developing embryo is extracted, along with portions of the fallopian tube itself, by the use of forceps or other instruments.[75] (4) "Radical surgical treatment" is necessary if the fallopian tube has ruptured and consists in a total salpingectomy or the removal of the entire affected fallopian tube and, with it, the unborn child.[76]

C. The Ethical and Religious Directives

In the 1971 set of *Ethical and Religious Directives for Catholic Health Care Facilities*, the bishops of the United States included the following directive, no. 16:

> In extrauterine pregnancy the affected part of the mother (e.g., cervix, ovary, or fallopian tube) may be removed, even though fetal death is foreseen, provided that (a) the affected part is presumed already to be so damaged and dangerously affected as to warrant its removal, and that (b) the operation is not just a separation of the embryo or fetus from its site within the part (which would be a direct abortion from a uterine appendage) and that (c) the operation cannot be postponed without notably increasing the danger to the mother.[77]

This directive clearly authorizes as morally licit the use of partial salpingectomy or total salpingectomy in order to safeguard the mother's life when there is grave danger of hemorrhaging from the fallopian-tube pregnancy. But it also clearly excludes use of a salpingostomy. At the time this directive was written, the management of tubal pregnancies by methotrexate was not known.

Yet the relevant directive in the 1994 *Ethical and Religious Directives for Catholic Health Care Services* is markedly different. It says simply: "In case of extrauterine pregnancy, no intervention is morally licit which constitutes a direct abortion" (no. 48).[78] But, theologians now ask, what constitutes a "direct abortion" in the management of tubal pregnancies?

D. Current Debates Over Management of Ectopic Pregnancies

In the first edition, I maintained that the salpingectomy was the only morally permissible, non-abortifacient way of coping with a tubal pregnancy. I rejected as abortifacient and hence immoral both salpingostomy and the use of methotrexate, repudiating the position defended by Albert Moraczewski, Patrick Clark, and others.[79]

I have since changed my mind and now accept the view held by Moraczewski and others. I have also now come to regard the use of salpingostomy and methotrexate as ways of coping with tubal pregnancies as "abortions as removal" and not as "abortion as killing," since the object specifying the act is not to kill the unborn child but to remove it from its place within the mother. Christopher Kaczor offers a good analysis of this matter, writing that

> removing the embryo from the fallopian tube in itself *is not* simply the same thing as intentionally killing. Although there is not yet an established procedure for facilitating this transfer, one can hope that advances in microsurgery and early detection of ectopic pregnancy would render possible both a preservation of embryonic human life as well as the reproductive capability of the fallopian tube. I believe that the removal of the embryo from its pathological site of implantation . . . is *implicitly* recognized as a morally good or indifferent action, considered by itself and independently of its effects (condition 1 of double effect), even by those who condemn these procedures. A number of respected ethicists who vigorously oppose removing the embryo alone, including William E. May, Eugene F. Diamond, Thomas Hilgers, and Kelly Bowring, nevertheless endorse efforts at embryo transplantation from the fallopian tube to the uterus. But such transplantation necessarily involves detaching the embryo from its location in the fallopian tube — which, if truly evil in itself and not merely from its effects, would be an act that is intrinsically evil and therefore never to

be performed regardless of the consequences. So at least implicitly, these authors do not hold that detaching the embryo from its pathological location in itself is intrinsically evil (or they should — to be consistent — condemn as intrinsically evil any effort to transplant an ectopic pregnancy into the uterus).[80]

Kaczor holds that the trophoblast is *not* a vital organ of the embryo. With Patrick Lee I disagree with him on this, but this is not central to justifying the procedure as removal and not intentional killing.

Conclusion to Chapter Five

This lengthy chapter has examined in detail the issue of abortion and respect for human life and its dignity. Human life is truly a gift, and a surpassing one at that, from God himself. It is indeed the "place" where we encounter God in our everyday lives. It is a *good of the person*, not a mere good **for** the person. If we are to love God, we must love our neighbor; and if we are to love our neighbor, we must respect the good of his or her life; and our neighbor includes the unborn child hidden in his or her mother's body (or, perhaps, in Petri dishes), no matter how small he or she may be. We ought never adopt by choice the proposal to take his or her life, to kill him or her. To intentionally kill an innocent person is always gravely immoral; to intentionally kill the innocent unborn is particularly heinous because of their utter dependence on others for the continuance of their existence. Their inviolable right to life makes no sense if adult members of the human species do not have the absolute obligation to forbear from intentionally killing them. But, as I have argued, all adult members of the human species have this obligation. In a certain way, the innocent unborn symbolize their adult brothers and sisters, for the latter must admit that, at one time, they, too, were "innocent unborn" human persons.

ENDNOTES FOR CHAPTER FIVE

1.   On this, see the helpful essay by Angel Rodriguez Luño, "La valutazione teologico-morale dell'aborto," in *Commento Interdisciplinare alla "Evangelium Vitae,"* under the direction and coordination of Ramon Lucas Lucas, Italian edition by Elio Sgreccia and Ramon Lucas Lucas (Vatican City: Libreria Editrice Vaticana, 1997), p. 419. As examples of older moral

manuals defining abortion as the expelling of a living but not yet viable fetus from the mother's womb, Luño refers to those by D. M. Pruemmer and H. Noldin.

In his *Manuale Theologiae Morale* (Friburgi Brisg./Rome: Herder, 1961), vol. 2, no. 137, Pruemmer defined abortion as "*eiectio immaturi foetus viventis ex utero matris*" (expelling of an immature living fetus from the mother's womb). In his *Summa Theologiae Moralis* (Oeniponte-Lipsiae: P. Rauch, 1941), vol. 2, no. 342, Noldin offered a similar definition, "*foetus abortus est eiectio immaturi ex utero matris*" (abortion is the expelling of an immature fetus from its mother's womb).

2. See Chapter One, above, pp. 27-28.

3. On this, see, for example, Germain Grisez, *Abortion: The Myths, the Realities, and the Arguments* (New York/Cleveland: Corpus Instrumentorum, 1970), pp. 137-156.

4. St. Basil the Great, *Epistles* 188, 2. *PG* 32.671. Indeed, he condemned as quibbling unworthy of Christians debates over the precise moment when the soul is infused, and in saying this he simply voiced the view of *all* the early Fathers.

5. On the Magisterium's teaching on this matter, see the excellent essay by Ignacio Carrasco de Paula, "The Respect Due to the Human Embryo: A Historical and Doctrinal Perspective," in *Identity and Statute (sic) of the Human Embryo: Proceedings of the Third Assembly of the Pontifical Academy for Life* (Vatican City, February 14-16, 1997), ed. Juan de Dios Vial Correa and Elio Sgreccia (Vatican City: Libreria Editrice Vaticana, 1998), pp. 48-74, esp. pp. 66-73. The title of the book should have "Status" where "Statute" is printed. An obvious error was made in the English version.

6. Pope Pius XII, "Address to the Biomedical Association of St. Luke," November 12, 1944, in *Discorsi e Radiomessagi di Sua Santità Pio XII* (Vatican City: Libreria Editrice Vaticana, 1945), 6 (1944-1945), p. 191; "Address to the Italian Catholic Union of Midwives," October 29, 1951, no. 2, in *Acta Apostolicae Sedis* 43 (1951), 838. In his "Address to the Biomedical Association of St. Luke" Pius had said: "We have on purpose always used the expression 'direct attack on the life of the innocent,' 'direct killing.' For if, for instance, the safety of the life of the mother-to-be, independently of her pregnant condition, should urgently require a surgical operation or other therapeutic treatment, which would have as a side effect, in no way willed or intended yet inevitable, the death of the fetus, then such an act could not any longer be called a *direct* attack on innocent life. With these conditions, the operation, like other similar medical interventions, can be allowed, always assuming that a good of great worth, such as

life, is at stake, and that it is not possible to delay until after the baby is born or to make use of some other effective remedy."

7. On this, see Chapter Two above, pp. 50-52. See also Pope John Paul II, encyclical *Veritatis splendor*, no. 78: *"The morality of the human act depends primarily and fundamentally on the 'object' rationally chosen by the deliberate will.*...The object of the act of willing is in fact a freely chosen kind of behavior. . . . By the object of a given moral act . . . one cannot mean a process or an event of the merely physical order, to be assessed on the basis of its ability to bring about a given state of affairs in the outside world. Rather, that object is the proximate end of a deliberate decision which determines the act of willing on the part of the acting person."

8. Nicanor Pier Austriaco, O.P., "On Static Eggs and Dynamic Embryos: A Systems Perspective," *The National Catholic Bioethics Quarterly* 2.4 (Winter 2002), 665.

9. Ibid, 665-666.

10. Ibid, 666.

11. Ibid, 666-667.

12. Patrick Lee and Robert George, "The First Fourteen Days of Life," *The New Atlantis* 13 (Summer 2006), 61-67.

13. Patrick Lee, *Abortion and Unborn Human Life* (Washington, DC: The Catholic University of America Press, 1997), and Robert George and Christopher Tollefsen, *Embryo: A Defense of Human Life* (New York: Doubleday, 2008). I am much indebted to Lee, George, and Tollefsen for material in the chapter.

14. Philip Wylie, *The Magic Animal* (Garden City, NY: Doubleday, 1968), p. 272. These characterizations are found in a particularly vitriolic passage, filled with invective against the notion of the sanctity of human life.

15. A claim made by the biologist Garrett Hardin, "Abortion — or Compulsory Pregnancy?" *Journal of Marriage and Family* (May 1968), 250. An obvious and insuperable difficulty with this way of describing the being in question is that it is alive and developing, whereas a blueprint is not.

16. A typical representative of this view is the late and widely influential ethicist Joseph Fletcher. See his essay, "New Beginnings of Life," in *The New Genetics and the Future of Man*, ed. Michael Hamilton (Grand Rapids: Eerdmans, 1972), p. 76. Such descriptions conceal rather than reveal the nature of the being in question.

17. This claim, made early in the twentieth century by the sexologist Havelock Ellis in his *Studies in the Psychology of Sex* (New York: 1924), 6.607, is quite common today and seems in fact to be a tenet of some leading fem-

inists. It is obviously false in view of the fact that every cell of the being that comes into existence at fertilization is identifiably quite different in nature from every cell of the mother.

18. Germain Grisez, *The Way of the Lord Jesus*, Vol. 2, *Living a Christian Life* (Quincy, IL: Franciscan Press, 1993), pp. 494-495.

19. Stephen Schwarz, *The Moral Question of Abortion* (Chicago: Loyola University Press, 1990), p. 73.

20. Ibid.

21. Marjorie Reiley Maguire, "Personhood, Covenant, and Abortion," in *Abortion and Catholicism: The American Debate*, ed. Patricia Beattie Jung and Thomas A. Shannon (New York: Crossroad, 1988), p. 109. Maguire's essay was originally published, it should be noted, in the 1983 volume of *The Annual of the Society of Christian Ethics* (Knoxville, TN: Society of Christian Ethics, 1983). Her essay, delivered at the annual convention of the Society, was among those judged worthy of publication in the Society's *Annual*. Others who hold this position include Pierre de Locht, former professor of moral theology at the Catholic University of Louvain, "Discussion," in *L'Avortement: Actes du Xieme colloque international de sexologie* (Louvain: Centre International Cardinal Suenens, 1968), 2.155; Louis Beinaert, S.J., "L'avortement est-il un infanticide?" *Etudes* 333 (1970), 520-523; Mary Warnock, "Do Human Cells Have Rights?" *Bioethics* 1 (1987), 2.

22. On this, see Grisez, "When Do People Begin?" *Proceedings of the American Catholic Philosophical Association* 63 (1989), 29; *Living a Christian Life*, p. 489.

23. See, in particular, Grisez, "When Do People Begin?" 27-47.

24. See Michael Tooley, *Abortion and Infanticide* (New York: Oxford University Press, 1983); Daniel Callahan, *Abortion: Law, Choice, and Morality* (New York: Macmillan, 1970), pp. 383-389, 497-498; Peter Singer, *Rethinking Life and Death: The Collapse of Our Traditional Ethics* (New York: St. Martin's Press, 1994).

25. See Singer, *Rethinking Life and Death*. Singer notes that the expression "speciesism," which "was coined by the Oxford psychologist Richard Ryder in 1970, has now entered the *Oxford English Dictionary*, where it is defined as 'discrimination against or exploitation of certain animal species by human beings, based on an assumption of mankind's superiority.' As the term suggests, there is a parallel between our attitudes to nonhuman animals, and the attitudes of racists to those they regard as belonging to an inferior race. In both cases, there is an inner group that justifies its exploitation of an outer group by reference to a distinction that *lacks real moral significance*" (p. 173; emphasis added). See also pp. 202-206, where Singer

elaborates on his "fifth new commandment: '*Do not discriminate on the basis of species.*'"

26. Lee, *Abortion and Unborn Human Life*, pp. 26-27, emphasis added.

27. This passage is found in a book dealing with the question of euthanasia, where debates over "personhood" similar to those over this issue in considering abortion are common. The book, authored by the members of a "Working Party" of the Linacre Centre of London, is entitled *Euthanasia, Clinical Practice and the Law*, ed. Luke Gormally (London: The Linacre Centre for Health Care Ethics, 1994), pp. 123-124. Among the members of the "Working Party," in addition to Gormally, were John Finnis and Elizabeth Anscombe.

28. Grisez, *Living a Christian Life*, p. 491; see "When Do People Begin?" 31-32. For another excellent defense of the proposition that membership in the human species is a sufficient criterion for personhood, see Lee, *Abortion and Unborn Human Life*, pp. 58-62.

29. For an excellent critique of the dualism underlying this position see Lee, *Abortion and Unborn Human Life*, pp. 32-37. See also Lee's essay, "Human Beings Are Animals," in *Natural Law and Moral Inquiry: Ethics, Metaphysics, and Politics in the Work of Germain Grisez*, ed. Robert P. George (Washington, DC: Georgetown University Press, 1998), pp. 135-151.

30. Grisez, *Living a Christian Life*, p. 490. In a footnote (no. 54), Grisez observes that both *Webster's New International Dictionary* and the *Oxford English Dictionary* say that a standard use of the term *person* is to refer to a living, human individual.

31. Grisez, *Living a Christian Life*, pp. 490-491; "When Do People Begin?" 30-31. See also *Euthanasia, Clinical Practice and the Law*, p. 41.

32. See the following: Joseph Donceel, S.J. "Immediate Animation and Delayed Hominization," *Theological Studies* 31 (1970), 76-105; Donceel, "A Liberal Catholic's View," in *Abortion and Catholicism: The American Debate*, pp. 48-53; Thomas A. Shannon and Allan B. Wolter, O.F.M., "Reflections on the Moral Status of the Pre-Embryo," *Theological Studies* 51 (1990), 603-636. Shannon and Wolter, in their efforts to rehabilitate the "delayed hominization" view, appeal to additional supposed facts made known by contemporary science.

33. For Grisez, see "When Do People Begin?" 33-34; *Living a Christian Life*, pp. 492-493. For Lee, see *Abortion and Unborn Human Life*, pp. 79-90. See also the following: Benedict Ashley, O.P., "A Critique of the Theory of Delayed Hominization," in *An Ethical Evaluation of Fetal Experimentation: An Interdisciplinary Study*, ed. Donald McCarthy (St. Louis: Pope John XXIII Medical-Moral Research and Education Center, 1976), pp.

113-133; Benedict Ashley, O.P. and Albert Moraczewski, O.P., "Is the Biological Subject of Human Rights Present from Conception?" in *The Fetal Tissue Issue*, ed. Peter Cataldo and Albert Moraczewski, O.P. (Braintree, MA: Pope John XXIII Medical-Moral Research and Education Center, 1994), pp. 33-60; Jean Siebenthal, "L'animation selon Thomas d'Aquin," in *L'Embryon: Un Homme. Actes du Congrès de Lausanne 1986* (Premier Congrès de la Societé Suisse de Bioetique 8 et 9 novembre 1986) (Lausanne: Centre de documentation civique, 1987), pp. 91-98; Mark Jordan, "Delayed Hominization: Reflections on Some Recent Catholic Claims for Delayed Hominization," *Theological Studies* 56 (1995), 743-763; Stephen J. Heaney, "Aquinas and the Presence of the Human Rational Soul in the Early Embryo," in *Abortion: A New Generation of Catholic Responses*, ed. Stephen J. Heaney (Braintree, MA: Pope John XXIII Medical-Moral Research and Education Center, 1992), pp. 43-72; Augustine Reagan, C.Ss.R., "The Human Conceptus and Personhood," *Studia Moralia* 30 (1992), 97-127.

34. Grisez, *Living a Christian Life*, pp. 492-493.

35. Siebenthal refers to the following Thomistic texts to show this: *Summa theologiae*, I, q. 118, a. 3; q. 76, a. 4 and a. 6, ad 1; III, q. 6, a. 4, ad 1; q. 2, a. 5.

36. Siebenthal, "L'animation selon Thomas d'Aquin," 96-97.

37. Among scholars who accept this view are the following: Baruch Brody, *Abortion and the Sanctity of Human Life: A Philosophical View* (Boston: Massachusetts Institute of Technology Press, 1975); Robert M. Veatch, "Definitions of Life and Death: Should There Be a Consistency?" in *Defining Human Life: Medical, Legal, and Ethical Implications*, ed. Margery W. Shaw and A. Edward Dondera (Ann Arbor, MI: AUPHA Press, 1983), pp. 99-113.

38. Lee, *Abortion and Unborn Human Life*, pp. 76-77.

39. See Grisez, "When Do People Begin?" 34; *Living a Christian Life*, pp. 493-494.

40. For this claim, see the following: Karl Rahner, S.J., "The Problem of Genetic Manipulation," in *Theological Investigations*, Vol. 9, *Writings of 1965-67: I*, tr. Graham Harrison (New York: Herder & Herder, 1972), p. 226; Lisa S. Cahill, "The Embryo and the Fetus: New Moral Contexts," *Theological Studies* 54 (1993), 124; Richard A. McCormick, S.J., "Who or What Is the Pre-embryo?" *Kennedy Institute of Bioethics Journal* 1 (1991), 3; Shannon and Wolter, "Reflections on the Moral Status of the Pre-Embryo," 618-619.

41. Shannon and Wolter, "Reflections on the Moral Status of the Pre-Embryo," 618, no. 60.

42. W. Jerome Bracken, C.P. "Is the Early Embryo a Person?" in *Life and Learning VIII: Proceedings of the Eighth University Faculty for Life Conference*, June 1998, ed. Joseph W. Koterski, S.J. (Washington, DC: University Faculty for Life, 1999), 443-467, where he cites a recent scientific study by D. Wilcox et al., "Incidence of Loss in Early Pregnancy," *The New England Journal of Medicine* 319/4 (July 28, 1988), 189-194, and others to challenge the claims frequently made.

43. Norman Ford, S.D.B., *When Did I Begin?: Conception of the Human Individual in History, Philosophy, and Science* (Cambridge/New York: Cambridge University Press, 1988).

44. Michael Coughlan, *The Vatican, the Embryo, and the Law* (Iowa City: University of Iowa Press, 1990).

45. In their superlative study, "Identity and Status of the Human Embryo: The Contributions of Biology," in *Identity and Statute (sic) of the Human Embryo*, in which they show the fatal flaws in the theory of Ford and others, Angelo Serra and Roberto Columbo note that the term "pre-embryo" was introduced into the literature in 1986 by A. McLaren. She and others (like Shannon and Wolter) who use this term claim that until approximately the fourteenth day after fertilization, all that occurs is the preparation of the protective and nutritional systems required for the future needs of the embryo, and that only at the fifteenth day after fertilization, when the "primitive streak" appears, does the embryo in the strict sense appear (see A. McLaren, "Prelude to Embryogenesis," in *Human Embryo Research: Yes or No?* the Ciba Foundation [New York: Tavistok, 1986], p. 12). Serra and Columbo, along with others, point out that the embryonic disk, which appears on the fifteenth day and to which McClaren gives such significance, is a structure "which derives from a further differentiation *of the embryoblast*, which is *already present* when the embryo as a *whole* provides, under genetic control, for a faster differentiation of the trophoblastic derivatives, which are extremely necessary for a correct and smooth progress of the body-building process. As a matter of fact," they continue, "the trophoblast and the embryoblast, both deriving from the zygote, simultaneously make their own way as a whole, according to a finely orchestrated program" (p. 167). Serra and Columbo thus conclude (with the majority of human embryologists), that it is not correct to distinguish between the so-called "pre-embryo" and the "embryo" proper. It is more scientifically accurate to speak of the "pre-implantation" embryo than of the "pre-embryo" when referring to the living human organism at the pre-implantation stage of development. It is here important to note that Ronan O'Rahilly, internationally regarded as one of the most outstanding human embryologists of our day, regards the term "pre-embryo"

as scientifically inaccurate and erroneous and refuses to use the term. See Ronan O'Rahilly and Fabiola Muller, *Human Embryology and Teratology* (New York: John Wiley & Sons, 1994), p. 55.

46. Shannon and Wolter, "Reflections on the Moral Status of the Pre-Embryo," refer to the work of C. A. Bedate and R. C. Cefalo, "The Zygote: To Be or Not to Be a Person," *Journal of Medicine and Philosophy* 14 (1989), 641-645.

47. Antoine Suarez, "Hydatidiform Moles and Teratomas Confirm the Human Identity of the Preimplantation Embryo," *Journal of Medicine and Philosophy* 15 (1990), 627. The same number of this journal carried an essay by Thomas J. Bole, III, "Zygotes, Souls, Substances, and Persons," ibid., 637-652. Bole criticized Suarez's essay on the grounds that normal zygotes have developed into partial hydatidiform moles (whereas Suarez argues that they cannot). Bole's claim, however, is contradicted by competent embryologists, for instance, Stanley J. Robboy, Marie A. Duggan, and Robert J. Kurnam, "The Female Reproductive System," *Pathology*, ed. Emmanuel Rubin and John L. Farber (2nd ed., Philadelphia: J. B. Lippincott, 1994), 967. On this, see Bracken, "Is the Early Embryo a Person?" p. 448.

48. See the following: Grisez, "When Do People Begin?" 35-40; *Living a Christian Life*, pp. 495-497; Lee, *Abortion and Unborn Human Life*, pp. 90-102; Ashley and Moraczewski, "Is the Biological Subject of Human Rights Present at Conception?" 33-60; Nicholas Tonti-Filippini, "A Critical Note," *The Linacre Quarterly* 56.3 (August 1989), 36-50; Anthony Fisher, O.P., "Individuogenesis and a Recent Book by Fr. Norman Ford," *Anthropotes: Rivista di studi sulla persona e la famiglia* 7 (1991), 199-244; Serra and Colombo, "Identity and Status of the Human Embryo: The Contribution of Biology," especially pp. 166-176.

49. R. Yanagimachi, "Mammalian Fertilization," in *The Physiology of Reproduction*, ed. E. Knobil, J. Neill et al. (New York: Raven Press, 1988), p. 135; cited by Grisez, "When Do People Begin?" 45, n. 49; *Living a Christian Life*, p. 495, n. 66. For Suarez, see his "Hydatidiform Moles..." (note 42).

50. Grisez, "When Do People Begin?" 37.

51. On this, see Lee, *Abortion and Unborn Human Life*, pp. 92-93.

52. Grisez, "When Do People Begin?" 38.

53. Ashley/Moraczewski, "Is the Biological Subject of Human Rights Present from Conception?" pp. 50-53.

54. Pope John Paul II, apostolic exhortation *Christifideles laici*, no. 51. See also his apostolic letter *Mulieris dignitatem*, no. 30: "The moral and spiritual strength of a woman is joined to her awareness that *God entrusts the human*

being to her in a special way. Of course, God entrusts every human being to each and every other human being. But this entrusting concerns women in a special way — precisely because of their femininity — and this in a particular way determines their vocation."

55. On this, see John Saward, *Redeemer in the Womb: Jesus Living in Mary* (San Francisco: Ignatius Press, 1993), in particular, pp. 165-168.

56. Sidney Callahan, "Abortion and the Sexual Agenda: A Case for Prolife Feminism," in *Abortion and Catholicism: The American Debate*, pp. 128-145, at 128-129.

57. Judith Jarvis Thomson, "In Defense of Abortion," *Philosophy and Public Affairs* (1970).

58. Here I have paraphrased Callahan's summary of these two arguments in "Abortion and the Sexual Agenda . . . ," pp. 128-129.

59. This was the analogy used by Thomson in her celebrated "defense" of abortion (cf. endnote 52).

60. Callahan, "Abortion and the Sexual Agenda . . . ," p. 131.

61. John Finnis, *Natural Law and Natural Rights* (Oxford/New York: Oxford University Press, at the Clarendon Press, 1980). Finnis's book is a volume in the Oxford Law Series. See pp. 199-205, "An Analysis of Rights Talk."

62. See endnote 57 above.

63. Here I follow Lee's summary, pp. 107-108, of Thomson's argument.

64. Ibid., pp. 113-116.

65. According to the principle of "double effect," it is permissible to "allow" or permit an evil to result from an act that is not intrinsically evil provided that this effect is not intended either as end or as means *and* that there is a "proportionate reason" for "permitting" or "allowing" the evil effect. Lee's argument is that, even if the abortions in question can legitimately be regarded as "removals" rather than "killings"— that is, the evil effect, the unborn child's death, is not intended either as end or as means — there is no "proportionate reason" for "permitting" or "allowing" the evil effect. On the contrary, there are serious moral reasons, based on justice, that require one *not* to "permit" this evil.

66. Lee, *Abortion and Unborn Human Life*, p. 116.

67. St. Thomas Aquinas, *Summa theologiae*, II-II, 64, 7.

68. Grisez, *Abortion: The Myths, the Realities, and the Arguments* (New York and Cleveland: Corpus Instrumentorum, 1970), pp. 340-346.

69. Ibid., pp. 345-346.

70. John Bruchalski, M.D., in an e-mail to William May, October 20, 2007.

71. John Finnis, Germain Grisez, and Joseph Boyle, Jr., " 'Direct' and 'Indirect': A Reply to Critics of Our Action Theory," *The Thomist* 61.1 (January 2001), 1-45.

72. John A. Rock, M.D., "Ectopic Pregnancy," in *TeLinde's Operative Gynecology* (Philadelphia: J. B. Lippincott, 1992), pp. 412-414. In 1970, approximately 17,800 ectopic pregnancies were reported in women aged 15 to 44; by 1980, the figure had risen to 52,000 women in this age group; today it is estimated that 1 pregnancy in every 60 is ectopic, with the rate increasing. It is ironic that among the causes of tubal pregnancies are *in vitro* fertilization (frequently resorted to as a way of providing children to women with blocked fallopian tubes) and the use of contraceptives.

73. Ibid., pp. 421-427.

74. J. Cannon and H. Jesionowska, "Methotrexate Treatment of Tubal Pregnancy," *Fertility and Sterility* 55 (June 1991), 1034.

75. Rock, "Ectopic Pregnancy," p. 427. See also Charles E. Cavagnaro III, "Treating Ectopic Pregnancy: A Moral Analysis," *The NaProEthics Forum* 3.6 (November 1998), 4.

76. Rock, p. 427; Cavagnaro, 4.

77. National Conference of Catholic Bishops, *Ethical and Religious Directives for Catholic Health Care Facilities* (Washington, DC: NCCB, 1971), no. 16.

78. National Conference of Catholic Bishops, *Ethical and Religious Directives for Catholic Health Care Services* (Washington, DC: NCCB, 1995), no. 48.

79. See William E. May, "The Management of Ectopic Pregnancies: A Moral Analysis," in *The Fetal Tissue Issue: Medical and Ethical Aspects*, ed. Peter J. Cataldo and Albert S. Moraczewski, O.P. (Braintree, MA: Pope John XXIII Medical-Moral Research and Education Center, 1994), pp. 121-148, esp. pp. 133-145. I believe that I was the first moral theologian to consider the use of methotrexate in the management of ectopic pregnancies.

80. Christopher Kazcor, "Ectopic Pregnancy and the Catholic Hospital," forthcoming in *Urged on By Christ: Catholic Health Care in Tension with Contemporary Culture: Proceedings of the 21st Workshop for Bishops* (Philadelphia, PA: National Catholic Bioethics Center, 2008). Professor Kazcor kindly sent me a copy of his fine article.

CHAPTER SIX

Experimentation on Human Subjects

This chapter will take up the morality of experimentation on human subjects. I will (1) introduce the topic and articulate and explain the cardinal principle governing human experimentation, namely, the principle of free and informed consent. I will then (2) examine the meaning and limits of proxy consent, in particular, proxy consent for non-therapeutic experiments to be carried out on incompetent human persons or those whom the late Paul Ramsey called "voiceless patients," and follow the analysis of this issue with a consideration of (3) research on the unborn, in particular embryo stem-cell research, (4) gene therapy, (5) prenatal and pre-implantation genetic screening, (6) genetic counseling, and (7) the human genome project.

1. Introduction: The Cardinal Principle of Free and Informed Consent[1]

One of the most unforgettable television newscasts I ever witnessed was a May 1973 CBS Special Report, "The Ultimate Experimental Animal: Man." It included a scene that struck me as especially illuminating, which well serves to introduce the question of experimenting on human beings. A black woman, who had been a prisoner in a Detroit jail, had participated in a program testing a new type of birth-control pill. This particular pill was known to the researchers to carry a high risk of causing cancer, but this fact was deliberately withheld from the women who had "volunteered" to participate in the program testing its effectiveness. When the woman learned, after her release from prison, that the pill she and other women had been taking posed a serious risk of causing cancer, she was outraged at having been "used," declaring to the CBS correspondent that she had been "treated like an animal."

Her reaction is very instructive. In saying that she had been treated like an animal and in being outraged at having been so treated, she voiced the conviction that human beings ought not to be treated like animals. She was not necessarily denying that she — with other human beings as well — is an animal (for, after all, we are); rather, she was affirming that a human being is an *animal with a difference*, an entity of moral worth, a subject of rights that demand respect and protection from the society in which one lives. She was saying, in a simple and unsophisticated way, what the philosopher Roger Wertheimer has called a "standard belief" among human beings. This is the belief that "being human has moral cachet; a human being has human status in virtue of being a human being";[2] that being a member of the human species has *moral* significance and has so because every member of the human species is a *person*, not a thing or mere animal.[3]

She was also affirming that any experiment performed on the "human animal" must, if it is to be rightly carried out, respect the truth that human beings are persons, beings of moral worth, subjects of rights rooted in their being and not conferred on them by others. She was affirming, at least implicitly, that no human being can be regarded simply a part subordinated to a larger whole, the society at large, but must be considered as a whole that cannot rightly be subordinated to the interests of others. Expressed in more philosophical terms, this woman was articulating what Karol Wojtyla called the "personalistic norm," which, "in its negative aspect, states that the person is the kind of good which does not admit of use and cannot be treated as an object of use and as such the means to an end," and which, "in its positive form . . . confirms this: the person is a good towards which the only adequate attitude is love."[4]

This is the cardinal point to be kept in mind as we consider the ethics of experimenting on human subjects. The moral worth of every human being from conception/fertilization until death is *the* crucial truth in considering this important topic in all its ramifications. That every human being *is* indeed a being of moral worth, a person of irreplaceable and priceless value, is a truth central to the Gospel and is eloquently proclaimed by the Church, as we have seen in our review of relevant magisterial documents in Chapter One. It is this truth alone that renders intelligible the cardinal principle in human experimentation, namely, the principle of free and informed consent, that "canon of loyalty," as Paul Ramsey terms it,[5] which is operative in all situations wherein one human person is the experimenter and another is his "co-adventurer" in the experiment.

A. Basic Types of Experimentation

Before we look into this principle and its meaning, however, it will be useful to distinguish different types of experimental situations. There are many types of such situations, but from the perspective of moral analysis the two most basic kinds are *therapeutic* and *non-therapeutic* or purely *research* experiments. Among the first can be included experiments whose purpose is to (1) diagnose an illness or condition afflicting a person, (2) alleviate or cure a malady from which the subject is suffering, and (3) prevent a person from becoming afflicted with a specifiable malady. Therapeutic experiments, in short, can be diagnostic, curative or alleviating, or preventive. Despite the differences in these kinds of experiments, all are therapeutic in that they are aimed at being of medical benefit to the subject experimented on. Some therapeutic experiments are *research* experiments in the sense that they study the effects of using diagnostic, prophylactic/therapeutic, or preventive methods that depart from ordinary medical practice, but nonetheless offer reasonable hope of success. Such research experiments are thus truly therapeutic insofar as they are designed not only to acquire knowledge but also *to be of benefit* for the subject.[6]

Non-therapeutic or purely research experiments are not, of themselves, designed to be of medical benefit to the subject. They are rather intended to further biomedical and behavioral research, to advance the frontiers of knowledge, and thus enable us eventually to develop new techniques for coping with the diverse maladies that plague humankind and thereby to enhance the common good. It is true that at times the subjects of such non-therapeutic experiments may be benefited in spiritual and psychological ways, but such benefits to the subject are incidental to the experiment (and experimenter!) as such, inasmuch as the experiment (and the experimenter) *intend* or *aim at* acquiring knowledge that *may* be beneficial to human beings in the future, whereas the therapeutic experiment is aimed at benefiting the subject of the experiment.

B. The Key Principle or "Canon of Loyalty": The Principle of Free and Informed Consent

The canon of loyalty that must be observed in experimental situations, whether therapeutic or non-therapeutic, is the principle of free and informed consent. This principle is at the heart of medical ethics and bioethics. It was eloquently expressed in the articles of the Nuremberg Code (1946-1949), and it is salutary today, a half-century later, to recall that this code was formulated when the memories of the atrocities carried out on human subjects by the Third Reich in the name of scientific research was fresh in the minds of men. According to the first article of the Nuremberg Code,

The voluntary consent of the human subject is absolutely essential. This means that the person involved should have legal capacity to
give consent; should be so situated as to be able to exercise free power
of choice, without the intervention of any element of force, fraud,
deceit, duress, overreaching, or other ulterior form of constraint or
coercion; and should have sufficient knowledge and comprehension of
the elements of the subject matter involved as to enable him to make
an understanding and enlightened decision. This latter element
requires that before the acceptance of an affirmative decision by the
experimental subject there should be made known to him the nature,
duration, and purpose of the experiment; the method and means by
which it is to be conducted; all the inconveniences and hazards reasonably to be expected; and the effects upon his health or person which
may probably come from his participation in the experiment.[7]

The moral demand that a human person who is to be the subject of an
experiment give free and informed consent is also embodied in the code of
ethics adopted by the World Health Organization in the *Declaration of
Helsinki* in 1964 and by the American Medical Association.[8] This principle is at the heart of traditional Jewish and Christian medical ethics, and has
been reaffirmed time and time again by the Magisterium of the Church.

**(1) *The Principle of Free and Informed Consent and Relevant Teaching
of the Magisterium***
As Gonzalo Herranz has emphasized, this principle was clearly recognized and affirmed by Catholic authors in the nineteenth century long
before it was articulated in the very first article of the Nuremberg Code in
1949. Herranz calls attention to the work of the French Catholic medical
doctor George Surbled, who clearly expressed this principle in the first edition (1891) of his *La morale dans ses rapports avec la médicine et l'hygiene,* and
to the vigorous affirmation by his predecessor Max Simon of the principle
of the supremacy of the human person over scientific research in his 1845
volume, *Déontologie Médicale ou des Devoirs des Médicins dans l'Etat Actuel
de la Civilisation.*[9]

The 1994 *Charter for Health Care Workers,* promulgated by the Pontifical Council for Pastoral Assistance to Health Care Workers, provides a
valuable summary of magisterial teaching on the need to secure the patient's
informed consent in number 72, citing liberally from and referring to relevant magisterial documents. Thus it will be useful here to present the text

of this number and in the endnotes refer to the magisterial documents either cited in the text of this number or referred to in the footnotes contained in it:

> To intervene medically, the health care worker should have the express or tacit consent of the patient. In fact [as Pope Pius XII affirmed], "he does not have a separate and independent right in relation to the patient. In general, he can act only if the patient explicitly or implicitly (directly or indirectly) authorizes him."[10] Without such authorization he gives himself an arbitrary power.[11] Besides the medical relationship there is a human one: dialogic, non-objective. The patient [as Pope John Paul II insists] "is not an anonymous individual" on whom medical expertise is practiced, but "a responsible person, who should be given the opportunity of personally choosing, and not be made to submit to the decisions and choices of others."[12] So that the choice may be made with full awareness and freedom, the patient should be given a precise idea of his illness and the therapeutic possibilities, with the risks, the problems and the consequences that they entail.[13] This means that the patient should be asked for an *informed consent*.[14]

(2) *Interpreting This Principle*

It is frequently difficult, if not impossible, as many authorities have pointed out,[15] to secure *fully* informed consent. They have noted that frequently it is not possible to explain to the person about to undergo an experiment all of the complications involved. At times, some hazards may not be known; at other times the persons to be subjected to the experiment may not be capable of understanding all the pertinent and known factors; at other times, full details of all possible hazards and complications might so terrify a person that he or she may become paralyzed in thought and unwilling to consent to a procedure that is really not hazardous and that offers solid hope of being beneficial.

This means that this cardinal principle or canon of loyalty, demanding the subject's free and informed consent, is to be understood as requiring "reasonably" free and "adequately" informed consent, and the reasonableness and adequacy are to be determined in accord with the Golden Rule of doing unto others as you would have them do unto you and not do unto them what you would not have them do to you. Ramsey puts matters this way: "A choice may be free and responsible despite the fact that it began in an emotional bias one way or another, and consent can be informed without being encyclopedic."[16] In their *Ethical and Religious Directives for Catholic Health Care Services* (1994), the bishops of the United States expressed the requirement of free and informed consent as follows: "Free and informed consent requires that the person or the person's surrogate [the issue of "proxy consent" will be explored below] receive all reasonable information about the essential nature of the proposed treatment and its benefits; its risks, side-effects, consequences, and cost; and any reasonable and morally legitimate alternatives, including no treatment at all."[17]

Basically, what is at stake here is *trust* between the subject and the doctor/researcher: trust that the doctor/researcher will *not* propose any experiment without communicating to the subject sufficient information for him or her to make an informed decision, for after all, it affects that person's life and health. Unfortunately today, this trust between patients and doctors/researchers has been to a great extent eroded for a wide variety of reasons, and it is imperative that such trust be restored. It can only be restored if doctors and researchers are willing, in informing subjects of proposed experiments, to shape their choices and actions in accord with the Golden Rule or basic principle of justice and fairness.[18]

This requirement, the canon of loyalty demanding reasonably free and informed consent, is imperative in *all* types of experimentation on human persons (who come to be at conception/fertilization and remain in being so long as they are living human bodies). The reason is rooted in the inviolability of the human person as a being of moral worth, as an entity surpassing in value the entire material-created world, the bearer of inalienable rights that must be recognized and respected by society and by all persons. As we have seen before, human beings are ends, not means, and all human beings are equal in their dignity as persons.[19] Ramsey has put the matter beautifully by saying, "No man is good enough to experiment upon another without his consent."[20] To experiment on a human subject without securing his consent is to treat him as a being who is no longer a person, no longer a being of moral worth, to make of him a means, not an end, to subordinate him to others, to deny his humanity.

With respect to medical treatments, there is one clear exception from the requirement of expressed consent, an exception which in no way weakens the normative demand governing medical practice by consent alone. This is the kind of case in which consent is reasonably presumed or implied when a person is in extreme danger and cannot explicitly give consent. As the *Charter for Health Care Workers* says, in extreme situations of this kind, "if there is a temporary loss of knowing and willing, the health care worker can act in virtue of *the principle of therapeutic trust*. . . . Should there be a permanent loss of knowing and willing, the health care worker can act in virtue of *the principle of responsibility for health care*, which obliges the health care worker to assume responsibility for the patient's health."[21] As Ramsey has said, "Indeed, we might say that if a doctor stops on the road to Jericho, instead of passing by on his way to read a research paper before a scientific gathering or to visit his regular, paying customers, he is self-selected as good enough to practice medicine without the needy man's expressed consent."[22]

(3) *Other Ethical Principles/Norms Governing Biomedical Research on Human Subjects*

Free and informed consent is not the only relevant moral principle to justify biomedical research on human subjects. Another key principle/norm is known as the "principle of descending order." The philosopher Hans Jonas suggested this principle in selecting subjects of research. It requires researchers to select the least vulnerable people as subjects.[23] The primary obligation is to protect *vulnerable persons* and to prevent taking advantage of them in "selecting" subjects of experimentation. Such subjects, of course, must give free and informed consent to the research project for which they are "selected" and for which they then volunteer. There are two major categories of "vulnerable persons." The first includes persons unable to give consent to experimentation: babies, born or unborn, and older persons who are mentally incompetent; the second group includes people vulnerable to manipulation or coercion (perhaps of a very subtle type) by others: for example, prisoners, residents of institutions, the poor, students attending institutes conducting research, etc. The criterion of descending order does not mean that vulnerable persons can never be rightly chosen or volunteer as subjects of biomedical research; it simply requires that research subjects be selected on the basis of justice. Benedict Ashley, O.P., and Kevin O'Rourke, O.P. offer the following general criterion relevant to this principle: "subjects should be selected so that risks and benefits will not fall unequally on one group in society.[24]

Two other good, sound subsidiary principles are formulated in Articles 9 and 10 of the Nuremberg Code. Article 9 states that "during the course of the experiment the human subject should be at liberty to bring the experiment to an end if he has reached the physical or mental state where continuation of the experiment seems to him to be impossible." Article 10 declares: "During the course of the experiment the scientist in charge must be prepared to terminate the experiment at any stage if he has probable cause to believe, in the exercise of good faith, superior skill and careful judgment required of him that a continuation of the experiment is likely to result in injury, disability or death to the experimental subject."[25]

2. Proxy Consent: Its Meaning, Justification, and Limits

There are many instances when it is impossible to secure adequately informed and free consent from the person who is to be the subject of the experimentation. It is obviously impossible to obtain such consent from incompetent human persons, the unborn, infants and children, the demented, etc., those whom Ramsey has called "voiceless patients."

A. Proxy Consent in the Therapeutic Situation

There is no serious debate among authorities — legal, medical, or moral — that proxy consent, i.e., consent given by another acting as a surrogate for the person on whom the experiment is to be performed, is justifiable when the experiment in question is therapeutic, that is, when it is designed to secure some benefit for the subject.

Frequently, the responsibilities of those who give proxy consent for therapeutic procedures on behalf of voiceless patients are described as making choices in accord with the incompetent individual's own preferences, if these are known, or else making these choices in accord with the "best interests" of the individual concerned if he or she had never expressed personal preferences, for instance, if one is acting as a proxy for an infant or for an adult who has never been able to exercise moral responsibility because of some anomaly. Thus the bishops of the United States declare that decisions made on behalf of an individual by a designated surrogate (or responsible family member) should "be faithful to Catholic moral principles and to the person's intentions and values [so long as these are compatible with Catholic moral principles], or if the person's intentions are unknown, to the person's best interests."[26]

I believe that the basic moral principle justifying "proxy" consent in the therapeutic situation is in fact the Golden Rule. We are to do unto others as we would have them do unto us and not do unto them what we would not have them do to us. If the health or life of a fellow human person for whom we have responsibility (as parents do for their children) is in danger and there are means that can be taken to protect and/or enhance that person's health and life and/or ameliorate his or her condition *without imposing grave burdens upon that person*, then we are morally obligated to authorize use of those means for protecting/preserving/enhancing/ameliorating the life and health of the person for whom we have responsibility. The *Charter for Health Care Workers*, I believe, expressed this requirement, rooted in the principle of the Golden Rule, in what it termed the *"principle of responsibility for health care."*[27]

In other words, I think that "proxy consent," when made on behalf of those who have never been able to articulate their own preferences with respect to the kind of therapeutic care they are willing to accept, is not so much "proxy consent," i.e., consent made in the name of another person (as godparents act as proxies for infants in consenting to baptism), as it is the *personal consent* of the one morally responsible for the care of the incompetent individual. In giving consent to *therapeutic* experiments, that is, those reasonably expected to *benefit* the subject, to protect his *goods*, on such incompetent persons, those giving it are not so much speaking in the name of those voiceless patients but are rather exercising their own proper moral responsibility.

If consent is given on behalf of a now incompetent person who, while competent, had expressed his or her preferences for the kind of therapeutic treatment he or she is willing to accept, then we are indeed speaking of "proxy consent," and the U. S. bishops are quite correct in saying that the choice made (the free consent given) ought to be faithful to person's intentions and values, *as long as such a choice is faithful to Catholic moral principles.* This issue will be taken up in greater depth in Chapter Seven, where we set forth the criteria to be observed in making moral choices regarding the kind of therapeutic medical treatment proposed to persons.

B. Voluntary Consent in the Non-Therapeutic Situation: Can This Ever Be Morally Required?

Before considering "proxy" consent to both therapeutic and non-therapeutic experimentation, it is necessary to consider the question whether there can be an *obligation* or *moral responsibility* for *competent persons* to volunteer as subjects in such experiments. For years I thought that there could be no such moral obligation and that volunteering to participate in such experimentation was an act of mercy, in the nature of a gift. But in preparing this paper and after discussing the matter with others, in particular Germain Grisez, I now believe that the principle of fairness can at times require a competent adult to choose freely to participate in biomedical non-therapeutic experiments under certain conditions. For instance, if one's personal physician asked one in the course of a routine medical examination to give a urine sample in a program designed to compare the urine of healthy adults with those suffering from a particular disease in order to test some hypothesis regarding treatment of the disease or of its symptoms, it seems that in fairness one could have a *moral* obligation to help out. In an instance of this kind, one can easily do something of benefit to fellow human persons with no cost or minimal cost to oneself. The situation is analogous, it seems, to that of a vigorous adult who sees a frail elderly person struggling to carry a suitcase across the street; fairness, rooted in the Golden Rule as understood in the Christian tradition, would normally require the vigorous adult to come to the frail, older person's aid. Although such a responsibility could not be legally mandated, it is reasonable to think that a moral obligation can exist for a competent adult to participate in non-therapeutic biomedical experimentation in situations of this kind. If, however, the non-therapeutic experiment imposes significant burdens or inconveniences, then fairness would not require one to volunteer as a research subject; one's free and informed choice to be a participant would indeed be an act of mercy, a "gift" of oneself.

C. Proxy Consent in the Non-Therapeutic Situation

Can "proxy" consent be justified in the non-therapeutic situation, i.e., when the proposed research/experiment/treatment is *not intended* to benefit the human subject of such procedures but rather to gain knowledge that may in the future be of great benefit to others? Here I will first review arguments advanced to justify and to oppose proxy consent in the non-therapeutic situation. I will then examine relevant magisterial teaching.

(1) *Arguments For and Against*

A major argument advanced to justify proxy consent in the non-therapeutic situation was proposed in the 1970s by the late Richard McCormick, S.J. His basic argument was that proxy consent in the *therapeutic* situation is justified precisely because parents and other surrogates can presume that the subjects themselves *would*, if they could, consent because they *ought* to consent by virtue of their moral obligation to protect their own life and health. Similarly, he argued, in *non-therapeutic* situations posing no significant risk or minimal risk and in which great good is promised, proxy consent for children and other non-competents is justified inasmuch as one can reasonably assume that the non-competent themselves *would* consent if they could because they would realize that they *ought* to consent to such experiments because of their social nature and obligation to promote the common good of society when they can do so with little effort and no danger or minimal risk to themselves.[28]

Paul Ramsey and I rejected McCormick's argument justifying proxy consent in both the therapeutic and the non-therapeutic situations precisely because there are no grounds for presuming that children and other non-competents *would*, if they *could*, consent in both situations because they would realize that they *ought* to do so. There is no need to infer, as did McCormick, that children and other non-competents have *any* moral obligations.[29] Precisely because they are non-competent, they are *not moral agents*, but they *are* persons who ought never to be used as mere means to ends extrinsic to themselves.[30] To treat them *as if* they were moral agents who had moral obligations to carry out, among them, to participate in non-therapeutic experiments promising great good at minimal or no significant risk, is to fail to recognize them for what, in truth, they *are*, namely, vulnerable, helpless human persons totally dependent on others.

I think that these considerations clearly show that McCormick's argument for justifying proxy consent to non-therapeutic experimentation is not at all valid. Although, as I noted earlier, competent adults could, under certain conditions, have a moral obligation to participate in certain kinds of non-therapeutic investigation, non-competent, "voiceless" persons can have no such obligation precisely because they have *no* moral obligations by reason of their condition.

With Ramsey I found McCormick's apologia for proxy consent in the non-therapeutic situation repugnant. In fact, from the 1970s until September 2002, when I presented an early draft of this paper at a meeting sponsored by the Pontifical Academy for Life in preparation for the plenary session of February 2003 and found my position sharply challenged, I firmly held the view that it is *never* morally right for others to give so-called "proxy" consent for non-competent, voiceless human persons to non-therapeutic research/experimentation. Basically, the argument supporting this conclusion — advanced in the 1970s and subsequently by Ramsey and me — holds that incompetent or "voiceless" human persons, by reason of their **dignity precisely as persons,** ought *never* be used as subjects in procedures that are non-therapeutic and are undertaken not for their benefit but for the benefit of others. According to this argument, even if the procedures may not "harm" them and may pose no significant risk, they are immoral because they violate their dignity as persons. Ramsey well expressed this position when he said:

To experiment on children [or other non-competent subjects] in ways that are not related to them as patients is already a sanitized form of barbarism; it already removes them from view and pays no attention to the faithfulness-claims which a child, simply by being a normal or sick or dying child, places upon us and upon medical care. . . . To attempt to consent for a child to be made an experimental subject is to treat the child as not a child. . . . Nontherapeutic, nondiagnostic, experimentation involving human subjects must be based on true consent if it is to proceed as a human enterprise. No child or incompetent adult can choose to become a participating member of medical undertakings, and no one else on earth should decide to subject those people to investigations having no relation to their own treatment. That is a canon of loyalty to them. This they claim simply by being a human child or incompetent.[31]

I was led to change my position unalterably opposing *all proxy consent to non-therapeutic procedures* because of the objections raised against it at a September 27-28, 2002, meeting of persons who had been invited to give papers at the Plenary Session of the Pontifical Academy for Life. I had prepared a paper on which this material is based, reaffirming my long-standing complete rejection of proxy consent in the non-therapeutic situation. Criticism given at that meeting, along with discussions I subsequently carried out with Germain Grisez, led me to conclude that although McCormick's *argument* to justify proxy consent on behalf of "voiceless" subjects in the non-therapeutic situation may be severely criticized for the reasons given, the position he took can be defended on other grounds. Some participants in the September 2002 meeting suggested one line of reasoning used to justify such "proxy" consent. The basic claim is that it would not be unreasonable — and therefore not contrary to objective moral standards — if parents, for instance, were to allow experimentation involving their children for the benefit of others if the experiment involves no significant risk. After all, parents frequently take their children, including babies, on automobile trips not undertaken for their benefit (e.g., to purchase some clothes for the mother), and such journeys surely involve some risks, but, after all, risks of this kind are acceptable both for oneself and for those for whom one cares. And other examples could be given. Hence, if it is not wrong for parents to act in this way in exercising responsible stewardship of their children, why would it be always immoral for them to consent to have their children participate in non-therapeutic research/experimentation?

I believe that Germain Grisez has clearly formulated this line of reasoning:

> People making decisions for someone who is not competent — for instance, parents for a child — *may not accept any significant risk (that is, any risk beyond the level of life's common risks) to a dependent's health for the sake of an experiment's possible benefit to others. For parents and others in charge of the noncompetent have a special responsibility to act in their personal interests, not to subordinate them to others. Nor can such subordination of a dependent's interests be an act of mercy, since mercy is self-sacrifice, not imposing sacrifice on someone for whom one is responsible.*[32]

I wish to note some important features of Grisez's presentation. First of all, he offers a clear definition/description of "significant" risk. He identifies as "significant" a risk that is "beyond the level of life's common risks" — e.g., such risks as riding in an automobile, crossing a street, etc. — "risks" which parents commonly take for their children when they have their children accompany them in a host of activities that are not intended to be of any direct benefit to the children themselves. Grisez thus provides us with a clearly defined criterion to help us determine whether a risk is "significant." Obviously, however, application of this criterion would vary depending on social/cultural conditions. Thus what constitutes "significant" risk in Manhattan would seem to be different from what constitutes "significant" risk in, say, Wagga Wagga, Australia.

Second, Grisez clearly believes that such parental consent in no way "subordinates" their children to the interests of others since he rejects such subordination. When conditions warrant parental consent (or consent by other guardians) to participation by those entrusted to their care in non-therapeutic experimentation, in other words, such consent is given in fidelity to the trust given them to protect the inviolable *dignity precisely as persons* of the non-competent persons for whose well-being they are responsible. Moreover, he explicitly rejects the claim that such subordination can be "an act of mercy, since mercy is self-sacrifice, not imposing sacrifice on someone for whom one is responsible."

After reflecting on the reasons advanced by those who considered my view too restrictive and not necessary to protect the inviolable dignity of "voiceless" persons, I have concluded that it would not be unreasonable for parents to allow their children to be subjects of non-therapeutic studies posing no "significant" risk (as defined above) and causing no significant inconvenience or burden to their children. They would not be treating them as mere objects of use or failing in their serious responsibility to protect their lives and health by all reasonable means.

I now believe that the view I defended for many years was, in fact, an overreaction to unethical experiments on non-competent persons and a fear, reasonable in itself, that the intrinsic dignity of such vulnerable persons was endangered by a desire to subordinate them to the interests of others.

"Proxy" consent in such situations is, of course, not true "proxy" consent, i.e., consent given in the name of the non-competent persons themselves. It is the personal consent of the parents or guardians of voiceless persons to permit those for whom they have a grave responsibility to participate in non-therapeutic experimentations if, and only if, such experimentations pose no "significant" risk, promise great benefit, and cannot be carried out on other subjects. As noted previously, I believe that children who have reached the "use of reason" can make free and informed decisions, and that, if so, parents ought to give their children sufficient information for them to make a free and informed choice in the matter and to answer any of their concerns and to retain veto power over their children's choices in this matter when they judge this necessary.

(2) *Relevant Magisterial Teaching*

With respect to *magisterial* teaching relevant to this matter, it is very important to consider (a) proxy consent to non-therapeutic experimentation on *unborn* human persons and (b) such experimentation on human persons *already born.*

The universal Magisterium of the Church rejects as absolutely immoral proxy consent to non-therapeutic experiments on *unborn human persons.* A key passage in *Donum vitae* of central importance regarding this matter is the following:

> As regards experimentation, and presupposing the general distinction between experimentation for purposes which are not directly therapeutic and experimentation which is clearly therapeutic for the subject himself, in the case in point [experimentation on human embryos and fetuses] one must also distinguish between experimentation carried out on embryos which are still alive and experimentation carried out on embryos which are dead. *If the embryos are living, whether viable or not, they must be respected just like any other human person; experimentation on embryos which is not directly therapeutic is illicit.* No objective, even though noble in itself, such as a foreseeable advan-

tage to science, to other human beings, or to society, can in any way justify experimentation on living human embryos or fetuses, whether viable or not, either inside or outside the mother's womb. The informed consent ordinarily required for clinical experimentation on adults cannot be granted by the parents, who may not freely dispose of the physical integrity or life of the unborn child. Moreover, experimentation on embryos and fetuses always involves risk, and indeed in most cases it involves the certain expectation of harm to their physical integrity or even their death. To use human embryos or fetuses as the object or instrument of experimentation constitutes a crime against their dignity as human beings having a right to the same respect that is due to the child already born and to every human person.[33]

When I first read this passage in 1987, and in the years to follow, I read it in the perspective of my position that regarded as immoral *all proxy consent* on behalf of "voiceless" persons to non-therapeutic experimentation precisely *because it violated their dignity as persons*. I thus *assumed* that the fundamental reason why *Donum vitae* absolutely repudiated proxy consent to non-therapeutic experimentation on the unborn was the same as my reason for repudiating it. Moreover, the text in question seemed capable of being interpreted in this way insofar as it prefaced its rejection of such consent by emphasizing the respect due to human embryos as persons equal in dignity to all other human persons. Moreover, I assumed that both *Donum vitae* and Pope John Paul II in the passage cited by *Donum vitae* considered non-therapeutic experimentation on human embryos — and indeed all human persons incapable of giving personal informed consent — to be immoral because such experimentation treated human embryos and other non-competent human persons as mere "objects" or "instruments" of use.

Thus, when I subsequently discovered that the U.S. bishops, who, with *Donum vitae* and Pope John Paul II, absolutely excluded as illicit proxy consent to non-therapeutic experiments on *unborn human persons*,[34] nonetheless *authorized* parents to give such consent to non-therapeutic experiments on children already born if the experiments poses no "significant risk to the person's well being,"[35] I accused them of unreasonably holding a "double standard," one for unborn children and another for children already born.[36] A position similar to that of the U.S. bishops was taken by the Australian hierarchy.[37] However, now, after changing my position regarding proxy consent to non-therapeutic experiments posing no "significant" risks to non-competent or "voiceless" persons, I realize that I was reading my views *into Donum vitae* and the passage from Pope John Paul II cited therein. I was guilty of *eisegesis* and failed to consider the possibility of interpreting the relevant texts differently. I now think that the fundamental reason why *Donum vitae* repudiates proxy consent to non-therapeutic experiments on *unborn human persons* is that "experimentation on embryos and fetuses *always* involves risk, and indeed in most cases it involves the certain expectation of harm to their physical integrity or even their death" (*Donum vitae*, 1.4; emphasis added). It is for this reason that *Donum vitae* also judges that such experimentation treats a living human embryo as a mere "object" or "instrument."

One might reasonably question why all non-therapeutic experiments on the unborn are illicit because of the serious risks they pose and why such experiments are justifiable on human persons already born. An unborn child cannot be a legitimate subject of a non-therapeutic experiment, but apparently the same child, minutes after birth, can be. This seems unreasonable. In answer to this reasonable question, I think it important to emphasize that parents and others who have responsibility to care for voiceless or non-competent persons can *not licitly* consent to their being subjects of non-therapeutic procedures *if these procedures pose "significant" risks*. I further maintain that newborn babies are very vulnerable subjects and that one can reasonably hold that non-therapeutic experiments performed on them would pose more than significant risks in comparison to any benefits to be expected.

(3) *Conclusion to "Proxy" Consent for Non-Competent or "Voiceless" Subjects to Participate in Non-Therapeutic Experimentations*

I maintain that "proxy" consent here is a misnomer, since the potential subjects are, precisely because they are non-competent or voiceless, incapable of giving consent, and no one should presume to give consent for them. The consent in question is the *personal* consent of parents and other guardians. The dignity proper to human beings precisely as persons and the dignity proper to them precisely as moral agents are both at stake. For parents and other guardians who might give consent for those under their care to participate in non-therapeutic experiments, the dignity primarily at stake is their dignity precisely as moral agents, who must respect fully the dignity precisely as persons of the voiceless, non-competent persons committed to their trust. If in their judgment, the proposed experimentation would not violate their charges' dignity precisely as persons, it would then not be unreasonable or a violation of the trust committed to them to give the necessary consent. A condition *sine qua non* if such consent is to be morally licit is precisely the requirement that the proposed experiment pose no "significant risk" (as this has been defined) to the persons committed to their care.

3. Research on the Unborn, in Particular, Embryonic Stem-Cell Research

The basic norm, clearly developed by *Donum vitae* (Vatican *Instruction on Respect for Human Life in its Origin and on the Dignity of Procreation*), as we saw in the previous section and also in Chapter One, rightly condemns as utterly immoral any non-therapeutic experimentation or research on human embryos. Any form of experimentation or research on a human embryo performed on it not for its own benefit but for that of others is unethical and gravely immoral, particularly if the experimentation is such as to gravely harm the unborn child. Any procedure whereby new human life is generated *in vitro* in order either to use it for implantation and gestation later on or to freeze it or to use it for experimental purposes is radically immoral and unjust, however good the motivation for doing so.

A. What Are Human Embryonic Stem Cells and Why Are They Sought for Research?

Today, embryonic stem-cell research is a matter of great interest. These are cells that develop very early in the human embryo after fertilization. They form the "inner cell mass" of the early embryo during the blastocyst stage, when the embryo is about to implant in the womb (the "outer mass" of the blastocyst is called the trophoblast and form the placenta and other supporting and vital organs needed for the development of the unborn child within the mother). These cells go on to form the body of the developing human person. Although they are not "totipotential," as are the cells organized into a unitary whole in the pre-implantation embryo, they are "pluripotential," since they have the capacity to develop into any of the 200 and more different kinds of cells that make up the adult human body. In theory, if these cells are extracted early enough during embryonic life, they can be cultured and manipulated to become the cells needed for specific therapeutic purposes. The cells thus produced can be transferred into an organ (e.g., the brain), where they can proliferate and replace or repair cells that are injured or dying because of some disease. With modern technology, there is reason to think that they can be designed to repair or replace muscle or brain cells, transplanted into human hearts or brains in order to treat such maladies as Parkinson's disease, Alzheimer's disease, and various heart diseases, and in this way restore health to many people.[38]

Advocates of human embryonic stem-cell research point to the following *technical advantages* of such research: (1) they are very flexible and may have potential to make any cell; (2) there is a never-ending supply — one embryonic stem-cell line can potentially provide an endless supply of cells with defined characteristics; and (3) they are readily available from embryos cryopreserved in *in vitro* fertilization clinics. They also admit that there are some *technical disadvantages*: (1) they are very difficult to differentiate uniformly into a target-type cell or tissue; (2) they are immunogenic — such cells are likely to be rejected after transplantation; and (3) they are tumorigenic — capable of forming tumors.[39] As Richard Doerflinger — whom I consider the most well-informed and intelligent lay (non-scientific) authority on stem-cell research — has said, human embryonic stem-cell lines "may develop genetic abnormalities preventing their use in humans for the foreseeable future."[40]

B. Why Research on Embryonic Stem Cells Is Gravely Immoral

Three principal methods, all of them intrinsically immoral, are currently being proposed for retrieving embryonic stem cells. The first is to induce the abortion of early embryos and retrieve their stem cells. The second is to produce embryos *in vitro* solely for the purpose of research, including stem-cell research. The third is to use the so-called spare embryos produced *in vitro* for infertility treatment and cryopreserved. All three of these methods require the *intentional* killing of unborn human children and are hence intrinsically evil. The persons anxious to obtain these cells want them *precisely because they are the cells of living human beings.* Were they the stem cells of canines, bovines, felines, simians, or dolphins, one would not want them (and members of People for the Ethical Treatment of Animals [PETA] and others would think it barbaric to kill embryonic dolphins or chimps or gorillas in order to get their stem cells). They thus frankly acknowledge that the beings they must kill are *human beings, members of the human species.*[41] But they claim that embryonic human beings are not *persons*, and that only persons have "rights." This claim, however, drives a wedge between *being a human being* and *being a person*, and requires those who distinguish sharply between the two to offer a non-arbitrary criterion to distinguish which members of the human species are persons and which are not. But this is impossible.

As a position paper prepared by Senator Sam Brownback of Kansas and released on July 1, 1999, rightly says: "The prospect of government-sponsored experiments to manipulate and destroy human embryos should make us all lie awake at night. That some individuals would be destroyed in the name of medical science constitutes a threat to us all."[42] Such experimentation and research is barbaric, disguised and hidden by utilitarian rhetoric and visions of the great good promised by being willing to close one's mind to the human dignity of the early unborn child, seeing in its place only "tissues" and "cells" with no inherent value.

C. Propaganda vs. Facts

Although some people — in particular, elites in our society, editorial writers for major news media, prominent academics and politicians — claim that embryonic stem-cell research has led to therapies for a host of dread diseases (diabetes, Parkinson's disease, various cancers, etc.), this is not the case. As a matter of fact, at present there are *no* therapeutic treatments making use of embryonic stem cells and *no* potential therapies are even in clinical trials. *Not a single human person has as yet benefited from such research!*

On the other hand, according to the National Institutes of Health and the National Marrow Donor Program,[43] adult stem cells are in established or experimental clinical use to treat human patients with several dozen conditions, including spinal cord injury, multiple sclerosis, cardiac problems, and stroke. For example, paralyzed human persons are being successfully treated with their own adult stem cells. The therapy, as developed by Dr. Carlos Lima in Portugal, uses a paralyzed person's own nasal stem cells and nerves, which are injected into his own spinal cord.[44] In fact, Richard Doerflinger, in a March 2007 article, listed "75 *New* Reasons to Reconsider the Alleged Need for Stem Cell Research that Destroys Human Embryos," noting "Recent Advances in Adult Stem Cell Research and Other Alternatives to Embryonic Stem Cell Research" made between June 2006 and February 2007.[45]

It is important to note that on October 27, 2004, a group of fifty-seven scientists sent a letter to Senator John Kerry, who was promoting embryonic stem-cell research in his campaign for president. In this letter, ignored by the major media, they pointed out the following: "25 years of research on mouse embryonic stem cells have produced limited indications of clinical benefit as well as indications of serious and potentially lethal side effects. Based on this evidence, claims of a safe and reliable treatment for any disease in humans are premature at best." They likewise affirmed that the clinical applications thus far made by using adult stem cells are producing "undoubted benefits" and are leading to a better understanding of "how and why they work so that they can be put to more uses."[46]

D. Legitimate Sources of Stem Cells for Research

As the previous section clearly indicates, adult stem cells — and these are found in newborns — can be, have been, and are being used already for therapeutic treatments. Obtaining such cells does not require the destruction of human embryos. As Edmund D. Pellegrino, M.D., among others, has pointed out, "Creditable laboratories have identified a wide variety of sources for pluripotential cells with the capability of embryonic stem cells. For example, stem cells from the bone marrow, placenta, or umbilical cord of live births are already in use in treating leukemia. Work currently in progress indicates that such cells can be altered to develop into cartilage and bone tissue and used in replacing diseased bone tissue.... [N]eural stem cells [have been] successfully isolated from living nerve tissue . . . and show promise for possible use in treating Parkinson's disease or brain injuries."[47] Since Pellegrino penned those lines, enormous advances have been made, as noted already, in therapies developed with use of adult stem cells.

Those advocating continued research on adult stem cells note the following *technical advantages*: (1) special adult stem cells from bone marrow and umbilical cords have been recently isolated that appear to be as flexible as embryonic types; (2) they are easier than embryonic stem cells to differentiate into specific kinds of cells or tissues; (3) they are not immunogenic — recipients who receive stem cells from their own cells and tissues will not reject transplants; (4) they are relatively easy to obtain; (5) they are non-tumoregenic.[48]

E. Proposed New Sources for Embryonic Stem Cells in Ways That Do Not Require the Killing of Human Beings During the Embryonic Stage of Their Existence

(1) *Pluripotent Stem Cells From Adult Skin Cells*

Undoubtedly, one of the most promising sources for pluripotent stem cells is adult skin cells. On November 20, 2007, both the *New York Times* and the *Washington Post* announced on their front pages that two teams of scientists had succeeded in turning human skin cells into what appear to be embryonic stem cells without making or destroying human embryos. The two teams were those at the University of Wisconsin, headed by James A. Thompson, and in Japan, headed by Shinya Yamanaka.

(2) *The President's Council on Bioethics 2005 "White Paper"*

In May 2005, the President's Council on Bioethics published a "white paper" entitled *Alternative Sources of Human Pluripotent Stem Cells*.[49] The Council was seeking ways of obtaining pluripotent stem cells by methods "that would meet the moral standard of not destroying or endangering human embryos in the process."[50] The Council identified four broad approaches. "The stem cells could be derived: (1) by extracting cells from embryos already dead; or (2) by non-harmful biopsy of living embryos; or (3) by extracting cells from artificially created non-embryonic but embryo-like cellular systems (engineered to lack the essential elements of embryogenesis but still capable of some cell division and growth); or (4) by dedifferentiation of somatic cells back to pluripotency."[51]

(3) *Hurlbut's Altered Nuclear Transfer Proposal*

Here I will summarize the third proposal presented at the Council's December 2004 meeting by Council Member Dr. William Hurlbut. He proposed a technique called "altered nuclear transfer" as a way of obtaining embryonic stem cells without destroying human embryos. He explained his proposal in "layman's language" in an interview with Kathryn Lopez in 2005 on *National Review on Line*. In it he said:

> Altered Nuclear Transfer seeks a morally acceptable means of producing pluripotent stem cells (the functional equivalent of embryonic stem cells) without the creation and destruction of human embryos.... ANT would employ the basic technology of nuclear transfer (SCNT), but with an alteration such that no embryo is created, yet pluripotent stem cells are produced.... ANT uses the technology of nuclear transfer, but with a preemptive alteration that assures that no embryo is created. The adult-cell nucleus is first altered before it is transferred into the egg. The alteration causes the adult-cell DNA to function in such a way that no embryo is generated, but pluripotent stem cells are produced. An embryo is "totipotent," capable of forming an organism, but embryonic stem cells are "pluripotent," capable of forming all the cell types of the body but not in the organized and coordinated pattern of a living being. ANT would directly create cells that are pluripotent but not totipotent.... ANT is a broad concept with a

range of specific approaches. The study by Rudolf Jaenisch involved the silencing of a gene crucial for early organization. Although the popular press portrayed the alteration as preventing the formation of the placenta, the failure of formation is at a far more fundamental level. The silenced gene, known by the name "Cdx2," is essential for the first cell differentiation and without it no basic body axes or body plan are ever established. It is reasonable to consider this alteration not a "deficiency" in an existing being, but an "insufficiency" that precludes the coherent organization that is the very defining character of an embryo.

There are other genes or combinations of genes that might also be used in ANT. One recent proposal, called ANT-OAR (oocyte-assisted reprogramming), would involve fast-forwarding gene-expression patterns directly to those that characterize embryonic stem cells. By "jump-starting" gene expression, one goes directly to a differentiated cell state and bypasses entirely the earlier developmental stages. This idea, put forward by Markus Grompe, director of the stem-cell program at Oregon Health Sciences, is the subject of current scientific research.[52]

Some claim that the entity Hurlbut creates is not a "pseudo-embryo" but rather a true but defective embryo. This objection was voiced by some but not all of the scholars attending, with Hurlbut, a scholars' forum in late April 2005 in Washington, DC, sponsored by the Westchester Institute for Ethics and the Human Person. But after Hurlbut explained his proposal in more detail, in particular the significance of the gene identified in his interview as "Cdx2," the majority of the scholars in attendance agreed that the entity in question is *not* a true embryo but a pseudo-embryo, i.e., it is *not a human person* and that therefore manipulating and even destroying it is in no way to kill an innocent human person.

(4) *Altered Nuclear Transfer-Oocyte Assisted Reprogramming*

This way of obtaining pluripotent stem cells with all the properties of embryonic stem cells is presented in full in the sources listed in the accompanying endnote.[53] It was initially proposed at the April 2005 Westchester Institute's Scholars Forum referred to earlier. Here I will provide a summary.

Many scientists are confident that ANT-OAR (altered nuclear transfer-oocyte assisted reprogramming) should allow us to produce pluripotent stem cells *directly* without creating or destroying human embryos. The nucleus of an adult body or somatic cell, containing a complete human genome, would be fused with an oocyte in a process similar to cloning. But, and this is the key point, before inserting the nucleus of this somatic cell, alterations would be made in its genes by epigenetic "reprogramming" so that the entity generated when the altered nucleus is fused with a denucleated oocyte is *not* totipotent, as is a human embryo, but rather pluripotent.

The ANT-OAR proposal introduces nanog and/or similar factors into the adult somatic cell *prior* to transfer of its nucleus into the denucleated oocyte. ANT-OAR positively instructs the adult nucleus (once inserted into the enucleated egg) to enter directly into a pluripotent state, without passing through any intervening stages of embryonic development. ANT-OAR proposes to use the cytoplasm of the oocyte to assist with the required reprogramming of the adult nucleus to the pluripotent state. As with cloning, the oocyte cytoplasm will "strip" the cellular type of the adult cell nucleus, reverting to an undifferentiated, more plastic state. Yet, unlike what happens in cloning, the adult cell nucleus will not be converted to a totipotent state (a state from which human embryonic development can proceed). Rather, as proposed, the alterations made to the adult nucleus will ensure that the cell produced by ANT-OAR enters immediately into a restricted, pluripotent state, without ever generating an embryo.

The proposal is for initial research using only non-human animal cells. This is most important. Those defending ANT-OAR do not want any experiments involving human oocytes to take place in the absence of experiments on non-human animals. If — and only if — such research establishes beyond a reasonable doubt that OAR can reliably be used to create pluripotent stem cells *without creating embryos* would we support research using human cells.

With others, I believe that animal research will confirm that embryogenesis does not occur with OAR. ANT-OAR thus seems a viable way of obtaining pluripotent stem cells, with all the technical advantages of embryonic stem cells, in a morally acceptable way, with no danger of killing unborn human persons for the good of others.

Some scholars think that the ANT-OAR proposal is justified by flawed reasoning and that in all likelihood the entity generated is *not* a pluripotent stem cell but is rather a severely damaged but true human embryo. This objection has been raised most vigorously by a group of scholars, in particular David L. Schindler and Adrian Walker, associated with the journal *Communio.*[54] I believe that the objections leveled against ANT-OAR have been adequately answered in detail by many,[55] preeminently by Edward

Furton, editor of *The National Catholic Bioethics Quarterly*,[56] Nicanor Austriaco, O.P.,[57] and E. Christian Brugger.[58] Interested readers may consult these sources for the debate.

(5) *Pluripotent Cells in Amniotic Fluid*

In the January 2007 issue of *Nature Biotechnology*, scientists at Wake Forest University School of Medicine in North Carolina reported that stem cells in the amniotic fluid, which surrounds babies in the womb, can turn into all the major tissue types — without any danger of forming tumors. The scientists also reported that these cells grow just as fast as embryonic stem cells (ESCs).

Because amniotic fluid-derived stem (AFS) cells are not derived from dissected embryos, they do not raise the moral issues raised by stem cells obtained by killing human embryos. In addition, it would be easy to create thousands of cell lines that could be used to produce tissues for regenerative medicine. "If you banked 100,000 specimens, you'd be able to provide cells for 99% of the U.S. population with a perfect match for genetic transplantation," according to Dr. Anthony Atala, the lead researcher.

The discovery was welcomed by other researchers. "If the cells can be extracted from the placenta, it's a very convenient way of getting large numbers of cell lines that repair all types of cells," said Ian Wilmut, one of Britain's leading stem cell and cloning experts. And, in a statement to *New Scientist*, Lyle Armstrong, of the University of Newcastle-upon-Tyne, in the United Kingdom, said: "It's likely that therapies will arise from cells like these way before they're available from ESCs."[59]

(6) *Pluripotent Stem Cells From Mice*

As reported in *BioEdge*, an Australian weekly pro-life journal,

> Three different groups reported last week that normal skin cells in mice can be reprogrammed to an embryonic state. "Neither eggs nor embryos are necessary. I've never worked with either," says Shinya Yamanaka of Kyoto University, who first unveiled the technique a year ago to sceptical colleagues.
>
> Now his results have been confirmed by two other teams, at the Whitehead Institute for Biomedical Research in Cambridge, Massachusetts, and the Harvard Stem Cell Institute. The reprogrammed cells meet all the tests of pluripotent cells — they form colonies, propagate continuously and form cancerous growths called teratomas, as

well as producing chimaeras. "Its unbelievable, just amazing," says Hans Schöler, a German stem cell expert. "For me, it's like Dolly. It's that type of an accomplishment."

What Yamanaka did was to take a mouse skin cell and introduce into it four proteins which trigger the expression of other genes to make it pluripotent. He calls the result induced pluripotent stem cells (iPS cells). "It's easy. There's no trick, no magic," he says. . . . Harvard researcher Chad Cowan says that it will change the field: "The most amazing thing about these papers is you now take this whole idea of reprogramming out of the hands of cloning specialists and put it into the hands of anyone who can do molecular and cell biology." Now the race is on to apply the technique to human cells. "We are working very hard — day and night," says Yamanaka. . . .

The ethical implications of this development were immediately seized upon by opponents of embryonic stem cell research. "Morally and practically, this new approach appears to be far superior," commented Richard Doerflinger, a spokesman for the US Catholic bishops conference. ~ New York Times, Jun 7; Nature, Jun 7; Science, Jun 8.[60]

4. Genetic Therapy

A. Gene Therapy: Its Definition and Types

"Gene therapy," as the Working Party of the [United Kingdom's] Catholic Bishops' Joint Committee on Bioethical Issues has said, "is the intentional alteration of genes in cells or tissues in such a way as to treat or prevent an inherited disorder, or to make another pathological condition more amenable to treatment." Continuing, the Working Party describes two of the basic types of such therapy: "Such intervention is termed *somatic* gene therapy if the alteration affects only the individual on whom it is carried out. If the intervention takes place on the germ-line cells — that is, sperm, ova, or their precursors — it is termed *germ-line* gene therapy, and will affect not only a particular individual but also his or her descendants."[61]

The goal of gene therapy is to treat human diseases by correcting the genetic defects underlying genetic maladies or by adding new genes to the patient in order to provide or enhance a given therapeutic operation.

In addition to these forms of gene *therapy*, there exists also the possibility of genetic *enhancement*, i.e., efforts to improve or enhance, by genetic engineering, characteristics such as size, skin color, intelligence, etc. Speaking of this possibility, W. French Anderson, one of the leading world authorities on gene therapy, had this to say: "To the extent that defects in these traits constitute truly damaging errors or disease, they ought to, and will, be treated with all the tools at our command [and efforts to treat these defects would then come under gene *therapy*]. But to the extent that they are not errors but rather normal human variations, the pursuit of forms of enhancement modification is fraught with risks for society." Anderson then goes on to enumerate some of these serious risks.[62] I will not consider here enhancement genetic engineering. At present, there are no good ethical reasons for attempting such engineering and many good moral reasons for not doing so; the medical hazards are as yet not even known: who decides and on what criteria, which genes to select for "enhancement," how one could avoid unjust discrimination in selecting those who would presumably benefit from such enhancement, etc.

Thus in what follows, attention focuses on gene *therapy,* and, in particular — for reasons to be given later — on *somatic gene therapy.*

B. How Gene Therapy "Works"

Today it is possible to treat or prevent a genetically based malady because of the breakthroughs that have occurred with ever-increasing frequency in molecular biology and DNA research over the past half-century. Each human cell, except for the mature red blood cell, has a nucleus containing *chromosomes.* Each chromosome is made up of DNA (deoxyribonucleic acid), which takes the form of a double-stranded helix, and attached to each strand of the helix is a series of alternating nucleotides called *bases.* DNA is the "genetic alphabet," and its bases are the "letters" of this alphabet. There are four, and only four, such bases or letters, namely, adenine (A), cytosine (C), guanine (G), and thymine (T), and the "words" of the genetic language or DNA are constructed of these "letters" or bases. The sequence of bases on either strand of the DNA constitutes a gene, the basic unit of heredity whereby traits are passed on from one generation to another.

Scientists now know a good deal about this genetic language. They realize that the substitution of even one "letter" for another can cause a cell to produce or not produce a given enzyme or protein essential for the normal functioning of the organism. If the organism is not functioning properly because of an error in the language of its DNA, it is possible, in light of new breakthroughs in molecular biology and recombinant DNA, to put the "right" letter into the pertinent genetic "word," to replace one that is "incorrect," etc., and in this way to correct a given genetically induced defect. In theory, such genetic therapeutic intervention can be done either to the body or somatic cells of the person afflicted with the malady — *somatic cell* therapy as described above — or to the germ cells of the persons transmitting the genetic traits to their offspring through generation of human life — *germ-line* therapy as described above.[63]

The major problem, once the "correct gene" has been designed or produced, is to get it into appropriate body cells of the person receiving the therapy.

C. Strategies for Gene Therapy

According to Anderson, there are three basic approaches to the genetic correction of diseases, namely, (1) *ex vivo*, (2) *in situ*, and (3) *in vivo*. The first requires the removal of cells from the patient, "correcting" them outside his body by inserting the normal gene and then returning the corrected cells to the patient. The second introduces the new, correct gene, directly into the site of the disease within the body of the patient, either in the form of a "virus vector" (on this, see below) or naked DNA. The third approach, not yet developed sufficiently for practical use, requires developing "vectors" that can be injected directly into the bloodstream and carry the therapeutic gene to the proper cell tissue safely and efficiently.[64]

In addition, Anderson notes that all current (c. 1995-2000) clinical protocols for gene therapy are based on the idea of adding a normal gene rather than replacing or correcting the malfunctioning gene present in the patient's body. This approach assumes that the newly added gene will be introduced into a site in the genome different from that of the defective gene, and that the new gene's expression will override the effects of the defective gene.[65]

D. Delivering Therapeutic Genes

The English Bishops' Working Group pointed out that effective gene therapy requires not only the recognition and isolation of the appropriate gene for effecting therapy but also an efficient delivery system. The latter — the delivery system — is called a *vector*.[66] Although the desired genes to be delivered into the cells of the patient needing therapy can be delivered by physical techniques (e.g., ingestion of an organic salt called calcium phosphate containing the appropriate DNA and the placing of DNA into fatty bubbles or liquid vesicles that can be fused with human body cells), such techniques have not as yet proved very effective. At present, the most effective way to deliver therapeutic genes is through the use of *viruses* and *viral vectors*.

Viruses have a natural tendency to enter human cells and insert their genetic information into the genome of the cells that they enter. Thus therapeutic gene cells, developed through recombinant DNA, can be inserted into various kinds of viruses capable of introducing their genetic information into target cells and allow those genes to become a permanent and functional part of the host-cell genome. The newly introduced gene is a new cellular gene of the patient. However, the viruses themselves can often have bad effects on the cells of the person into whom they are introduced. But, again as a result of the advances made in molecular cellular biology, it is now possible to inactivate or remove deleterious viral genes, replacing them with the desired therapeutic genetic material.[67]

This type of genetic *somatic cell* therapy has proved beneficial and successful in the treatment of several genetically based diseases (e.g., cystic fibrosis, adenosine deaminase deficiency [ADA] — a genetic disorder caused by the lack of the gene product adenosine deaminase and leading to abnormality of bone marrow cells and thus giving rise to serious infections), and there is hope that as time goes on more and more genetically based diseases can be treated by somatic cell therapy.

E. The Morality of Somatic Cell Gene Therapy

Somatic gene therapy raises problems similar to those posed by other forms of treatment. Such therapy is morally warranted as long as the risks posed by this new type of therapy are not significant when compared with the reasonable expectation that employment of such therapy will indeed bring great benefit *to the patient*. Somatic cell gene therapy is today, of course, *experimental* in nature and does not constitute "standard" treatment. As with other experimental procedures (e.g., as kidney transplants were when they were first initiated), there is reason for reserving such therapy for serious diseases for which there is no satisfactory alternative treatment.[68] There is urgent need that, wherever possible, attempts at somatic therapy on human persons be preceded by studies on animals.

There is the possibility that somatic gene therapy may have side effects, possibly deleterious, affecting the germ-line or gametic cells. Such risk is not limited to gene therapy, as other medical treatments can risk harming the children conceived while their mothers, in particular, are undergoing treatment. To reduce the risk of unintentionally harming progeny, some have recommended, as Helen Watt has observed, that female patients participating in trials of somatic cell therapy be required to use contraceptives.[69] As Watt goes on to note, correctly, "Those who recognize the use of contraception as incompatible with sexual integrity will wish to recommend, instead, the use of natural family planning — always assuming there really is no appreciable risk of transmitting an effect to the germ line."[70]

In the next section of this chapter, devoted to prenatal and pre-implantation screening, I will consider the morality of somatic gene therapy on the pre-implantation embryo.

F. Germ-Line "Therapy"

At present, such "therapy" seems unrealizable, and the risks entailed, particularly if human subjects (and their progeny — for such "therapy" affects not only particular individuals but all their descendants) are involved, are far too great, and even unknown, to warrant its use. Much more research must be done on animals before one can even begin to think of morally licit applications of such "therapy." The problems and risks raised by germ-line therapy are such as to provide serious grounds for thinking that it should never be carried out. Watt describes these serious risks — to the immediate subject, to future generations, to the human embryos that would no doubt be used for purely research purposes, etc. — in great detail in her excellent article, and I refer readers interested in pursuing the matter to it.[71] Such therapy is *not* to be regarded in any way as intrinsically evil. It is simply that at present, with other pressing health needs and in view of the serious and unresolved problems and unknown risks raised by this line of therapy, it would be better to leave it alone. But it might perhaps be morally licit in the future, once sufficient studies have been done on animals and there is reasonable hope that the terrible risks such therapy raises both for the individuals immediately affected and for their descendants can be avoided or minimized.

5. Prenatal and Pre-Implantation Screening

A. Prenatal Diagnosis and Screening

As Thomas Hilgers, M.D., has said, "Prenatal diagnosis is as old as obstetrics and having babies."[72] Its original purpose was to help protect the health and life of both the unborn child and its mother. It had as its major emphasis the diagnosis or assessment of conditions to assist the physician in helping the unborn child to a more normal and healthy life.

With the development of sonography, which allowed one to see into the uterus and to observe the development of the embryo/fetus, and an explosion of technological tools helpful in diagnosing — such as amniocentesis or chorionic villus sampling (CVS) — it is now possible to identify and evaluate at least 20 different chromosome anomalies and 700 to 1,000 different biochemical or molecular conditions with a genetic base.[73]

(1) Moral Misuse of Prenatal Screening

When the possibility of terminating a pregnancy became legal in the United States in 1973, the pressure for accurate diagnosis grew, and the legal penalty imposed on obstetricians for failing to warn or diagnose fetal anomalies became a driving force in obstetric care. As a result of this pressure, the stated objective of prenatal diagnosis today is "to offer the widest range of informed choice to couples at risk of having children with an abnormality, and to allow such couples the opportunity to achieve a healthy family by avoiding the birth of affected children through selected abortion."[74] In fact, as Hilgers notes, in a recent review of the practice of fetal testing, one leading advocate of such testing declared, in a statement which seems to summarize current attitudes of Western medicine, that "the advantages of ever-earlier prenatal testing seem obvious. The sooner a problem is detected, the sooner therapy or termination can be undertaken."[75] Commenting on this author's statement, Hilgers says: "While lip service is given to 'therapy,' it is clear that 'termination' or abortion is the overwhelming approach utilized as a result of these [screening] programs. . . . [O]ver the last 35 years, we have moved, in prenatal diagnosis, from making a diagnosis for the purposes of assisting the patient (in this case the fetus), to making a diagnosis so that the patient can be eliminated. This shift has already taken place and, to a great extent, has taken a strong hold in medical practice."[76]

This does not mean, however, that prenatal diagnosis as such is immoral. Diagnostic information is not of itself morally wrong. But a great many of the diagnostic procedures now available are used primarily to detect, as soon possible, whether an unborn child suffers from a malady such as Down syndrome, Trisomy 18 or Trisomy 13, spina bifida, or Tay-Sachs disease. All women are now offered a blood test designed to detect neural tube defects (such as those that cause spina bifida), and physicians who fail to offer the tests in areas where proper follow-up is available (practically the entire United States) are liable to malpractice suits.[77] A set of tests is now available for detecting chromosomal defects such as Down syndrome: amniocentesis, chorionic villus sampling, and sampling of maternal serum alpha-fetoprotein (MSAFP). Amniocentesis involves removal of a small amount of amniotic fluid, containing cells from the fetus, by the use of a hollow needle inserted into the amniotic sac. This procedure for the purpose of analyzing the chromosomes of the fetus is usually performed at about the sixteenth week of gestation, and it requires approximately three to four weeks to obtain results of the chromosomal testing. Chorionic villus sampling can be performed much earlier in pregnancy. MSAFP tests the maternal serum. If the alpha-fetoprotein in this serum is high, this indicates an increased risk of neural tube defects and requires further study. If the AFP is low, this indicates an increased risk of Down syndrome or other chromosome disorders.

The MSAFP test has now been expanded to look for the presence of two other substances (estriol and HCG), making the test far more sensitive. This so-called triple test makes it much easier to detect Down syndrome — better than 80 percent of such unborn children can be identified by this test, which also, incidentally, has a high false positive rate (i.e., the identifying of unborn children as being afflicted with Down syndrome when in reality they are not). The usual outcome is the recommendation that those unborn children identified as "abnormal" be terminated or aborted.[78]

(2) Morally Good Uses of Prenatal Testing

As noted already, prenatal diagnosis as such is useful and can be put to good use. Hilgers says that, for the most part, invasive procedures which jeopardize the embryo and fetus (e.g., amniocentesis) are medically unnecessary in medical practice in which neither the doctor nor the patient is willing to abort. He says that in some select kinds of cases, having adequate knowledge of the child's condition can be useful in guiding proper medically therapeutic treatment of the unborn child. Diagnostic ultrasound, he argues, is noninvasive and is probably not sufficiently employed to afford proper management of pregnancies.[79]

Prenatal diagnosis can be very valuable. For example, by detecting neural tube anomalies such as spina bifida it is frequently possible to engage in therapeutic actions on the developing embryo in the womb. For example, a shunt can be inserted into the child's brain and fluid causing pressure on the brain drained from it, thus providing great benefit to a child suffering from spina bifida. In fact, at a hearing at the U.S. Senate some years ago sponsored by pro-life Senator Gordon Humphrey, I witnessed testimony from a couple with their physician and their child — now born and resting on her mother's lap — in which they described the wonderful surgery that had been done on the child while still in the womb, a therapeutic intervention indicated after prenatal diagnosis had shown that she suffered from a neural tube defect and that fluids were building up in her cranium, exerting pressure on her brain. This timely intervention was successful in minimizing the harm this child suffered.

(3) Conclusion

Magisterial teaching provides solid guidance regarding prenatal diagnosis. In *Donum vitae* (I, 2), the Congregation for the Doctrine of the Faith declared such diagnosis "permissible if the methods used, with the consent of the parents who have been adequately instructed, safeguard the life and integrity of the embryo and its mother and does not subject them to disproportionate risks. But this diagnosis is gravely opposed to the moral law when it is done with the thought of possibly inducing an abortion depending upon the results: a diagnosis which shows the existence of a malformation or a hereditary illness must not be the equivalent of a death-sentence." Similar teaching is found in other relevant magisterial documents, such as John Paul II's *Evangelium vitae*, the Pontifical Council for Pastoral Assistance to Health Care Workers' *Charter for Health Care Workers*, and the U.S. bishops' *Ethical and Religious Directives for Catholic Health Care Services.*[80]

Baumiller has observed that, because the contemporary attitude (described above so well by Hilgers) is to "terminate" the life of an unborn child identified by modern methods of prenatal diagnosis as suffering a serious anomaly, "most medical centers with a moral concern about the sacredness of all life have traditionally not offered prenatal diagnostic services. Patients are commonly sent to centers where a pro-life stance is not expected. . . . Thus Catholic hospitals and those who practice obstetrics have too frequently abandoned those people most in need of support. That support must be to affirm the sanctity of human life. Prenatal diagnosis offers information to a woman, a couple; such information is good because it delineates reality."[81] A true challenge is here presented to the Catholic health care community.

B. Pre-Implantation Diagnosis and Screening

The treatment of this issue can be relatively brief. Pre-implantation diagnosis and screening of human embryos have grown out of the technology of *in vitro* fertilization and, as Hilgers has put it, "the challenge to clinicians and investigators to improve the 'take home baby rate.' "[82] Embryos subject to such screening/diagnosis come from two sources. The first and by far the largest source of embryos subject to pre-implantation diagnosis is *in vitro* fertilization, and the principal aim of such screening/diagnosis is to determine whether embryos in question are at risk of suffering from some serious (or perhaps not so serious) disease or anomaly and, if so identified, to "terminate" their lives by refusing to implant them in their mothers' wombs (or the wombs of "surrogates"). Diagnosis and screening for such purposes (along with the way in which these tiny humans have been "produced") is utterly immoral, as the *Vatican Instruction on Respect for Human Life in Its Origin and on the Dignity of Procreation* (*Donum vitae*) made crystal clear — and as we saw in reviewing this document in Chapter One.

Another source of embryos for pre-implantation diagnosis/screening is pre-implantation embryos flushed from the uterus by uterine lavage.[83] This procedure is usually done to seek out embryos at high risk and then "terminate them."

Pre-implantation diagnosis can, however, have truly *therapeutic ends* in view. For instance, it is possible to use gene therapy on a pre-implantation embryo to correct a possible serious malady. Thus on February 3, 2000, the *London Times* (I happened to be in London at the time) reported that doctors had helped a married couple who had already had one child who suffered from cystic fibrosis to have a child free of this disease, despite the fact that they stood at risk of having another child so afflicted. What they had done was to have the couple provide the ovum and sperm, fertilize these gametic cells *in vitro*, and then subject the developing pre-implantation embryo to a test to see whether or not it carried the genes responsible for cystic fibrosis. It did. But then the physicians introduced a viral vector carrying a gene to "correct" this problem, and they succeeded in doing so. The child was then implanted in the mother's womb, and approximately nine months later (early February 2000) a baby girl was born, one totally free of cystic fibrosis.

Here the moral problem is that this child was not conceived in the mother's womb after a marital act but was rather "produced" in the laboratory in a petri dish and, had the gene therapy not been successful, the pre-implantation embryo would have been "discarded" and not implanted in the mother's womb.

But would it be immoral to remove an early, pre-implantation embryo from the womb by uterine lavage if there is serious reason to think that it suffers from a serious genetic malady that could be cured by the introduction of the "right" gene through gene somatic cell therapy?

The Magisterium has not addressed this issue. Although *Donum vitae* condemns *in vitro* fertilization and the freezing of embryos (cryopreservation), "even when carried out in order to preserve the life of an embryo," as

246 CATHOLIC BIOETHICS AND THE GIFT OF HUMAN LIFE

an offense contrary to human dignity because this exposes the embryo to grave risks of harm (cf. *Donum vitae*, I, 6), it had previously acknowledged, as we have seen already in discussing *prenatal* diagnosis, that if such diagnosis respects the embryo's life and is directed toward its safeguarding, it can be morally licit (cf. ibid., I, 2). Thus might it not be in conformity with magisterial teaching to remove an early embryo from the womb by uterine lavage, if there is serious reason for believing it subject to a devastating genetic disease, and, if there are good reasons for thinking that gene somatic line therapy would be successful, deliver the "correct" genes to the embryo, and then re-introduce it into the mother's womb for implantation? It seems to me that this may be a valid moral option.[84]

6. Genetic Counseling

In their *Ethical and Religious Directives for Catholic Health Care Services*, the U.S. bishops state: "Genetic counseling may be provided in order to promote responsible parenthood and to prepare for the proper treatment and care of children with genetic defects, in accordance with Catholic moral teaching and the intrinsic rights and obligations of married couples regarding the transmission of life" (no. 54). Genetic counseling, therefore, is morally legitimate in itself.

The need for such counseling is growing, as today we know that many, many diseases and anomalies affecting human persons are genetically based. In fact, a genetic component has been identified for over 4,000 diseases, disorders, and traits,[85] and as the Human Genome Project (see below) advances, and after virtual completion, more and more such diseases may be identified. As a result, today many persons, particularly married couples, are legitimately concerned to know whether or not there is likelihood that any children they may generate may be afflicted by some serious genetically induced malady. The moral issue concerns the *kind* of counseling to be given.

Today, in our secular society, many think that if genetic testing shows that a couple is at high risk of conceiving a child afflicted by a serious genetically based malady, that couple ought to take effective steps to prevent either the conception or birth of such a child. By effective steps for preventing conception, moreover, they mean various contraceptive procedures, in particular tubal ligation, and by effective steps for preventing birth, should tests *in utero* show that the child is, or may well be, afflicted by such a malady, they mean abortion. They may also recommend artificial insemination by a donor, *in vitro* fertilization (followed by pre-implantation diagnosis, with "termination" of embryos identified as afflicted by a genetic malady), and other immoral methods of coping with the dangers that genetic testing may indicate. Obviously, a morally upright person cannot offer such "counseling."

Germain Grisez has provided very practical guidance for morally upright counselors, in particular, physicians who might be asked by their patients for advice on these matters. Obviously, a Catholic physician/counselor, or any morally upright counselor, should tell potential patients that he or she is committed to the good of human life and will never advise anyone to even consider contraception, sterilization, abortion, *in vitro* fertilization, etc. Because of the current climate in our society, physicians and others who refuse to provide such counseling may be vulnerable to legal malpractice suits. They ought therefore to seek competent legal advice. Grisez also makes the following practical suggestion:

> You may be able to minimize your vulnerability arising from your nonconformity [to secular standards] by not only telling those who come to you where you stand but having them read, and perhaps even sign, a carefully drafted summary of your position on matters where your standards of good practice will diverge from those the courts would be likely to use. Without anticipating the legal advice you will receive, I think such a summary probably should include a clear statement that, as a matter of principle, you will not prescribe contraceptives, do sterilizations, or perform abortions; you will give no medical advice regarding these matters and no information about their availability; and in respect to these matters you will not refer patients to others from whom they might obtain any service, advice, or information that, as matter of principle, you would not provide personally.[86]

This seems eminently good, practical advice for counselors.

If a couple seeking counsel is not married, the results of a genetic test would either remove reasons for concern or disclose a reason, not necessarily conclusive but surely worth considering, for either abstaining from marriage or continuing one's search for a spouse. If the couple is married, negative results of genetic testing would, of course, allay any fears they might have. But if the tests disclosed that there were indeed risks of conceiving a child who would be afflicted by a genetic malady, the couple would then need helpful counseling. Above, a morally wrong kind of counseling was excluded.

The choice whether to accept the risk and seek to generate life through the conjugal act or to avoid doing so by the practice of periodic continence is, of course, the responsibility of the couple. The Magisterium of the Church clearly recognizes that the likelihood of generating a child who might suffer from a serious genetic illness provides a *serious* reason for deciding not to have a child for either a certain or indefinite period of time.[87] The couple might legitimately reach the conclusion (and their counselor might well concur and indeed recommend) that running the risk would either be unfair to others or that they either could not fulfill or would be seriously tempted to omit fulfilling the responsibilities they would incur in caring for a child afflicted by the malady. Such a conclusion and/or recommendation would not be immoral.

However, the couple might conclude (and their counselor might well agree and recommend) that they courageously agree to accept the risk and by doing so firmly commit themselves to carry out the responsibilities that they would incur should their child indeed be afflicted by the malady in question. Although some people, particularly in our secular culture, might argue that if a couple deliberately risks having a child who might suffer from a serious malady such as cystic fibrosis, they are being unjust, either to the child exposed to such a risk or to the larger society (which will have to help in providing suitable health care), or to both. I believe that those who argue this way are mistaken. If the child is generated, a new and precious human person has come into existence, and his or her life is of surpassing value and contributes to the common good. Frequently, the burdens such a child might himself suffer and present for others are highly exaggerated, while the possible benefits of the child's life, to itself, its parents, and to society as a whole, are ignored or minimized. Thus, as Grisez correctly says, "one cannot rule out the possibility that a couple could rightly decide that they need not abstain from possibly fertile intercourse, despite the probability that a child will be afflicted with a severe disease, genetic or other. Moreover, in the case of genetic diseases, a couple accept not only more or less risk; avoiding parenthood on this basis means also forgoing children who would themselves be healthy, though perhaps carriers of the genetic defect."[88]

7. The Human Genome Project

The genome is the sum of the genetic material that defines a biological species. The Human Genome Project (HGP) is an international research program whose goal is to map in detail the positions of genes on their respective chromosomes, to determine the complete nucleotide sequence of human DNA, and to localize the estimated 50,000-100,000 genes on each of the 46 human chromosomes within the human genome.[89] By late June 2000, this vast project was completed.

Human genome studies of genetically related disorders and diseases are of tremendous importance not only to scientists and physicians but to everyone. The major *moral* question is how this knowledge will be used. It can obviously be used to develop new kinds of genetic therapy, and it may perhaps become feasible to attempt some kinds of germ-line therapy that would not raise grave moral objections.

The greatest (and legitimate) fear people have is that, if genetic testing made possible by the HGP showed them susceptible to or carriers of serious genetic maladies, they would experience prejudicial and indeed unjust treatment from those who learn of their genetic defects or dispositions. Such unjust treatment could be extended by parents to children whose genetic propensities become known to them, by employers and potential employers, by health care providers and insurance companies, and by the government. The possibility exists that some individuals would not be allowed to marry or to have children, that efforts to make sterilization and abortion compulsory would be made, etc.

But these potential problems are not *per se* the result of the Human Genome Project, which in itself is essentially a research project intended to enrich the human community by expanding its knowledge. The problems lie in the human heart and will, not in the HGP.

ENDNOTES FOR CHAPTER SIX

1. In the introduction and first two parts of this chapter, I have adapted, with substantive additions and developments, some material from my earlier book, *Human Existence, Medicine, and Ethics: Reflections on Human Life* (Chicago: Franciscan Herald Press, 1977), Chapter One, "Experimenting on Human Subjects." The matter presented here, however, is in essence a complete reworking of the issue.

2. Roger Wertheimer, "Philosophy on Humanity," in *Abortion: Pro and Con*, ed. Robert L. Perkins (Cambridge, MA: Schenkmann, 1975), pp. 107-108.

3. Today, of course, many influential authors explicitly claim that membership in the human species has absolutely *no* moral significance and that

those who claim that it does are guilty of "speciesism." Among the more prominent and better-known advocates of this view are Michael Tooley (see his *Abortion and Infanticide* [Oxford and New York: Oxford, at the Clarendon Press, 1983], esp. pp. 61-76), Peter Singer (see his *Rethinking Life and Death: The Collapse of Our Traditional Ethics* [New York: St. Martin's Press, 1994], esp. pp. 202-206, and Joseph Fletcher, "Indicators of Humanhood," *Hastings Center Report* 2 (November 1972), 1-4. This denigration of the moral worth of human beings, a cornerstone of the "culture of death," was criticized above in Chapter Five. One of the finest philosophical rebuttals of this position is given by Patrick Lee, *Abortion and Unborn Human Life* (Washington, DC: The Catholic University of America Press, 1997), Chapter One.

4. Karol Wojtyla, *Love and Responsibility*, trans. H. Willetts (New York: Farrar, Straus, Giroux, 1981), p. 41.

5. Paul Ramsey, *The Patient as Person: Explorations in Medical Ethics* (New Haven and London: Yale University Press, 1970), Chapter One, "Consent as a Canon of Loyalty with Special Reference to Children in Medical Investigation," pp. 1-58. This chapter is *must* reading on this subject.

6. See, for example, Benedict Ashley, O.P., and Kevin O'Rourke, O.P., *Health Care Ethics: A Theological Analysis* (4th ed., Washington, DC: Georgetown University Press, 1997), pp. 345-346.

7. Articles of the Nuremberg Tribunal, article 1; cited by Ramsey, *The Patient as Person*, p. 1.

8. The text of the *Declaration of Helsinki* can be found in Henry K. Beecher, *Research and the Individual* (Boston: Little, Brown, and Co., 1970), p. 227.

9. Gonzalo Herranz, "Christian Contributions to the Ethics of Biomedical Investigation: An Historical Perspective," in *Ethics of Biomedical Research in a Christian Vision: Proceedings of the Ninth Assembly of the Pontifical Academy for Life* (Vatican City, 24-26, February 2003), eds. Juan de Dios Vial Correa and Elio Sgreccia (Vatican City: Libreria Editrice Vaticana, 2003), pp. 126-145.

10. Here the *Charter* refers to Pius XII, "To the Doctors of the G. Mendel Institute," Nov. 24, 1957, in *AAS* 49 (1957), 1031. Pius XII spoke about this topic many times. A useful collection of his addresses on this subject can be found in *The Pope Speaks* 1.3 and 1.4 (1954). Among his principal addresses are those to the First International Congress on the Histopathology of the Nervous System (September 14, 1952), the Sixteenth International Congress of Military Medicine (October 19, 1953), and the Eighth Congress of the World Medical Association (September 30, 1954).

11. In a footnote at this point, the *Charter* quotes from the following passage from the Pontifical Council *Cor Unum*'s "Some Ethical Questions Relating to the Gravely Ill and the Dying" (June 27, 1981): "The patient cannot be the object of decisions which he will not make, or, if he is not able to do so, which he could not approve. The 'person,' primarily responsible for his own life, should be the center of any assisting intervention: others are there to help him, not to replace him." The full text of this document is found in *Enchiridion Vaticanum 7, Documenti ufficiali della Santa Sede 1980-1981* (Bologna: EDB, 1985), 1137, no. 2.1, 2.

12. The *Charter* cites this text from Pope John Paul II's Address to the World Congress of Catholic Doctors, October 3, 1982, published in *Insegnamenti di Giovanni Paolo II* 5.3 (Vatican City: Libreria Editrice Vaticana, 1983), p. 673, no. 4.

13. Here the *Charter* refers to Pope John Paul II's Address to the Participants at Two Congresses on Medicine and Surgery, October 27, 1980, published in *Insegnamenti di Giovanni Paolo II* 3.2 (Vatican City: Libreria Editrice Vaticana, 1981), pp. 1008-1009, no. 5.

14. The text of no. 72 of the *Charter* can be found in Pontifical Council for Pastoral Assistance to Health Care Workers, *Charter for Health Care Workers* (Boston: Pauline Books and Media, 1995), pp. 70-71.

15. For instance, Henry K. Beecher, *Research and the Individual*, pp. 18-19, 121ff.

16. Ramsey, *The Patient as Person*, p. 3.

17. National Conference of Catholic Bishops, *Ethical and Religious Directives for Catholic Health Care Services* (Washington, DC: United States Catholic Conference, 1995), no. 27.

18. In *The Patient as Person*, p. 8, footnote 6, Ramsey notes that "Sir Harold Himsworth said (1953) that the Hippocratic Oath can be given in a single sentence: *Act always so as to increase trust* (quoted by Ross G. Mitchell, 'The Child and Experimental Medicine,' *British Medical Journal* 4, no. 1 [March 21, 1964]: 726). This might better read: *Act always so as not to abuse trust; act always so as to exhibit faithfulness,* to deserve and inspire trust."

19. On this, I have already referred to the "personalistic norm" articulated by Karol Wojtyla in *Love and Responsibility*. Other excellent and eloquent defenses of the inviolable dignity of all human beings, all human persons, are set forth by Jacques Maritain, *The Person and the Common Good* (New York: Charles Scribner's Sons, 1947), Chapter 3; Mortimer Adler, *The Difference of Man and the Difference It Makes* (New York: Meridian, 1968).

20. Ramsey, *The Patient as Person*, p. 7.

21. Pontifical Council for Pastoral Assistance to Health Care Workers, *Charter for Health Care Workers*, p. 72, no. 73.

22. Ramsey, *The Patient as Person*, pp. 7-8.

23. Hans Jonas, "Philosophical Reflections on Experimenting with Human Subjects," in *Philosophical Essays: From Current Creed to Technological Man* (Chicago: University of Chicago Press, 1980), pp. 105-131.

24. See Ashley-O'Rourke, *HealthCare Ethics* (4th ed.), p. 346, where they identify this as the 4th Principle of Research on Human Subjects.

25. Pontifical Council for Pastoral Assistance to Health Care Workers, *Charter for Health Care Workers*, p.72, no. 73.

26. Ibid., p. 77, no. 81.

27. Ibid., p. 77, no. 81. Here the internal citation is from the same address of Pope John Paul II, ibid.

28. Richard McCormick, S.J., *How Brave a New World? Dilemmas in Bioethics* (Garden City, NY: Doubleday, 1981), chapter four, "Proxy Consent in the Experimental Situation," pp. 61-62; and chapter six, "Sharing in Sociality: Children and Experimentation," pp. 87-98. Chapter four had originally been published in *Perspectives in Biology and Medicine* 18 (1974), 2-20; chapter six had originally been published in *Hastings Center Report* 5:3 (May 1975), 26-31.

29. Here I want to note that I believe, with others, that as children grow they become capable of exercising their intellect and power of free choice. According to the *Code of Canon Law*, "minors," i.e., individuals under eighteen years of age, "on completion of the seventh year . . . [are] presumed to have the use of reason" (*"Minor . . . expleto autem septennio, usum rationis habere praesumitur"*) (canon 97.2). Those who have reached the use of reason, I believe, can give personal free and informed consent to be subjects of non-therapeutic as well as therapeutic research/experiments. However, I believe that the parents of minor children can veto such authorization.

30. On this, see my essay, *Experimenting on Human Subjects, The Linacre Quarterly* 41:3 (November 1974), 238-252, and also my *Human Existence, Medicine, and Ethics: Reflections on Human Life* (Chicago: Franciscan Herald Press, 1977), pp. 21-28; Ramsey, *A Reply to Richard McCormick: The Enforcement of Morals: Nontherapeutic Research on Children*.

31. Ramsey, *The Patient as Person*, pp. 12-14.

32. Germain Grisez, *The Way of the Lord Jesus*, Vol. 2, *Living a Christian Life* (Quincy, IL: Franciscan University Press, 1993); emphasis added.

33. Congregation for the Doctrine of the Faith, *Donum vitae* (1987), 1.4, *AAS* 80 (1988), 81-83. Italics in the original. At this point a footnote, no. 29, is given. It reads: "Cf. Pope John Paul II, Address to a Meeting of the Pontifical Academy of Sciences, October 23, 1982: *AAS* 75 (1983), 37: 'I condemn, in the most explicit and formal way, experimental manipulations of the human embryo, since the human being, from conception to death, cannot be exploited for any purpose whatsoever.' "

34. See National Conference of Catholic Bishops, *Ethical and Religious Directives for Catholic Health Care Services*, no. 51: "Non-therapeutic experiments on a living embryo or fetus are not permitted, even with the consent of the parents." See also *Charter for Health Care Workers*, no. 82.

35. Ibid., no. 31, which reads in part: "In instances of nontherapeutic experimentation, the surrogate can give this consent *only if the experiment entails no significant risk to the person's well being*" (emphasis added).

36. I made this accusation in the first edition of this book.

37. See the Australian bishops' *Code of Ethical Standards for Catholic Health and Aged Services in Australia*. In no. 6.6 of this document, we read: "Research involving vulnerable people must only be undertaken when the knowledge to be obtained is sufficiently important to warrant involving such vulnerable people and this knowledge cannot be obtained by other means.... *Non-therapeutic experimentation must involve no significant risk at all*" (emphasis added).

38. A good presentation of this matter is given by Edmund D. Pellegrino, M.D., "Human Embryos and the Stem Cell Controversy," *The NaProEthics Forum* 4.6 (November 1999), 2-3. See also Edward J. Furton and Micheline M. Mathews-Roth, M.D., "Stem Cell Research and the Human Embryo, Part One," *Ethics & Medics* 24.8 (August 1999), 1-2.

39. On this, see testimony of Rev. Tadeusz Pacholczyk given July 30, 2005, to the Pennsylvania Conference of Catholic Bishops; see http://www.pacatholic.org/statements/stemcellresearch.html.

40. Doerflinger, in a letter to the U.S. House of Representative made public April 29, 2004. See http://www.catholicnews.com/data/stories/cns/0403293.htm. Among Doerflinger's important essays on stem-cell research published between 1999 and 2006 are the following: "Human Cloning and Embryonic Stem Cell Research after Seoul," in *The National Catholic Bioethics Quarterly*, Vol. 6, No. 2 (Summer 2006), 339-350 (reprinting congressional testimony of March 7, 2006); "The Many Casualties of Cloning," *The New Atlantis* (Spring 2006), 60-70; "Cloning Chaos," National Review Online (December 13, 2005), at www.nationalreview.com/comment/doerflinger200512130824.asp; "Confronting Technology

at the Beginning of Life: A Morally Grounded Policy Agenda for the
United States," in Charles Colson and Nigel Cameron (eds.), *Human Dig-
nity in the Biotech Century: A Christian Vision for Public Policy* (Downers
Grove, IL: InterVarsity Press 2004), pp. 221-239; "Experimentation on
Human Subjects and Stem Cell Research," in Kevin T. McMahon, S.T.D.
(ed.), *Moral Issues in Catholic Health Care* (Philadelphia, PA: Saint Charles
Borromeo Seminary 2004), pp. 93-107; "Retrospective and Prospective:
The Public Policy Debate on Embryo Research," in Nicholas C. Lund-
Molfese and Michael L. Kelly (eds.), *Human Dignity and Reproductive
Technology* (Lanham, MD: University Press of America 2003), pp. 97-109;
"Testimony on Embryo Research and Related Issues," in *The National
Catholic Bioethics Quarterly*, Vol. 3, No. 4 (Winter 2003), 767-786; "The
Ethics and Policy of Embryonic Stem Cell Research: A Catholic Perspec-
tive," in Nancy E. Snow (ed.), *Stem Cell Research: New Frontiers in Science
and Ethics* (Notre Dame, IN: University of Notre Dame Press, 2003), pp.
143-166; "The science and politics of stem cell research," in L. Gormally
(ed.), *Culture of Life — Culture of Death* (London: The Linacre Centre,
2002), pp. 299-307; "The Policy and Politics of Embryonic Stem Cell
Research," *The National Catholic Bioethics Quarterly*, Vol. 1, No. 2 (Summer 2001), 135-143; "The Ethics of Funding Embryonic Stem Cell
Research: A Catholic Viewpoint," in *Kennedy Institute of Ethics Journal*,
Vol. 9, No. 2 (June 1999), 137-150.

41. See, for example, Nicholas Wade, "Embryo Cell Research: A Clash of Values," *New York Times*, Friday, July 2, 1999, A21.

42. Cited in ibid.

43. See *Congressional Record*, September 9, 2004, pp. H6956-7.

44. See *The Weekly Standard*, December 22, 2004. See http://stemcellresearch.
org for new breakthroughs using adult stem cells for therapeutic purposes.

45. For this article, see http://www.stemcellresearch.org/alternatives/75new
reasons.pdf.

46. For this letter, see www.stemcellresearch.org/pr/kerry.pdf.

47. Pellegrino, "Human Embryos and the Stem Cell Controversy," 3. Pelle-
grino cites the following scientific sources to support his affirmations: P.
Rubinstein et al., "Outcomes Among 526 Recipients of Placental-Blood
Transplants from Unrelated Donors," *New England Journal of Medicine*
399 (November 26, 2998), 1565-1577; R. Lewis, "Human Mesenchyma
Stem Cells Differentiate in the Lab," *The Scientist* 13 (April 12, 1999),
1ff.; Claire Lowry, "Adult Human Brain Stem Cells Reproduce In Vitro,"
UniSci Science and Research News, April 28, 1999.

48. On this, see Rev. Tadeusz Pacholczyk, cf. endnote 39 above.

49. The President's Council on Bioethics, *Alternative Sources of Human Pluripotent Stem Cells: A White Paper* (Washington, DC: The President's Council on Bioethics, 2005).

50. Ibid., p. 2.

51. Ibid., p. 3.

52. For this interview, see http://www.nationalreview.com/interrogatory/hurlbut200512060850.asp. Hurlbut offers a more technical presentation of his proposal in "Altered Nuclear Transfer as a Morally Acceptable Means for the Procurement of Human Embryonic Stem Cells," *Perspectives in Biology and Medicine*, Vol. 48, No. 2 (Spring 2005), 211–228.

53. See "The Moral Retrieval of ES Cells," *Ethics & Medics*, 30.7 (July 2005), 1-2; *Origins*, July 7, 2005, 26ff.; See also http://www.eppc.org/publications/pubID.2374/pub_detail.asp.

54. See the following: David L. Schindler, "Biotechnology and the Givenness of the Good: Posing Properly the Moral Questions Regarding Human Dignity," *Communio* 31.4 (Winter 2004), 612-644; Adrian Walker, "Altered Nuclear Transfer: A Philosophical Critique," ibid., 649-684; Adrian Walker, "A Way Around the Cloning Objection Against ANT? A Brief Response to the Joint Statement on the Production of Pluripotent Stem Cells by Oocyte Assisted Reprogramming," ibid., 32.1 (Spring 2005), 188-194; Schindler, "A Response to the Joint Statement 'Production of Pluripotent Stem Cells by Oocyte Assisted Reprogramming,'" ibid., 32.2 (Summer 2005).

55. The following scholars have endorsed ANT-OAR: Hadley Arkes, Ph.D.; Rev. Nicanor Pier Giorgio Austriaco, O.P., Ph.D.; Rev. Thomas Berg, L.C., Ph.D.; E. Christian Brugger, D. Phil.; Nigel M. de S. Cameron, Ph.D.; Joseph Capizzi, Ph. D.; Maureen L. Condic, Ph.D.; Samuel B. Condic, M.A.; Rev. Kevin T. FitzGerald, S.J., Ph.D.; Rev. Kevin Flannery, S.J., D.Phil.; Edward J. Furton, Ph.D.; Robert George, Ph.D.; Timothy George, Th.D.; Alfonso Gómez-Lobo, Dr. phil.; Germain Grisez, Ph.D.; Markus Grompe, M.D.; John M. Haas, Ph.D.; Robert Hamerton-Kelly, Th.D.; John Collins Harvey, M.D., Ph.D.; Paul J. Hoehner, M.D., M.A., FAHA; William B. Hurlbut, M.D.; John F. Kilner, Ph.D.; Patrick Lee, Ph.D.; William E. May, Ph.D.; Rev. Gonzalo Miranda, L.C., Ph.L., S.T.D.; C. Ben Mitchell, Ph.D.; Most Reverend John J. Myers, J.C.D., D.D.; Chris Oleson, Ph.D.; Rev. Tad Pacholczyk, Ph.D.; Rev. Peter F. Ryan, S.J., S.T.D.; William L. Saunders, J.D.; David Stevens, M.D., M.A.; Rev. Msgr. Stuart W. Swetland, S.T.D.; M. Edward Whelan III, J.D.; Rev. Thomas Williams, L.C., Ph.L., S.T.D.

56. Edward Furton, "A Defense of Oocyte-Assisted Reprogramming," *The National Catholic Bioethics Quarterly* 5.3 (Autumn 2005), 465-468, at 467-468.

57. Nicanor Austriaco, "Are Teratomas Embryos or Non-Embryos? A Criterion for Oocyte-Assisted Reprogramming," *The National Catholic Bioethics Quarterly* 5.3 (Autumn 2005).

58. E. Christian Brugger, "ANT-OAR: A Morally Acceptable Means for Deriving Pluripotent Stem Cells: A Reply to Criticisms," *Communio* 32 (Winter 2005), 753-769.

59. For this, see *BioEdge* 234 (January 9, 2007).

60. See *BioEdge* 253 (June 13, 2007).

61. *Genetic Intervention on Human Subjects: The Report of a Working Party of the Catholic Bishops' Joint Committee on Bioethical Issues* (London: The Catholic Bishops' Joint Committee on Bioethical Issues, 1996), p. 6. Members of the Working Party were Dr. A. P. Cole (Chairman), Rev. John Henry, John Duddington, Dr. Ian Jessiman, Dr. John McLean, Agneta Sutton, and Dr. Helen Watt.

62. W. French Anderson, "Gene Therapy. I. Strategies for Gene Therapy," *Encyclopedia of Bioethics*, 911.

63. On all this, see *Genetic Intervention on Human Subjects*, pp. 6-15; Anderson, "Genetic Therapy," in *The New Genetics and the Future of Man*, ed. Michael Hamilton (Grand Rapids, MI: Eerdmans, 1972) pp. 109-117.

64. Anderson, "Gene Therapy. I. Strategies for Gene Therapy," 908.

65. Ibid.

66. Ibid., 909f.; *Genetic Intervention on Human Subjects*, p. 12.

67. Anderson, "Gene Therapy I. Strategies for Gene Therapy," 909f.

68. See L. Archer, "Genetic Testing and Gene Therapy," in *Man-Made Man: Ethical and Legal Issues in Genetics*, eds. P. Doherty and A. Sutton (Dublin: Open Air, 1997), p. 38.

69. This is recommended, for instance, by the British Gene Therapy Advisory Committee in its *First Annual Report November 1993-December 1994* (London: Health Departments of the United Kingdom, 1995), pp. 5-6. Helen Watt calls attention to this in her very helpful essay, "Human Gene Therapy: Ethical Aspects," in *Human Genome, Human Person, and the Society of the Future: Proceedings of the Fourth Assembly of the Pontifical Academy for Life* (Vatican City, February 23-25, 1998), eds. Juan de Dios Vial Correa and Elio Sgreccia (Vatican City: Libreria Editrice Vaticana, 1999), p. 256, footnote 6.

70. Watt, "Human Gene Therapy: Ethical Aspects," p. 256.

71. Ibid., pp. 256-268.

72. Thomas W. Hilgers, M.D., "Prenatal and Pre-Implantation Genetic Diagnosis: Duty or Eugenic Prelude?" in *Human Genome, Human Person, and the Society of the Future*, p. 172.

73. Ibid. Hilgers provides a detailed description of various methods of prenatal testing, accurately assessing their moral value, on pp. 175-185.

74. R. Penkenth, "The Scope of Preimplantation Diagnosis," in *Preconception and Preimplantation Diagnosis of Human Genetic Disease*, ed. R. G. Edwards (Cambridge: Cambridge University Press, 1993), p. 82. Cited by Hilgers, "Prenatal and Pre-Implantation Screening," p. 174, note 1.

75. E. Jauniaux, "Fetal Testing in the First Trimester of Pregnancy," *The Female Patient* 22 (1997), 51-52, cited by Hilgers, "Prenatal and Pre-Implantation Screening," p. 186.

76. Hilgers, "Prenatal and Pre-Implantation Screening," p. 186.

77. On this, see Robert C. Baumiller, S.J., "Prenatal Diagnosis," *Ethics & Medics* 20.11 (November 1995), 3. Baumiller also provides a brief synoptic description of major kinds of prenatal diagnosis.

78. Ibid., 3; see Hilgers, "Prenatal and Pre-Implantation Screening," pp. 178-179.

79. Ibid., pp. 186-187.

80. Thus in *Evangelium vitae*, no. 14, Pope John Paul II says: "Prenatal diagnosis, which presents no moral objections if carried out in order to identify the medical treatment which may be needed by the child in the womb, all too often becomes an opportunity for proposing and procuring an abortion. . . ." See *Charter for Health Care Workers*, nos. 59-61, and *Ethical and Religious Directives for Catholic Health Care Services*, no. 50.

81. Baumiller, "Prenatal Diagnosis," 4.

82. Hilgers, "Prenatal and Pre-Implantation Genetic Diagnosis," p. 184.

83. Hilgers notes this possibility on p. 184. The procedure is described more fully by Dr. Alan Handyside. See June Berlfein, "The Earliest Warning," *Discover* (February, 1992), 14.

84. On this, see Albert Moraczewski, "Genes and Pandora's Box," *Ethics & Medics* 18.3 (March 1993), 2.

85. See John Haas, "Human Genetics," *Ethics & Medics* 21.2 (February 1996), 1-2.

86. Germain Grisez, *The Way of the Lord Jesus*, Vol. 3, *Difficult Moral Questions* (Quincy, IL: Franciscan Press, 1997), p. 300.

87. See, for example, Pope Paul VI, encyclical *Humanae vitae*, no. 10.

88. Grisez, *Difficult Moral Questions*, p. 302.

89. On this, see Albert Moraczewski, "Genes and Ethics," *Ethics & Medics* 16.5 (May 1991), 2; see also National Institutes of Health Web site: http://www.nhgri.nih.gov/HGP/, "The Human Genome Project," 2/16/2000.

CHAPTER SEVEN

Euthanasia, Assisted Suicide, and Care of the Dying

Introduction: The Contemporary Movement for Euthanasia and Assisted Suicide

In 1935, the first Voluntary Euthanasia Society was founded in London, and a Euthanasia Society was established in the United States in 1938, but by the early 1970s neither had had much success in gaining support. At the beginning of 1975, the U.S. Euthanasia Society was reactivated as the Society for the Right to Die, and by the beginning of the 1990s support for euthanasia and physician-assisted suicide in the English-speaking world had grown enormously. Public opinion polls in the United States and Britain during the last decade have shown increasing willingness to sanction euthanasia and assisted suicide both morally and legally, and those agitating for change are no longer, as Daniel Callahan, president of the Hastings Center (an influential think tank on bioethical issues), has noted, "a small minority, the usual reformist suspects, but a larger, more influential group of academics, physicians, legislators, judges, and well-placed and well-organized lay people."[1]

To account for this "sea change" in public opinion, Callahan points to:

A growing fear of a long, lingering death, the consequence of changes in the way people die occasioned by more chronic illness and more death in old age; the publicity given to a number of cases where seemingly conservative resistance kept people alive longer than most people found tolerable; ... the AIDS epidemic, with its well publicized cases of young people dying miserable deaths from a particularly noxious and degrading disease ...; the potent Anglo-American movement toward greater self-determination and autonomy — fostered most explicitly on the political left but implicitly abetted ... by the libertarian strains so prominently espoused by conservatives for free market solutions to social problems, and perhaps a diminished willingness on the part of many to accept the pain and suffering of dying as an acceptable fact of life.[2]

The reasons Callahan cites have undoubtedly contributed to the growing success the movement is enjoying.[3] Note, in particular, that he singles out the emphasis on autonomy in contemporary society and an unwillingness to accept pain and suffering. In his encyclical *Evangelium vitae*, Pope John Paul II points to an exaggerated and false understanding of individual autonomy and to hedonism as critical factors contributing to the "culture of death" (cf. *Evangelium vitae*, nos. 20, 23). I believe that another major factor helping to win acceptance of euthanasia and assisted suicide is the idea that *personal* life, as distinct from "merely" biological life, requires exercisable cognitive abilities. This dualistic understanding leads many to conclude that once an individual no longer has such exercisable abilities or when there is danger that they will be lost because of disease or illness, then that individual's biological life is of no value to him or her and that he or she is better off dead than alive; one's life is no longer worth living. Another contributing factor, I believe, is the acceptance of abortion. It is frequently justified on the grounds that the life destroyed is merely "biologically human" and not "personal," and it is at times resorted to as a kind of "mercy killing" or euthanasia of unborn children diagnosed as suffering from maladies that will, so it is alleged, make their lives burdensome and miserable.

Pope John Paul II offers insights into the reasons accounting for the appeal euthanasia has for many today. Thus he writes in *Evangelium vitae*:

> In the sick person the sense of anguish, of severe discomfort, and even of desperation brought on by intense and prolonged suffering can be a decisive factor. Such a situation can threaten the already fragile equilibrium of an individual's personal and family life, with the result that, on the one hand, the sick person, despite the help of increasingly effective medical and social assistance, risks feeling overwhelmed by his or her own frailty; and on the other hand, those close to the sick person can be moved by an understandable even if misguided compassion. All this is aggravated by a cultural climate which fails to perceive any meaning or value in suffering, but rather considers suffering the epitome of evil, to be eliminated at all costs . . . [and assumes] a certain Promethean attitude which leads people to think that they can control life and death by taking the decisions about them into their own hands. . . . As well as for reasons of a misguided pity at

the sight of the patient's suffering, euthanasia is sometimes justified by the utilitarian motive of avoiding costs which bring no return and weigh heavily on society. Thus it is proposed to eliminate malformed babies, the severely handicapped, the disabled, the elderly, especially when they are not self-sufficient, and the terminally ill. (no. 15)

Although euthanasia and physician-assisted suicide are becoming more and more accepted as morally right and legally necessary, these forms of intentional killing of the innocent remain intrinsically immoral. The *Catechism of the Catholic Church*, referring to the Vatican *Declaration on Euthanasia*, ably summarizes what Catholic faith holds. It recognizes that "whatever its motives and means, direct euthanasia consists in putting an end to the lives of handicapped, sick, or dying persons," and is therefore "morally unacceptable" (no. 2277). Continuing, it declares: "Thus an act or omission which, of itself or by intention, causes death in order to eliminate suffering constitutes a murder gravely contrary to the dignity of the human person and to the respect due to the living God, his Creator. The error of judgment into which one can fall in good faith does not change the nature of this murderous act, which must always be forbidden and excluded" (ibid.).

In this chapter I will proceed as follows. (1) I will clarify the terminology used in debates over euthanasia. (2) I will set forth the major arguments given to support what I call the "ethics of euthanasia," including the argument to gain legal approval of voluntary active euthanasia. (3) I will offer a critique of the "ethics of euthanasia" and show why a willingness intentionally to kill a human person is absolutely incompatible with respect for his dignity as a person. (4) I will develop what I will call the "ethics of benemortasia" or of caring, and only caring, for the dying. In developing this alternative to the "ethics of euthanasia," I will identify criteria that help us to distinguish between "ordinary" or "proportionate" medical treatments and "extraordinary" or "disproportionate" treatments. The former are morally required, whereas the latter can, and at times ought to, rightly be refused. (5) I will then take up the care to be given persons who are judged to be permanently unconscious or in the so-called persistent vegetative state. I will conclude (6) with a discussion of living wills and advance directives.

1. Clarifying the Terminology

The Vatican *Declaration on Euthanasia* (1980) defines euthanasia as "an action or an omission which of itself or by intention causes death, in order that all suffering may in this way be eliminated. Euthanasia's terms of reference, then, are to be found in the intention of the will and of the methods used" (Part II). This is a very clear and precise definition, explicitly and rightly noting that one can kill another "in order that all suffering may in this way be eliminated" by acts of *omission* as well as by acts of *commission*. This is most important to recognize, because advocates of euthanasia seek to win support by claiming that so-called passive euthanasia, which for them encompasses "allowing" a person to die of some underlying pathology by withholding or withdrawing medical treatments, is already regarded as morally and legally permissible and that, therefore, "active" euthanasia ought also to be recognized as morally and legally permissible.[4] This is completely false.

The term "euthanasia" is derived from the combination of two Greek words, *eu* (good or well) and *thanasia* (death), and originally meant a good or happy death. But today, as the Vatican *Declaration on Euthanasia* makes clear, it has acquired the meaning of "mercy killing." In fact the revised edition of *The Random House College Dictionary* gives the following as the first meaning of "euthanasia": "1. Also called **mercy killing**, the act of putting to death painlessly a person suffering from an incurable and painful disease or condition."[5]

Euthanasia takes the following forms: 1. *Active euthanasia* (at times called "direct" or "positive" euthanasia), in which someone intentionally chooses to kill a person by an act of commission. Active euthanasia can be either (a) *voluntary active euthanasia*, when it is performed on persons who give free and informed consent to being killed mercifully; (b) *nonvoluntary active euthanasia*, when performed on individuals who are not capable of giving free and informed consent to being killed mercifully; or (c) *involuntary active euthanasia*, when done to individuals who refuse to give free and informed consent to being killed mercifully but who nonetheless are so killed. 2. *Passive euthanasia* (at times called "indirect" or "negative" euthanasia), in which someone brings about the death of a person for merciful reasons by an act of omission, i.e., by withholding or withdrawing medical treatments that could preserve that person's life precisely in order to bring death about. Like active euthanasia, passive euthanasia can also be (a) *voluntary*, when the person killed gives free and informed consent to the withholding or withdrawing of treatments precisely as a way of bringing about his or her own death; (b) *nonvoluntary*, when the person so killed is incompetent and incapable of giving consent; or (c) *involuntary*, when the person so killed refuses to consent to the withholding or withdrawing of life-preserving treatments.[6]

Today the euthanasia movement is principally concerned with establishing the moral rightness and legal permissibility of *active voluntary euthanasia*, claiming erroneously that *passive euthanasia*, both voluntary and nonvoluntary, has already been recognized as morally and legally permissible. Many euthanasia advocates are also agitating for acceptance of *active nonvoluntary euthanasia*, and, as will be seen, they clearly hold it to be the morally right way of "treating" many incompetent patients.

Physician-assisted suicide is accurately defined by one of its champions, Dr. Timothy E. Quill, as "the act of making a means of suicide (such as a prescription for barbiturates) available to a patient who is otherwise physically capable of suicide, and who subsequently acts on his or her own. It is distinguished from voluntary euthanasia, where the physician not only makes the means available but is the actual agent of death upon the patient's request."[7] Thus the principal difference between euthanasia and assisted suicide is that in euthanasia a person other than the one killed is the principal cause of the killing whereas in assisted suicide the person killed is himself or herself the principal cause while the physician or other person (spouse, etc.) formally cooperates in the killing act and is, as it were, an instrumental cause. Since it is usually a physician who "assists" in the suicide, the expression "physician-assisted suicide" is most common in the literature. The most prominent practitioner and advocate of physician-assisted suicide, of course, is the notorious Dr. Jack Kevorkian,[8] popularly known as "Dr. Death," who was convicted of murder and sentenced to prison in 1999.

Since the moral and juridical issues regarding physician-assisted suicide are basically the same as those regarding euthanasia, in what follows I will speak only of euthanasia and the ethics of euthanasia. The rationale justifying physician-assisted suicide is the same as that underlying euthanasia. Those in favor of euthanasia support physician-assisted suicide, while those rejecting it as intrinsically immoral similarly repudiate physician-assisted suicide.

Note, above all, that active euthanasia, brought about by an act of commission, and passive euthanasia, achieved through an act of omission, are morally the same. Each is the *intentional killing* of an innocent human person for reasons of mercy. Such *intentional killing* of an innocent person for reasons of mercy is completely different from the choice (intention) to withhold or withdraw medical treatments from a person because the *treatments* in question are either useless or burdensome, realizing that the person will die without such treatments. In euthanasia, one chooses to kill either by an act of commission or of omission because one judges that the *life* of the person to be killed is either useless or excessively burdensome and that the person is better off dead than alive. In what I shall call "benemortasia," one refuses to kill a person because one respects his or her life as something incomparably good; one rather chooses to withhold or withdraw *treatments* that are either futile (useless) or impose unnecessary burdens upon the dying person. This is a key distinction, frequently ignored today, that will be developed further in this chapter.

2. The "Ethics of Euthanasia"

The "ethics of euthanasia" has been developed by a great many persons. Although the euthanasia movement began in the 1930s,[9] it picked up momentum in the 1970s, particularly after the Supreme Court's *Roe v. Wade* abortion decision in 1973, and the 1970s witnessed a host of books and articles setting forth the rationale underlying euthanasia.[10] The arguments advanced in the 1990s (another decade of great agitation for the euthanasia movement) are rooted in the same ideology.[11] I will first consider the rationale underlying the drive for voluntary active euthanasia and then the rationale underlying the movement for nonvoluntary active euthanasia.

A. Voluntary Active Euthanasia

(1) *The "Principle of Autonomy"*
The argument justifying voluntary active euthanasia morally and also for sanctioning it by law is fundamentally the following: In voluntary active euthanasia, the patient, even if not terminally ill, gives free and informed consent to being killed mercifully. The patient wants to die. The patient's desire to die is, moreover, understandable because of the pain and/or suffering experienced. Pain relievers may not be wholly effective in eliminating pain and other discomforts, including embarrassment, humiliation arising from the illness, a desire to alleviate the burdens his or her care imposes on others, etc. The patient has reached a mature and settled judgment that he or she is better off dead than alive. Since the person to be killed mercifully gives free and informed consent to being killed, no injustice will be done. Respect for this person's integrity and autonomy require one to honor his or her request to die. In fact, not to do so is not only to fail to respect the person's autonomy and dignity, it is to compel him or her to live in a way he or she believes is a horrible mockery of all he or she

holds dear and to force him or her to die a miserable, pain-ridden death. Thus the request of such persons to be killed ought to be honored; carrying it out is, in fact, an act of kindness or beneficence. Not only is voluntary active euthanasia morally right, but it ought also to be protected by law. To continue its prohibition is cruel to those who are made to suffer needlessly and infringes on the liberty of those who would choose to be killed or to kill in order to prevent needless suffering.[12] Indeed, as several champions of voluntary active euthanasia put matters, "death control, like birth control, is a matter of human dignity. Without it persons become puppets."[13]

From this we can see that the major argument given to justify voluntary active euthanasia is rooted in the premise that human persons are autonomous, i.e., that their freedom of self-determination includes the freedom to choose to be killed when doing so is judged reasonable on the grounds that they are better off dead than alive, that their lives are no longer of any value to them, and that others have the duty to respect their choice to be killed mercifully rather than bear the indignity of a life no longer worth living. Meaningful human dignity, in this understanding, consists in the ability to control one's own life and death and to determine the manner of one's demise.[14]

Voluntary active euthanasia, therefore, is justified on an alleged "principle of personal autonomy," or on the right of persons to be in control of their own life and death. As Singer puts it, linking the right to die to the right to life, "the most important aspect of having a right to life is that one can choose whether or not to invoke it. We value the protection given by the right to life only when we want to go on living. No one can fear being killed at his or her own persistent, informed and autonomous request."[15]

(2) "Personal" Life vs. "Biological" Life

But voluntary active euthanasia also rests on the dualistic presupposition, implicit if not explicit, that physical, bodily life is radically distinct from "personal" life. The former is merely "biological" in nature; the latter, personal or meaningful life, consists in the exercisable ability to communicate, to make judgments, to reason. This dualistic presupposition is, as we will see, more central to the defense of nonvoluntary euthanasia, but it is likewise prominent in the defense of voluntary active euthanasia mounted by many of its more ardent advocates. Thus Fletcher, elaborating on the right of autonomous persons to exercise their dominion over physical nature, including bodily life and its processes, had this to say:

Physical nature — the body and its members, our organs and their functions — all of these things are a part of "what is over against us," and if we live by the rules and conditions set in physiology or another *it* we are not *thou*. . . . Freedom, knowledge, choice, responsibility — all these things of personal or moral stature are in us, not *out there*. Physical nature is what is over against us, out there. It represents the world of *its*.[16]

Similarly, Maguire rails against the "physicalistic ethic that left moral man at the mercy of his biology" and condemned him to "await the good pleasure of biochemical and organic factors and allow these to determine the time and manner of his demise." Technological man, Maguire continues, now realizes that he has the moral right to intervene "creatively" and "to terminate his life through either positive action [active voluntary euthanasia] or calculated benign neglect [passive voluntary euthanasia] rather than await in awe the dispositions of organic tissues."[17] Similarly, Harris and Singer sharply distinguish mere biological life from personal life, claiming that persons have a right to choose death rather than become depersonalized through debilitating illnesses.[18]

B. Nonvoluntary Euthanasia

Although the contemporary legal battle is over voluntary active euthanasia, advocates of the "ethics of euthanasia" likewise maintain that nonvoluntary euthanasia is also the right moral choice to make on behalf of many incompetent patients, and that this ought to be legally permissible. As noted earlier, "nonvoluntary" euthanasia is used to describe the mercy killing of patients who are *not capable* of giving or withholding consent to being killed mercifully, but whose lives are judged no longer of any value to them.

(1) *"Quality of Life" Judgments Justifying Nonvoluntary Euthanasia*

Two major arguments are given to justify nonvoluntary euthanasia or the mercy killing of incompetent individuals. The first is based on the "quality of life" and the judgment that an incompetent person's life is no longer of any value to him or to her and that killing such a person is a benefit rather than a harm. Arguments based on "quality of life" judgments have been advanced by many euthanasia supporters. Among the more ardent advocates of nonvoluntary euthanasia, in particular the "beneficent" mercy killing of handicapped newborns, are Glanville Williams, Marvin Kohl, H. Tristram Englehardt, Jr., Robert F. Weir, Anthony Shaw, Raymond S. Duff, and A. G. M. Campbell.[19] Frequently, nonvoluntary euthanasia, particularly in the case of newborns, is administered by withholding or withdrawing life-preserving measures (including feeding, even by mouth, e.g., some celebrated cases of Down syndrome babies killed by "benign" neglect). The life-preserving measures are withheld or withdrawn precisely as a means of bringing about death, and the killing is justified on the grounds that the individuals killed are, because of their low quality of life, better off dead than alive. Different advocates of nonvoluntary euthanasia based on a poor quality of life differ greatly, however, in identifying "criteria" to determine whether one's quality of life is so bad that death is a benefit and not a harm. Although quite frequently nonvoluntary euthanasia is accomplished by an act of omission (so-called passive euthanasia), its advocates hold that active euthanasia is also morally justifiable, and preferable to passive euthanasia because the former is quicker than the lingering death frequently resulting from nontreatment.[20]

The basic argument is simply this: one can determine that an individual's quality of life is so poor that continued existence is for that person not a benefit but a burden. Thus, killing that person is an act of benevolence or kindness, for by killing that person, whose life has been judged to be no longer worth living, one is doing something good.

(2) *Nonpersonhood and Nonvoluntary Euthanasia*

The justification of nonvoluntary euthanasia based on "quality of life" judgments does not deny the personhood of those to be killed mercifully. Another argument to justify nonvoluntary euthanasia, whether by an act of commission (active) or by one of omission (passive), is that those killed are either not yet persons or are no longer persons. Thus their intentional killing can be likened to the killing of other animals for reasons of mercy.

Joseph Fletcher, Michael Tooley, and Peter Singer are among the most vociferous champions of this latter claim (these authors, and many others, likewise justify abortion, as we saw in a previous chapter, on the grounds that the unborn cannot be regarded as persons).[21] They argue that abortion is frequently justified because intrauterine examination has disclosed that the unborn entity suffers from some serious (or not too serious) malady (e.g., Down syndrome, Tay-Sachs disease, cystic fibrosis, etc.), and that one ought to prevent its birth and subsequent experience of a life not worth living, what one could call euthanasia of the unborn. But at times, prenatal examination does not take place or fails to detect some serious (or not too serious) malady. Since both the unborn and the newborn are not, in their judgment, persons because they lack exercisable cognitive abilities, their parents ought to have the right to kill them to spare such infants a burdensome life.

Here it is worth noting that John Harris, a leading advocate of euthanasia, justified the withholding of nutrition and hydration by means of tubes to Tony Bland, an Englishman said to be in the so-called persistent vegetative state, on the grounds that Bland could no longer be considered a "person" because he had no exercisable cognitive faculties and was hence "no longer capable of possessing any interests at all" — an ability which Harris deems necessary if an entity is to be regarded as a "person" — and that, consequently, "death was in his best interests." Harris held that the withdrawing of tubally provided food and hydration from Bland was done precisely in order to bring about his death — a clear case of nonvoluntary euthanasia.[22] In another section of this chapter I will discuss in more detail the care to be given persons in the so-called persistent vegetative state, and we will see that some hold that withholding or withdrawing the provision of food and hydration from such persons is justified as the withholding or withdrawing of *useless* and/or *burdensome* treatment, with the subsequent death not intended, and not as an act of euthanasia by an act of omission. But Harris clearly sees such withholding or withdrawing of nutrition and hydration as the *intentional* killing of a human being who is no longer to be regarded as a person, as an act of nonvoluntary but justified euthanasia.

C. The Legal or Jurisprudential Issue

Although the champions of euthanasia approve of both voluntary and nonvoluntary euthanasia, whether active or passive, as morally good choices that ought to be legally permissible, the major goal of euthanasia supporters today is to win legal approval of voluntary active euthanasia. At present, the law of homicide (at least in the United States) protects the lives of all innocent human persons who have survived birth by strictly prohibiting intentionally killing them. Thus the law now regards active euthanasia, even if voluntary, as criminal homicide. This accounts for the great contemporary agitation clamoring for a change in the legal status. Here I will merely summarize the basic argument advanced by apologists for euthanasia to effect a change in the law. It can be stated as follows:

> By definition, if euthanasia is voluntary, the person to be killed mercifully gives free and informed consent to being killed; hence killing him or her does no injustice. The person's desire to be killed

mercifully is reasonable in view of the suffering and/or pain and/or humiliation he or she experiences; at times others, too, are suffering terribly, psychologically, or economically, or both. Killing this person, who after all, freely consents to being killed and may even be begging to be killed, is thus a reasonable way to end all this suffering. Although some people in our society regard such killing as immoral for various reasons, it would be cruel and unjust to impose their values on those who freely choose to be killed and on those who seek to compassionately execute their choice. Thus voluntary active euthanasia ought to be legally permissible.

This argument would seem to find legal support in the understanding of the Fourteenth Amendment undergirding the 1992 Supreme Court decision in *Planned Parenthood v. Casey*. In that case, Justices Souter, Kennedy, and O'Connor gave as one of the major reasons for reaffirming the "central holding" of *Roe v. Wade* the meaning of "liberty" in the Fourteenth Amendment. According to them, matters "involving the most intimate and personal choices a person may make in a lifetime, choices central to personal dignity and autonomy, are central to the liberty protected by the Fourteenth Amendment. At the heart of liberty is the right to define one's own concept of existence, of meaning, of the universe, and of the mystery of human life."[23] Fortunately, the drive to legalize voluntary active euthanasia has not yet succeeded.

D. Summary and Conclusion: The "Ethics of Euthanasia"

Arthur Dyck, a Protestant theologian teaching at Harvard University, is a champion of innocent human life, both prior to birth and through the whole of life until death. In my opinion, Professor Dyck gives us one of the most accurate and succinct summaries of the major claims upon which the "ethics of euthanasia" is based — claims he subsequently countered with the truths underlying what he called the "ethics of benemortasia." According to Dyck, the case for active voluntary euthanasia rests on the following presuppositions:

(1) that the dignity that attaches to personhood by reason of the freedom to make moral choices demands also the freedom to take one's life or to have it taken when this freedom is absent or lost; (2) that there is such a thing as a life not worth living, a life that lacks dignity, whether by reason of distress, illness, physical or mental handicaps, or even sheer despair or whatever reason; (3) that what is sacred

or supreme in value is the "human dignity" that resides in the rational capacity to choose to control life and death.[24]

The first and third of these presuppositions, taken together, constitute the so-called principle of autonomy invoked by so many today to provide a moral and jurisprudential justification of euthanasia. The second of these presuppositions is also at the heart of the alleged justification of nonvoluntary euthanasia, along with the claim that some of the non-competent individuals who are to be killed mercifully are not persons because they lack exercisable cognitive abilities. This second presupposition implies a dualism, one that regards physical, bodily life as an instrumental good: a good *for* the person, not a good *of* the person, and thus different in kind from the truly *personal* goods that perfect the person and are thus goods *of* the person, goods such as knowledge, free choice, meaningful interpersonal relationships, etc., i.e., goods whose very being depends on consciousness.

3. Critique of the "Ethics of Euthanasia"

Here I will focus on the following: (A) the claim that voluntary euthanasia is justified by human autonomy, (B) the contention that nonvoluntary euthanasia is justified on the basis of "quality of life" judgments, (C) the dualism underlying the entire euthanasia movement, and (D) the reasons why voluntary active euthanasia ought not to be legalized.

A. Autonomy and Voluntary Euthanasia vs. the Sanctity of Life

As we have seen, the basic argument for voluntary euthanasia is this: the person to be killed mercifully gives free and informed consent to being killed in this way. He chooses death, regarding it as a benefit. In doing so, he is simply exercising his autonomy. Respect for this autonomy should therefore lead others, including doctors, to confer the benefit of a merciful death on him.

But a doctor, even one not opposed in principle to euthanasia, would refuse to kill a patient, even if the patient begged to be killed, if he thought that the patient still had a worthwhile life to live. Thus, as the authors of a superb study prepared by a group of British Catholics rightly point out, "*it is precisely the judgement that a patient no longer has a worthwhile life which will seem to justify euthanasia,*" and, continuing, they affirm: "*But precisely that contention is inconsistent with recognising the continuing worth and dignity of the patient's life.*"[25] In a magnificent passage, these authors then show why this is so:

In any apparent conflict between, on the one hand, the requirement that we do not deny equal human dignity and respect for the
sanctity of human life and, on the other, the putative claims of respect
for autonomy, the principle of the sanctity of human life must always
trump those claims. For recognition of equal human dignity is fundamental to recognition of all human beings as subjects of justice. There
is no authentic conflict between rightly respecting the sanctity of
human life and rightly respecting autonomy. The exercise of human
autonomy in giving shape, direction, and character to a human life is
not a source of value and dignity at *odds* with the fundamental source
of human worth and dignity in human nature itself. For . . . what makes
it reasonable to recognise human nature as the source of our basic
worth and dignity as human beings is the fact that our nature in its
development is intrinsically directed to human fulfilment and human
good. And what best makes sense of the ideal of respect for autonomy
is the role played by free choice in the achievement of that fulfilment
to which our nature is directed; for self-determining choice is integral
to that achievement. But if the moral significance of autonomy is
understood in that way, then the value of autonomy is derivative from,
and reflective of, that which gives value to our humanity. So it should
be clear that the claims of autonomy cannot properly extend to
choices, which are inconsistent with recognising the basic worth and
dignity of every human being.[26]

In other words, human autonomy (self-determination) is not unlimited.
Its *rightful* exercise enables us to achieve our fulfillment, our perfection,
but it is subservient to our *good as persons*. I have cited this passage at length
not only because it is, in my opinion, so powerful, but also because much
that is said in it fits in beautifully with Pope John Paul II's correct understanding of legitimate human autonomy and the role that a false notion of
autonomy has played in the development of the "culture of death."

Legitimate human autonomy, or self-government, is rooted in our
capacity to determine our lives in and through our self-determining acts of
free choice. Pope John Paul II, as we saw in Chapter Two, emphasized the
truth that "it is precisely through his acts that man attains perfection [= the
"fulfillment" referred to in the above passage] as man, as one who is called
to seek his Creator of his own accord and freely to arrive at full and blessed
perfection by cleaving to him" (*Veritatis splendor*, no. 71). Our freely chosen
deeds, as the Pope stresses, "do not produce a change merely in the state of

affairs outside of man, but, to the extent that they are deliberate choices, they give moral definition to the very person who performs them, determining his *profound spiritual traits*" (no. 71). They are a *"decision about oneself* and a setting of one's own life for or against the Good, for or against the Truth, and ultimately, for or against God" (no. 65). In other words, as we saw in Chapter Two, we *give to ourselves our identity as moral beings in and through the actions we freely choose to do.*

Moreover, as John Paul II likewise rightly stressed, human freedom of choice, our legitimate autonomy, must be guided, if we are to exercise it rightly, by the *truth*. Human freedom and autonomy are not unlimited, creative of the moral order. Human freedom is exercised rightly and in a way conducive to human fulfillment or perfection only when guided by the *truth*. This truth is rooted ultimately in God's wise and loving plan for human existence, the eternal law, and God has so made us that we are capable of participating actively in this wise and loving plan through our knowledge of the practical truths necessary to guide our choices so that they can lead us to our perfection, and our knowledge of these truths is what we know as natural law (*Veritatis splendor*, nos. 38-45; cf. Chapter Two, pp. 58-61). When human autonomy is conceived as the creator and arbiter of good and evil, of right and wrong, we are no longer able to guide our choices by the truth but only by subjective and changing human opinions (cf. *Veritatis splendor*, nos. 35-37), and human autonomy, so conceived, gives birth to the "culture of death" (cf. *Evangelium vitae*, no. 19).

In short, human autonomy, human freedom of choice, is limited. It is valued precisely because we can exercise it with a view to our flourishing or fulfillment as persons living in communion with others. By exercising it in accord with the truth, we choose in such a way that we give to ourselves our identity as persons willing to respect the truth and to shape our lives in accord with it. If our choices seriously undermine in us our capacity to flourish as human persons, and if, *a fortiori*, they aim to damage aspects of this capacity in others, there is no reason to respect such choices. And the intentional killing of ourselves or others, no matter what the reason, is a choice that sets us against the inherent goodness of human life, of this great and incomparable good gift that God has given us. In choosing to *kill*, moreover, we give to ourselves the identity of *killers*. This is the reason, as Vatican II reminds us, why morally bad choices, such as the choice to *kill* innocent human life, not only poison society and dishonor the Creator, but "harm their perpetrators more than those who are harmed by them" (*Gaudium et spes*, no. 27).

B. "Quality of Life" Judgments and Justice

We have seen that two principal arguments are advanced to justify non-voluntary euthanasia. One claims that the individuals to be killed mercifully, although certainly members of the human species, are no longer to be regarded as persons because they lack presently exercisable cognitive faculties, etc. Since this claim has been sufficiently refuted in the chapter on abortion, it is not necessary to discuss it here.

The second asserts that even if we grant that the individuals to be killed mercifully are indeed persons, their "quality of life" is so poor that life is no longer of any benefit to them, and that death can be regarded as a kindly release from a burdensome and/or useless existence demeaning to human persons. This claim is utterly incompatible with the justice due to human persons. "Quality of life" judgments are inescapably arbitrary and unjust. Different authors assign different qualities that one needs to possess "meaningful" life, and the same authors at times list different qualities in different apologias for their position. More significantly, the qualities alleged to make life worthwhile (intelligence, ability to respond to stimuli, awareness of others, etc.) all admit of enormous differences in degree. But some cutoff point has to be assigned, above which the quality of life is "meaningful," and below which it is not, so that death can be mercifully administered. Such cutoff points are arbitrarily asserted, with different authors assigning different "weight" to different factors and different degrees of ability within the chosen criteria. It is evident that this way of determining who should live and who should die is utterly arbitrary and unjust.[27]

C. Dualism and Euthanasia

Advocates of euthanasia are in essence dualists. They regard human persons as consciously experiencing subjects, free to do as they choose, whose bodily life is merely an instrumental good, a good *for* persons, i.e., consciously experiencing subjects. When this life becomes burdensome, it is, for them, no longer of value; it is rather a burden that the experiencing subject is free to set aside. As the authors of *Euthanasia, Clinical Practice and the Law* so perceptively say, "propaganda puts into the mouth of the potential, theoretical suicide [or advocate of euthanasia]: 'I belong to myself, and I can set conditions on which I will consent to go on living.' Life is regarded as a good or bad hotel, which must not be too bad to be worth staying in."[28] But our bodily life is integral to our lives as persons; it is not something foreign to it. Human persons are bodily persons, and bodily life is not merely, as we saw in a previous chapter, a useful or instrumental good *for* the person, but it is rather integral to the human person, an aspect of his or her *being*. One cannot respect a human person without respecting his or her bodily life.

The dualism underlying euthanasia is false. Human persons are bodily beings, whose bodies are integral to their being as persons. When God created human persons, "male and female he created them" (Gn 1:27), i.e., men and women of flesh and blood. He did not create conscious minds to which he then added a body as an afterthought. Moreover, when the Father's only-begotten Son, his uncreated Word, became man to show us how deeply God loves us, he did not become a conscious mind using a body as his instrument; rather, he became "living flesh" (*sarx egeneto*, as the Greek of John 1:14 reads). Although human persons are *more* than their bodies because their life-giving principle, the principle that makes their bodies to be *human* bodies, is a spiritual soul, they are nonetheless *bodies, living flesh*. If a person breaks his or her arm, he does not damage his property or break an "instrument"; he or she hurts *himself* or *herself*.

The bodily life of a human person, however heavily burdened it may be, is still that person's life, his very being. To attack one's life is to attack one's person. One cannot kill a person's body without killing the person. Although the latter's soul is immortal, the soul is not the "I," the self,[29] for the self is a unit of body and soul. Christians believe that Christ has conquered death, so that death has lost its sting. But death itself is not good; it is the deprivation of life, and life is a good, and an incalculable good *of* the person. To judge that a person's life no longer has any value, that it is worthless, is to judge that a *person* no longer has any value, that a *person* is worthless.

Here it is worth recalling what Dr. Leo Alexander, who took part in the Nuremberg trials after World War II, had to say about "medical science under dictatorship." After a careful study of the "culture of death" characteristic of the Third Reich, he showed that it has its origins in the acceptance of mercy killing. He concluded: "Whatever proportion these crimes [of the Nazis] finally assumed, it became evident to all who investigated them that they had started from small beginnings. . . . It started with the acceptance of the attitude, basic in the euthanasia movement, *that there is such a thing as a life not worthy to be lived.*"[30]

D. Voluntary Active Euthanasia and the Law

We have already seen the major argument advanced to secure the legalization of voluntary active euthanasia, namely, that it is not unjust because the person to be killed freely consents to being so killed and that its legal proscription violates their liberty and the liberty of those who want, compassionately, to honor their request to be killed mercifully.

The basic counterargument, advanced with great skill by Grisez and Boyle, can be summarized as follows. Legalizing euthanasia without stringent governmental regulation would inevitably be unjust because some persons who would not freely consent to being killed mercifully would surely be pressured or coerced into giving consent to such killing, and these persons would unjustly be deprived of the protection that the current law of homicide extends to them. But to avoid this kind of injustice, strict governmental regulation would be indispensable. But government involvement, including the use of tax monies, for this purpose would infringe on the liberty of all those citizens who find such killing abhorrent and who do not wish their government to be involved in such killing, undertaken, moreover, not for the *common* good, but to serve the *private* interests of individuals. Legalizing euthanasia without government regulation would unjustly endanger the lives of those who might then be pressured into giving consent to being killed mercifully; legalizing it with strict governmental supervision would infringe on the liberty of others; since voluntary active euthanasia cannot be legalized without causing injustice to those to be killed or unjustly infringing on the liberty of citizens who find government involvement in such killing for some individuals' private good repugnant, it cannot be legalized without doing injustice. Therefore, it ought not be legalized.[31]

4. The "Ethics of Benemortasia"

"Benemortasia" is a term meaning a "good" or "happy" "death" (from the Latin, *bene* [good] and *mortasia* [death]), coined by Arthur Dyck of Harvard University, who, as we have seen already, vigorously opposes the "ethics of euthanasia." A similar term, "agathanasia" (from the Greek *agathos, agathe* [good] and *thanasia* [death]), was coined by the late Paul Ramsey, for many years professor of Christian ethics at Princeton University and a champion of the culture of life vs. the culture of death.[32]

I believe that the "ethics of benemortasia" can be adequately set forth by reflecting on and developing the following truths: (1) it is always wrong, and utterly incompatible with love for God and neighbor, intentionally to kill innocent human life; (2) in caring for the dying, a proper love for life requires one to make use of "ordinary" or "proportionate" means of preserving life, but one is free to withhold or withdraw "extraordinary" or "disproportionate" means of doing so.

A. The Intrinsic Good of Human Life and the Evil of Intentional Killing

We believe, and rightly so, that human persons are radically different in kind from other animals and that, because they are, they are beings of moral worth, whose lives are precious. The ultimate reason why human life is precious is that it is a good and great gift of God, a created participation in his life. He has given it to us to guard and protect, to be its stewards. But "why," the authors of *Euthanasia, Clinical Practice and the Law*, inquire, "cannot we stewards of our life return it to its rightful owner when the indications are that it has served its purpose and that God is recalling it to himself? Why cannot we then hasten death?" Their answer to this question is eloquent:

> The Christian response is that one's stewardship of one's life does not include the choice to terminate the stewardship itself. We did not ourselves participate in initiating the gift and task of that stewardship; we could not accept it on conditions chosen by us. Why God should have brought us (or anyone) into existence as "persons created for their own sake" is deeply mysterious. So we should not be particularly surprised if we also find it mysterious that God sees meaning and value in every part — even the most miserable and reduced — of the lifespan he allots us. But that God can and does is central to the faith of Israel and to Christian faith. His ways are not our ways, and the particular workings of his purposes are inscrutable to us. The conditions of our stewardship, then, are provided by God's commandments or "mandates." Men and women can come (though not without the risk of uncertainty and confusion) to a knowledge of those commandments by a conscientious exercise of "natural" reason, i.e., even without the benefit of God's self-disclosure. . . . In that self-disclosure there is revealed a commandment which, as explained through Scripture and the tradition of the Church, forbids us to intend to terminate our life. It has always been Christian belief that that expression of God's will holds good in all the circumstances and conditions of life. . . . We are all in the hands of a loving God who has given us each a life to be lived out in loving worship of him and in loving service of our neighbour, in preparation for a further life of perfect fulfillment

with the God of all love and consolation. . . . The ultimate source of the dignity and inviolability of the human being is God's creative love and loving purpose, which are at the depth of the mystery of every human person, and uniquely for everyone.[33]

The life God has given us includes our bodily life, which is integral to our *being* as human persons. So true is this that "to regard the body as a prison, or as an instrument or detachable launching rocket of the *real* person, is incompatible with the faith in which incarnation and redemption are central. . . . The good of human life, protected by God, is the good of bodily life. One cannot justify an attack on that life, even in one's own person, by arguing that one's bodily life is useless or an encumbrance to one's *real* vocation as a person. Reverence for that bodily life is thus integral to one's earthly existence."[34]

As John Paul II reminds us in *Veritatis splendor*, love for our neighbor requires us to respect our neighbor's *good*, and we can do this only by respecting his *goods*, the goods perfective of him at the various levels of his existence, goods such as *life* itself (cf. nos. 12, 13). One cannot love one's neighbor if one judges the neighbor to be better off dead than alive, if one *wills* that he or she be dead.

B. Criteria for Distinguishing Between "Ordinary" ("Proportionate") and "Extraordinary" ("Disproportionate") Treatments

(1) *Relevant Church Teaching and Its Interpretation*
Two major documents of the Church's Magisterium clearly distinguish between "ordinary" or "proportionate" treatments — i.e., treatments that one is morally obliged to use in order to respect the dignity of human life and rightly to exercise one's stewardship of it — and "extraordinary" or "disproportionate" treatments — i.e., treatments that one is at liberty to withhold or withdraw in exercising stewardship over one's own or another's life. We reviewed the teaching in one of these documents, the Vatican *Declaration on Euthanasia* (1980) in Chapter One, and here we will note its relevance. The other document is a 1957 address of Pope Pius XII to a congress of anesthesiologists. In the course of his remarks, Pius had this to say:

> . . . normally one is held to use only ordinary means [to prolong life]
> — according to the circumstances of persons, places, times, and cul-
> ture — that is to say, means that do not involve any grave burden for

oneself or another. A stricter obligation would be too burdensome for most men and would render the attainment of the higher, more important good too difficult. Life, health, all temporal activities are in fact subordinated to spiritual ends. On the other hand, one is not forbidden to take more than the strictly necessary steps to preserve life and health, so long as he does not fail in some more important duty.[35]

This statement of Pius XII is obviously relevant to the distinction between "ordinary" and "extraordinary" means of treatment and to the criteria for determining whether or not it is morally appropriate to withhold or withdraw treatment. Here he indicates that "ordinary" medical treatment is that kind of treatment which offers reasonable hope of benefiting the subject without imposing unacceptable burdens on the subject or others, whereas "extraordinary" medical treatment is treatment which imposes unacceptable burdens on the subject and/or others. The Pope did not himself address the *specific* criteria for distinguishing between treatments that are ordinary and those that are extraordinary. Rather, he outlined a general approach that seems clear enough, but one which obviously requires more specification.

(2) *Interpreting Pius XII's Statement: Kevin O'Rourke's View Criticized*
A crucial issue in interpreting this statement by Pius XII has to do with the proper understanding of what he meant when he said that life, i.e., physical, bodily life, is subordinated to "spiritual ends." Here I want to call attention to and criticize the way Kevin O'Rourke, O.P., interprets this passage of Pius XII (he applies this interpretation to the treatment to be given persons said to be in the "persistent vegetative state"). O'Rourke maintains that Pius XII's emphasis on the supremacy of the spiritual goal of human life

specifies more clearly the terms "ordinary" and "extraordinary." A more adequate and complete explanation of "ordinary" means to prolong life would be: those means which are obligatory because they *enable* a person to strive for the spiritual purpose of life. "Extraordinary" means would seem to be: those means which are optional because they are *ineffective* or a grave burden in helping a person strive for the spiritual purpose of life.[36]

I would agree, for reasons to be set forth below, that a means is extraordinary if it *imposes* a "grave burden" on a person and prevents him or her from striving for the spiritual purpose of life. Thus if a proposed medical treatment has a high risk of rendering a person permanently unconscious, the person could rightly refuse the treatment, preferring to live out his or her life consciously. The burden this proposed treatment would impose on the person is truly excessive.

But O'Rourke errs seriously when he claims that a means is "ordinary" only if it *enables* a person to pursue this goal and that it is "extraordinary" and hence not obligatory if it is *ineffective* in helping a person strive for the spiritual goal of life. He errs seriously because there are many people, including some seriously mentally impaired infants and children and some elderly people who are "not with it," who are not actually able to make judgments and choices and thus incapable of pursuing the "spiritual goal of life." But these unfortunate human beings are still persons; their lives are still good and of value, and it is good for them to be alive. If they should fall sick or be in danger of death, they surely have a right to some kinds of medical treatments that would preserve their lives, even if these treatments would be *ineffective* in helping them pursue the spiritual goal of life. Thus, for example, if elderly persons no longer mentally competent or infants suffering from trisomy 21 (a disorder entailing severe mental incapacity and leading to an early death) were to cut an artery, one could not simply allow them to bleed to death; or, if they should break their arm, one could not omit putting it into a cast so that it could be healed. But these "treatments" would not *enable* them to pursue the spiritual goal of life and they would be *ineffective* for that purpose, and on O'Rourke's analysis would thus be "extraordinary" and not obligatory. But this is surely false.

A proper interpretation of Pius's statement, as noted above, is that treatments which would *prevent* a person from pursuing the spiritual goal of life, *disabling* him or her, would be truly "extraordinary" because of the terrible burden it would impose upon them. But preventing a non-competent patient from bleeding to death, repairing his or her broken limbs, giving him or her antibiotics to combat severe flu, etc., would surely be "ordinary" and mandatory treatments. In O'Rourke's exegesis of the text, they would not be. Thus I regard his interpretation as seriously defective and tending to the view that bodily life is merely an instrumental good *for* the person, not a good *of* the person.[37]

The other major magisterial document is the Vatican *Declaration on Euthanasia*. While unequivocally condemning suicide and all forms of euthanasia as absolutely immoral, this document reaffirmed traditional Catholic teaching that one is not obliged to use all possible means to preserve and prolong human life. It referred to the distinction between "ordinary" and "extraordinary" means of preserving life, noting that the imprecision of these terms is the cause of some ambiguity and that, therefore, some more recent writers have suggested that the term "proportionate" be used to designate means which are morally obligatory and that the term "disproportionate" be used to designate means which are not morally obligatory. It stated that no matter what terms are used, it will nonetheless be possible to make a correct judgment "by studying the type of treatment to be used, its degree of complexity or risk, its cost and the possibility of using it, and comparing these elements with the result that can be expected, taking into account the state of the sick person and his or her physical and moral resources" (sect. IV).

Moreover, the same document maintained that "one cannot impose on anyone the obligation to have recourse to a technique which is already in use but which carries a risk or is burdensome. Such a refusal is not the equivalent of suicide; on the contrary, it should be considered as an acceptance of the human condition, or a wish to avoid the application of a medical procedure disproportionate to the results which can be expected, or a desire not to impose excessive expense on the family or community" (ibid.). In addition, it says that "when inevitable death is imminent in spite of the means used, it is permitted in conscience to take the decision to refuse forms of treatment which would only secure a precarious and burdensome prolongation of life, so long as the normal care due to a sick person in similar cases is not interrupted" (ibid.).

The precise interpretation of these statements will occupy us more fully below.

(3) Legitimate vs. Illegitimate "Quality of Life" Judgments

Note that the Vatican *Declaration* affirms that in assessing treatments it is proper to take "into account the state of the sick person and his or her physical and moral resources." Here the *Declaration* makes it clear that, although it is *always* gravely immoral to kill a person mercifully because one judges that the "quality" of his or her life is so wretched that he or she would be better off dead than alive, it is legitimate to consider the "quality" of his or her life *in relationship to specific kinds of treatments* for a person *in that condition*, i.e., with that "quality of life." What would not be too risky, painful, burdensome, etc., for an otherwise healthy teenager or adult might well be so for persons suffering from advanced stages of lethal diseases, etc. Thus, for instance, an amputation of a limb would not be "disproportionate" or "extraordinary" for an otherwise vigorous youth or mature adult but would be so for someone suffering from advanced pancreatic cancer or something similar. Such "quality of life" judgments, which bear on the uselessness or burdensomeness of specific kinds of *treatments* for persons in *specific kinds of conditions*, are not the same as "quality of life" judgments asserting that those persons' *lives* are no longer of any value.[38] The late John R. Connery, S.J., summed this matter up well when he said that while the Catholic tradition has repudiated a quality of life ethic which would deny persons needed medical care simply on the basis of the poor quality of their lives, it nonetheless "allowed quality of life considerations in decisions about prolonging life *if they were related to the means themselves.*"[39]

(4) *Richard McCormick's "Quality of Life" Position*

In two exceptionally influential essays,[40] Richard McCormick, S.J., insisted that it is not possible to judge which treatments are "extraordinary" and hence not morally obligatory without necessarily making "value of life" judgments. "There has been a tendency, " he wrote, "to shift the problem from the means to reverse the dying process to the quality of life sustained or preserved.... Granted that we can easily save the life, *what kind of life are we saving?*"[41] According to McCormick, bodily, physical life, while indeed "basic" and "precious," is a relative good, one "to be preserved precisely as the condition of these other values [interpersonal relationships]. It is these other values and possibilities which found the duty to preserve physical life and also dictate the limits of this duty."[42] In his view, the Judeo-Christian tradition holds that "the meaning, substance, and consummation of life are to be found in human *relationships* and the qualities of justice, respect, concern, compassion and support that surround them."[43] Because this is so, one can judge that bodily life is not a value to be preserved when the potential for these relationships has been lost or if it can never be attained. He maintains that "when in human judgment this potentiality [for human relationships] is totally absent or would be, because of the condition of the individual, totally subordinated to the mere effort for survival, that life can be said to have achieved its potential."[44] He claims that the reason for withholding or withdrawing a treatment is based on a judgment about the quality of life which the treatment will preserve. Thus he writes: "Often it is the kind of, the quality of, the life thus saved (painful, poverty-stricken, and deprived, away from home and friends, oppressive) that establishes the means as extraordinary. *That* type of life would be an excessive hardship for the individual."[45]

There are very serious problems with McCormick's proposal. The principal one is that there is a vast difference between concluding that a particular *treatment* is excessively burdensome and hence "extraordinary" and not morally required for this particular patient, taking into account his condition or "quality of life" relative to the treatment proposed, and concluding that someone's *life* is excessively burdensome. Pius XII and the Vatican *Declaration* direct our attention to the nature of the *treatments* to be used, taking into account the patient's physical and moral resources. McCormick *redirects* our attention to the quality of the person's *life* that the proposed treatments would preserve. McCormick then judges that person's *life* as the burden. The burden to be lifted is the person's life, not the proposed or presently used treatment. McCormick's proposal, consequently, is not compatible with the teaching of these magisterial documents. It seems clearly dualistic, regarding physical, bodily life as a useful good, a condition for the experiencing of truly personal goods, and not itself a *personal good*.

(5) Criteria for Determining Whether Treatments Are "Ordinary" ("Proportionate") or "Extraordinary" ("Disproportionate")

We will be helped to discover the criteria for withholding or withdrawing treatments (= criteria for distinguishing between "ordinary/proportionate" and "extraordinary/disproportionate" treatments) by first considering non-suicidal reasons for refusing treatment. As Grisez and Boyle have noted,

> Individuals who are competent can refuse treatment upon themselves without the intent to end their own lives, which would be their motive if they appraised their future prospects and decided that they would be better off dead. Such refusal of treatment, including treatment without which life will be shortened, can be based upon *objectionable features of the treatment itself, its side effects, and its negative consequences*. An individual who has no desire to die can take such factors into account and decide that life without treatment, so long as life lasts, will be better than life with it. Such a decision is not a choice of death.[46]

A human person, in short, can refuse a treatment — choose that it be withheld or withdrawn — without adopting by choice a proposal to kill himself or herself. The treatment refusal is based on the judgment that the treatment itself, or its side effects or deleterious consequences, are so burdensome that undergoing the treatment is not morally obligatory. The treatment in question is truly "extraordinary/disproportionate" since the burdens it imposes far exceed the benefits likely to result from its use.

What are some major reasons for refusing treatment on these grounds? Here, too, Grisez and Boyle offer helpful criteria that flesh out the general guidelines given by Pius XII and the Vatican *Declaration.* They write:

> First, sometimes treatment is experimental or risky; . . . second, some treatment is itself painful or brings about other experienced conditions which are undesirable; . . . third, in many cases, the requirements for the application of medical care would interfere with the activities and experiences which one desires during the time [of life] remaining; . . . fourth, many persons object to certain forms of care on the basis of some principle [for example, Jehovah's Witnesses refuse blood transfusions because they believe that this is immoral, the equivalent of taking life, and others refuse organ transplants from the newly dead because they fear that the organs were taken while the "donor" was still alive]; . . . fifth, there is a variety of reasons why persons find medical care psychologically repugnant; . . . sixth, in many cases medical care for one individual makes very severe demands upon others.[47]

To the reasons for making a given treatment unduly burdensome assigned by Grisez and Boyle in the above paragraph, we can add the cost of some medical treatments; one is not obligated to bankrupt his or her family in order to undergo a treatment. All these factors are *objectively discernible features in the treatment itself, its side effects, and its negative consequences that impose undue burdens on the patient and/or others.* One can rightly reject such treatments and withhold them or withdraw them. The choice to do so is not suicidal, not rooted in the "ethics of euthanasia" but rather in the "ethics of benemortasia." We could say that *excessive burdensomeness* is the major criterion for determining whether a proposed treatment is "extraordinary/disproportionate." Excessive burdensomeness is, as it were, the genus, and species of such burdensomeness include the treatment's riskiness, its bad side effects and bad consequences on the life of the person, the excessive pain of the treatment, treatments judged morally or psychologically repugnant, and excessive expense that would imperil the economic security of the patient, the patient's family, and/or the community. Withholding or withdrawing such treatments is not a choice to kill oneself or another for merciful reasons. It is *not* euthanasia. One does not judge a *life* excessively burdensome; one judges a *treatment* excessively burdensome. And, as we have seen already, in making this judgment, the "physical and moral resources of the patient" — his or her "quality of life" in *that* sense — can rightly be taken into account.

In addition to the criterion of *burdensomeness*, another criterion that enables us to judge whether a given treatment, for a given patient, is "extraordinary/disproportionate" and hence not morally required is the criterion of *usefulness*. In the Catholic tradition, a means has been judged useless in the strict sense if the benefits it promises are nil or useless in a wider sense if the benefits conferred are insignificant in comparison to the burdens it imposes.

The authors of *Euthanasia, Clinical Practice and the Law* provide a very detailed analysis of the reasons why a competent patient may rightly refuse treatment. In addition to excessive risk or financial cost, they identify four potentially acceptable reasons for rejecting treatment because it is "extraordinary/disproportionate." These are: "a) the burdens attendant on treatment impress one as more than one can cope with; b) the burdens attendant on treatment seem hardly warranted by the promised benefits; c) treatment is not worthwhile because a dying patient has reason to think that he no longer has an obligation to seek to prolong his life; d) treatment is straightforwardly futile, i.e., inappropriate to the biological nature of one's condition, as, for example, when putatively curative treatment is offered to someone in an irreversible state of dying."[48]

In summary, we can say that the two principal criteria for determining whether to withhold or withdraw a treatment because it is "extraordinary/disproportionate" are *burdensomeness* and *uselessness*. The former is the major criterion, insofar as the relative uselessness of many treatments is contingent upon the burdens they impose when compared with the benefits they bring. But what is most important is that these criteria draw attention to the *burdensomeness* and/or *uselessness* of the means used to preserve life. They do not lead one to conclude that treatments are to be withheld or withdrawn because of a judgment that the patient's *life* is either burdensome or useless — and this, as we have seen, is the judgment reached in the "ethics of euthanasia." Judgments of the burdensomeness and/or uselessness of treatments are compatible with a respect and love for the dignity of human life, which is *always* a precious good, a gift from God, no matter how heavily burdened it may be.

C. Summary: The Presuppositions of the "Ethics of Benemortasia"

A fitting conclusion for this section is provided, I believe, by Arthur Dyck, who, as we have seen, coined the term "benemortasia." Just as he ably set forth the presuppositions underlying the "ethics of euthanasia," so he also neatly expressed the presuppositions underlying the "ethics of benemortasia." These are:

1. A human being's life is not solely at the disposal of that person; every human life is part of a human community that is held together in part by respect for life and love for the lives of its members.
2. The dignity of the person, by reason of his freedom of choice, includes the freedom of dying persons to refuse non-curative, death-preventing interventions, but it does not include the freedom to choose death and to set one's will against life.
3. Every life has some worth. Life itself is a precious good; it is an intrinsic good, a good *of* the person, not merely a useful or instrumental good, a good *for* the person.
4. The supreme good is God himself, to whom the dying and those who care for the dying are responsible.[49]

5. Caring for the Permanently Unconscious and Persons in the "Persistent Vegetative State"

Introduction
I will (a) comment on the so-called *persistent* vegetative state; (b) summarize responses by U.S. Catholic bishops and theologians to the issue prior to Pope John Paul II's important address of March 20, 2004; (c) present John Paul II's address and its significance; (d) consider the negative responses given to it by a large number of American theologians; (e) give my own defense of the Holy Father's position, showing how unfounded are the objections leveled against it; and (f) take up the document on this subject issued by the Congregation for the Doctrine of the Faith in August 2007.

A. Comments on the " 'Persistent' Vegetative State"
At the end of International Congress "Life-Sustaining Treatments and Vegetative State: Scientific Advances and Ethical Dilemmas" (Rome, March 17-20, 2004), the World Federation of Catholic Medical Associations (FIAMC) issued a statement in which the scientists who participated in the Congress offered several considerations regarding the nature of this alleged "state," among them the following:

1) Vegetative State (VS) is a state of unresponsiveness, currently defined as a condition marked by: a state of vigilance, some alternation of sleep/wake cycles, absence of signs of awareness of self and of surroundings, lack of behavioural responses to stimuli from the environment, maintenance of autonomic and other brain functions.

2) VS must be clearly distinguished from: encephalic death, coma, "locked-in" syndrome, minimally conscious state. VS cannot be simply equalled to cortical death either, considering that in VS patients islands of cortical tissue which may even be quite large can keep functioning.

3) In general, VS patients do not require any technological support in order to maintain their vital functions.

4) VS patients cannot in any way be considered terminal patients, since their condition can be stable and enduring.

5) VS diagnosis is still clinical in nature and requires careful and prolonged observation, carried out by specialized and experienced personnel, using specific assessment standardized for VS patients in an optimum controlled environment. Medical literature, in fact, shows diagnostic errors in a substantially high proportion of cases. For this reason, when needed, all available modern technologies should be used to substantiate the diagnosis.

6) Modern neuroimaging techniques demonstrated the persistence of cortical activity and response to certain kinds of stimuli, including painful stimuli, in VS patients. Although it is not possible to determine the subjective quality of such perceptions, some elementary discriminatory processes between meaningful and neutral stimuli seem to be nevertheless possible.

7) No single investigation method available today allows us to predict, in individual cases, who will recover and who will not among VS patients.

8) Until today, statistical prognostic indexes regarding VS have been obtained from studies quite limited as to number of cases considered and duration of observation. Therefore, the use of adjectives like "permanent" referred to VS should be discouraged, by indicating only the cause and duration of VS.[50]

Note that in no. 8, the scientists who participated in this important congress explicitly declare that the adjective "permanent" *not* be used to describe the condition because such use is not warranted by the facts. Note also that in no. 6, the scientists indicate that persons in the "vegetative" state may be able to experience pain.

The October 15, 2007, issue of the *New Yorker* magazine carried an article by Jerome Groopman that confirmed the findings of the medical scientists given above.[51]

B. Responses Prior to Pope John Paul II's Address

In the accompanying footnote, I identify responses by some major secular sources to this issue[52] in order to focus on responses by U.S. Catholic bishops and theologians.

(1) *Responses by U.S. Bishops*

The bishops of the United States gave contradictory answers. Although directive no. 58 of the *Ethical and Religious Directives for Catholic Health Care Services* (November 1994) clearly affirms that one ought to presume that nourishment so provided be given such persons "as long as this is of sufficient benefit to outweigh the burdens involved to the patient," some individual bishops and the Texas Conference of Catholic Bishops had earlier concluded that doing so is futile and useless. The Texas bishops, who did not provide extensive argument, claimed that someone in PVS was "stricken with a lethal pathology which, without artificial nutrition and hydration will lead to death." They held that withholding or withdrawing artificially provided food from such persons "is simply acknowledging the fact that the person has come to the end of his or her pilgrimage and should not be impeded [by artificially provided food] from taking the final step."[53] Some individual bishops issued statements of a similar nature.[54]

On the other hand, in 1992 the Committee for Pro-Life Activities of the NCCB prepared a document that surveyed relevant medical literature dealing with the issue and different positions taken by moral theologians. The Pro-Life Committee explicitly stated that it did not find persuasive the rationale of some theologians that since persons in the PVS condition can no longer pursue the spiritual goal of life, feeding them artificially is futile and/or unduly burdensome. The Committee concluded: "We hold for a presumption in favor of providing medically assisted nutrition and hydration to patients who need it, which presumption would yield in cases where such procedures have no medically reasonable hope of sustaining life or pose excessive risks or burdens."[55]

John Paul II singled out this paper for praise in a talk to a group of U.S. bishops on their *ad limina* visit to the Vatican in 1998.[56]

Even before this, in 1992, the Pennsylvania bishops had issued a somewhat similar document, replete with references to pertinent medical literature, declaring: "As a general conclusion, in almost every instance there is an obligation to continue supplying nutrition and hydration to the unconscious patient. There are situations in which this is not the case [e.g., when the patient can no longer assimilate the food and its provision is hence useless], but these are exceptions and should not be made into the rule." In their judgment, artificially providing food to PVS patients is "clearly beneficial in terms of preservation of life" and does not add a "serious burden" in the vast majority of cases. Consequently, it is in principle morally obligatory.[57]

Several individual bishops and other conferences of bishops issued statements reaching similar conclusions as the Pro-Life Committee and the Pennsylvania bishops.[58]

(2) The Theological Position Claiming That Tubal Feeding of PVS Patients Is Not Morally Required

The leading proponent of this position was Kevin O'Rourke, O.P.[59] O'Rourke claimed that his view was rooted in the teaching of Pope Pius XII. In an important address to a congress of anesthesiologists, Pius had said:

> ... normally one is held to use only ordinary means [to prolong life] — according to the circumstances of persons, places, times, and culture — that is to say, means that do not involve any grave burdens for oneself or another. A more strict obligation would be too burdensome for most men and would render the attainment of the higher, more important good too difficult. Life, health, all temporal activities are in fact subordinated to spiritual ends. On the other hand, one is not forbidden to take more than the strictly necessary steps to preserve life and health, as long as he does not fail in some more serious duty.[60]

O'Rourke claimed that the Pope' emphasis on the spiritual goal of life

specifies more clearly the terms "ordinary" and "extraordinary." A more adequate and complete explanation of "ordinary" means to prolong life would be: those means which are obligatory because they enable a person to strive for the spiritual purpose of life. "Extraordinary" means would seem to be those means which are optional because they are ineffective or a grave burden in helping a person strive for the spiritual purpose of life.[61]

As pointed out earlier in this chapter, while O'Rourke correctly interpreted the teaching of Pius XII by saying that a means is extraordinary if it *imposes* a grave burden on a person and prevents him from pursuing the spiritual goal of life, he erred greatly when he claimed that a means is extraordinary when it is "*ineffective* ... in helping a person strive for the spiritual purpose of life" and that a means is ordinary precisely and *only* insofar as it enables a person to strive for the spiritual purpose of life. Many people, including some seriously handicapped children and mentally impaired adults, are incapable of pursuing the spiritual goal of life. People with very severe mental disabilities cannot do so because in order to do so a person must be able to make judgments and free choices. But these unfortunate human beings are still persons; their lives are still good, and it is good for them to be alive. If they should fall sick or be otherwise in danger of death, they surely have a right to "ordinary" care, and others have a serious moral responsibility to protect and preserve their lives unless the efforts to do so are themselves futile or excessively burdensome. Thus, for example, if an elderly person suffering from a malady that renders him incompetent and incapable of engaging in specifically human acts should suffer a cut artery and be in danger of dying because of loss of blood, it would surely be morally obligatory to stop the bleeding by appropriate means. Such means are surely "ordinary" or "proportionate." Yet, on O'Rourke's analysis, they would be "extraordinary" inasmuch as they would in no way be *effective* in helping this person pursue the spiritual purpose of life.

Applying his understanding of Pius XII's teaching to persons said to be in the PVS condition, O'Rourke maintained that since these individuals are not capable of pursuing the spiritual goal of life and since feeding them tubally is ineffective in helping them do so, then such feeding is not required. He also claimed that such individuals are suffering from a "fatal pathology" and that all one does by "feeding" such persons tubally is to preserve "mere physiological functioning." His associate Benedict Ashley, O.P., shared this position.[62]

(3) *The Position Holding That Artificially Providing Food to PVS Persons Is Obligatory*

This view, like that of *Ethical and Religious Directives*, of the Pennsylvania bishops and the Pro-Life Committee of the National Conference of Catholic Bishops, holds that artificially providing food to permanently unconscious persons (those in the PVS state) is to be regarded ordinarily as morally obligatory insofar as it is neither useless nor unduly burdensome. With several others I developed this view in "Feeding and Hydrating the Permanently Unconscious and Other Vulnerable Persons."[63]

We began by articulating major presuppositions and principles, among them: that human bodily life is a great good; that it is personal, not subpersonal; that it is inherently good, not merely instrumentally so; that no matter how heavily burdened, such life remains a good.

We held that withholding/withdrawing various forms of preserving life, including the provision of food and water by tubal means, is morally permissible *if* the means employed is either useless or excessively burdensome. We affirmed that it is useless or relatively so if the benefits provided are nil or insignificant in comparison to the burdens imposed, and that it is excessively burdensome if benefits offered are not worth pursuing for one or more objective reasons: too painful, too damaging to the person's bodily life and functioning, too restrictive of the patient's liberty and preferred activities, too suppressive of the person's mental life, too expensive, etc.

We acknowledged explicitly that "*if it is really useless or excessively burdensome* to provide someone with nutrition and hydration, then these means may rightly be withheld or withdrawn, *provided* that this omission does not carry out a proposal to end the person's life but rather is chosen to avoid the useless effort or the excessive burden of continuing to provide the food and fluids."[64] However, after examining the issue, we judged that tubally providing food and hydration to the permanently unconscious and other vulnerable persons was neither useless nor excessively burdensome and that consequently it ought to be given. We thus concluded:

> [I]n the ordinary circumstances of life in our society today, it is not morally right, nor ought it to be legally permissible, to withhold or withdraw nutrition and hydration provided by artificial means to the permanently unconscious or other categories of seriously debilitated but nonterminal persons. Rather, food and fluids are universally needed for the preservation of life, and can generally be provided without the burdens and expense of more aggressive means of supporting life. Therefore, both morality and law should recognize a strong presumption in favor of their use.[65]

We also argued that by caring for such persons in this way another good, that of human solidarity, was served.[66]

Since some — for example, O'Rourke — argued that the expense entailed in feeding PVS patients must realistically be regarded as terribly burdensome in our society,[67] we acknowledged that no one would want his family bankrupted in order to provide him with tubally assisted feeding. But does this mean that O'Rourke is correct? At present, the cost for taking care of PVS patients is usually covered in great part by insurance or other programs. But one cannot legitimately avoid excessive expense (if this does become an issue) by *abandoning care for the person and by intentionally bringing his death about by starvation.* There are morally legitimate ways to reduce the cost of care. Persons put into the situation of caring for a loved one in the PVS state or other conditions are not obliged to have them cared for in highly expensive hospitals or nursing homes (if insurance and governmental help are inadequate). They can remove them from these costly institutions, take them home, and do the best they can with the help of such services as hospice care, volunteers from the parish or neighborhood, etc. The high standards of care possible in expensive institutions might not be possible, but one can still maintain solidarity with the person, doing what one can, including providing food and nourishment by tubal means (not too difficult to do once begun, even at home). One does not have to endure undue financial burdens.

C. Pope John Paul II's Address of March 20, 2004

(1) *Context and Key Themes*
This address, given at the conclusion of the International Congress "Life-Sustaining Treatments and Vegetative State: Scientific Advances and Ethical Dilemmas," co-sponsored by the Pontifical Academy for Life and the International Federation of Catholic Medical Associations, was based on the latest medical and scientific findings relevant to the "vegetative" state.[68]

Among the principal ideas Pope John Paul articulated are the following:

1. *"A man, even if seriously ill or disabled in the exercise of his highest functions, is and always will be a man,* and he will never become a 'vegetable' or an 'animal' " (no. 3; emphasis in original).
2. *The right of the sick person, even one in the vegetative state, to basic health care.* Such care includes "nutrition, hydration, cleanliness, warmth, etc." and "appropriate rehabilitative care" and monitoring "for clinical signs of eventual recovery" (no. 4).
3. *The moral obligation,* in principle, *to provide food and water to persons in the "vegetative" state by tubal means:* "I should like to underline how the administration of food and water, even when provided by artificial means, always represents a *natural means* of preserving life, not a medical act. Its use, furthermore, should be considered, in principle, *ordinary and proportionate,* and as such morally obligatory, insofar as and until it is seen to have attained its proper

finality, which in the present case consists in providing nourishment to the patient and alleviation of his suffering" (no. 4; emphasis in original).

4. *The need to resist making a person's life contingent on its quality:* "[I]t is not enough to reaffirm the general principle according to which the value of a man's life cannot be made subordinate to any judgment of its quality. . . ; it is necessary to promote the *taking of positive actions* as a stand against pressures to withdraw hydration and nutrition as a way to put an end to the lives of these patients" (no. 6; emphasis in original).

5. *The principle of solidarity:* "It is necessary, above all, *to support those families* who have had one of their loved ones struck down by this terrible clinical condition" (no. 6; emphasis added).

(2) *Comments*

John Paul II emphasized that the providing of food and water even by artificial means is to be regarded "*in principle*" (emphasis added) "*'ordinary' and 'proportionate'* and as such morally obligatory." Thus, although such provision is obligatory in principle, the Pope allowed for those cases in which the provision of nutrition and hydration would not be appropriate, either because they would not be metabolized adequately or because their mode of delivery would be gravely burdensome.

As the Australian bishops have noted, "the Pope's statement does not explore the question whether artificial feeding involves a medical act or treatment with respect to insertion and monitoring of the feeding tube. While the act of feeding a person is not itself a medical act, the insertion of a tube, monitoring of the tube and patient, and prescription of the substances to be provided do involve a degree of medical and/or nursing expertise. To insert a feeding tube is a medical decision subject to the normal criteria for medical intervention."[69] I bring this up because some may claim that, since providing food/water by tubal means requires a medical act to insert the tube, such feeding is itself a medical treatment and not an act of caring. This is not true. But the insertion of a feeding tube, particularly through enteral and not perienteral means, is neither futile nor burdensome in almost all cases.

D. Negative Responses to This Address

The principal negative responses to John Paul II's address were the following: it marked "a significant departure from the Roman Catholic bioethical tradition,"[70] it was not in conformity with the 1980 Vatican *Declaration on Euthanasia*,[71] and was not so primarily because it imposes excessively severe burdens on the families of such persons.[72] Thus John Paris, S.J., claimed that the Pope's talk ran counter to over 400 years of Church teaching, mandated use of excessively burdensome means, was probably written not by the Pope but by Bishop Elio Sgreccia, who "represents the radical right-to-life segment of thinking."[73] Edward Sunshine found the Pope's address so utterly incompatible with the 1980 *Declaration on Euthanasia* that it is "merely an assertion of ecclesiastical authority, with little grounding in reason,"[74] and John Tuohey likened it to a faulty thesis proposal by a graduate student ignorant of traditional Catholic teaching.[75] Boston College moral theologian Lisa Sowle Cahill asserted apodictically that John Paul II was *not* the author of the document and like others contended that it is simply incompatible with traditional Catholic teaching.[76]

Christopher Kaczor has summarized and challenged essays by O'Rourke, Jean deBlois, Tuohey, Cahill, Thomas Shannon, and others dissenting from John Paul's address in the Autumn 2007 issue of *The National Catholic Bioethics Quarterly*.[77]

The claim that John Paul II imposes grave burdens on the families of persons in the "vegetative" state is, in fact, the position taken by O'Rourke, Ashley, and Jean deBlois in the fifth edition of *HealthCare Ethics*.[78] In this edition, Ashley and O'Rourke abandon their claim that feeding/hydrating persons like Terri Schiavo is not required because doing so does not enable them to pursue the spiritual end of life — the argument they had earlier advanced. In this edition, they *claim* that they accept John Paul II's position "in principle." They note that even the Pope allows removal of feeding/hydrating such persons if doing so is in fact either futile or burdensome. This is true. But Ashley-O'Rourke-deBlois continue by making claims that are simply false and then insinuating that such feeding is usually very burdensome on the *families* of such persons and that therefore it can be rightly withheld or withdrawn.

They claim (p. 197) that their interpretation of the papal address is "supported by the National Catholic Bioethics Center," with a reference to its statement of April 23, 2004. However, their positions are **not** the same — in fact, the NCBC issued a special newsletter emphasizing that the position taken by Ashley et al. differs profoundly from its own. Ashley et al. say that their view is not supported by the "incommensurable goods theory" that "makes physical life always a benefit except when the person is actually dying" (p. 197). Since this is the theory common to Germain Grisez, myself, and others, I can say that they misrepresent our position and here truly show their hand, for we hold that "physical life" (bodily life) is *always a precious good of the person* even *when the person is dying.* Although this life may be burdened, it is itself always a precious gift from God.

If we link our authors' rejection of the view of those holding the "incommensurable goods theory" with their claim, in speaking of the Schiavo case, that feeding/hydrating individuals said to be in the "vegetative state" preserves merely physiological life, we can see how their own interpretation of the March 20, 2004, address is mistaken.[79]

Like others who rejected John Paul II's address, they claim that it imposes grave burdens on the families of persons in the "vegetative state." I answer this objection below.

E. My Defense of John Paul II's Address

(1) *Compatibility of the March 20 Address With "Traditional Catholic Teaching"*

In *Evangelium vitae*, John Paul II explicitly appealed to the *Declaration on Euthanasia* to distinguish euthanasia "from the decision to forgo . . . medical procedures which no longer correspond to the real situation of the patient, either because they are by now disproportionate to any expected results or because they impose an excessive burden on the patient and his family. . . . To forgo extraordinary or disproportionate means is not the equivalent of suicide or euthanasia; it rather expresses acceptance of the human condition in the face of death" (no. 65). Thus John Paul II obviously judged it appropriate to withhold or withdraw the provision of nutrition and hydration for legitimate reasons (futility, excessive burdensomeness). Moreover, his teaching in no way requires that tubally assisted feeding and hydration be maintained at all costs, but only when the *benefits such assistance provides are present and no excessive burdens are imposed.* If in particular instances such feeding/hydration would not effectively preserve life or alleviate suffering, it would lack its beneficial effect and would be futile.

Some months after his March 20, 2004, address, as noted above, John Paul delivered another address on November 12, 2004, in which he once again reaffirmed the Catholic tradition according to which aggressive treatment, i.e., treatment that "is ineffective or obviously disproportionate to the aims of sustaining life or recovering health," may be withheld or withdrawn. He then went on to speak of the need to continue "palliative care," especially for patients with terminal diseases.[80] This address is in perfect conformity with, and in no way contrary to, his teaching on March 20 of the same year on the obligation, in principle, to provide food and hydration to the permanently unconscious *"insofar as and until it is seen to have attained its proper finality*, which in the present case consists in *providing nourishment to the patient and alleviation of his suffering"* (March 20 address, no. 3; emphasis added).

His statement is fully compatible with the *Ethical and Religious Directives for Catholic Health Care Services*, no. 58 — "There should be a presumption in favor of providing nutrition and hydration to all patients, *including patients who require medically assisted nutrition and hydration, as long as this is of sufficient benefit to outweigh the burdens involved to the patient"* (emphasis added) — and with the documents on this issue prepared by the Pennsylvania Conference of Bishops and the Committee for Pro-Life Activities of the USCCB. How then is it opposed to the Catholic tradition?

(2) Does John Paul II Impose Excessively Grave Burdens on Families?

Does the Pope's teaching, as some American theologians assert, impose grave burdens on the families of those whose lives are sustained by providing them tubally with food and water even when they are not consciously aware of themselves or others? Simply *feeding/hydrating* the permanently unconscious surely does not impose burdens on families or other caregivers, just as *feeding* those paralyzed from the neck down or suffering loss of all limbs does not impose excessive burdens on caregivers. The burden they carry is not caused by the *feeding* but rather by the seriously debilitating condition of those for whom they care. But this is a burden that must in justice be accepted by others. Would those opposing John Paul II claim that we should stop feeding the demented, the paralyzed, quadruple amputees, and individuals who are simply "not with it"?

Moreover, withholding or withdrawing tubally provided food and water would not eliminate the burden of caregivers; only the *death* of those cared for would end the burden. Germain Grisez, after noting that, as the permanently unconscious person's loved ones witness what is done to provide food and other care, they experience a great and undeniable burden, correctly said:

> Of course, this burden will be eliminated if food is withheld, but only because the comatose person will be eliminated. Thus, to decide not to feed a comatose person in order to end the burden and his or her loved one's experience is to choose to kill that person in order to end the miserable state in which he or she now lives.[81]

John Paul II himself was keenly aware of the great hardship that families of PVS patients endure in caring for them. He thus outlined some important positive steps to help these patients and their families, and "... to stand against pressures to withdraw hydration and nutrition as a way to put an end to the lives of these patients" (no. 6). John Paul II suggested the following concrete practical ways to help:

> ... the creation of a network of awakening centers with special treatment and rehabilitation programs; financial support and home assistance for families when patients are moved back home at the end of intensive rehabilitation programs; the establishment of facilities which can accommodate those cases in which there is no family able to deal with the problem or to provide "breaks" for those families who are at risk of psychological and moral burnout. (no. 6)

Such steps would demonstrate society's concern and love for these seriously impaired individuals. From a specifically Christian perspective, they would give powerful testimony to the faithfulness and selflessness of Christian love, which continues to be expressed even when those who receive it can show no appreciation — even when they are apparently totally unaware of this loving presence. For in providing care only to those who can thank us and return the favor, do we not already have our reward?

(F) Definitive Defense by the Congregation for the Doctrine of the Faith's August 1, 2007, "Responses to Certain Questions of the United States Conference of Catholic Bishops Concerning Artificial Nutrition and Hydration"

This brief document and the Commentary attached to it are luminously clear. I will thus reproduce the texts here in full. It is very unusual for the CDF to issue explanatory commentaries on its brief responses to questions raised by bishops. The texts are as follows:

Responses to Certain Questions of the United States Conference of Catholic Bishops Concerning Artificial Nutrition and Hydration

First question: Is the administration of food and water (whether by natural or artificial means) to a patient in a "vegetative state" morally obligatory except when they cannot be assimilated by the patient's body or cannot be administered to the patient without causing significant physical discomfort?

Response: Yes. The administration of food and water even by artificial means is, in principle, an ordinary and proportionate means of preserving life. It is therefore obligatory to the extent to which, and for as long as, it is shown to accomplish its proper finality, which is the hydration and nourishment of the patient. In this way suffering and death by starvation and dehydration are prevented.

Second question: When nutrition and hydration are being supplied by artificial means to a patient in a "permanent vegetative state," may they be discontinued when competent physicians judge with moral certainty that the patient will never recover consciousness?

Response: No. A patient in a "permanent vegetative state" is a person with fundamental human dignity and must, therefore, receive ordinary and proportionate care which includes, in principle, the administration of water and food even by artificial means.

The Supreme Pontiff Benedict XVI, at the Audience granted to the undersigned Cardinal Prefect of the Congregation for the Doctrine of the Faith, approved these Responses, adopted in the Ordinary Session of the Congregation, and ordered their publication.

Rome, from the Offices of the Congregation for the Doctrine of the Faith, August 1, 2007.

William Cardinal Levada
Prefect
Angelo Amato, S.D.B.
Titular Archbishop of Sila
Secretary

Commentary

The Congregation for the Doctrine of the Faith has formulated responses to questions presented by His Excellency the Most Reverend William S. Skylstad, President of the United States Conference of Catholic Bishops, in a letter of July 11, 2005, regarding the nutrition and hydration of patients in the condition commonly called a "vegetative state." The object of the questions was whether the nutrition and hydration of such patients, especially if provided by artificial means, would constitute an excessively heavy burden for the patients, for their relatives, or for the health care system, to the point where it could be considered, also in the light of the moral teaching of the Church, a means that is extraordinary or disproportionate and therefore not morally obligatory.

The Address of Pope Pius XII to a Congress on Anesthesiology, given on November 24, 1957, is often invoked in favor of the possibility of abandoning the nutrition and hydration of such patients. In this address, the Pope restated two general ethical principles. On the one hand, natural reason and Christian morality teach that, in the case of a grave illness, the patient and those caring for him or her have the right and the duty to provide the care necessary to preserve health and life. On the other hand, this duty in general includes only the use of those means which, considering all the circumstances, are ordinary, that is to say, which do not impose an extraordinary burden on the patient or on others. A more severe obligation would be too burdensome for the majority of persons and would make it too difficult to attain more important goods. Life, health and all temporal activities are subordinate to spiritual ends. Naturally, one is not forbidden to do more than is strictly obligatory to preserve life and health, on condition that one does not neglect more important duties.

One should note, first of all, that the answers given by Pius XII referred to the use and interruption of techniques of resuscitation. However, the case in question has nothing to do with such techniques. Patients in a "vegetative state" breathe spontaneously, digest food naturally, carry on other metabolic functions, and are in a stable situation. But they are not able to feed themselves. If they are not provided artificially with food and liquids, they will die, and the cause of their death will be neither an illness nor the "vegetative state" itself, but solely starvation and dehydration. At the same time, the artificial administration of water and food generally does not impose a heavy burden either on the patient or on his or her relatives. It does not involve excessive expense; it is within the capacity of an average health care system, does not of itself require hospitalization, and is proportionate to accomplishing its purpose, which is to keep the patient from dying of starvation and dehydration. It is not, nor is it meant to be, a treatment that cures the patient, but is rather ordinary care aimed at the preservation of life.

What may become a notable burden is when the "vegetative state" of a family member is prolonged over time. It is a burden like that of caring for a quadriplegic, someone with serious mental illness, with advanced Alzheimer's disease, and so on. Such persons need continuous assistance for months or even for years. But the principle formulated by Pius XII cannot, for obvious reasons, be interpreted as meaning that in such cases those patients, whose ordinary care imposes a real burden on their families, may licitly be left to take care of themselves and thus abandoned to die. This is not the sense in which Pius XII spoke of extraordinary means.

Everything leads to the conclusion that the first part of the principle enunciated by Pius XII should be applied to patients in a "vegetative state": in the case of a serious illness, there is the right and the duty to provide the care necessary for preserving health and life. The development of the teaching of the Church's Magisterium, which has closely followed the progress of medicine and the questions which this has raised, fully confirms this conclusion.

The *Declaration on Euthanasia*, published by the Congregation for the Doctrine of the Faith on May 5, 1980, explained the distinction between proportionate and disproportionate means, and between therapeutic treatments and the normal care due to the sick person: "When inevitable death is imminent in spite of the means used, it is permitted in conscience to take the decision to refuse forms of treatment that would only secure a precarious and burdensome prolongation of life, so long as the normal care due to the sick person in similar cases is not interrupted" (Part IV). Still less can one interrupt the ordinary means of care for patients who are not facing an imminent death, as is generally the case of those in a "vegetative state"; for these people, it would be precisely the interruption of the ordinary means of care which would be the cause of their death.

On June 27, 1981, the Pontifical Council *Cor Unum* published a document entitled *Some Ethical Questions Relating to the Gravely Ill and the Dying*, in which, among other things, it is stated that "There remains the strict obligation to administer at all costs those means which are called 'minimal': that is, those that normally and in usual conditions are aimed at maintaining life (nourishment, blood transfusions, injections, etc.). The discontinuation of these minimal measures would mean in effect willing the end of the patient's life" (no. 2.4.4.).

In an address to participants in an international course on forms of human preleukemia on November 15, 1985, Pope John Paul II, recalling the *Declaration on Euthanasia*, stated clearly that, in virtue of the principle of proportionate care, one may not relinquish "the commitment to valid treatment for sustaining life nor assistance with the normal means of preserving life," which certainly includes the administration of food and liquids. The Pope also noted that those omissions are not licit which are aimed "at shortening life in order to spare the patient or his family from suffering."

In 1995 the Pontifical Council for Pastoral Assistance to Health Care Workers published the *Charter for Health Care Workers*, paragraph 120 of which explicitly affirms: "The administration of food and liquids, even artificially, is part of the normal treatment always due to the patient when this is not burdensome for him or her; their undue interruption can have the meaning of real and true euthanasia."

The address of John Paul II to a group of bishops from the United States of America on an *ad limina* visit, on October 2, 1998, is quite explicit: nutrition and hydration are to be considered as normal care and ordinary means for the preservation of life. It is not acceptable to interrupt them or to withhold them, if from that decision the death of the patient will follow. This would be euthanasia by omission (cf. no. 4).

In his address of March 20, 2004, to the participants of an International Congress on "Life-sustaining Treatments and the Vegetative State: scientific progress and ethical dilemmas," John Paul II confirmed in very clear terms what had been said in the documents cited above, clarifying also their correct interpretation. The Pope stressed the following points:

1) "The term *permanent vegetative state* has been coined to indicate the condition of those patients whose 'vegetative state' continues for over a year. Actually, there is no different diagnosis that corresponds to such a definition, but only a conventional prognostic judgment, relative to the fact that the recovery of patients, statistically speaking, is ever more difficult as the condition of vegetative state is prolonged in time" (no. 2) (Terminology concerning the different phases and forms of the "vegetative state" continues to be discussed, but this is not important for the moral judgment involved).

2) In response to those who doubt the "human quality" of patients in a "permanent vegetative state," it is necessary to reaffirm that "the intrinsic value and personal dignity of every human being do not change, no matter what the concrete circumstances of his or her life. *A man, even if seriously ill or disabled in the exercise of his*

highest functions, is and always will be a man, and he will never become a 'vegetable' or an 'animal' " (no. 3).

3) "The sick person in a vegetative state, awaiting recovery or a natural end, still has the right to basic health care (nutrition, hydration, cleanliness, warmth, etc.), and to the prevention of complications related to his confinement to bed. He also has the right to appropriate rehabilitative care and to be monitored for clinical signs of possible recovery. I should like particularly to underline how the administration of water and food, even when provided by artificial means, always represents a *natural means* of preserving life, not a *medical act.* Its use, furthermore, should be considered, in principle, *ordinary* and *proportionate,* and as such morally obligatory, to the extent to which, and for as long as, it is shown to accomplish its proper finality, which in the present case consists in providing nourishment to the patient and alleviation of his suffering" (no. 4).

4) The preceding documents were taken up and interpreted in this way: "The obligation to provide the 'normal care due to the sick in such cases' (Congregation for the Doctrine of the Faith, *Declaration on Euthanasia,* p. IV) includes, in fact, the use of nutrition and hydration (cf. Pontifical Council *Cor Unum, Some Ethical Questions Relating to the Gravely Ill and the Dying,* no. 2, 4, 4; Pontifical Council for Pastoral Assistance to Health Care Workers, *Charter for Health Care Workers,* no. 120). The evaluation of probabilities, founded on waning hopes for recovery when the vegetative state is prolonged beyond a year, cannot ethically justify the cessation or interruption of *minimal care* for the patient, including nutrition and hydration. Death by starvation or dehydration is, in fact, the only possible outcome as a result of their withdrawal. In this sense it ends up becoming, if done knowingly and willingly, true and proper euthanasia by omission" (n. 4).

Therefore, the Responses now given by the Congregation for the Doctrine of the Faith continue the direction of the documents of the Holy See cited above, and in particular the Address of John Paul II of March 20, 2004. The basic points are two. It is stated, first of all, that the provision of water and food, even by artificial means, is in principle an ordinary and proportionate means of preserving life for patients in a "vegetative state": "It is therefore obligatory, to the extent to which, and for as long as, it is shown to accomplish its proper finality, which is the hydration and nourishment of the patient." It is made clear, secondly, that this ordinary means of sustaining life is to be provided also to those in a "permanent vegetative state," since these are persons with their fundamental human dignity. When stating that the administration of food and water is morally obligatory *in principle*, the Congregation for the Doctrine of the Faith does not exclude the possibility that, in very remote places or in situations of extreme poverty, the artificial provision of food and water may be physically impossible, and then *ad impossibilia nemo tenetur*. However, the obligation to offer the minimal treatments that are available remains in place, as well as that of obtaining, if possible, the means necessary for an adequate support of life. Nor is the possibility excluded that, due to emerging complications, a patient may be unable to assimilate food and liquids, so that their provision becomes altogether useless. Finally, the possibility is not absolutely excluded that, in some rare cases, artificial nourishment and hydration may be excessively burdensome for the patient or may cause significant physical discomfort, for example resulting from complications in the use of the means employed.

These exceptional cases, however, take nothing away from the general ethical criterion, according to which the provision of water and food, even by artificial means, always represents a *natural means* for preserving life, and is not a *therapeutic treatment*. Its use should therefore be considered *ordinary and proportionate*, even when the "vegetative state" is prolonged.

---

6. Advance Directives

An advance directive is a document by which a person makes provision for health care decisions in the event that, in the future, he or she is no longer competent to make such decisions for himself or herself. Advance directives are of two main types: (1) the "living will" and (2) the "durable power of attorney for health care." A third type of advance directive (3) is a hybrid of these two.

A. The Living Will
This is a signed, witnessed or notarized document that allows a patient to direct that specified life-sustaining treatments be withheld or withdrawn if the patient is in a terminal condition and unable to make health care

decisions. Since an attending physician who may be unfamiliar with the signer's wishes and values has the authority to carry out the directives of the will, its terms may be interpreted in a way not envisioned by its signer. Moreover, the language used in such documents is often vague and general, and fails to distinguish clearly the difference between a suicidal intention (to forgo treatment precisely as a way of ending one's life) and the non-suicidal intention to forgo treatment because of the treatment's uselessness or burdensomeness. Frequently, models of a living will are promoted by supporters of euthanasia, using language that is easy to interpret in a way favorable to euthanasia. Because of these features of the so-called living will — a document prepared in advance of the time when one will be in a situation calling for careful judgment about the appropriateness or non-appropriateness of specific treatments — it seems to me (and to others who have examined this issue far more deeply than I) that it is not advisable to make use of a "living will" as an advance directive regarding one's health care.

B. The Durable Power of Attorney

This is a signed, witnessed or notarized document in which the signer designates an agent to make health care decisions for himself or herself in the event that he or she becomes incompetent. The agent must, of course, be chosen with great care since the agent will have great power and authority to make decisions about whether health care is to be provided, withheld, or withdrawn. The signer of such a document has the obligation to discuss his or her values, wishes, and instructions with the agent before and at the time the document is signed, and the agent must be willing to respect and carry out the signer's wishes.

The major advantage of appointing a health care decisions agent is that it leaves decision making in the hands of a person of one's own choosing. Obviously, a Catholic will choose only someone who respects and lives up to the Church's teaching on the dignity of human life. The Catholic Conference for the District of Columbia issued a pastoral letter containing a set of criteria for selecting a health care agent with the power of attorney. These are most useful, in my opinion. Thus I here reproduce them:

- Appoint someone who has the strength of character to make good judgments in painful circumstances.
- Appoint someone who you know you can trust to make decisions on the basis of the Church's teaching. The prudent person will select an agent who will act as he or she would have acted in whatever circumstances evolve.

- No one should agree to act as an agent for another person if that person would expect or require the agent to make decisions which disregard the teaching of the Church. It is not morally acceptable to carry out immoral decisions on behalf of someone else. No agent and no physician should ever feel obliged to act contrary to their well-informed consciences, even on behalf of another person.
- Appoint someone who is likely to be available to care for you in the distant future. . . . [I]t may be advisable to name alternate agents, in the event that your first choice proves unable or unwilling to act for you when the need arises.
- Discuss the specifics of your directive with the person whom you wish to choose as your agent. . . .
- Generally avoid: 1. Stating that you wish to reject certain treatments under all circumstances except in case of imminent death or when one's present medical condition makes it clear in advance that such treatments would be futile; 2. Stating without qualification that you want medical remedies restricted in the event that you become permanently unconscious or terminally ill. Such stipulation can amount to providing a premature self-diagnosis. You should allow your health care agent and physician latitude to offer you appropriate care based on your actual condition.
- Include a provision regarding treatment at the time of imminent death. Recall that the Church allows a person on the verge of death to refuse a treatment which would result in only a burdensome prolongation of life. Your advance directive should authorize your agent to observe this norm.
- Periodically review the provisions of your directive. . . . Make copies of your directive and distribute them to your agent and each of your health care providers and anyone else you deem appropriate.[82]

The International Task Force on Euthanasia and Assisted Suicide has developed a very worthwhile document called the "Protective Medical Decisions Document" (PMDD). This is a durable power of attorney for health care documents specifically prohibiting suicide, assisted suicide, and euthanasia. It is a document fully compatible with Catholic teaching. Among its provisions are the following:

> I wish to receive medical treatment appropriate to my condition which offers a reasonable hope of benefit. I direct that food and water be provided to me unless death is inevitable and truly imminent so that

the effort to sustain my life is futile or unless I am unable to assimilate food or fluids. I ask that, even in the face of death, I be provided with ordinary nursing and medical care, including pain relief, appropriate to my condition. Nothing should be done which will directly and intentionally cause my death, nor should anything be omitted when such omissions would directly and intentionally cause my death. Euthanasia (an action or omission which of itself or by intent causes death), whether by commission or omission, is not permitted.[83]

In conclusion, I advise persons not to sign living wills, which are vigorously promoted by euthanasia advocates. Rather, appoint a person whom you trust to be your agent by giving him or her durable power of attorney. Consider making use of the Protective Medical Decisions Document available from the International Anti-Euthanasia Task Force.[84]

ENDNOTES FOR CHAPTER SEVEN

1. Daniel Callahan, "Foreword" to *Euthanasia Examined: Ethical, Clinical and Legal Perspectives*, ed. John Keown (Cambridge: Cambridge University Press, 1995), pp. xiii-xiv.

2. Ibid., p. xiv.

3. On factors contributing to acceptance of the euthanasia movement, see also Patrick Nowell-Smith, "In Favour of Voluntary Euthanasia," in *Principles of Health Care Ethics*, ed. Raanan Gillon (New York: John Wiley & Sons, 1994), pp. 754-755.

4. See, for example, the following: Nowell-Smith, "In Favour of Voluntary Euthanasia," pp. 751-761; Joseph Fletcher, "Ethics and Euthanasia," *American Journal of Nursing* 73 (April 1973), reprinted in *To Live and To Die*, ed. Robert H. Williams (New York: Springer Verlag, 1973).

5. The *Random House College Dictionary* (rev. ed., New York: Random House, 1996), p. 456.

6. On this, see Germain Grisez and Joseph Boyle, *Life and Death With Liberty and Justice: A Contribution to the Euthanasia Debate* (Notre Dame, IN: University of Notre Dame Press, 1979), pp. 86-87. This excellent work, now two decades old, remains one of the finest studies available to show that respect for the intrinsic goodness of human bodily life absolutely proscribes euthanasia of any kind. I am in great debt to the authors, whose work, unfortunately, has never received the attention it merits for both its moral and jurisprudential arguments against euthanasia.

7. Timothy E. Quill, "Death and Dignity," in *Last Rights: Assisted Suicide and Euthanasia Debated*, ed. Michael M. Ulhmann (Washington, DC/Grand Rapids, MI: Ethics and Public Policy Center/William B. Eerdmans Publishing Co., 1998), pp. 327-328. Quill's essay originally appeared in his book *Death and Dignity: Making Choices and Taking Charge* (New York: Norton, 1993).

8. See Jack Kevorkian, "A Fail-safe Model for Justifiable Medically Assisted Suicide," in *Last Rights*, pp. 263-296; originally published in *American Journal of Forensic Psychiatry* 13.1 (1992).

9. Among the early advocates of euthanasia were Glanville Williams, an English lawyer, and Joseph Fletcher, at that time an Anglican clergyman. Glanville's most important work advocating euthanasia was his *Sanctity of Life and the Criminal Law* (New York: Alfred A. Knopf, 1957). Fletcher devoted a chapter defending euthanasia in his *Morals and Medicine* (Boston: Beacon Press, 1960), a work reprinted in the 1970s and 1980s. During the 1970s, Fletcher wrote frequently in defense of euthanasia (see endnote 10).

10. Three authors in particular wrote extensively (and influentially) on the subject, namely, Joseph Fletcher (a professor at the Episcopal Theological School in Cambridge, MA, and later at the University of Virginia), Daniel Maguire (a Catholic theologian teaching at Marquette University), and Marvin Kohl (a philosopher at the State University of New York in Buffalo). Among Fletcher's writings on the subject at this time were: "Ethics and Euthanasia" (see endnote 4); "The Patient's Right to Die," in *Euthanasia and the Right to Death*, ed. A. B. Downing (London: Peter Owen, 1969), pp. 66-69; and "The 'Right' to Life and the 'Right' to Die," in *Beneficent Euthanasia*, ed. Marvin Kohl (Buffalo: Prometheus Books, 1975). Maguire authored a book and several essays, among them *Death by Choice* (New York: Doubleday, 1974); "The Freedom to Die," in *New Theology No. 10*, ed. Martin Marty and Dean Peerman (New York: Macmillan, 1974); and "A Catholic View of Mercy Killing," in *Beneficent Euthanasia*. Among Kohl's contributions to the literature was his essay "Voluntary Beneficent Euthanasia" in the volume he edited, *Beneficent Euthanasia*. That volume ended with "A Plea for Beneficent Euthanasia," pp. 233-236, written by Kohl and Paul Kurtz (editor of the *Humanist*) and signed by Fletcher, Maguire, several Nobel laureates, physicians, religious leaders, and academics.

11. More contemporary articulations of the "ethics of euthanasia" include the following: Patrick Nowell-Smith, "In Favour of Voluntary Euthanasia," in *Principles of Health Care Ethics* (see endnote 3 for details), pp. 751-762; John Harris, "Euthanasia and the Value of Life," in *Euthanasia Examined* (see endnote 1 for details), pp. 6-22; Jean Davis, "The Case for Legalising Voluntary Euthanasia," in ibid., pp. 83-95; Ronald Dworkin, *Life's Domin-*

ion: An Argument About Abortion, Euthanasia, and Individual Freedom (New York: Harper, 1993); Dworkin, "Do We Have a Right to Die?" in *Last Rights* (see endnote 7 for details), pp. 75-94; Peter Singer, *Rethinking Life and Death: The Collapse of Our Traditional Ethics* (New York: St. Martin's Press, 1995); Derek Humphrey and Ann Wickett, *The Right to Die: Understanding Euthanasia* (New York: Harper & Row, 1988).

12. This, in essence, is the argument advanced by a host of writers. See, for instance, Kohl, "Voluntary Beneficent Euthanasia," esp. pp. 131-133, where he emphasizes that voluntary euthanasia is rooted in a respect for the dignity of the person to control his or her own life; Fletcher, "Ethics and Euthanasia," "The 'Right' to Life and the 'Right' to Die"; Maguire, "The Freedom to Die." Dworkin believes it is tyrannical to oppose a person's well-considered decision to ask to be killed mercifully: "making someone die in a way... that he believes [is] a horrifying contradiction of his life, is a devastating, odious form of tyranny" (*Life's Dominion...*, p. 217). See also Harris, "Euthanasia and the Value of Life," pp. 14-16.

13. Fletcher, "The Patient's Right to Die," p. 69. See also Maguire, "The Freedom to Die," pp. 188-189.

14. Thus Kohl, one of the leading proponents of "beneficent euthanasia," distinguishes sharply between the dignity human beings have by reason of their nature as members of the human species — he refers to this as dignity — and the dignity human persons have insofar as they are capable of controlling their own lives — dignity— and his contention is that it is dignity that is at stake in the issue of euthanasia and that this dignity justifies the "right to die" and to choose to be killed mercifully, a choice that others are obliged to respect. See his "Voluntary Beneficent Euthanasia," pp. 132-133.

15. Singer, *Rethinking Life and Death*, pp. 218-219.

16. Fletcher, *Morals and Medicine*, p. 211.

17. Maguire, "The Freedom to Die," pp. 188-189. It is instructive to note that both Fletcher and Maguire explicitly link the freedom to choose death (in euthanasia) to the freedom to control conception by contraceptive methods. This helps one see the link between acceptance of contraception and the "culture of death." See Chapter Four.

18. Harris, "Euthanasia and the Value of Life," pp. 8-9; Singer, *Rethinking Life and Death*, pp. 180-183, 202-206.

19. Marvin Kohl, *The Morality of Killing: Sanctity of Life, Abortion and Euthanasia* (Atlantic Highlands, NJ: Humanities Press, 1974), pp. 81-96; Glanville Williams, *Sanctity of Life*, p. 316; Williams, "Euthanasia," *Medico-Legal Journal* 41 (1973), 22; H. Tristram Englehardt, Jr., "Ethical Issues in Aiding the Death of Young Children," in *Beneficent Euthanasia,*

pp. 180-192; Robert F. Weir, *Selected Nontreatment of Handicapped New-borns* (New York: Oxford University Press, 1984), esp. pp. 188-223; Anthony Shaw, "Dilemmas of 'Informed Consent' in Children," in *Death, Dying, and Euthanasia*, ed. Dennis J. Horan and David Mall (Frederick, MD: University Publications of America, 1984), pp. 75-90; Raymond S. Duff and A. G. M. Campbell, "Moral and Ethical Dilemmas in the Special-Care Nursery," in *Death, Dying, and Euthanasia*, pp. 91-104.

20. See, for example, Weir, *Selective Nontreatment of Handicapped Newborns*, pp. 215-221.

21. Fletcher, "Indicators of Humanhood: A Tentative Profile of Man," *Hastings Center Report* 2 (November 1972), 1; "Four Indicators of Humanhood — The Enquiry Matures," *Hastings Center Report* 4 (December 1974), 5-7; Tooley, "Abortion and Infanticide," *Philosophy and Public Affairs* 2 (1972), 37-65, esp. 44-48; Singer, *Rethinking Life and Death*, pp. 202-206.

22. Harris, "Euthanasia and the Value of Life," pp. 7-8, 17-18.

23. Supreme Court of the United States, *Planned Parenthood of Southeastern Pennsylvania et al. v. Robert P. Casey*, June 29, 1992, p. 9. An excellent analysis and critique of this decision is Russell Hittinger, "Et Tu, Justice Kennedy?" *Crisis* 10.8 (September 1992), 16-22.

24. Arthur Dyck, "Beneficent Euthanasia and Benemortasia: Alternative Views of Mercy," in *Beneficent Euthanasia*, p. 127.

25. *Euthanasia, Clinical Practice and the Law*, ed. Luke Gormally (London: The Linacre Centre for Health Care Ethics, 1994), pp. 131, 132; emphasis, including bold face, in the original. The first part of this truly excellent volume upholding the sanctity of life and providing devastating criticism of the rationale to justify euthanasia contains a reprint of the important Linacre Centre Working Party Report, whereas the second part contains the submission made on behalf of The Linacre Centre to House of Lords' Select Committee on Medical Ethics. Among the members of the Working Party were Luke Gormally, John Mahoney, S.J., G. E. M. Anscombe, and John Finnis.

26. Ibid., p. 132.

27. The best treatment of the injustice of "quality of life" criteria for determining who should live and who should die is given by Grisez and Boyle in *Life and Death With Liberty and Justice*, chapter 6.

28. *Euthanasia, Clinical Practice and the Law*, p. 42.

29. As St. Thomas says, commenting on St. Paul's teaching on the resurrection of the body, "*anima mea non est ego*" ("my soul is not me") (*In 1 Cor. 15*).

30. Leo Alexander, "Medical Science Under Dictatorship," in *Death, Dying, and Euthanasia*, p. 584. Alexander's essay, which should be read by every-

one who wants to understand the evil of euthanasia, originally appeared in the *New England Journal of Medicine* 241 (1949), 39-47.

31. See Grisez and Boyle, *Life and Death With Liberty and Justice* (Notre Dame, IN: University of Notre Dame Press, 1978), pp. 154-168.

32. Ramsey proposed the term "agathanasia" in his long essay, "On (Only) Caring for the Dying" in his *Patient as Person* (New Haven: Yale University Press, 1970), pp. 113-164. Dyck developed his analogous notion of "benemortasia" in two essays: "An Alternative to an Ethics of Euthanasia," in *To Live and To Die*, pp. 98-112, and in "Beneficent Euthanasia and Benemortasia: Alternative Views of Mercy," in *Beneficent Euthanasia*, pp. 117-129.

33. *Euthanasia, Clinical Practice and the Law*, pp. 53-54.

34. Ibid., p. 55.

35. Pope Pius XII, "The Prolongation of Life: An Address to an International Congress of Anesthesiologists," as reprinted in *Death, Dying, and Euthanasia*, p. 284.

36. Kevin O'Rourke, O.P., "Evolution of Church Teaching on the Prolongation of Life," *Health Progress* (January-February 1988), 32; emphasis added. O'Rourke set forth the same understanding of Pope Pius's statement in the following essays: "The A.M.A. Statement on Tubal Feeding: An Ethical Analysis," *America* (November 22, 1988), 321-323, an essay that the Society for the Right to Die, an advocacy group for legalizing euthanasia subsequently saw fit to reprint in its newsletter; "Should Nutrition and Hydration Be Provided to Permanently Unconscious and Other Mentally Disabled Persons?" *Issues in Law and Medicine* 5 (1989), 181-196; "On the Care of 'Vegetative' Patients," *Ethics & Medics* 24.4 (April 1999), 3-4; 24.5 (May 1999), 1-2. The same position is also set forth by O'Rourke in the work he co-authored with Benedict Ashley, O.P., *Health Care Ethics* (4th ed., Washington, DC: Georgetown University Press, 1997), pp. 421-426.

37. My interpretation of O'Rourke's position (and it is important to note it is shared by Benedict Ashley, O.P., as endnote 36 clearly shows) is correct. It is precisely the interpretation given it by one who finds it the correct way of understanding what Pius XII meant, namely, Thomas F. Schindler, S.S., director of ethics at Mercy Health Services in Farmington, MI. Schindler, who considers O'Rourke's position "excellent," concludes that "we should no longer state the ethical obligation as one of 'prolonging life.' Rather, we should refer to the obligation of maintaining a life 'capable of reaching life's spiritual goals' or 'capable of realizing life's purposes.'" ("Implications of Prolonging Life," *Health Progress* [April 1988], 12). This, it seems to me, is definitely a "quality of life" view subject to the kind of criticism given above in discussing the "ethics of euthanasia." A similar position is taken

by Richard M. Gula, S.S., "Quality of Life: A Focus on the Patient's Total Good," *Health Progress* (July-August 1988), 34-39, 84.

38. This matter is very clearly discussed in *Euthanasia, Clinical Practice and the Law*, pp. 43-45. See also Grisez and Boyle, *Life and Death With Liberty and Justice*, pp. 260-269.

39. John R. Connery, S.J., "Prolonging Life: Its Duty and Its Limits," in *Moral Responsibility in Prolonging Life Decisions*, ed. Donald McCarthy and Albert Moraczewski, O.P. (St. Louis: Pope John XXIII Medical-Moral Research and Education Center, 1981), p. 133.

40. Richard McCormick, S.J., "To Save or Let Die: The Dilemma of Modern Medicine," published simultaneously in *Journal of the American Medical Association* 229 (1974), 171-176, and *America* 130 (July 7, 1974), 6-10, and reprinted in McCormick's *How Brave a New World? Dilemmas in Bioethics* (Garden City: Doubleday, 1981), pp. 339-351, and "The Quality of Life, the Sanctity of Life," *Hastings Center Report* 8.1 (1978), 30-36, reprinted in *How Brave a New World?*, pp. 383-401. References will be to these essays as found in *How Brave a New World?*

41. "To Save or Let Die," in *How Brave a New World?*, p. 345 (emphasis added).

42. Ibid.

43. Ibid., p. 346.

44. Ibid., p. 349.

45. Ibid., p. 347; emphasis in original.

46. Grisez and Boyle, *Life and Death With Liberty and Justice*, p. 260.

47. Ibid., pp. 268-269.

48. *Euthanasia, Clinical Practice and the Law*, p. 66.

49. Dyck, "An Alternative to an Ethics of Euthanasia," in *To Live and To Die*, pp. 111-112; Dyck provides a similar list, omitting the fourth, in "Beneficent Euthanasia and Benemortasia: Alternative View of Mercy," in *Beneficent Euthanasia*, pp. 128-129. I have modified somewhat his way of articulating these presuppositions.

50. FIAMC and Pontifical Academy for Life, "Joint Statement on the Vegetative State," available at http://www.vatican.va/roman_curia/pontifical_academies/acdlife/documents/rc_pont-acd_life_doc_20040320_joint-statement-veget-state_en.html.

51. Jerome Groopman, "Silent Minds: Scan Technology and Vegetative Patients," *New Yorker*, October 15, 2007.

52. In 1981, the Ethical and Judicial Council of the American Medical Association declared it ethical to withdraw all means of life support, including

such feeding, "where a terminally ill patient's coma is beyond doubt irreversible" (American Medical Association, Judicial Council, *Current Opinions of the Judicial Council of the American Medical Association: Including the Principles of Medical Ethics and Rules of the Judicial Council* [Chicago: American Medical Association, 1981], p. 9, par. 2.11). The President's Commission for the Study of Ethical Problems in Medicine and Biomedical and Behavioral Research addressed this issue in its 1983 monograph on foregoing life-sustaining treatments, concluding that the decision to provide or forego tube feeding of PVS patients was best made by the patient's surrogates and not by the courts and that foregoing all treatment, including tubally administered food and hydration, was an ethically legitimate option (President's Commission for the Study of Ethical Problems in Medicine and Biomedical and Behavioral Research, *Deciding to Forego Life-Sustaining Treatment: Ethical, Medical, and Legal Issues in Treatment Decisions* [Washington, DC: U.S. Government Printing Office, 1983], pp. 171-196). Among organizations issuing guidelines favoring the withholding of tubal feeding from PVS patients were the American Academy of Neurology ("Position of the American Academy of Neurology on certain aspects of the care and management of the persistent vegetative state patient," *Neurology* 39 [1989], 125-126) and American Medical Association ("Persistent Vegetative State and the Decision to Withdraw or Withhold Life Support," *Journal of the American Medical Association* 263 [1990], 426-430. It should be noted that a significant number of the individuals who drafted statements of this kind think that "personhood" is lost if an individual is no longer capable of exercising cognitive abilities.

53. Texas Conference of Catholic Bishops, "On Withdrawing Artificial Nutrition and Hydration" (May 7, 1990), in *Origins: NC News Service* 20 (1990), 53-55. It should be noted that two of the eighteen members of the Texas Conference of Catholic Bishops refused to sign this statement, and that one Texas bishop, René Gracída of Corpus Christi, published an extensive critique of it, "Interim Pastoral Statement on Artificial Feeding and Hydration: A Critique," published originally in the May 25, 1990, edition of [Corpus Christi] *Diocesan Press.*

54. See, for example, the Most Reverend Louis Gelineau, Bishop of Providence, RI, "On Removing Nutrition and Water from a Comatose Woman" (January 10, 1988), in *Origins: NC News Service* 17 (1988), 546-547.

55. Committee for Pro-Life Activities, National Conference of Catholic Bishops, *Nutrition and Hydration: Moral and Pastoral Reflections* (Washington, DC: United States Catholic Conference, 1992), Publication No. 516-X, p. 7. The document was also printed in *Origins: NC News Service* 21 (1992), 705-711; the citation is found at 711.

56. John Paul II, "Building a Culture of Life," "Ad Limina" Address to the Bishops of California, Nevada and Hawaii (October 2, 1998), *Origins* 18.18 (October 15, 1098), no. 4.

57. Pennsylvania Conference of Catholic Bishops, "Nutrition and Hydration: Moral Considerations," in *Origins: NC News Service* 21 (1992), 542-553.

58. See, for example, the following: New Jersey State Catholic Conference, " 'Friend-of-the-Court Brief to the New Jersey Supreme Court': Providing Food and Fluids to Severely Brain Damaged Patients" (November 3, 1987), in *Origins: NC News Service* 16 (1987), 542-553; the Most Reverend James McHugh, Bishop of Camden, NJ, "Artificially Assisted Nutrition and Hydration" (September 21, 1989), in *Origins: NC News Service* 19 (1989), 314-316. The episcopal conferences of Missouri and Florida also issued statements on this matter, as did the Most Reverend John Myers of Peoria. One researcher, Thomas Shannon (who himself holds that providing food artificially to PVS patients is not obligatory) sent a questionnaire to the ordinaries of U.S. dioceses on the matter. Seventy-eight ordinaries responded, offering conflicting and contradictory directives, often prepared by diocesan bioethics committees or hospital committees within the diocese. Shannon summarizes his findings in an essay coauthored with James Walter, "The PVS Patient and the Forgoing/Withdrawing of Medical Nutrition and Hydration," *Theological Studies* 49 (1988), 623-647, reprinted in *Quality of Life: The New Medical Dilemma*, ed. James J. Walter and Thomas A. Shannon (New York: Paulist, 1990), 203-223; the summary of Shannon's survey is found on pp. 204-210.

59. Between 1986 and 2001, O'Rourke presented his view in many places. See the following: "The A.M.A. Statement on Tube-Feeding: An Ethical Analysis," *America* 155 (1986), 321-333, 333; "Evolution of Church Teaching on Prolonging Life," *Health Progress* 59 (1988), 28-35; "Should Nutrition and Hydration Be Provided to Permanently Unconscious and Other Mentally Disabled Persons?" *Issues in Law & Medicine* 5 (1989), 181-196; "Open Letter to Bishop McHugh: Father Kevin O'Rourke on Hydration and Nutrition," *Origins: NC News Service* 19 (1989), 351-352; "On the Care of 'Vegetative' Patients," *Ethics & Medics* 24.4 (April 1999), 3-4, and 24.5 (May 1999), 1-2; with Benedict Ashley, O.P., in their book *Health Care Ethics* (4th ed., Washington, DC: Georgetown University Press, 1997), pp. 421-426; with Patrick Norris, O.P., "Care of PVS Patients: Catholic Opinion in the United States," *Linacre Quarterly* 68.3 (August 2001), 201-217.

60. Pope Pius XII, "The Prolongation of Life: Allocution to the International Congress of Anesthesiologists" (November 24, 1957), in *The Pope Speaks* 4 (1958), 396.

61. Kevin O'Rourke, "Evolution of Church Teaching on the Prolongation of Life," 32.

62. See their *Health Care Ethics*, pp. 421-426.

63. See *Issues in Law & Medicine*, Vol. 3, No. 2 (Winter, 1987), 203-217. The authors were listed as: William E. May, Robert Barry, O.P., Msgr. Orville Griese, Germain Grisez, Brian Johnstone, C.Ss.R., Thomas J. Marzen, J.D., Bishop James T. McHugh, S.T.D., Gilbert Meilaender, Ph.D., Mark Siegler, M.D., and Msgr. William Smith. Subsequently, ninety-eight other scholars, including Paul Ramsey, Robert George, and Hadley Arkes, signed the statement and their names are printed on pp. 212-217.

64. May et al., "Feeding and Hydrating the Permanently Unconscious," 209.

65. Ibid, 211.

66. This point has been further developed by one of the co-authors, Germain Grisez, who, in a later work, has said that "life-sustaining care for [persons] severely handicapped does have a human and Christian significance in addition to the one it would derive precisely from the inherent goodness of their lives. This additional significance is . . . profoundly real, just as is the significance of [a husband's faithfulness to a permanently unconscious] wife, which continues to benefit not only the person being cared for but the one giving care" (Grisez, *Difficult Moral Questions* [Quincy, IL: Franciscan Press, 1997], p. 223).

67. O'Rourke, "Open Letter to Bishop McHugh: Father Kevin O'Rourke on Hydration and Nutrition," 351-352.

68. On this, see the brief review of the Congress's work given by Richard Doerflinger, "John Paul II on the 'Vegetative' State: An Important Papal Speech," *Ethics & Medics* 29.6 (June 2004), 3. Doerflinger himself was a participant at the Congress.

69. Australian bishops, "Briefing Note on the Obligation to Provide Nutrition and Hydration," 09-05-04, available at http://www.acbc.catholic.org.au/documents/2004090316.pdf.

70. On this, see Thomas A. Shannon and James J. Walter, "Implications of the Papal Allocution on Feeding Tubes," *Hastings Center Report* 34.4 (July-August 2004), 18-20, at 18; see also Ronald Hamel and Michael Panicola, "Must We Preserve Life?" *America* (April 19-26, 2004) 6-13; John Tuohey, "The Pope on PVS: Does JP II's statement make the grade?" *Commonweal* 131.12 (June 18, 2004).

71. Shannon and Walter, "Implications. . ."

72. See, for example, Sister Jean deBlois, "Prolonging Life or Interrupting Dying? Opinions Differ on Artificial Nutrition and Hydration," Aquinas

Institute, Spring 2004 Newsletter, http://www.ai.edu (unfortunately, this is no longer posted online), and John Paris, S.J., "No Moral Sense," in an interview with Brian Braiker of *Newsweek* (March 23, 2005) and available on http://www.newsweek.com/id/48970.

73. Paris, "No Moral Sense."

74. Edward R. Sunshine, "Truncating Catholic Tradition," *National Catholic Reporter*, April 8, 2004, at http://natcath.org/NCR_Online/archives2/2005b/040805/040805k.php.

75. Tuohey, "The Pope on PVS."

76. Lisa Sowle Cahill, "Catholicism, Death and Modern Medicine," *America* (April 25, 2005), 14-17.

77. Christopher Kaczor, "Notes & Abstracts: Philosophy and Theology," *The National Catholic Bioethics Quarterly* 7.3 (Autumn 2007), 595-600.

78. Benedict Ashley, Jean deBlois, Kevin O'Rourke, *HealthCare Ethics* (5th ed., Washington, DC: Georgetown University Press, 2006).

79. For an extensive critique of the 5th edition of *HealthCare Ethics*, see my review essay of the book in *The National Catholic Bioethics Quarterly* 7.2 (Summer 2007), 409-417.

80. The text of John Paul II's address of November 12, 2004, to the 19th International Conference of the Pontifical Council for Health Pastoral Care is available at http://www.vatican.va/holy_father/john_paul_ii/speeches/2004/november/documents/hf_jp-ii_spe_20041112_pc-hlthwork_en.html.

81. Germain Grisez, "Should Nutrition and Hydration Be Provided to Permanently Unconscious and Other Mentally Disabled Persons"? *Issues in Law & Medicine* 5.2 (Fall 1989), 171.

82. Roman Catholic Bishops of the District of Columbia (His Eminence James Cardinal Hickey, the Most Rev. Alvaro Corrada, the Most Rev. Leonard Olivier), *Care of the Sick and Dying: A Pastoral Letter* (Washington, DC: The District of Columbia Catholic Conference, 1994), pp. 26-28.

83. International Task Force on Euthanasia and Assisted Suicide, "Protective Medical Decisions Document," P.O. Box 760, Steubenville, OH 43952; http://www.internationaltaskforce.org/.

84. Ibid.

CHAPTER EIGHT

Defining Death and Organ Transplantation

The first edition of this book, in which I accepted D. Alan Shewmon's critique of the "brain death" criterion for determining that a person had died, was published in September 2000. While the book was at press, Pope John Paul II gave an address on August 29, 2000, to the Eighteenth International Congress of the Transplant Society. In it, he said that the "so-called 'neurological' criterion... namely, the *complete* and *irreversible* cessation of all brain activity, if rigorously applied, does not seem to conflict with the essential elements of a sound anthropology" and that therefore healthcare workers can use these criteria for ascertaining death with "moral certainty" (no. 5). But he also maintained that it was the task of scientists and doctors, not the Magisterium or theologians, to develop criteria to determine whether death has in fact occurred. It will obviously be important to consider this address in depth in this revised version of the chapter written prior to that address.

I will proceed as follows. After an introduction, I will (1) summarize the state of the question up to August 2000; (2) examine John Paul II's August 29, 2000, statement and Shewmon's reflections thereon; (3) summarize recent developments in the debate over brain death, focusing on discussions at two open meetings of the President's Council on Bioethics in September and November 2007, at the second of which Shewmon presented his position; (4) offer an evaluative conclusion of that debate; (5) note significant developments in early 2008; and (6) consider the question of transplants between living persons.

Introduction

A current issue of crucial importance focuses on the definition of death and on criteria for determining that a person has died. This issue is critical because it is possible to save the lives of persons who are threatened by death because one or more of their vital organs — the heart, lungs, liver, etc. — no longer function. Although paired vital organs such as kidneys can be provided for them by living donors — organ transplants from the living will be taken up in the concluding section of this chapter — such donors cannot be used as the source of unpaired vital organs such as the heart, but a possible source for such organs (and of paired vital organs as well) is the "body" of a person who has just died. But organ transplants from a cadaver *must* take place almost immediately after death. Were the transplantation delayed, the organs in question would quickly deteriorate and would no longer be of any help in preserving the lives of those in need of them.

In the legitimate desire to obtain a life-saving organ for a fellow human being whose life can be saved by transplant surgery, it is necessary to strenuously resist any temptation to diminish care of a dying person because he or she happens to be a prospective donor. This is the reason why the World Medical Assembly, at a 1968 meeting in Sydney, Australia, accepted the principle that there be complete separation of authority and responsibility between the physician or group of physicians charged with caring for the dying person and the physician or group of physicians whose task is to care for the person in need of an organ. It is for this reason that one of the provisions of the Uniform Anatomical Gift Act is the following:

> The time of death shall be determined by a physician who attends the donor at his death, or, if none, the physician who certifies the death. This physician shall *not* participate in the procedures for removing or transplanting a part.[1]

Our rightful concern in the practical order to protect the dignity of the dying person is paralleled, or *ought* to be paralleled, in the intellectual order with a concern to separate the question of defining death and the use of organs for transplants. The late Paul Ramsey forcefully made this point when he said:

> If in the practical order we need to separate between the physician who is responsible for the care of a prospective donor, and the physician who is responsible for a prospective recipient, do we not need in the intellectual order to keep the question of the definition of death equally discrete from the use of organs in transplantations? If only the physician responsible for a dying man should make the determination that he has died, with no "help" from the medical team

that has in its care a man who needs a borrowed organ, should not also the definition of death and the tests for it that he uses be ones that he thinks are sound or were agreed to by the profession without having transplantation in view? There would be too little protection of life attained in the practical order by entirely separating the authority and responsibility of the teams of physicians if the definition of death and the tests used for it have already been significantly invaded by the requirements of transplant therapy. If no person's death should *for this purpose* be hastened, then the definition of death should not *for this purpose* be updated, or the procedures for stating that a man has died be revised as a means of affording easier access to organs.[2]

Ramsey eloquently emphasizes our absolute obligation to respect and care for our fellow human beings, especially those who are dying. Because of contemporary developments in medical technology, it is becoming more and more difficult to die and to determine whether the body before us is, in truth, a *living human body* (and therefore a living human person) or a cadaver (the mortal remains of a *once* living human body). The concern to redefine "death" and to establish criteria for determining that death has, in fact, occurred has in large measure been caused by this twofold difficulty.[3]

It would be foolish to ignore the fact that attempts to "update" death have not also been greatly influenced by the enormous strides in transplant surgery and the need to find suitable organs. Indeed, many influential persons today claim that a human person is "dead" when the functioning of the neocortex of the brain is irreversibly lost, so the individual can no longer engage in the cognitive/affective activities specific to human persons. On this view, an individual living human body capable of breathing, circulating blood, and assimilating nourishment on its own, without the aid of any technological instrumentation, may well be a living human body but it cannot be regarded as a "person" because it is not capable of doing what persons do; on this view, the "person," i.e., the being endowed with rights, is already dead and the non-personal living body can be regarded as a cadaver, a corpse, and hence a potential source of vital organs for those in need of such. This way of viewing death, dualistic in nature and utilitarian in practice, is utterly inimical both to the Christian understanding of human life and to sound philosophy. Many people, nonetheless, advocate it today.[4]

1. The State of the Question Up to 2000

A. Pope John Paul II on Death Prior to 2000

John Paul II presented his thoughts on this issue at some length in his "Discourse of John Paul II to the Participants of the Working Group" of the working group of the Pontifical Academy of Sciences. He took up three matters of critical importance in bioethics and indeed in human existence, namely, (1) the value of human life, including bodily life; (2) the definition of death; and (3) the death of a human person and organ transplantation. Here I will not present his address at length but summarize the major teachings he developed in it. The text of this address is found in *Working Group on the Determination of Brain Death and Its Relationship to Human Death* (December 10-14, 1989) (Pontificiae Academiae Scientiarum Scripta Varia, 83; eds. R. J. White, H. Angstwurm, and I. Carrasco de Paula [Vatican City: Pontifical Academy of Sciences, 1992]).

(1) *The Value of Human Life, Including Bodily Life*
The value of human life "springs from what is spiritual in man"; the body "receives from the spiritual principle — which . . . makes it what it is — a supreme dignity, a kind of reflection of the Absolute. The body is that of a person, a being which is open to superior values, a being capable of fulfillment in the knowledge and love of God. . . ." Here the Pope is in effect saying: *Every living human body is a living human person.*

(2) *The Definition of Death*
Although it is not easy to define death in a way acceptable to everyone, John Paul II says "it occurs when the spiritual principle which assures the unity of the individual can no longer exercise its functions in and upon the organism, whose elements, left to themselves, disintegrate." Theologically speaking, death occurs when the soul is separated from the body, for then the body is no longer *a living human body, a person*, but the mortal remains of a person. But John Paul makes it clear that the *human person is an embodied being; that the body is integral to the human person*, for he declares: "Unlike animals, man knows that he must die *and he perceives this as an affront to his dignity. Although in the flesh he is mortal, he also realizes that he ought not to die, because he carries within himself an openness, an aspiration towards the eternal.*" In short, death is the ultimate indignity to the human person, for the person dies, not merely his body.

(3) *Human Death and Organ Transplants*

John Paul emphasizes that it is absolutely necessary to make sure that a person is really dead before one seeks to use his organs for the good of others. He identifies two tasks: one concerning scientists, analysts, and scholars, whose responsibility it is to determine as precisely as possible the moment of death and the indisputable signs of death; the second one concerns moralists, philosophers, and theologians, who must exercise prudence in finding the correct solutions to new problems and new aspects of age-old problems in light of new data. *Note that the Holy Father explicitly maintains that scientists, not theologians or philosophers, have the responsibility and competence to determine when death has taken place and the indisputable signs that it has. Nor is it the competence of the Magisterium to make a judgment on this scientific issue.*

B. The Conclusions of the "Working Group" of Scientists

The major conclusions or "final considerations" of the scientific members of the Working Group of the Pontifical Academy of Sciences centered on: (1) the clinical definition of death; (2) clinical indications that death has occurred; and (3) the artificial prolongation of organ functions in the event of brain death. Here I summarize these major conclusions. The text of the "Working Group" is found in *Working Group on the Artificial Prolongation of Life and the Determination of the Exact Moment of Death* (Vatican City: Pontifical Academy of Sciences, 1986).

(1) *The Clinical Definition of Death*

"A person is dead when there has been total and irreversible loss of all capacity for integrating and coordinating physical and mental functions of the body as a unit." I think this definition fits in well with a commonsense understanding of death and harmonizes with the Judeo-Christian tradition. Shewmon, whose challenge to brain death is considered next, supports the idea that death necessarily entails loss of the integrative unity of the body and sees this as in harmony with Aristotelian-Thomistic thought.

(2) *Clinical Indications That Death Has Occurred*

Death, as clinically defined, in fact has occurred when: "a) spontaneous cardiac and respiratory functions have irreversibly ceased, which rapidly leads to a total and irreversible loss of all brain functions, or b) there has been an irreversible cessation of all brain functions, even if cardiac and respiratory functions which would have ceased have been maintained artificially." The Working Group in 1989 thus concluded, as did a similar Working Group in 1985, that "the establishment of total and irreversible loss of all brain function is the true medical criterion of death."

(3) *Artificial Prolongation of Organ Functions*
If brain death has occurred, "artificial respiration can prolong cardiac function for a limited time, thus permitting a short period of survival for organs for the possibility of transplantation. This is possible only in cases of complete irreversible loss of all brain functions (brain death)."

Thus participants in the 1989 Working Group of the Pontifical Academy of Sciences agreed that a human person can be truly declared dead once it has been established that "there has been an irreversible cessation of all brain functions" and that it is morally proper, once a person has been declared dead by reason of brain death, to use artificial means to prolong cardiac function for a limited time in order to preserve vital organs for transplantation.

C. The Rationale for Identifying "Brain Death" With Human Death

(1) *Historical Background*
The "clinical definition" of death advanced by the Working Group of the Pontifical Academy of Sciences harmonizes with the truth that a human person is a bodily being and that a living human body is a person. What makes the body *to be* human and alive is its vital principle, the soul. And although the soul is immaterial, the human person is not, for the human person is a body-person, a biological organism, a living whole. The human person is *more* than his body, because he is capable, by reason of his vital principle, of nonmaterial acts — knowing the truth and making free choices. But the human person is nonetheless inescapably and essentially a *body person*, not a *spirit person* — and when the body dies, the person dies. As the Working Group's definition makes clear, a *living human body is a person*, and, conversely, *a dead human body is a dead person*, i.e., is no longer a person but rather the mortal remains of a person. We can truly say that death is the irreversible cessation of the integrated organic functioning that is characteristic of the living human body as a whole.

Before the middle of the twentieth century, there was no major dispute over the criteria for determining that a person had died because the integrated organic functioning characteristic of the body as a whole had irreversibly ceased. A person was judged to be dead when his heart stopped beating and his blood stopped circulating, when he stopped breathing, etc. However, beginning with the development of more effective artificial respirators and subsequent breakthroughs in medical technology and life-support systems, troubling and serious questions were raised about the traditional ways of declaring a person dead.

(2) *The Consensus on "Brain Death": The Report of the President's Commission*
Beginning in the 1960s, the medical community responded to the difficulties noted above by developing new criteria for determining that a person has, in fact, died. Despite differences among the proposals made, a consensus emerged (one accepted by the Working Group of the Pontifical Academy of Sciences in 1985 and again in 1989) that the total and irreversible absence of the function of the entire brain is as valid a criterion for determining that death has occurred as the traditionally accepted cardiorespiratory indications of death. In the United States, this consensus was well articulated by the members of the U.S. President's Commission for the Study of Ethical Problems in Medicine and Biomedical and Behavioral Research in its 1981 report.

This important Commission *explicitly* rejected efforts to define death in terms of the irreversible cessation of the function of the neocortex of the brain (on this view of death, persons said to be in the PVS condition could be declared dead!). But they advocated statutory enactment of a Uniform Definition of Death Act (subsequently enacted in more than half of all U.S. jurisdictions). This act, supported by the U.S. President's Commission, provides that an individual who has sustained either (1) irreversible cessation of circulatory and respiratory functions or (2) irreversible cessation of all functions of the entire brain, including the brain stem, is dead.[5]

(3) *The Presuppositions Underlying This Consensus*
As several commentators have noted, the statute proposed by the President's Commission first of all presupposes that "death" is understood to mean the death of a human being or human person *as a whole, as a unified organism*. A common misunderstanding of brain death is to regard it designating the death of an organ and not of the whole organism. The truth is that organs can cease functioning. But what *dies* is the living organism whose organ or organs have ceased to function. Another central presupposition underlying this approach to understanding death is that we must be

able to draw a line between those who are alive and those who are dead. Although *dying* is a process insofar as not all parts of the body "die" at the same time (fingernails and hair, for instance, continue to grow some time after the human person whose fingernails and hair they were is dead), death is not a process but the definite termination of the life of a living being.[6] The line drawn by the President's Commission and the Uniform Definition of Death Act is arbitrary in the sense that it is the choice, by competent authorities, of one proposal among others, but it is by no means arbitrary insofar as it is rooted in the reasonable belief that once either circulatory/respiratory functions *or* the functions of the *entire brain* have irreversibly ceased, one can be confident that a once living human person is dead.

A final presupposition on which this consensus depends is the belief that the *brain is the central integrating organ of the human body* in human beings who have advanced beyond the embryonic stage. Since the brain is the central integrator or critical organ of the whole human body, its destruction or irreversible nonfunctioning necessarily entails loss of somatic integrative unity, a thermodynamic "point of no return," a literal "dis-integration" of the organism as a whole.[7]

Confirmation of the belief that the brain is the central integrating organ of the whole human body is provided, defenders of the brain-death criterion emphasized, by the fact that the bodily functions and organs of those declared brain dead simply cannot be kept alive, even by advanced mechanical means, for very long. Rather, they inevitably and promptly collapse and deteriorate despite the most aggressive therapy and efforts to resuscitate. The following citations from authoritative sources suffice to illustrate this:

> Even with extraordinary medical care, these [somatic] functions [e.g., circulation of blood] cannot be sustained indefinitely — typically, no longer than several days.[8]
>
> Despite all efforts to maintain the donor's circulation, irreversible cardiac arrest usually occurs within 48 to 72 hours of brain death in adults, although it may take as long as 10 days in children. Indeed, general acceptance of the concept of brain death depended on this close temporal association between brain death and cardiac arrest.[9]
>
> What was clearly established in the early 1980s was that no patient in apneic coma declared brain dead . . . had ever failed to develops asystole [absolute cessation of blood pressure, etc.] within a rela-

tively short time. That fundamental insight remains as valid today [1996] as it was twenty years ago.[10]

It was in this way that the concept, rationale for, and consensus on brain death developed.

D. Alan Shewmon's Challenge to "Brain Death"

Here I will summarize the thought on this matter that D. Alan Shewmon, a pediatric neurologist acknowledged to be an authority on the function of the brain, developed by the year 2000 in a series of articles, four of which are listed in the accompanying note.[11] In these and other essays, Shewmon presented the reasons, based on empirical evidence, leading him to abandon the concept of brain death. Shewmon, who himself had accepted this concept, is now certain that it cannot be sustained.

(1) *Evidence Challenging the Claim That the Brain Is the Central Integrating Organ*

After citing authorities claiming that once there is total and irreversible cessation of the functioning of the whole brain all other systems inevitably collapse quickly despite the most aggressive efforts to restore such functioning, Shewmon draws on recent research, much of it his own, showing beyond a doubt — in particular in the case of T.K., a boy who survived for seventeen years (at the time of my writing the first edition of this book, the year 2000; he has since died, after surviving more than two decades after being declared brain dead) — that this is simply not true. Shewmon has more recently set forth in great detail the condition of T.K. and two other long-term survivors of brain death, and later in this chapter I will summarize his presentation of this evidence at a meeting of the President's Council on Bioethics on November 9, 2007.

Such empirical evidence, Shewmon argues, *falsifies* the claim that the brain is the central integrating organ of the entire human body. Summarizing, Shewmon says that these data

> teach us several lessons: (1) "Brain death" does *not* necessarily lead to imminent cardiac arrest despite all treatment [the "evidence" repeatedly advanced to support acceptance of "brain death"]. (2) The heterogeneity of survival duration is largely explainable by non-brain factors. Moreover, the process of brain damage leading up to "brain death" frequently induces secondary damage to heart and lungs. Therefore, the tendency to early cardiac arrest in the majority of patients is

attributable more to *somatic* factors than to mere absence of brain activity *per se*. (3) The first few weeks are especially precarious. But those who make it through tend to stabilize, no longer requiring sophisticated technological support. Some have even been discharged home on a ventilator. Although some personhood-consciousness reductionists might try to argue that these are not human *persons*, no one can seriously claim that they are not living human *organisms*, living human *beings*.[12]

(2) Criteria for Determining the "Integrative Unity" of the Human Body
Shewmon argues that we must first *define* "integrative unity" and then examine the body for *properties relevant to the definition*. He proposes two operational definitions: (i) "integrative unity" is possessed by an organism if it possesses at least one emergent holistic level property, i.e., a property deriving from the mutual interaction of the parts and is predicable only of the entire composite, and (ii) any body requiring less technological assistance to maintain its vital functions than some other body that is a living whole must possess at least as much robust integrative unity and hence also be a living whole. In light of these criteria, Shewmon concludes that the brain, far from serving as a "central integrator," is rather a modulator or fine-tuner protecting an implicitly *already existing*, intrinsically mediated somatic unity. "Integrative unity is *not* a top-down imposition from a 'central integrator' on an otherwise unintegrated collection of organs.... Rather, it is a *non-localized, holistic property* founded on the mutual interaction among all parts of the body."
    In light of this, Shewmon offers "new criteria" for determining death.

(3) New Criteria for Determining That Death Has Occurred.
Shewmon agrees that death of a living organism is the irreversible loss of the integrative unity of the body. The *anatomical criterion* that this has occurred now shifts from a single focus (the brain) "to the entire body and consists in a critical degree of molecular-level damage throughout the body, beyond a thermodynamical 'point of no return.'" The *clinical tests* to show that this has happened shift from ones indicating loss of brain function to those manifesting "thermodynamically supracritical microstructural damage diffusely throughout the body." Since a *sine qua non* of opposition to entropy is energy, generated by chemical respiration, and since a *sine qua non* of somatic integration is circulation of blood, a clinical test for the "point of no return" is "sustained cessation of circulation of oxygenated blood."

Shewmon believes that twenty to thirty minutes of complete cessation of such circulation at normothermia are enough to show that the "point of no return" has been reached. Is Shewmon's proposal for determining that death has occurred, the "circulatory-respiratory" test, the same as the traditional "cardio-pulmonary" test? He says no because neither spontaneous heartbeat nor breathing through the lungs is necessary for life (the cardio-pulmonary test). He thus thinks his proposal is a "conceptual advance," bringing our criterion and tests for death more in line with the basic concept of death.[13]

2. Pope John Paul II's Address of August 29, 2000, and Shewmon's Commentary Thereon

A. Pope John Paul II's Address of August 29, 2000, to the Eighteenth Meeting of the Transplantation Society

(1) *The Text of the Papal Address*
The text of John Paul II's address is reproduced in full.

Distinguished Ladies and Gentlemen,

1. I am happy to greet all of you at this International Congress, which has brought you together for a reflection on the complex and delicate theme of transplants. I thank Professor Raffaello Cortesini and Professor Oscar Salvatierra for their kind words, and I extend a special greeting to the Italian Authorities present.

To all of you I express my gratitude for your kind invitation to take part in this meeting and I very much appreciate the serious consideration you are giving to the moral teaching of the Church. With respect for science and being attentive above all to the law of God, the Church has no other aim but the integral good of the human person.

Transplants are a great step forward in science's service of man, and not a few people today owe their lives to an organ transplant. Increasingly, the technique of transplants has proven to be a valid means of attaining the primary goal of all medicine — the service of human life. That is why in the Encyclical Letter *Evangelium Vitae* I suggested that one way of nurturing a genuine culture of life "is the donation of organs, performed in an ethically acceptable manner, with a view to offering a chance of health and even of life itself to the sick who sometimes have no other hope" (no. 86).

2. As with all human advancement, this particular field of medical science, for all the hope of health and life it offers to many, also presents *certain critical issues* that need to be examined in the light of a discerning anthropological and ethical reflection.

In this area of medical science too the fundamental criterion must be *the defense and promotion of the integral good of the human person*, in keeping with that unique dignity which is ours by virtue of our humanity. Consequently, it is evident that every medical procedure performed on the human person is subject to limits: not just the limits of what it is technically possible, but also limits determined by respect for human nature itself, understood in its fullness: "what is technically possible is not for that reason alone morally admissible" (Congregation for the Doctrine of the Faith, *Donum Vitae*, 4).

3. It must first be emphasized, as I observed on another occasion, that every organ transplant has its source in a decision of great ethical value: "the decision to offer without reward a part of one's own body for the health and well-being of another person" (*Address to the Participants in a Congress on Organ Transplants*, June 20, 1991, no. 3). Here precisely lies the nobility of the gesture, a gesture which is a genuine act of love. It is not just a matter of giving away something that belongs to us but of giving something of ourselves, for "by virtue of its substantial union with a spiritual soul, the human body cannot be considered as a mere complex of tissues, organs and functions . . . rather it is a constitutive part of the person who manifests and expresses himself through it" (Congregation for the Doctrine of the Faith, *Donum Vitae*, 3).

Accordingly, any procedure which tends to commercialize human organs or to consider them as items of exchange or trade must be considered morally unacceptable, because to use the body as an "object" is to violate the dignity of the human person.

This first point has an immediate consequence of great ethical import: *the need for informed consent*. The human "authenticity" of such a decisive gesture requires that individuals be properly informed about the processes involved, in order to be in a position to consent or decline in a free and conscientious manner. The consent of relatives has its own ethical validity in the absence of a decision on the part of the donor. Naturally, an analogous consent should be given by the recipients of donated organs.

4. Acknowledgement of the unique dignity of the human person has a further underlying consequence: *vital organs which occur singly in the body can be removed only after death*, that is from the body of someone who is certainly dead. This requirement is self-evident, since to act otherwise would mean intentionally to cause the death of the donor in disposing of his organs. This gives rise to one of the most debated issues in contemporary bioethics, as well as to serious concerns in the minds of ordinary people. I refer to the problem of *ascertaining the fact of death*. When can a person be considered dead with complete certainty?

In this regard, it is helpful to recall that *the death of the person* is a single event, consisting in the total disintegration of that unitary and integrated whole that is the personal self. It results from the separation of the life-principle (or soul) from the corporal reality of the person. The death of the person, understood in this primary sense, is an event which *no scientific technique or empirical method can identify directly.*

Yet human experience shows that once death occurs *certain biological signs inevitably follow*, which medicine has learnt to recognize with increasing precision. In this sense, the "criteria" for ascertaining death used by medicine today should not be understood as the technical-scientific determination of the *exact moment* of a person's death, but as a scientifically secure means of identifying *the biological signs that a person has indeed died.*

5. It is a well-known fact that for some time certain scientific approaches to ascertaining death have shifted the emphasis from the traditional cardio-respiratory signs to the so-called *"neurological" criterion*. Specifically, this consists in establishing, according to clearly determined parameters commonly held by the international scientific community, the complete and irreversible cessation of all brain activity (in the cerebrum, cerebellum and brain stem). This is then considered the sign that the individual organism has lost its integrative capacity.

With regard to the parameters used today for ascertaining death — whether the "encephalic" signs or the more traditional cardio-respiratory signs — the Church does not make technical decisions. She limits herself to the Gospel duty of comparing the data offered by medical science with the Christian understanding of the unity of the person, bringing out the similarities and the possible conflicts capable of endangering respect for human dignity.

Here it can be said that the criterion adopted in more recent times for ascertaining the fact of death, namely the *complete* and *irreversible* cessation of all brain activity, if rigorously applied, does not seem to conflict with the essential elements of a sound anthropology. Therefore a health-worker professionally responsible for ascertaining death can use these criteria in each individual case as the basis for arriving at that degree of assurance in ethical judgment which moral teaching describes as "moral certainty." This moral certainty is considered the necessary and sufficient basis for an ethically correct course of action. Only where such certainty exists, and where informed consent has already been given by the donor or the donor's legitimate representatives, is it morally right to initiate the technical procedures required for the removal of organs for transplant.

6. Another question of great ethical significance is that of *the allocation of donated organs* through waiting-lists and the assignment of priorities. Despite efforts to promote the practice of organ-donation, the resources available in many countries are currently insufficient to meet medical needs. Hence there is a need to compile waiting-lists for transplants on the basis of clear and properly reasoned criteria.

From the moral standpoint, an obvious principle of justice requires that the criteria for assigning donated organs should in no way be "discriminatory" (i.e., based on age, sex, race, religion, social standing, etc.) or "utilitarian" (i.e., based on work capacity, social usefulness, etc.). Instead, in determining who should have precedence in receiving an organ, *judgments should be made on the basis of immunological and clinical factors*. Any other criterion would prove wholly arbitrary and subjective, and would fail to recognize the intrinsic value of each human person as such, a value that is independent of any external circumstances.

7. A final issue concerns a possible alternative solution to the problem of finding human organs for transplantation, something still very much in the experimental stage, namely *xenotransplants*, that is, organ transplants from other animal species.

It is not my intention to explore in detail the problems connected with this form of intervention. I would merely recall that already in 1956 Pope Pius XII raised the question of their legitimacy. He did so when commenting on the scientific possibility, then being presaged, of transplanting animal corneas to humans. His response is still enlightening for us today: in principle, he stated, for a *xenotransplant* to be licit, the transplanted organ must not impair the integrity of the psychological or genetic identity of the person receiving it; and there must also be a proven biological possibility that the transplant will be successful and will not expose the recipient to inordinate risk (cf. *Address to the Italian Association of Cornea Donors and to Clinical Oculists and Legal Medical Practitioners*, May 14, 1956).

8. In concluding, I express the hope that, thanks to the work of so many generous and highly-trained people, scientific and technological research in the field of transplants will continue to progress, and extend to *experimentation with new therapies which can replace organ transplants*, as some recent developments in prosthetics seem to promise. In any event, methods that fail to respect the dignity and value of the person must always be avoided. I am thinking in particular of attempts at human cloning with a view to obtaining organs for transplants: these techniques, insofar as they involve the manipulation and destruction of human embryos, are not morally acceptable, even when their proposed goal is good in itself. Science itself points to other forms of *therapeutic intervention* which would not involve cloning or the use of embryonic cells, but rather would make use of stem cells taken from adults. This is the direction that research must follow if it wishes to respect the dignity of each and every human being, even at the embryonic stage.

In addressing these varied issues, *the contribution of philosophers and theologians* is important. Their careful and competent reflection on the ethical problems associated with transplant therapy can help to clarify the criteria for assessing what kinds of transplants are morally acceptable and under what conditions, especially with regard to the protection of each individual's personal identity.

I am confident that social, political and educational leaders will renew their commitment to fostering a genuine culture of generosity and solidarity. There is a need to instill in people's hearts, especially in the hearts of the young, a genuine and deep appreciation of the need for brotherly love, a love that can find expression in the decision to become an organ donor.

May the Lord sustain each one of you in your work, and guide you in the service of authentic human progress. I accompany this wish with my Blessing.

---

(2) Comment

John Paul II rightly regards organ donation, when *"performed in an ethically acceptable manner,"* as a great act of self-giving love, when it is organ donation from a cadaver or from a living person. He also emphasizes that the human person is a unified whole composed of body and of soul. *The human body,* he stresses in citing a text from *Donum vitae, "is a constitutive part of the person who manifests and expresses himself through it,"* a truth absolutely central to his famous "theology of the body."

Precisely because of the transcendent dignity of the human person, he insists that *"vital organs which occur singly in the body can be removed only after death,* that is from the body of someone who is certainly dead [emphasis in original]. *This requirement is self-evident, since to act otherwise would mean intentionally to cause the death of the donor in disposing of his organs* [emphasis added]." Here I wish to note that in *Evangelium vitae* John Paul II had *defined* abortion as the "intentional *killing* of an unborn child," whereas in the past theologians had *defined* abortion as the "intentional *removal* of an unborn child from its site within the mother's body" (see the discussion of this issue in Chapter Five, above). Thus a question that needs to be considered later is whether the distinction made between "intentional *killing*" and "intentional *removal*" might have relevance to procuring vital organs from certain specifiable persons in the very process of dying.

John Paul II likewise affirmed: *"[T]he death of the person* is a single event, consisting in the total disintegration of that unitary and integrated whole that is the personal self. It results from the separation of the life-principle (or soul) from the corporal reality of the person. The death of the person, understood in this primary sense, is an event which *no scientific technique or empirical method can identify directly."* This passage shows, first, that *death is in a very real sense a mystery and that it cannot be directly identified.* It also shows that John Paul II, like most people, regarded death as an *event,* a once-and-for-all occurrence and not as a process. Nonetheless, as he then continued, "human experience shows that once death occurs *certain biological signs inevitably follow,* which medicine has learnt to recognize with increasing precision. In this sense, the 'criteria' for ascertaining death used by medicine today should not be understood as the technical-scientific determination of the *exact moment* of a person's death, but as a scientifically secure means of identifying *the biological signs that a person has indeed died.*" This is extraordinarily important. *Empirical and scientific techniques, although not competent to identify a person's death directly, are competent to identify biological signs that can give us assurance that a person is dead,* and this, of course, is supremely important if we can morally procure vital organs only from a person known to be dead.

The Pope then notes that modern approaches to ascertaining death have shifted the emphasis from the traditional cardio-respiratory signs to the so-called *neurological criterion,* which consists in establishing the complete and irreversible cessation of *all* brain activity, and that this is now considered the sign that the individual organism has lost its integrative capacity or, in other words, has died. In noting this, however, he likewise takes pains to stress that "*the Church does not make technical decisions* [emphasis added]... [but] limits herself to the Gospel duty of comparing the data offered by medical science with the Christian understanding of the unity of the person." He then goes on to affirm, in perhaps the central teaching of this address, "the criterion adopted in more recent times for ascertaining the fact of death, namely the *complete* and *irreversible* [emphasis in original] cessation of all brain activity, if rigorously applied, does not *seem* [emphasis added] to conflict with the essential elements of a sound anthropology. *Therefore a health-worker professionally responsible for ascertaining death can use these criteria in each individual case as the basis for arriving at that degree of assurance in ethical judgment which moral teaching describes as 'moral certainty'* [emphasis added]. This moral certainty is considered the necessary and sufficient basis for an ethically correct course of action. Only where such certainty exists, and where informed consent has already been given by the donor or the donor's legitimate representatives, is it morally right to initiate the technical procedures required for the removal of organs for transplant."

B. Shewmon's Commentary on the Holy Father's Address[14]
Shewmon points out that many interpret the Pope's address as though it could be summarized in the following syllogism:

(A) The proper concept of human death is "a single event, consisting in the total disintegration of that unitary and integrated whole that is the personal self. It results from the separation of the life-principle (or soul) from the corporal reality of the person." (par 4)

(B) "The so-called 'neurological criterion' " (par 5) reliably indicates that a patient is no longer an integrated whole.

(C) Therefore, "the so-called 'neurological criterion' " reliably identifies that the person is dead, making it "ethically correct" ("morally right") to remove vital organs for transplant. (par 5)

Shewmon believes that a careful reading of the document does not support this interpretation because what the Pontiff said is "subtly but critically different in the minor premise and conclusion and can be summarized in the following quasi-syllogism (differences highlighted in italics)":

(A) The proper concept of human death is "a single event, consisting in the total disintegration of that unitary and integrated whole that is the personal self. It results from the separation of the life-principle (or soul) from the corporal reality of the person." (par 4)

(B) *There is a consensus among the "international scientific community" that* "The so-called 'neurological criterion' " (par 5) reliably indicates that a patient is no longer an integrated whole. (par 5)

(C) Therefore, *health professionals can have a "moral certainty" that* the person is dead, making it "ethically correct" ("morally right") to remove vital organs for transplant. (par 5)

Since both the Pope and the Pontifical Academy of Sciences reject the mere loss of consciousness *per se*, even if permanent, as a sufficient condition for considering someone dead, Shewmon then points out that "If, therefore, the Pope considers 'the so-called "neurologic" criterion' (par 5) a valid indicator of human death, it must be on the basis of the irreversible loss of *both* all mental capacity *and* the physiological unity of the body as indicators of the loss of body-soul unity. If a human body is alive as a biological organism, even if permanently unconscious, then it is necessarily vivified by a human life-principle (or soul), and we have simply an unconscious living person, not a live nonperson or a corpse."

He then notes that significantly the Pope never used the ambiguous term "brain death" but referred to the "so-called 'neurological' criterion" for death and then specified what this entailed as understood by the "consensus" of the international scientific community. Note, too, that the Pope did *not* say that this "*is* the sign" that death has occurred but rather that "this is *considered* the sign." By whom? Obviously, Shewmon says, by that community. The Pope then went on to say that using this criterion "does not *seem* to conflict with the essential elements of a sound anthropology" (par 5).

Shewmon is sure the Pope "would express grave concern about possible 'conflict with... sound anthropology'" *if* the international scientific community did not in fact consider this a true sign that a person was dead because a true consensus on this matter was lacking, and he then shows that there is no such authentic consensus among scientists by referring to numerous peer-reviewed articles published between 1993 and 2001[15] and summarizing recent international congresses on brain death, in particular those that took place in Havana, Cuba, in 1996 and 2000. Those meetings, he points out, "surely constitute the most representative gathering of the 'international scientific community' of experts in this field." Since the first such symposium in 1992, he continued, "there has been a definite shift of opinion away from the biological 'organism-as-a-whole' rationale to the philosophical "personhood" rationale (i.e., death of the 'person' by virtue of permanent loss of consciousness despite a biologically live body), and an increasing number of participants have publicly disavowed the organism/unity rationale as sufficiently contradicted now by empirical evidence."

He draws attention to a passage in John Paul II's address that corresponds in "technical and stylistic detail" to one particular outmoded notion of brain death. The passage in question reads as follows: "It is a well-known fact that for some time certain scientific approaches to ascertaining death have shifted the emphasis from the traditional cardio-respiratory signs to the so-called 'neurological' criterion. ... [T]he irreversible cessation of all brain activity... is then considered the sign that the individual organism has lost its integrative capacity" (par 5). Shewmon's comment on this passage is very important:

> This is the old notion, popularized in the 1970s by lawyer-ethicist Alexander Capron (Capron, 1987a; Capron and Kass, 1972), that BD is exactly the same bodily state as good-old-fashioned death, but merely that the traditional cardiopulmonary signs have been "masked" by artificial ventilatory and cardiovascular support — a view that figured prominently in the US President's Commission report 1981 (of which Mr. Capron was executive director). Although it sounds good, it does not withstand physiological or logical scrutiny (cf. Capron's ineffective response to an incisive letter to the editor [Capron, 1987b; Youngner, 1987]). This way of conceptualizing BD, in terms of an alternate set of post-factum "signs" of the same singular phenomenon that the "traditional signs" indicate, completely fell by the wayside by

the turn of the 1990s. It is not that death somehow occurs, and because the artificial support of ventilation and circulation masks the traditional signs of death, physicians need some non-cardiopulmonary sign that it has occurred. For one thing, BD and traditional death are very different physiological states. In BD the heart beats spontaneously and most non-brain organs and tissues function perfectly well and interact appropriately with each other; what is artificially supported is merely ventilation and often blood pressure and fluid balance. This is simply not the same physiological state as an old-fashioned corpse, so it is erroneous to speak of two alternative post-factum signs for the same state.

Shewmon believes that passage in the Pope's address likely derived from "one or more prestigious consultants from the 'older' generation who were intimately familiar with the pre-1990s BD literature and debate but who were out of date with current thinking on the topic or who ... cannot filter out or 'cannot understand' the more recent critiques of a position upon which they built prestigious careers."

Shewmon thinks that, "given the information he seems to have had, what he [the Pope] said in his discourse was perfectly reasonable." But he rightly wonders how that discourse might have differed had the Pope been better informed of the technical aspects of the controversy and able to judge the scientific merits of traditional BD dogma for himself.

At the conclusion of his commentary, Shewmon says:

> Apart from being guided by the Holy Spirit in matters of faith and morals, Pope John Paul II is a very wise and intelligent man, who knows perfectly well that the medical-biological aspects of diagnosing death are outside the competence of the Church and within the competence of the medical profession. He knows perfectly well that the Church has no authority to settle controversies of an empirical nature related to BD, and he does not pretend to do so. Rather, he has stated the Church's perennial teaching about the nature of human life and death, and has deferred to what he has been given to believe is the prevailing consensus of medical science concerning the somatic pathophysiology of patients with dead brains, concluding that this (supposed) consensus is compatible with the Church's teaching about the nature of human life and death. That is far from a Magisterial endorsement of empirical claims. Moreover, his statement leaves open the possibility that, if the neuroscientific community accepts the

mounting evidence against the somatic-unity rationale and shifts to explaining BD as a loss of "personhood" from a live human organism, the Magisterium could (and should) correspondingly revise its assessment and declare that such a criterion for death not only *does* "seem to conflict with the essential elements of sound anthropology" but *clearly* conflicts with them. I believe that sufficient evidence is already available but remains poorly known and poorly understood by the general medical community, and even less known and understood by the Holy Father, who has more pressing things on his agenda than the study of clinical neuroscience.

That Shewmon is correct about this I will now show by examining the work of the United States President's Council for Bioethics in its "white paper" entitled "Controversies in the Determination of Death." Before closing this section, however, it is important to recall that Pope John Paul II definitively affirmed that it was the task and responsibility of scientists and doctors to determine the criteria sufficient to allow us to know that a person has died, and is not within the competence or the responsibility of the Magisterium, theologians, and philosophers.

3. Important Recent Developments in the Debate Over "Brain Death"

Of these recent developments, I believe that the most important is found in the work of the United States President's Council on Bioethics in its white paper identified above. After examining this work, I will review some important recent essays by James DuBois and Shewmon, and then draw my conclusions.

A. The President's Council on Bioethics

At present (late December 2007), the final approved version of Council's white paper has not been published; it may appear early in 2008 and if so I hope to be able to revise this section accordingly. The Council's next meeting is scheduled for March 2008. A revised draft of the document was prepared on September 26, 2007, shortly after the September 6 meeting. It is not permissible to cite directly from that draft, but I can cite from the transcript of the Council's discussion of that draft's immediate predecessor at the September 6 meeting.[16] I was not personally present at that meeting, but I was present at the November 9, 2007, meeting, when Shewmon, at the invitation of Council members, presented his views and answered questions.[17] These transcripts provide us with a good grasp of the different views of the Council members.

(1) *Meeting of September 6, 2007*

The transcript makes it clear that Leon Kass, who had been the first president of the Council (now presided over by Edmund Pellegrino), and who at that time was still serving as a member (he has since resigned), was the principal architect of the document under discussion.

Council Member Diana Schaub opened the discussion by asking Kass several penetrating questions. She spoke as follows:

> This report, "Controversies in the Determination of Death," does a fine job of setting forth the evolution of thinking about the standards for determining death. It traces the emergence of an alternative neurological standard of death in the 1970s to supplement the traditional cardiopulmonary standard and examines the continuing challenges to that standard. . . . Even if the neurological standard was in part motivated by a desire to create the heart-beating dead-donor category, the question still remains: Is the category a true one? Are there heart-beating cadavers and ventilated corpses such that we need a neurological basis for the determination of death? . . . [T]he report takes up this question in Chapter 4, first laying out *the reasons for doubt that were posed originally by Hans Jonas and elaborated and updated more recently by Shewmon* and then, most ambitiously, attempting to answer those doubts and defend the neurological standard with a new and better biologically-based rationale [emphasis added].

Note that the report — the draft of the white paper — acknowledges that Shewmon raised such serious doubts about the older rationale used to justify the "neurological standard" that a "new and better biologically-based rationale" to justify that standard was required. In fact, the draft maintained that Shewmon argued forcefully that patients who are positively and reliably diagnosed with brain death continue to exhibit *many* functions that are "somatically integrative," correctly noting that the brain is *not* the *integrator* of the body's many and varied functions.

But what is the "new and better biologically-based rationale" used to defend the neurological or brain death criterion? Schaub, a political scientist by profession, questioning Kass, summarized it as follows and expressed perplexity over it:

Instead of looking internally at the presence or loss of somatic integration, the report suggests that we look at the organism's relation to the external world. A living organism is in need of and open to commerce and exchange with its environment. Spontaneous breathing is a crucial manifestation of such openness. The report even states that this "commerce with the surrounding world" is "the definitive 'work' of an organism." When the drive for such commerce is irreversibly gone, as in total brain dysfunction, then the individual is dead. I don't know quite what to make of this argument.... [I]t seems to me odd to say that the wholeness of a living organism hinges on its needy openness. Apparently the wholeness of organic life is not whole in the sense of complete or unified. But even granting that organisms have a needy, outward-directed mode of being, is it correct to say that satisfying this need is the definitive work of an organism?... Most astonishing, I thought, were the cases of pregnant women diagnosed with total brain dysfunction whose bodies continued to provide support to the developing fetus for days and even months. My uncertainty about the line between life and death would ... have inclined me to resist the neurological standard back in the 1970s. However, that same uncertainty leaves me inclined today to accept the settled, majority view of the medical profession.

Although perplexed, Schaub seems here to accept the "new and better biologically-based rationale" on the authority of those scientists and medical doctors who, like Kass, proposed it. Before Kass had opportunity to reply, there was a discussion among some medical doctors who are Council members, Floyd Bloom and Daniel Foster, regarding Shewmon's competence. Council Members Robert George, Alfonso Gomez-Lobo, and, later, Gilbert Meilaender, William Hurlbut, and Peter Lawler, assured Bloom and Foster of Shewmon's super credentials and urged that he be invited to a subsequent Council meeting.

When Kass responded to Schaub, he pointed out that he was now offering to the Council a longer version, a "beefed up" new argument to defend the neurological standard, and this version was incorporated into the draft released shortly thereafter, on September 26. He suggested that the trouble with the brain-death criterion started "when people tried to articulate the justification for this in terms of some understanding of why the complete dysfunction of the entire brain constitutes the equivalence of the death of the organism as a whole." Later, because of an influential paper by

J. L. Bernat, the concept of integration took very great prominence, and that concept, Kass said, is behind some of the major objections that Shewmon levels. He granted that much of what Shewmon says is "very interesting," but said that he himself was not convinced, even in the presence of the kind of holistic activity that Shewmon shows does occur.

He then commented on Schaub's opening series of questions, acknowledging the need to strengthen the new argument and suggesting that the Council ought not talk about integration but about "work," "the essential work, of the organism," namely, "its capacity to maintain itself, and that activity of self-maintenance requires, on the one hand, an inner drive to do so, the ability to act on the environment at least minimally to provide that without which there could be no organic life, and some kind of responsiveness to the world, at least minimal responsiveness." Without that foundation, one cannot claim that an organism manifesting integral bodily functioning is truly a living human body. He concluded that the Council's report, with the new argument beefed up, "stands a chance of rescuing the criteria giving it a sounder, not foolproof, but a sounder philosophical defense in which Shewmon's objections can be acknowledged and bypassed." We will later see Shewmon's critique of this new argument. Here I simply observe that even Kass, its author, did not present a demonstrative but rather what he called a "sounder, not foolproof," basis for the brain-death concept.

Rebecca Dreisser, a lawyer, declared, in a very revealing statement, that "organ transplantation is a benefit to society that we want to maintain *even if we cannot know that the donors are dead*" (emphasis added). This is very significant; it shows a very utilitarian mentality.

William Hurlbut, M.D., of Stanford University, noted how well regarded Shewmon, whom he knows personally, is in medical circles. He had problems with Kass's rationale and wanted Bloom to say clearly what he thought was inadequate about Shewmon's ideas and how he would define the integrated unity of the organism, and to ask Kass what he might say about the species-typical dimensions of commerce and whether there might be something specific to human beings that the Council might focus on.

Bloom, in responding to Hurlbut, had a revealing comment. He claimed that "when the brain isn't there, it doesn't matter what the rest of the body is doing. That person [sic] is never going to be a person." He suggested that Terri Schiavo was dead as a person when she was permanently unconscious. This shows that Bloom adopts what is known as the "higher brain" definition of death; when the neocortex is not functioning, the "person" is dead, even though there is a living human body. As we will see, he made this position even more evident in his response to Shewmon's presentation at the November meeting.

Responding to Bloom, Kass said that no one would say that Terri Schiavo was dead. "She might have been dead as a 'person,' whatever that means. But no one would have buried her. One might have been warranted or not in taking the feeding tube out, but that was a decision to discontinue life-sustaining treatment, not a question about pronouncing her dead." He did not adequately respond to Hurlbut's question.

Peter Lawler, a philosopher, thought Shewmon cast real doubt about the brain-death criterion. He had demonstrated that integrated, somatic functioning, which was the basis of the earlier consensus on brain death, is very questionable because an argument can be made that the organism continues to have that kind of integrated, somatic functioning even if the brain is *not* working. "So why would anyone care about this?... Because some people want to give the most expansive possible definition of life. When in doubt, go with life.... I do think people of good will are shaken by Shewmon." Moreover, he continued, Kass's argument for a need for openness is open to question "because it's so... philosophic and... so complicated... and perhaps so questionable in its own way.... [D]oes it really provide what we really need to extinguish the doubt or were we wrong to think there was doubt that needed to be extinguished?"

After interventions by George and others regarding Shewmon's expertise, Schaub posed a quick and difficult question to Kass, namely, "Why wouldn't we say that things like the sexual maturation of a BD child [Shewmon demonstratively shows this has occurred] or the gestation of a fetus, how is that not indicative of the presence of a drive to self-preservation and, not only self-preservation, but the next generation?" Kass's reply did not, it seems to me, adequately answer this question but simply asserted that his "first impulse would be to say that if you could perfuse and ventilate a corpse so that it becomes simply an, as it were, incubator for a life that happens to reside there rather than see it as the continued work of what would have been the mother, I imagine it would be possible to sustain fetal life in lots of unnatural places and this would be one of the first such." There was further discussion of this by Foster and Schaub, and then Lawler spoke again. Emphasizing that "the whole premise of this report is that Shewmon's challenge is important," he pointed to a paragraph in the draft of the white paper under discussion: "[T]otal brain dysfunction can... continue to serve as a criterion for declaring death, not because it necessarily indicates complete loss of integrated somatic functioning, but because it is a sign that this organism can no longer engage in the sort of work that defines living things." He said he was 98 percent persuaded by it.

Much more was said at this meeting, but here I have provided a fairly substantive report of what was discussed.

(2) *Meeting of November 9, 2007*

In his opening comments, Shewmon observed that one version of brain death is loss of essential human properties or personhood, restricted primarily to advocates of "higher brain death" or "neocortical death." He pointed out that this is the implicit rationale of many advocates of whole brain death today. When asked why they really think brain death is death, they will claim that it's because there's no person when there is permanent unconsciousness. He pointed out that Fred Plum, M.D., a major figure in American neurology who has written extensively about issues of coma and brain death, noted in one of his textbooks that individuals who had been declared brain dead actually expired because of "spontaneous cardiac arrest" or because of the discontinuation of respiratory assistance, making it obvious that Plum did not consider these people dead by virtue of their brain being destroyed, but rather they died as organisms when the respirator was discontinued or they had a spontaneous cardiac arrest. Moreover, Ronald Cranford, M.D., another very famous neurologist who has written extensively on brain death, had the following revealing comments to make on brain death in an article about the so-called vegetative state: "It seems, then, that permanently unconscious patients have characteristics of both the living and the dead. It would be tempting to call them dead and then retrospectively apply the principles of death as society has done with brain death."

Shewmon then went into a detailed description, using videotape, of several cases of individuals diagnosed as brain dead, who survived as living organisms for prolonged periods of time. One was a fourteen-year-old boy in California who had jumped onto the hood of a slowly moving car, fallen off, hit his head against the concrete, and within four days was brain dead, certified by a full neurological exam and an apnea test. His parents, deeply religious, refused to accept that this was death and insisted that the doctors continue life support. The doctors, to avoid an ugly confrontation, made an agreement that the parents accepted to withdraw all support except for the ventilator and basic fluids for forty-eight hours, and that if the child then passed away, that was an indication of God's will. The doctors were

convinced he would surely be dead by then. But to their surprise, he survived the forty-eight hours of simple fluids and ventilator support, and they
were in an awkward position to continue support. They transferred him to
a skilled nursing facility with the diagnosis of brain death. Since in California he was legally dead, the nursing facility was very confused and con-
tacted Shewmon, who examined the boy and concurred with the diagnosis
of brain death. Amazingly, while in this condition the boy began pubertal
changes, dying at sixty-three days from an untreated pneumonia.

Shewmon presented three other cases; two had already been described
in his previous publications, and the third was from a Japanese publication;
he had, however, opportunity personally to examine the person and work
with his doctors in Japan. I will here consider only the first of these, the
famous case of T.K., and the third.

T.K. is the world-record survivor in the state of brain death. He con-
tracted Haemophilus influenzae meningitis at age four and a half years.
Because he was under five, no formal diagnosis of brain death was made
under guidelines at that time. But Shewmon was convinced that he was
brain dead. He then elaborated on the evidence for brain death because
one criticism leveled against him was that he had made an incorrect diagnosis. Shewmon wanted to assure the President's Council that there was
superabundant evidence of the correctness of his diagnosis. Shewmon
demonstrated that for the rest of his life in this state T.K. had no cranial
nerve reflexes, no spontaneous respiration, including off of the ventilator for
up to a minute for purposes of changing tracheostomy, etc. On day two, he
had sudden onset of profound hypothermia and of diabetes insipidus, both
complications of brain death, and there was no other reason that he would
have had these symptoms on day two. He had four EEGs on brain death
day zero, which Shewmon called the day of onset of brain death; again, the
next day; again, on day 841; and again on day 4,202. All these EEGs were
absolutely flat at maximal sensitivity. Continuing, Shewmon said:

> He had a CT scan on brain death day nine, which showed exten-
> sive subarachnoid hemorrhage, diffuse, severe cerebral edema with
> obliteration of the ventricles and cisterns. And he had splitting of the
> cranial sutures. The intracranial pressure was so high that his already
> fused cranial sutures at age four split apart.... Multiple independent
> neurology consults reiterated the lack of neurological function, includ-
> ing my own exam, which I videotaped and will show you in a second,
> on brain death day 4,969. A few months after that exam when he was

13 and a half years into the state of brain death, they did an MRI scan, which I'll show you, also, an MR angiogram and multi-modality evoked potentials, which I'll show you. Finally, if anybody still had any doubts, he passed away a couple of years ago, and an autopsy was performed — a brain-only autopsy, which showed no identifiable brain structures, including brain stem structures, and I will show you that, as well. So there's no question that this child was brain dead. He was transferred from the ICU to a regular pediatric ward on day 504, and he was discharged after seven and a half years in this condition. He was discharged to a rehab facility and then to home, and he had four brief hospitalizations during the rest of his time in this condition. He expired after 20 and a half years in the state of brain death. Thirty-seven percent of that time he was in the hospital, 53 percent was at home, and 10 percent was in a rehab facility or skilled nursing facility.

Shewmon next summarized holistic properties that his body demonstrated: homeostasis of fluid balance, electrolytes, energy balance, etc., without monitoring and without frequent adjustment based on that monitoring; temperature maintenance, proportional growth, and teleological wound healing from surgical procedures or from minor abrasions or from infections; cardiovascular and autonomic regulation, heart rate, and capillary skin changes. T.K. had various infections, pneumonia, urinary tract infection, sinusitis, and with ordinary antibiotics got through all of that.

These were all, Shewmon maintained, holistic properties because they are not properties of any one organ or organ system, but properties of the organism as a whole. Shewmon showed videos providing evidence of his autonomic reactivity and hyperactive reflexes. T.K. had what is called a triple flexion response where one elicits the Babinski reflex, and the entire legs at hip, knee, and ankle will withdraw. When Shewmon pinched T.K.'s shoulder, his leg moved, showing integration within the spinal cord across levels of spinal cord. When covers were removed from him, he got goose bumps and mottling of the skin.

The third case was a Japanese boy who became brain dead at age thirteen months from a necrotizing encephalopathy of presumed viral etiology. He has now been brain dead for seven years, 78 percent of that time which has been in the hospital and 22 percent at home. He has had three EEGs on day one, day 297, and day 1,617, all of them isoelectric; three brain stem auditory evoked responses, all of them showing no response; a SPECT scan, showing no intracranial blood flow; five CTs and four MRI scans, all showing progressive disintegration of the brain to disorganized fluids and membranes without identifiable brain structures.

Shewmon showed his growth charts at three years old, at four years old, at five years eight months old (when Shewmon first saw him and confirmed the lack of brain functions), and at eight years old. Shewmon said he thought Council members would agree that if any biologist were put in front of this boy and not primed about any brain-death debate but simply asked to examine this and tell us if this is a living organism or not, any biologist would say, "Well, of course this is a living organism. This is a comatose apneic living organism."

I will now take up Council member Floyd Bloom's revealing questions/comments and Shewmon's response. Bloom said almost immediately, in order to make matters clear: "*I belong to that reductionistic biological group of people such as the ones you quote, starting with our beloved, distinguished Fred Plum and ending with Dr. Cranford, all of whom will take the position that a person in that state without the capacity for consciousness may have a living body but is not a person* [emphasis added]. . . . I don't understand why that is not correct. The fact that the brainless [bodies in your examples] . . . *may be alive in some aspects in no way eliminates the fact that they are still dead as human beings* [emphasis added]."

Then, in a statement manifesting hostility to Catholic teaching, Bloom declared: "[Y]ou go on to say, then, that *the key difference between Catholic anthropology and person mind/brain reductionism, of which I would happily agree to be known as a member, 'The former admits of such a notion as a permanently unconscious person, while the latter does not.' And I would say that's accurate for my position*" (emphasis added).

Shewmon's reply is worth citing at some length:

> I think it's very interesting that you say that you are in the camp with Dr. Plum and Cranford and so on because this is exactly the point I was making in my talk, that more and more people who understand this issue very thoroughly have gotten away from the mainstream biological rationale for brain death and admit that the only coherent rationale is, indeed, this philosophical position regarding the relationship between personhood and consciousness. . . . [W]hen I was presenting this at the International Symposium on Brain Death and Coma in Havana some years ago, Dr. Plum was there, and during the question-and-answer session he said exactly what you quoted there, that, "Okay, I admit from your evidence that this is a living human

organism, but is it a human person?" And so practically the whole audience at that meeting of all experts in this issue was kind of split down the middle about the philosophy of personhood. And you had a lot of people saying, "If there's no consciousness[,] there's no person," and others saying, "An unconscious person is not an oxymoron. You can have an unconscious person, including a permanently unconscious person, and as long as the biological organism is living, then there's a living organism and a living unconscious person.". . . [T]here was no meeting of the minds once this philosophical divide was clarified. But what I found very interesting was there was general agreement that the biological rationale didn't hold water anymore. And so I considered my presentation a success because I wasn't there to argue philosophy but to present this biological evidence, which was new at the time and I think now seems to be generally accepted. . . . [T]he view that you explained in line with Plum and Cranford I don't see adopted in the White Paper. That's very interesting that you say that because the White Paper doesn't reflect that at all.

I think that we must conclude from all this testimony the following: (1) knowledgeable members of the Council competent to judge the work of doctors/scientists clearly judge that Shewmon has already falsified the rationale commonly accepted to support the "neurological" criterion and therefore (2) attempted to develop a new and stronger rationale to support that criterion; (3) Shewmon is absolutely correct in claiming that adherents of brain death *now* accept the "higher brain death" criterion — according to them the "person" no longer exists when exercisable cognitive abilities are lost, even if their "bodies" continue to live even without ventilators, etc.

B. Other Developments

Among other important recent developments, I here consider two. The first is Shewmon's own post-2000 position regarding determination of death, and the other the views expressed by James DuBois, most recently in an issue of *The National Catholic Bioethics Quarterly* principally devoted to the question of brain death.

(1) *Shewmon's Post-2000 Position*

One essay in which Shewmon develops this is in his article "The Dead Donor Rule: Lessons from Linguistics," *Kennedy Institute of Ethics Journal*.[18] This article, published in 2004, marks a shift in Shewmon's position. Up until then, he had held that the "correct concept of death must be species-nonspe-cific, applicable to all living things," even after his rejection of the " 'organ-ism as a whole' or 'integrative unity' rationale for 'brain death.' " Shewmon now believes, largely because of his discovery that the concepts of death in cultures with no linguistic equivalent to the English word "death" differ from the concept of death in languages with such equivalents, that we should "abandon the search for criteria for the universally 'true' moment of death, as there is no single, context-independent 'true' moment of death. Rather there are various moments of *state discontinuity*," of which one, depending on the clinical circumstances of the dying person and the behavioral and ethical issues of those standing around, will stand out as particularly striking and/or ethically determining, analogous to proposals when "death behaviors" are appropriate (290-291). Among these "death behaviors," the removal of vital organs is the one for which precise timing is most critical. "Regarding trans-plantation of unpaired vital organs — or both of paired vital organs — the DDR [Dead Donor Rule] reflects the belief of many that the critical ethical question is: 'Is the donor dead?' But if there is no one, true 'moment' of death in an absolute sense, but rather a multiplicity of moments, any one of which might serve as a reasonable demarcation for a particular context, how does one decide which is more appropriate for the context of transplantation?" (291).[19]

In a key passage he then writes:

> "Is the patient dead?" not only is the wrong question to ask on the practical, physical level; it is not even a meaningful one when asked on a microscopic time-scale in the transition between life and death. . . . *The question that really matters is: If one extirpates such-and-such organ(s) in such-and-such a way, does one kill or harm the patient? Although the verb "to kill" implicitly involves a dichotomous notion of life and death, it also involves causality and intentionality. The latter aspects make it possi-ble in some situations to bypass the fuzzy, intrinsically undecidable border between life and death, so that one can be morally certain of "not killing" even without first having to determine which side of the life-death bound-ary the donor is on at the time."* (292; italics in original)

Note well that Shewmon does not *deny* that death is a once-and-for-all event. He simply thinks that it is not medically possible to identity the "true" moment of death. His claim is that our use of the word could corre-late with many different events and that selecting a particular biological event is arbitrary and that therefore we should focus on the question whether extirpation of vital organs will kill or cause the death of a person. He continues: "I believe . . . that there is a profound and critical difference between killing and letting die, as well as between intending and foreseeing death, even if in some pairs of examples the physical acts or omissions might look outwardly identical. I also believe that the principle of double effect is valid and necessary for bioethics" Shewmon then restricts his discussion to the ideal DCD (= Donation after Cardiac Death) context. This assumes the legitimacy of stopping life support (independent of transplant considerations), truly informed consent, lack of conflict of interest, medical certainty that apnea will occur once the ventilator is discontinued, etc. Shewmon thus suggests that it may be possible, using the principle of double effect, to "remove" vital organs from a dying person *without intentionally killing that person*, analogous to the situation, discussed in Chapter Five, to "removing" a nonviable embryo/fetus from its site within the mother's body without intentionally killing the unborn child.

Shewmon identifies certain types of "state discontinuity" by using the symbols E1, E2, etc. He had identified these states earlier in his article. Here they need to be described so that readers will understand his discussion of organ transplants in the ideal DCD context:

- E1 = Expiration (ex-spiration) and is the death scenario common prior to the ICU era when the terminally ill person was at home and breathed his or her "last."
- E2 = Final Asystole, a death scenario often taking place in a hospital when a do-not-resuscitate order is in place for a dying person. The person stops breathing, and finally the EKG (electrocardiogram) goes flat. Let us call the latter event E2.
- E3 = Loss of Potential for Cardiac Autoresuscitation. This seems to be of interest only in the context of non-heart-beating organ donors (NCBD) or more commonly today donation after cardiac death (DCD).
- E4 = Loss of Potential for Interventional Resuscitation. On this view this loss is "irreversible" despite use of all technological means.
- E5 = Onset of Permanent Loss of Consciousness. This is the analog of E2 in the neurological domain, occurring five to ten seconds after permanent cessation of blood flow to the brain. If there is no moral obligation to try to restore consciousness, and especially if there is an obligation not to try, then E5 is also analogous to E3.

- E6 = Loss of Potential for Recovery of Consciousness. This corresponds to what has been identified as a permanent vegetative state.
- E7 = Irreversible Loss of All Brain Function. This is the state of discontinuity widely adopted, i.e., irreversible cessation of the functioning of the entire brain.

Shewmon writes: "When the ventilator is withdrawn in the operating room, the first E to occur will be E1, final apnea; then will ensue E2, E3, E4, and E6 in that order (Presumable E5 has already taken place whether from primary brain damage or from sedation for the procedure)." Our question now should be not which E represents "true death," but "Beyond which of these events does the removal of organs X, Y, Z neither kill nor harm the patient, even in the physical sense of accelerating the dying process." The answer depends on which organs we are talking about. If we are talking about vital organs other than the heart and lungs, i.e., both kidneys, the whole liver, "removing them even before E1 will neither cause nor hasten death, because, in the *ideal* DCD context under discussion, by the time the loss of those organs might exert even the tiniest systemic effect, all the E's would have supervened long before. . . . Thus for transplantation of noncardiopulmonary organs, it is utterly irrelevant ethically whether 'brain death' is 'really death,' or whether the Pittsburgh protocol 2 minutes of asystole[20] is 'really death,' or whether any other physical event is 'really death.' Such questions are both malformulated and ethically beside the point" (293-294).

But for transplanting heart and/or lungs, the moral requirement that we "do no harm" by their extirpation is much more difficult to determine. Shewmon *suggests* a procedure that would allow the extirpation of these vital organs *before disconnecting* the ventilator insofar as "once circulation has effectively ceased due to the effect of progressive hypoxia on the heart, the dying or decaying process continues just the same regardless of whether the nonbeating heart and nonfunctioning lungs remain physically in the circulationless body" (294).

He then adds a most important disclaimer:

The foregoing discussion *does not* [emphasis added] constitute advocacy of any particular transplantation protocol. It addresses the very precise and limited question of whether it is possible in principle to remove vital organs without causing or hastening death or violating the time-honored injunction *primum non nocere*. My conclusion is yes, it is possible in principle. *But before deciding whether it would be*

*prudent to put this principle into practice in today's society, many other fac-
tors, which are outside the scope of this paper, must be considered, such as
whether donor consent can be guaranteed to be truly informed and free;
whether, in the case at hand, apnea off life support can be predicted with
medical and moral certainty; whether such eviscerating procedures respect
human dignity even if they might not cause or hasten death, whether the
risk of public misperception that this is utilitarian killing can be minimized
and so on. If the answer to one or more of these "whethers" is a "no,"... then
it behooves us to hold off implementing the otherwise intrinsically ethical
procedure until all the circumstantial details are worked out* [emphasis
added]. (296)

I will return to this in my conclusion.

(2) James DuBois's Views

As noted before, Vol. 7, No. 3 (Autumn 2007) of *The National Catholic
Bioethics Quarterly* featured articles on the determination of death. In my
opinion, the most significant was James Dubois's "Avoiding Common Pitfalls in the Determination of Death" (545-563), in which he recapitulates
many ideas he had previously set forth in his essay "Is Organ Procurement
Causing the Death of Patients."[21]

First I offer a summary of "Is Organ Procurement Causing the Death
of Patients" and then of "Avoiding Common Pitfalls in the Determination
of Death."

"Is Organ Procurement..." has two parts. In **Part I**, DuBois offers a
philosophical foundation for the UDDA (Uniform Declaration of Death
Act) by examining death *per se* and then brain death and NHBD (Non-
Heart Beating Donors; also designated as DCD or Donation after Cardiac
Death) criteria for determining death. DuBois argues that many of the
debates over death "can be bypassed by changing the terms of the debate,"
for "what matters most is not death as a process or an event but *death as a
state*" (emphasis added). Why? Because "understanding death as a state
allows us to determine death in a *functional* [emphasis in original] manner... compatible with the needs of law and medicine and, in principle,
consistent with many commonsense and religious views of death" (23).[22]

In **Part II**, DuBois examines objections arising from ignoring or rejecting the distinction between killing and letting die and the principle of double effect (PDE); but his concern is whether use of the drug Heparin to thin
the donor's blood or other anticoagulants may knowingly cause death, and

he argues, using the PDE, to defend use of Heparin. He concludes his introduction by saying: "If successful, this article will do more than show that our current transplant practices do not cause the death of donors. By clarifying the lines between life and death, on the one hand, and between intentionally killing and unintentionally hastening death, on the other, we might restore a sense that proposals to drop the dead donor rule are radical recommendations to cross lines we have never crossed before" (23-24).[23]

In "Avoiding Common Pitfalls in the Determination of Death," DuBois begins with a presentation of specific sources of concerns about determining death in organ donation, preeminently the claims, with which he disagrees, that brain-death criteria are wrong (e.g., Shewmon), and that DCD (NHBD) protocols involve killing donors (e.g., Trog and others) (546-548). He then gives **Seven Guidelines for the Determination of Death** (548-558), the first two being "*1. Focus on Death as a State, Not an Event or Process*" and "*2. Rely on a Description of the State of Death Based on Medical Experience Rather Than an A Priori Definition of Death.*" We saw this before. Here he notes that the Shewmons (D. Alan and Elizabeth in "The Semiotics of Death and Its Medical Indications," in *Brain Death and Disorders of Consciousness* [New York: Springer Science, 2004], pp. 89-114) "have offered evidence that calls into question the usefulness of such a definition [i.e., the brain-death definition of death]," but he in effect bypasses the Shewmon critique and focuses on *the state of the dead body*, declaring, "[D]o we really need theoretical definitions of death?" and observing that "as the Shewmons have notably argued, theoretical definitions of death do not directly 'lead to' or generate specific criteria such that we can directly observe death." He then goes on to say, "As a general rule it is better to begin with a non-controversial description of the state of dead bodies, a description of the biological signs of death like those offered by the UDDA [Uniform Definition of Death Act]. In the following three points [3, 4, 5] I will try to develop such a description — one in keeping with the UDDA" (550-551).

He then turns to "*3. Focus on a Loss of Functions, Not Structural Damage*"; "*4. Focus on a Permanent Loss of Function, Not Irreversibility in All Possible Worlds*"; and "*5. Distinguish between Relevant Functions and Irrelevant (or Masking) Biological Activities*. In these sections, DuBois largely reaffirms views set forth in his 2001 article in *Issues in Law and Medicine*. I want, however, to note some features of his presentation in some of these sections. In (4), where he is mainly concerned with declaring DCD (NHBD) donors dead, he affirms: "[I]t is reasonable that the *determination* of death by a physician should involve some irreversibility or permanency criterion. But the primary reason for this is not metaphysical but rather ethical: we do not want to treat a body as dead if we should attempt resuscitation (as in cases of unexpected cardiac arrest) or if there is a chance that nature has not yet run its course" (555). But, as he had argued in cases of DCD, the choice has been made not to attempt resuscitation, and the minutes allowed after death is declared prior to extirpation of vital organs suffice to assure us that nature has run its course. In (5), he considers what he calls a "focal" description of death — "one that involves the loss of all major functions, not just neurolog-ical functions, and that includes an appropriate notion of permanency." He then affirms: "[W]e can describe the death of a human being *as a state of widespread nonfunctioning — including the loss of neurological functions (par-ticularly consciousness and brain-stem reflexes), circulation, and respiration — which naturally becomes permanent after a few minutes.* Because the key func-tions are interdependent, the state of death may be determined by focusing on any one of them, most commonly circulatory or neurological functions." Continuing, he notes that while it is difficult to operationalize the "disinte-gration of the entire organism as a whole," "our intuition tells us that it is possible, even if sometimes difficult, to distinguish between the life of an organism and the life of isolated organ cells" (555-556). In (5), defending brain death, he notes, with Kenneth Iserson, that in brain death the body is physiologically decapitated, and that one has no trouble in affirming that a decapitated body is dead. If one rejects the idea that a physiologically decap-itated body is dead, "one is left with a conclusion repugnant to common sense and good metaphysics, namely, that both a severed head and a decap-itated body are living substances if separately maintained alive," and in a footnote he points out that the Shewmons hold this view (557).

His point in "*6. Consider That a 'Meaningful' Death May Be a 'Good Death'*" is that in the death/organ donation of DCD (NHBD) patients we have a meaningful and good death, and in "*7. Determining Death Is an Act of Practical Reasoning in Which Ethical and Metaphysical Considerations Rightly Mix*," he emphasizes that doctors are practical persons, not philoso-phers, but that they are also concerned with ethics. Hence "while we must be careful to ensure that utilitarian concerns do not compromise the integrity of determinations of death, we also should not condemn the com-mingling of ethics and metaphysics in the determination of death" (558).

I think that I have provided a substantive and accurate summary of DuBois' thought. Although he and the Shewmons agree on many points, the basic difference is that Dubois holds the brain-death criterion whereas the Shewmons do not. Moreover, it seems to me that DuBois defends the brain-death criterion as proposed in the understanding that had become the widespread consensus, i.e., based on the rationale that the President's Council concurred in acknowledging that Shewmon's critique had so seriously called it into question that a new and stronger rationale was needed.

4. Evaluative Conclusion to This Debate

I am convinced that Shewmon has definitively shown that the brain-death criterion, even in the "beefed-up" version of the alleged "stronger" rationale developed by Kass and others to support it, is false and cannot be safely used. I also think that although it may, *in principle*, be possible to extirpate vital paired or unpaired organs from individuals in the dying process *without intentionally killing them*, it would be most imprudent to put into practice the protocols Shewmon suggested in his "Dead Donor" article. As Shewmon himself declared, at the end of that essay:

> [B]efore deciding whether it would be prudent to put this principle into practice in today's society, many other factors, which are outside the scope of this paper, must be considered, such as whether donor consent can be guaranteed to be truly informed and free; whether, in the case at hand, apnea off life support can be predicted with medical and moral certainty; whether such eviscerating procedures respect human dignity even if they might not cause or hasten death, whether the risk of public misperception that this is utilitarian killing can be minimized and so on. If the answer to one or more of these "whethers" is a "no,"... then it behooves us to hold off implementing the otherwise intrinsically ethical procedure until all the circumstantial details are worked out.

I think the answer to some of these "whethers" is "no," in particular to the risk of public misperception that this is utilitarian killing. Our culture unfortunately already is subject to a dualistic understanding that severs the "person" from his or her own body and operates on a proportionalistic, consequentialistic moral methodology. Moreover, transplant surgery of vital organs is surely not "ordinary" or "proportionate" or morally obligatory treatment. No human person has the "right" to such organs, although I fear some today claim that they do. We must resist this move.

5. Significant Developments in the First Part of 2008

The first four sections of this revised chapter were completed shortly before Christmas 2007. I am writing this section at the end of April 2008. To me the most significant developments regarding brain death in the early part of this year took place at an exceptionally important two-day "Scholars Forum" on brain death in which I participated. The Forum was sponsored by the Westchester Institute for Ethics and the Human Person, under the direction of Thomas Berg, L.C., and was held on April 10-11 in Washington, DC.

There I learned that at a meeting a short time prior to the Forum, the President's Council on Bioethics had approved its white paper on the subject of brain death, and this white paper will be made public in June 2008. Since the document is not in the public domain at present, I cannot refer directly to it. I was told that it supports the concept of brain death. However, precisely because of Dr. Alan Shewmon's critique of the reasoning used to justify that concept, as Leon Kass reported in the September 6, 2007, meeting summarized in Section 3 of this chapter, the Council's white paper adopts the new reasoning to support this concept outlined by Kass at that meeting and also summarized in Section 3.

At the opening session of the Forum, Shewmon presented the empirical evidence and reasoning that led him to abandon his acceptance of the concept of brain death. In it, he developed in detail the evidence summarized in Sections 1 through 4 above. Since the Forum was a private meeting of scholars, I will not summarize the discussions that took place. My concern is to show how they forced me to revise my own views.

Prior to the Forum, I held that the organism in question is undoubtedly a human organism, i.e., the body of a living human person. However, during the intense discussions/debates over this issue, a philosophical argument, rooted in the Thomistic tradition, was presented that very seriously undermined my conviction. I can summarize the argument, as I understand it, in this way. A brain is a necessary organ for sensory activities, and also for rational activities — after all, a key Thomistic principle is that "nothing is in the intellect that is not first in some way in the senses." If this is so, then it follows that an entity lacking a brain simply cannot be a mammalian, much less a human, organism because not only can it not engage in sensory activities (a prerequisite for rational activities) but also, unlike a human person in the embryonic stage, it lacks the radical capacity to do so. Thus the organism in question must be subhuman and even submammalian. The person has indeed died and a substantial change has occurred.

Although I was almost persuaded by this argument, I wondered whether it might be possible that although a human organism without a brain does not have the capacity to *exercise* its sensory and intellectual powers, it might still have the radical capacity or "active potency" to engage in sensory and intellectual activities. But after thinking this over and asking colleagues whose judgment I respect about the matter, I have come to the conclusion that a post-embryonic brainless organism simply does not have the active potency or radical capacity to generate a brain. Thus I must now also conclude that "bodies" that really are brain dead are *not* human or even mammalian.

Nonetheless, I do not consider the issues raised by Shewmon to be settled. There are very good reasons to question the validity of the standard diagnostic criteria to determine brain death. Moreover, they do not correspond to the statutory definitions of death patterned after the Uniform Determination of Death Act, insofar as they do not require all functions of the brain to be absent, and they explicitly allow some functions of the brain to be present (e.g., hypothalamic functions). Thus when can we know with moral certitude that a human person is in fact brain dead and that one can "retrieve" his vital organs to save the life of another?

I believe that the entire community, and all who seek to shape their choices and actions in accord with the truth, owes Dr. Shewmon a debt of gratitude. His work is of great importance. At present, I am of an unsettled view. I now accept of brain death as a valid conclusion of the argument given above, but just how do we know with moral certitude that a person is in fact brain dead? That for me is still an unresolved matter.

6. Organ Transplants From the Living (*Inter Vivos*)

Today the transplanting of vital organs, such as a kidney, a portion of the liver, etc., from one living person to another in desperate need of a vital organ is commonplace. We intuitively and instinctively judge that the giving of a part of one's own body to help a gravely or even mortally ill fellow human person is not only morally justifiable but an act of heroic charity.

The Magisterium of the Church praises the self-giving of vital organs by living persons. Pope John Paul II has frequently remarked on the moral liceity of the self-giving of vital organs, and he has likewise clearly indicated the limits of such self-giving. Thus, in his Address to the First International

Congress of the Society for Organ Sharing, he said, first, that "a transplant, and even a simple blood transfusion, is not like other operations. It must not be separated from the donor's act of self-giving, from the love that gives life. The physician should always be conscious of the particular nobility of his work; he becomes the mediator of something especially significant, the *gift of self* which one person has made . . . so that another might live." He then articulated the norm: "A person can only donate that of which he can deprive himself without serious danger or harm to his own life or personal identity, and for a just and proportionate reason."[24]

The *Catechism of the Catholic Church*, in taking up organ transplants *inter vivos*, says: "*Organ transplants* are in conformity with the moral law if the physical and psychological dangers and risks to the donor are proportionate to the good that is sought for the recipient."[25] And finally, the bishops of the United States declare: "The transplantation of organs from living donors is morally permissible when such a donation will not sacrifice or seriously impair any essential bodily function and the anticipated benefit to the recipient is proportionate to the harm done to the donor. . . . [T]he freedom of the prospective donor must be respected."[26]

Nonetheless, the proper way to justify organ donations from living persons is a matter of debate among Catholic theologians. In fact, when this kind of surgery became possible around the middle of the twentieth century, it stirred controversy among them.[27] Some leading theologians of the time, among them Marcellino Zalba, S.J., wondered how one could justify a procedure in which a healthy human person (the donor) willingly suffers mutilating surgery and the risk of health problems, perhaps serious ones, in the future when his own life and health are not imperiled. The mutilating surgery could hardly be regarded as therapeutic for the donor and hence could not, in their judgment, be justified by the principle of totality, according to which one could justify the mutilation of one's own person (e.g., the amputation of a gangrenous limb or the excision of cancerous testicles) in order to protect one's own life.[28]

Gerald Kelly, S.J., provides the reasons why he and theologians of his day concluded that the principle of totality could not be used to justify such procedures: "This principle [that of totality] can be applied only when there is the subordination of part to whole that exists in the natural body. No such subordination exists between human persons or between the individual and society. Each person is a distinct entity, with a distinct finality. No matter how lowly his condition, he is not subordinated to others in the order of being."[29] Some theologians, nonetheless, sought to justify organ transplants *inter vivos* by "extending" the principle of totality. A radical presentation of this line of thinking, extending the principle to embrace the total good of the person, including the "spiritual" good of the donor, who allegedly benefits spiritually by the self-giving of his vital organs, was presented by Martin Nolan, O.S.A.[30] His attempted justification, rooted in a dualistic understanding of the human person, was soundly criticized by others, in particular by the great Protestant ethicist, Paul Ramsey, who characterized it as the "sticky benefits" theory.[31] In addition, Pope Pius XII, who had himself invoked the principle of totality to justify mutilating surgery on one's own person when necessary to protect the person's health and life as a whole, explicitly declared that this principle could not be used to justify organ transplants among the living.[32]

Realizing that organ transplants among the living cannot be justified by the totality principle, other theologians, preeminently Gerald Kelly, S.J., followed the lead first suggested by Bert Cunningham, C.M., in his doctoral dissertation, *The Morality of Organic Transplantation* (Washington, DC: The Catholic University of America Press, 1944), that the self-giving of one's own vital organs could be justified by the principle of fraternal charity or love when doing so is of great benefit to the recipient, with the proviso that the harm suffered by the donor is limited and morally acceptable. This view, endorsed and developed by Kelly, was soon accepted by many moral theologians. They distinguished between *anatomical* and *functional* integrity, arguing that only the latter was necessary for bodily and personal integrity.

Some theologians, preeminently Germain Grisez, argue that organ transplants from the living can be justified by the principle of double effect. According to this principle, an action having two effects — one good, the other bad — is morally good provided that the action is not morally wrong for other reasons, that the evil is not intended, that the evil is not the means to the good, and that there is a "proportionate reason" for tolerating or accepting the bad effect. Grisez argues, correctly in my opinion, that the "principle of totality" is itself, if analyzed properly, an instance of double effect. However, the *physical* "directness" of the causing of harm and the *physical* "indirectness" of the causing of the benefit led many theologians to think that a special principle was needed to justify the "mutilation" involved in necessary surgical interventions on one's own body (the malfunctioning or diseased organ, e.g., the gall bladder, was first removed physically, causing a "mutilation" before the healing would take place).

But if we analyze the matter from a moral perspective, we can see that the "object" morally specifying the chosen act (on this see *Veritatis splendor*, no. 78) is not the harm done to the person but rather the removal of the organ or part of the body, with, as its resulting effects, the "mutilation" (the evil effect) and the "protection" or "restoration" of health (the good effect). Thus, in analyzing morally the reason why one is justified in submitting to "mutilating" surgery to protect one's own life and health, Grisez writes:

> It can be morally good and even obligatory to remove a part of the body essential to some physiological or psychic function, when doing so of itself also protects or promotes health: the detriment to function may not be intended as a means to the other end, but may only be accepted as a side effect. For example, a person sometimes should consent to the cutting off of an infected or cancerous limb or nonvital organ when that is necessary to prevent the infection or cancer from doing great harm to the body as a whole. Indeed, this is so even when the part removed is itself healthy, if removing it has natural consequences which are necessary for the health of the body as a whole and which cannot be brought about in another way. For example, a man suffering from breast cancer may consent to the surgical removal of his normal testicles in order to stop the hormones which are aggravating the cancer.[33]

Similarly, Grisez argues, the same norms can be applied to the self-giving of vital organs. The morality of giving them depends on how the freely chosen act relates one to the relevant goods: healthy functioning and life itself. If the harm (including the mutilation) suffered by the donor — but in no way *intended* either by him or those involved in the transplant — does not impair his functional integrity, the evil suffered is an unintended side-effect of an act of self-giving. However, were the donor's own functional integrity and hence his own health and life to be impaired, the choice would be to impede or damage his own health as a means to some good end, but one can never intend or choose evil for the sake of good to come.[34]

Although theologians differ among themselves on the proper way to justify the self-giving of vital organs by living donors, today all agree that it is morally permissible, under given conditions, for live donors to donate paired organs to those who are in need of them. Moreover, the Church's Magisterium praises those who generously give such organs, while at the same time clearly noting the limitations of such self giving.

ENDNOTES FOR CHAPTER EIGHT

1. "Uniform Anatomical Gift Act, Section 7 (b)," as printed in Alfred M. Sadler, Jr., M.D., Blair L. Sadler, LL.B., and E. Blythe Stason, J.D., "The Uniform Anatomical Gift Act: A Model for Reform," *Journal of the American Medical Association* 206 (December 9, 1968), 2506.

2. Paul Ramsey, *The Patient as Person* (New Haven: Yale University Press, 1970), p.103.

3. On this, see Ronald E. Cranford, "Death, Definition and Determination of. I. Criteria for Death," *Encyclopedia of Bioethics*, ed. Warren T. Reich (2nd rev. ed., New York: McGraw-Hill, Inc., 1995), 529.

4. See, for example, E. T. Bartlett and S. J. Younger, "Human death and destruction of the neocortex," in *Death: Beyond Whole-Brain Criteria*, ed. R. M. Zaner (Dordrecht/Boston: Kluwer Academic Publishers, 1988), pp. 199-215; Robert M. Veatch, "The Impending Collapse of the Whole-Brain Definition of Death," *Hastings Center Report* 23.4 (July-August 1993), 18-24. As we shall see later, in summarizing discussions at the September and November 2007 meetings of the President's Council on Bioethics, several members of this prestigious body who had been advocates of "brain death" are now strong supporters of this position.

5. U.S. President's Commission for the Study of Ethical Problems in Medicine and Biomedical and Behavioral Research, *Defining Death: Medical, Legal, and Ethical Issues in the Determination of Death* (Washington, DC: U.S. Government Printing Office, 1981), p. 41.

6. See, for instance, Alexander Morgan Capron, "Death, Definition and Determination of. II. Legal Issues in Pronouncing Death," *Encyclopedia of Bioethics*, 536.

7. Among authorities articulating this view are the following: (1) U.S. President's Commission for the Study of Ethical Problems in Medicine and Biomedical and Behavioral Research, *Defining Death*...; (2) J. L. Bernat, *Ethical Issues in Neurology* (Boston: Butterworth-Heinemann, 1994), pp. 113-143; (3) Pontifical Academy of Sciences, *Determination of Brain Death*..., pp. 81-82.

8. U.S. President's Commission..., *Defining Death*..., p. 35.

9. B. E. Soifer, A. W. Geib, "The Multiple Organ Donor: Identification and Management," *Annals of Internal Medicine* 110 (1989), 814-823.

10. Pallis C. Harley, *ABC of Brainstem Death* (London: BMJ Publishing Group, 1996). I owe references nos. 6, 7, 8 to D. Alan Shewmon, who

refers to them in his essay, "Chronic 'brain death': Meta-analysis and conceptual consequences," *Neurology* 51 (December 1998), 1538.

11. (1) "Recovery from 'Brain Death': A Neurologist's Apologia," *The Linacre Quarterly* (February 1997), 30-96; (2) " 'Brainstem Death,' 'Brain Death' and Death: A Critical Re-Evaluation of the Purported Evidence," *Issues in Law & Medicine* 14.2 (1998), 125-145; (3) "Chronic 'Brain Death': Meta-analysis and conceptual consequences," *Neurology* 51 (December 1998), 1538-1545; (4) "Determining the Moment of Death: New Evidence, New Controversies" — this essay, delivered at a conference on bioethics at the Universidad de Navarra in October 1999 was later published under the title "Determinación del momento de la muerte: nuevas evidencias, nuevas controversias" in Ana Marta González González, Elena Postigo Solana, and Susana Aulestiarte Jiménez (eds.), *Vivir y Morir con Dignidad Temas fundamentales de Bioética en una sociedad plural* (Pamplona, Spain, EUNSA: Ediciones Universidad de Navarra, 2002), pp. 153-171. The second essay noted was adapted from a lecture Shewmon gave at the Linacre Centre for Health Care Ethics Twentieth Anniversary International Conference, July 28-31, 1997, at Queen's College, Cambridge University. That lecture has now been published under the title "Is It Reasonable to Use the UK Protocol for the Clinical Diagnosis of 'Brain Stem Death' as a Basis for Diagnosing Death?" in *Issues for a Catholic Bioethic: Proceedings of the International Conference to Celebrate the Twentieth Anniversary of the Foundation of the Linacre Centre 28-31 July 1997*, ed. Luke Gormally (London: The Linacre Centre, 1999), pp. 315-333. Shewmon briefly set forth his position in his essay "Definitions of Death, the Persistent Vegetative State, and Anencephaly," in *The Bishop and the Future of Catholic Health Care: Proceedings of the Sixteenth Workshop for Bishops*, ed. Daniel P. Maher (Braintree, MA: Pope John XXIII Medical-Moral Research and Education Center, 1997), pp. 136-153.

12. Shewmon, "Brainstem Death, Brain Death and Death...," 136.

13. Among them he lists the following: C. A. Machado, "A new definition of death based on basic mechanisms of consciousness generation in human beings," in C. Machado, ed., *Brain Death: Proceedings of the Second International Conference on Brain Death: Havana, Cuba,, February 27- March 1, 1996* (Amsterdam: Elsevier, 1995), pp. 57-88; R. D. Truog, "Is it time to abandon brain death?" *Hastings Center Report* 27 (1997), 29-37; along with several of his own essays and others.

14. Shewmon's comments on Pope John Paul's address have not been published. He drafted them for several people who had asked him to do so, and he has given me permission to refer to them here.

15. Among them he lists the following: C. A. Machado, "A new definition of death based on basic mechanisms of consciousness generation in human beings," in C. Machado, ed., *Brain Death: Proceedings of the Second International Conference on Brain Death: Havana, Cuba, February 27–March 1, 1996* (Amsterdam: Elsevier, 1995), pp. 57-88; R. D. Truog, "Is it time to abandon brain death?" *Hastings Center Report* 27 (1997), 29-37; along with several of his own essays and others.

16. This transcript can be downloaded from http://www.bioethics.gov/tran scripts/sept07/sept6.html.

17. This transcript can be downloaded from http://www.bioethics.gov/tran scripts/nov07/nov9.html.

18. Kennedy Institute of Ethics Journal 14.3 (2004), 277-300.

19. Another essay in which his new position is developed is one he co-authored with his wife, Elizabeth Seitz Shewmon, "The Semiotics of Death and Its Medical Applications," in *Brain Death and Disorders of Consciousness*, eds. C. Machedo and D. Alan Shewmon (New York: Springer Science, 2004), pp 89-114.

20. This is described at length in Phyllis Graser's article, "Donation After Cardiac Death," *The National Catholic Bioethics Quarterly* 7.3 (Autumn 2007), 527-544.

21. *Issues in Law and Medicine*, 18.2 (Summer 2002), 21-43.

22. Shewmon, in his article on the Dead Donor Rule, agrees with DuBois that death be regarded as a *state* and that medically it is impossible to determine the "true" moment of death. But while DuBois thinks that what matters is "not whether" death is an event or a process, but death as a state," Shewmon thinks that what really matters is whether "organ procurements cause the death of the patient." They differ in that DuBois thinks we can have moral certainty that non-heart-beating donors (NHBD or DCD) are already dead, accepting the brain-death criteria, whereas Shewmon does not. At least that is how I understand their difference.

23. Writing in 2002, DuBois, as footnote 2 of his essay shows, is thinking of authors like Robert Trog and Norman Fost who would drop the rule and admit that we are indeed killing donors and justify our doing so. Note that Shewmon, who rejects the dead donor rule in his 2004 article, does *not* conclude that we are killing donors but argues that the extirpation of vital organs from NHBDs does *not kill them and that their deaths are foreseen but unintended side effects of the extirpation of their organs.*

24. Pope John Paul II, Address to the First International Congress of the Society for Organ Sharing, *L'Osservatore Romano*, English ed. (June 24, 1991), 2.

25. *Catechism of the Catholic Church*, no. 2296. **NB:** Here I give the text as required by the "Modifications from the *Editio Typica*" (based on the definitive Latin text promulgated on September 8, 1997). The text found in editions of the *Catechism* prior to that date is somewhat different.

26. National Conference of Catholic Bishops, *Ethical and Religious Directives for Catholic Health Care Services* (Washington, DC: United States Catholic Conference, 1995), directive no. 30.

27. For a discussion of the debates that took place, see a series of articles by Gerald Kelly, S.J., in *Theological Studies* 16 (1955) 391-396; 17 (1956) 341-344, 557-561; 18 (1957) 228-230, 570-572.

28. On the "principle of totality" see John Gallagher, C.S.B., "The Principle of Totality: Man's Stewardship of His Body," in *Moral Theology Today: Certitudes and Doubts*, ed. Donald G. McCarthy (St. Louis, MO: Pope John XXIII Medical-Moral Research and Education Center, 1984), pp. 217-242.

29. Gerald Kelly, S.J., *Medico-Moral Problems* (St. Louis, MO: The Catholic Hospital Association, 1957), p. 247.

30. Martin Nolan, O.S.A., "The Principle of Totality in Moral Theology," in *Absolutes in Moral Theology?*, ed. Charles E. Curran (Washington, DC: Corpus Books, 1968), pp. 232-248.

31. Paul Ramsey, *The Patient as Person: Explorations in Medical Ethics* (New Haven, CT: Yale University Press, 1970), chapter 4, "The Self-Giving of Vital Organs," pp. 165-197, in particular pp. 178-181.

32. See, for example, Pope Pius XII, "Allocution to a Group of Eye Specialists" (May 14, 1956), as found in *The Human Body: Papal Teaching*, selected and arranged by the Monks of Solesmes (Boston: St. Paul Editions, 1960), nn. 645ff.

33. Germain Grisez, *The Way of the Lord Jesus*, Vol. 2, *Living a Christian Life* (Quincy, IL: Franciscan Press, 1993), p. 542.

34. Here I paraphrase and in some ways modify ibid., p. 543.

Bibliography and
Resources

NOTE

The endnotes for each chapter provide extensive bibliographical references for the issues specific to each chapter. Here I provide information on (1) a Select Bibliography of Texts, Encyclopedias, and Anthologies, (2) a list of important Journals and Periodicals, and (3) Centers and Web sites of Particular Value for Catholic Perspectives on Bioethics.

Select Bibliography of Texts, Encyclopedias, and Anthologies

Ashcroft, Richard Edmund, Angus Dawson, Heather Draper, and John McMillan, eds., *Principles of Health Care Ethics*. 2nd ed. Philadelphia: J. P. Lippincott, 2007. The first edition of this massive work of over 800 pages was edited by Raanon Gillan. The best item in it is a brilliant essay by John Finnis and Anthony Fisher, O.P., "Theology and the Four Principles of Ethics," a devastating and accurate critique of the highly influential work of Beauchamp and Childress referred to below.

Ashley, Benedict, O.P., Kevin O'Rourke, O.P., and Jean deBlois, C.S.J., *Health Care Ethics: A Theological Analysis*. 5th ed. Washington, DC: Georgetown University Press, 2007. In my opinion the fourth edition is superior to the fifth. For a review of the fifth edition see my "Review Essay" in *The National Catholic Bioethics Quarterly* 7.2 (Summer 2007), 409-417.

―――. *Ethics of Health Care: An Introductory Textbook*. 2nd ed. Washington, DC: Georgetown University Press, 1994.

Beauchamp, Thomas, and James Childress, *Principles of Biomedical Ethics*. 3rd ed. New York: Oxford University Press, 1994. This is a widely used and highly influential work; in it, personal autonomy trumps everything.

Cataldo, Peter, and Albert S. Moraczewski, O.P., eds. *Catholic Health Care Ethics: A Manual for Ethics Committees*. Braintree, MA: National Catholic Bioethics Center, 2002. This is very useful and new material that can be inserted easily. (This was published in a binder divided into sections so that new material can be easily inserted.) The Center has since moved to Philadelphia.

Griese, Orville, *Catholic Identity in Health Care: Principles and Practice.* Braintree, MA: Pope John XXIII Medical-Moral Research and Education Center, 1987.

Grisez, Germain, *The Way of the Lord Jesus.* Vol. 2, *Living a Christian Life.* Quincy, IL: Franciscan Press, 1993. Chapter Eight of this volume, entitled "Life, Health, and Bodily Inviolability," is a short and excellent treatise on bioethics, pp. 459-552.

———. *The Way of the Lord Jesus.* Vol. 3, *Difficult Moral Questions.* Quincy, IL: Franciscan Press, 1997. Many of the questions analyzed in detail by Grisez in this volume concern bioethical issues.

McCormick, Richard A., S.J., *How Brave a New World? Dilemmas in Bioethics.* Garden City, NY: Doubleday, 1978. Although dated, this work embodies a proportionalist method of making moral judgments incompatible with Catholic teaching. It is, however, very influential.

———. *The Critical Calling: Reflections on Moral Dilemmas Since Vatican II.* Washington, DC: Georgetown University Press, 1989. The same comments as given previously apply here.

Post, Stephen Garrad, ed. *Encyclopedia of Bioethics.* 3rd rev. ed. New York: McGraw-Hill, 2005. Five volumes paginated consecutively. The first edition was published in 1978. This is basically oriented in a secularist direction. In the first edition, there was an entry on "Marriage." This is now called "Marriage and Other Significant Relationships."

Ramsey, Paul, *The Patient as Person.* New Haven: Yale University Press, 1970. Although an old work, it is still one of the best despite a few problematic positions.

———. *Ethics at the Edges of Life: Medical and Legal Intersections.* New Haven: Yale University Press, 1978. Another superlative work.

Shannon, Thomas A., ed. *Basic Writings of the Key Ethical Questions That Surround the Major Biological Possibilities and Problems.* 4th ed. New York: Paulist Press, 1993. Biased toward proportionalism.

Smith, Janet, and Christopher Kaczor. *Life Issues, Medical Choices: Questions and Answers for Catholics.* Cincinnati, OH: Servant Book from St. Anthony Messenger, 2007. This brief work is written clearly and is fully in accord with Catholic teaching.

Walters, Leroy, ed., *Bibliography of Bioethics.* Detroit: Gale Research Co., 1975-present. An annual bibliography, the most complete of its kind, classified systematically.

Important Journals and Periodicals

BioEdge. This is a very helpful weekly newsletter summarizing current developments in bioethics from a deeply Catholic perspective. It is published by Australasian Bioethics Information, whose Web site is http://www.australasianbioethics.org. It is headquartered in Australia.

Catholic Medical Quarterly: Journal of the Guild of Catholic Doctors. A quarterly journal published by the Guild of Catholic Doctors in England.

Ethics & Medics: The Bulletin of the National Catholic Bioethics Center on Moral Issues in the Health Care Sciences. Inaugurated in 1975, this is a very useful monthly periodical, ordinarily four pages in length and containing two brief but significant essays on an issue in bioethics. It is published by the National Catholic Bioethics Center (formerly called the Pope John XXIII Medical-Moral Research and Education Center).

Hastings Center Report. This is published bimonthly by the Hastings Center, a nonpartisan organization that carries out educational and research programs on ethical issues in medicine. In addition to the bimonthly *Report*, the Center issues occasional studies on selected topics.

Health Progress. This journal, formerly called *Hospital Progress*, is published ten times a year by the Catholic Health Association of the United States.

Issues in Law and Medicine. This is a quarterly publication of the National Legal Center for the Medically Dependent and Disabled, Inc., the Horatio P. Storer Foundation, Inc., and the American Academy of Medical Ethics, Inc. Essays in this journal are uniformly of high scholarly quality and pro-life in orientation.

Journal of the American Medical Association (JAMA). A weekly, professional journal for physicians; many articles are quite technical; others deal with ethical issues from various perspectives, unfortunately too often utilitarian in nature.

Linacre Quarterly. This is the official publication of the Catholic Medical Association, formerly called the National Federation of Catholic Physicians' Guilds.

The NaProEthics Forum. Bimonthly publication of the Pope Paul VI Institute, Omaha, Nebraska, this was published regularly for several years but is no longer being published. That is unfortunate, as it carried good material.

The National Catholic Bioethics Quarterly. Published by the National Catholic Bioethics Center (see below) and edited by Edward Furton, this is without a doubt the premier scholarly quarterly on bioethical

issues published under Catholic auspices. It is must reading for anyone seriously interested in the issues taken up in this book.
New England Journal of Medicine. This is a very prestigious and scholarly
weekly journal. Articles are frequently very technical; most ethical
issues are addressed from a secularist point of view but at times some
very excellent pieces appear.

Centers and Web Sites of Particular Value for Catholic Perspectives on Bioethics

The most important center for Catholic perspectives on bioethics in the
United States is the **National Catholic Bioethics Center,** formerly called the
Pope John XXIII Medical-Moral Research and Education Center. It publishes its bulletin, *Ethics & Medics,* and numerous monographs on bioethical
issues. For many years, it has sponsored, with the help of the Knights of
Columbus, workshops on specific topics in bioethics for the bishops of the
United States, Canada, and Latin America, publishing papers given at these
workshops in volumes of proceedings. John Haas is the current president of
the Center. Its Web site is http://www.ncbcenter.org.

Another very important center for Catholic perspectives on bioethics
is the **Linacre Centre**. Now a little over a quarter of a century old, the Centre has sponsored excellent research in bioethics. Among its publications is
its Working Party Report on Euthanasia, *Euthanasia, Clinical Practice and
the Law,* edited by Luke Gormally, and cited frequently in the endnotes of
Chapter Seven. Luke Gormally was its founder and first director; Helen
Watt is currently its director. Its Web site is http://www.linacre.org.

The **Center for Health Care Ethics**, while representing the Catholic
tradition, seeks dialogue with the many other ethical traditions represented
in the United States. Its Web site is http://chce.slu.edu.

The **Joseph P. and Rose F. Kennedy Institute of Ethics**, although
located on the campus of a major Catholic university (Georgetown), does
not, on the whole, support magisterial teaching and presents a wide variety of views on bioethical matters. Currently a very strong Catholic voice
is found in Professor John Keown, an Englishman who is widely known
and respected as an authority on euthanasia and assisted suicide. Its Web
site is http://kennedyinstitute.georgetown.edu/index.htm.

Additional Web Sites

In addition to the Web sites noted above, the following organizations, with their Web sites, are valuable resources for those interested in Catholic perspectives on bioethics.

Culture of Life Foundation: http://www.culture-of-life.org. This is an excellent source for relevant essays and other information on contraception, abortion, the generation of human life, euthanasia, etc.

International Federation of Catholic Medical Associations: http://frblin.club.fr/fiamc/welcome.html. Another good source.

International Task Force on Euthanasia and Assisted Suicide: http://www.iaetf.org. An excellent source for material on euthanasia and allied subjects.

Pontifical Academy for Life: http://www.academiavita.org/portal. jsp?lang=english. A very important source. Publications of the Academy are most significant and helpful.

Pontifical Academy of Sciences: http://www.vatican.va/roman_curia/ pontifical_academies/acdscien. Another very important source.

Pontifical Council for Health Pastoral Care: http://www.health pastoral.org. Also important.

United States Conference of Catholic Bishops Pro-Life Office: http://www.nccbuscc.org/prolife. This is the source for many very important articles, etc.

Center for Bioethics and Culture Network: http://www.cbc-network.org. Under the leadership of Jennifer Lahl, this non-Catholic center is a valuable source of information supporting pro-life activities.

President's Council on Bioethics: http://www.bioethics.gov. The first chairman of this important body was Leon Kass; its current director is Edmund Pellegrino, M.D. It publishes excellent documents on life issues and transcripts of its sessions can be downloaded.

Coalition of Americans for Research Ethics: Do No Harm: http://www.stemcellresearch.org. This is the best source for information on stem cell research, adamantly opposed to killing human beings in their embryonic stage in order to obtain pluripotent stem cells.

Center for Bioethics and Human Dignity: http://www.cbhd.org. This Center, located at Trinity International University in Deerfield, Illinois, is a pro-life Protestant bioethics organization completely opposed to abortion, euthanasia, etc. It publishes an important journal and issues newsletters regularly that are of help.

Index

252; requires quality-of-life judgments, 281f, 310
McHugh, Bishop James, on care of
"vegetative" patients. 312, 313
McLaren, A., introduced term "pre-
embryo," 308
McLaughlin, David, reproductive technologies, 115, 116
Meilaender, Gilbert, defends contraception, but opposes abortion, 127,
156; care of "vegetative" patients,
313
methotrexate (MTX), debate over use
in coping with ectopic pregnancies, 201ff
Missouri bishops, care of "vegetative"
patients, 312
Montagu, Ashley, totally severs sex
from procreation, 135, 159
moral judgment, steps in making true,
62ff
moral norms, absolute, 61ff; how
known, 61ff
Moraczewski, Albert, O.P., critique of
delayed hominization view, 180,
207; critique of twinning argument, 185, 193, 209,; defends
MTX and salpingostomy for coping with tubal pregnancies, 201f;
human genome project
Mosier, Alicia, contraception, anti-life,
129f, 142, 157, 160
Myers, Bishop John, care of "vegetative"
patients, 313

N
natural family planning (NFP), underlying anthropological presuppositions, 132, 139f
natural law, first principles of, 56; fulfilled through Christ's redemptive
work, 63ff; normative truths of,
58ff; participation in eternal law,
56f

Neuchterlein, James, defends contraception but opposes abortion,
127f, 156
New Jersey bishops, care of "vegetative"
patients, 313
Nicaea, Council of, eternal Word
"begotten, not made," relevance
to reproductive technologies, 87
Nolan, Mark, O.S.B., inaccurate use of
principle of totality to justify
organ transplants *inter vivos*, 355,
360; supports contraceptive sterilization, 162
Noldin, H., definition of abortion, 203
nonvoluntary euthanasia, alleged non-
personhood of one to be killed,
267f; apologia for, 266ff; based on
poor quality of life, 266f
Nowell-Smith, Patrick, euthanasia
advocate, 305; euthanasia movement, 305
Nuechterlein, James, defense of contraception, 126f, 156, 161
Nuremberg Code, principle of informed
and free consent, 215f, 259

O
object, of human act, primary source of
moral specification of moral acts,
52ff
O'Connor, Sandra Day, opinion in
Planned Parenthood v. Casey, 269,
308
O'Donnell, Thomas, S.J., procedures for
"assisting" the conjugal act, 118,
119
ordinary/extraordinary distinction (or
proportionate/disproportionate
distinction), criteria for determining, 277ff; criteria for determining, relevant magisterial teaching,
277f; *see also* burdensomeness
organ transplants, from the dead, in
principle justifiable, 314; in practice, not possible to know with

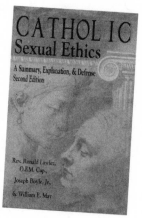
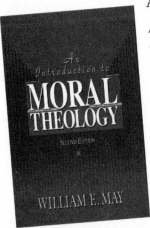